The Search for Labour
Market Flexibility

THE SEARCH FOR LABOUR MARKET FLEXIBILITY

The European Economies in Transition

Edited by

ROBERT BOYER

CLARENDON PRESS · OXFORD

1988

Oxford University Press, Walton Street, Oxford OX2 6DP

Oxford New York Toronto
Delhi Bombay Calcutta Madras Karachi
Petaling Jaya Singapore Hong Kong Tokyo
Nairobi Dar es Salaam Cape Town
Melbourne Auckland

and associated companies in
Berlin Ibadan

Oxford is a trade mark of Oxford University Press

Published in the United States
by Oxford University Press, New York

First published in French by
Editions La Découverte in 1986

British Library Cataloguing in Publication Data
La flexibilite du travail en Europe.
The Search for labour market flexibility
: the European economies in transition.
1. Western Europe. Labour market.
Effects, 1970–1987 of economic change
I. Boyer, Robert
331.12'094
ISBN 0–19–828560–4

Library of Congress Cataloging in Publication Data
The Search for labour market flexibility : the European economies in
transition / edited by Robert Boyer.
p. cm
1. Industrial relations—Europe. 2. Industrial relations–
–Government policy—Europe. 3. Social security—Europe. I. Boyer,
Robert.
HD8376.5.S42 1988 331'.094—dc19 87–34802
ISBN 0–19–828560–4

Set by Hope Services, Abingdon
Printed and bound in
Great Britain by Biddles Ltd
Guildford & Kings Lynn

FOREWORD

How is it possible to manage economic and social flexibility? This appears to be one of the most pressing questions facing European economies, as they deal with the dire effects of the international crisis. Some see a greater flexibility of rules and regulations, and a reform of the institutional and legal framework regarding social security and labour relations, as the best means of combating excessively rigid systems which seem to give rise to high unit costs of production that cannot be sustained in the face of international competition. For others — and, in particular, for a number of European trade unions — the mere idea of flexibility is denounced as the ideology of management which tends to undermine the social gains of recent years. However, as this study shows, systems of social security as well as labour relations have changed considerably since 1973 in all the European countries. 'Convergence' is not the correct term to use, but the same difficulties in regulating the relationship between the production of goods and services and the various means of income redistribution have appeared everywhere in the context of a general slow-down of economic growth. At the same time, innovation and far-reaching processes of change are now taking place in all the European economies.

How can we make the most of this? That is the principal subject of this study; it is a question that has always seemed central to the economists of the European Federation for Economic Research (FERE), who are the authors of this book.

FERE was set up in 1982, on the initiative of several European research centres, to study and carry out research on the European economy and its place in the world economy. It consists of seven research centres in seven countries: CEPREMAP in France, the Department of Applied Economics at the University of Cambridge in Britain, ISMERI in Italy, SEVI in Belgium, FEWP at the University of Bremen in West Germany, the University of Santiago de Compostella in Spain, and ESRI in Ireland. For almost three years, meetings involving researchers from these different centres were held, thanks to support from the French Ministry of Research and Technology, the Commission of the European Communities, and, more recently, the Commissariat Général du Plan and the Caisse de Dépôts et Consignations in France.

The initial work of the Federation focused on five broad issues: economic recovery and financial constraints; the redistribution of income and inflation; the restructuring of systems of production and trade practices; relations between the European economies and the rest of the world; and the development of new instruments for regulating national and international economic systems.

Readers will form their own ideas as to the relevance of the challenge that was taken up by the researchers of FERE: to compare developments in internal forms of economic and social organization in each country, in order to identify similarities or differences in the impact of the international crisis on each country, and to assess the various reactions to it.

In addition to this purely comparative analysis, the aim was to evaluate in a coherent way the capacity of Europe, apparently in decline as an economic and commercial power, to fulfil its potential as the premier market in the world. For this reason, it was decided to analyse the means adopted in each country to enable it to adapt to the international economic situation and to combat the crisis within a coherent general framework.

The approach adopted is that of 'regulation', developed by a group of researchers who were initially interested in long-term changes in the French and US economies. They accordingly evolved a method of study combining an historical approach with an institutional and statistical analysis, even going so far as to attempt to model the changes taking place. This led to the history of each country being divided into periods denoting the main stages of development of a mass production economy, which then led to the change in the economy in the present crisis being studied in the same way.

Such an approach allows us to focus the analysis on one particular aspect of this change that is fundamental as regards regulation: that is, changes in the system of wage/labour relations, by which is meant all those processes that are reflected in institutional and legal relations, that affect methods of production and redistribution, and that govern employment in present-day capitalism.

The decision to begin by studying changes in the system of wage/labour relations — rather than, for example, the restructuring of systems of production, problems of trade, or public spending — is based on two observations which seemed to be common to the researchers in the Federation. On the one hand, related to the questions noted above regarding social flexibility, forms of organization of the labour market and industrial relations seem to be undergoing changes during this crisis. On the other hand, despite vast political differences, the governments of countries in Europe are at present experiencing great difficulties, which in some degree are similar, in managing these changes. Higher unemployment, stagnation of demand, and labour market segmentation, but also the emergence and consolidation of less secure jobs and the gradual breakdown in the social consensus that facilitated postwar growth, have contributed to the problem. The papers in this book strengthen the notion that the various economies of Europe have experienced similar changes. It is as if, in crisis, they were looking for new forms of flexibility, new ways to adapt more quickly to economic fluctuations. The question that clearly arises is whether and to what extent these developments are subject to social (and of course political) control; a further question that needs analysis is who benefits from these changes? Could we identify concrete policies of 'offensive' flexibility at a European level or a national level in each country? One answer, suggested by the work presented here, seems that the need to adapt will result in as many attempts to deal with the crisis being made within firms and other organizations as are made by a process of collective negotiation.

Equally, in so far as certain developments are common to Europe as a whole, ought we not, at least in part, to raise the question of imposing 'social control' of economic developments, starting from the notion of Europe as a 'social entity'?

This book, which consists of seven national studies and a synthesis, presents the results of work carried out by a multinational team co-ordinated by Robert Boyer with the support of Michele Salvati. It was presented in provisional form in September 1984 in Paris to around a hundred interested people, including Robert Lion, Director General of the Caisse des Dépôts, Henri Guillaume, Commissaire Général du Plan, Pancrazio de Pasquale, President of the Regional Commission of the European Parliament, and the late Professor Lord Kaldor.

The analysis in the book has benefited from the comments and observations made at that conference, and we hope that it may initiate an informed debate on the relationship between the economy and society in the Europe of the 1980s.

FRANÇOIS DE LAVERGNE
President of FERE

CONTENTS

TABLES

FIGURES

Part I

The Evolution of Wage/Labour Relations
in Seven European Countries

1

Wage/Labour Relations, Growth, and Crisis: A Hidden Dialectic

Robert Boyer

1. Changes in Labour Relations: The Root of the Crisis and Economic Policy-making

During the 1960s, economic policy discussions focused on the comparative efficiency of budgetary and monetary mechanisms in keeping developed economies close to full employment without inflation. Now, in the mid-1980s, the scenario has radically altered: traditional methods of economic management are still being used, but in a restrictive way, to reduce inflation even at the cost of a huge, long-term increase in unemployment. The more fundamental objective is to foster *structural change* so that sustained growth may be regained. According to government priorities, this task is entrusted either to the market, to deregulation, and the combating of 'rigidity', or, although increasingly rarely, to economic planning, an expansion of the public sector, and the welfare state.

Since the early 1980s, many have identified problems of labour relations as bearing the major responsibility for stagnation during the crisis, with the result that firms and governments have come to question and sometimes substantially to revise their policies. The aim of this book is to introduce certain concepts which may prove useful for studying the links between changes in labour relations and macroeconomic developments. Previous studies have explored these issues, taking account of the long-run dynamic of US and French capitalism (see Bibliography). These same concepts will be used to analyse changes that have taken place over the past decade in seven European countries, and to outline some responses to the following questions:

- Have the same kinds of institutional and economic change occurred in the different countries, or *have national responses to the crisis differed significantly?*
- *What factors explain these changes* — the deepening of the international crisis, the development of institutional restrictions on the operation of the labour market in the postwar period, or changes in economic policy priorities?

- If the quest for *greater flexibility* in labour markets has been common to all, what specific form does it take in different European countries?
- Does this strategy contribute to a reduction in unemployment, and does it ultimately define a *new configuration of labour relations* which might lead to a way out of the crisis?

Each of the authors of the national surveys (Chapters 2–8) has contributed his knowledge of specific economic, political, and social developments in his country and has approached the study from his own particular perspective. Nevertheless, all the analyses form part of a general investigation into the concepts of wage/labour relations and the method of regulation as a way of perceiving the linkages between certain types of labour relations and the growth of the economy. But there is nothing rigid about the use of this analytical framework, if only because the result of this comparative international research has been not merely to chart similarities and differences between European countries, but also to bring to light *new theoretical problems*.

The objective of this chapter is to introduce the relevant concepts, by considering the role played by labour markets in economic growth in postwar Europe. It raises one key question, central to the various analyses contained in this book: are the institutional forms of the labour market homogeneous or heterogeneous?

2. Growth in European Countries and Wage/Labour Relations: Some Historical Facts

In the early 1950s it was generally feared that the interwar trend towards stagnation would recur, and that once reconstruction had been completed, European economies would return to their long-term growth rate of around 2 per cent a year. As we now know, such fears were groundless, since most industrialized countries grew by around 5 per cent a year between 1950 and 1973. The population explosion accounts for only a minor part of this acceleration, which derived mainly from a rapid long-term growth in productivity.

2.1. Simultaneous changes in production and consumption norms

It is necessary to explain why capital accumulation, which had taken such a disastrous turn during the 1930s, was able to continue for more than a quarter of a century without a major crisis. One explanation springs naturally to mind: the countries of Europe, ruined and partially destroyed by the war, had the opportunity of achieving the productivity levels of the US economy. There is little doubt that the technological, as well as organizational and industrial, features of the 'American model' played a pivotal role in the recovery of these countries: the United States blazed a trail that the other economies were to follow as best they could in the light of the possibilities provided by the current socio-political climate and their inherited cultural traditions.

Most comparisions of productivity levels confirm the tendency of Japan and most European countries gradually to catch up with the United States. There was, however, nothing automatic about such a relationship, as is illustrated, on the one hand, by the stagnation of relative productivity in the United Kingdom and, on the other, by the very different trends in European economies after 1973.

The American model not only permeated methods of producing (production norms), but it also affected our way of life (consumption norms).[1] Between the two world wars the European countries had 'imported' the former without having been able to introduce the latter, even though such altered consumption norms were vital to the completion of the macroeconomic cycle; an inadequacy of effective demand despite a huge increase in mass production was a familiar feature of the 1929 crisis. After 1950, however, the reason why predictions of stagnation were disproved was that *mass consumption* developed in tandem with the modernization of productive systems (see, e.g., Bertrand, 1981; Boyer, 1979b).

Thus, per capita consumption almost doubled from 1960 to 1977 in countries such as France and Germany. The United Kingdom lagged behind somewhat, possibly because the life-style there had already altered after the First World War, or because the country was suffering the consequences of its attempts to increase productivity. Consumer expenditure began to take on characteristics remarkably similar to those in the United States, and patterns of consumption in the European countries began to converge in a process extremely similar to that already experienced with production structures. This parallel between a rapid change in production norms and a transformation of consumption norms was a distinctive new feature of the postwar period.

But does this then mean that what lies behind successful evolution is technology? The harnessing of technological potential is not, in fact, a convincing explanation. Modern methods of organizing production were available as long ago as the 1920s, and so were certain durable goods: why did the postwar pattern of development not catch on then?

---

[1] The originator of these terms was M. Agglietta (1976), who carried out an analysis of the US economy in the 1970s.

Robert Boyer

2.2. *A New Deal between wage-earners, employers, and governments*

One explanation undoubtedly lies in the economic mechanisms by which gains in productivity are apportioned. Between 1920 and 1930, the effect of the upsurge in productivity accompanying the spread of Taylorism (see Section 4) was to reduce the need for industrial employment and to depress real wages, on account of the broadly competitive mechanisms that prevailed in the United States and in most other countries at that time. Given that there was insufficient unearned income to ensure that consumption kept pace with mass production, the logic of the market inevitably restored compatibility between production and demand by means of a huge fall in prices, economic activity, and profits.

Since the 1950s, however, the situation has been quite different because of the extremely clear parallel between the growth in industrial productivity and the rise in real wages. Of course, such a parallel was already evident during the second half of the nineteenth century, but it was now operating at a particularly high rate of growth without being interrupted by periodic depressions. Moreover, it became rarer and rarer for nominal prices to fall, thereby reducing the short-term imbalance between production and sales. Instead, adjustments increasingly took the form of productivity gains being handed on to those groups that provided mass consumption: first and foremost, wage-earners. Indeed, in recent years wage-earning has become the dominant form of productive activity, which means that in the countries of continental Europe waged work is gradually reaching the proportions long known in the United States and the United Kingdom.

Cumulative growth gives rise to a circular process of economic development: a high level of investment permits industrial modernization and reconstruction and hence yields major potential productivity gains, while the workers are willing to accept the new systems of labour organization and to leave the initiative for them in the hands of employers, focusing their demands on increased real wages. Since the Second World War disputes have, *de facto* if not *de jure*, ended in compromise, with managers selecting the methods of production and wage-earners receiving a share of the 'dividends of progress', i.e. the productivity gains thereby obtained. Consequently, the growth of real-wage income matches that of productive capacity in the consumption sector (housing, cars, other durable goods, etc.) and calls in return for more investment, which mobilizes the sectors producing capital goods. As long as the capital coefficient is roughly stable — or even if it declines — a stable distribution of income implies a more or less constant rate of profit. A cumulative process becomes possible: rapid growth is fostered by a stable relationship between wages and profits and consumption and

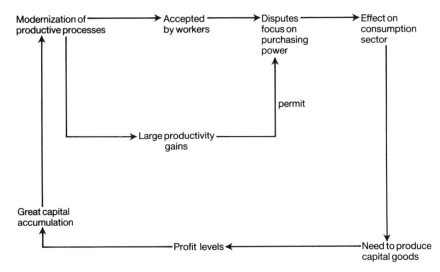

FIG. 1.1 How the establishment of new wage/labour relations has been central to the growth of European economies since the Second World War.

investment.[2] Fig. 1.1 outlines the logic of the links in this virtuous growth process.

Two fundamental characteristics of labour relations lie behind the virtuous circle of productivity–growth–investment–consumption:

- Workers and their trade unions accept the imperative of modernization, which is left to the discretion of company managers.

- Labour disputes focus on nominal wage rises, so that these vary according to anticipated productivity gains and inflation.

3. An Interpretation in Terms of Wage/Labour Relations and Methods of Regulation

The above features could undoubtedly be incorporated in the traditional approach to analysing the labour market. But that approach has the drawback of implying the existence of a timeless, universal logic, in which imbalances and crises are due solely to violations of the principles of pure and perfect competition. The likelihood of nominal wages increasing while unemployment is high and still rising is ruled out *a priori* by standard neoclassical theory: only the monopoly power of trade unions, the

[2] This process has been analysed, and later formalized, by Bertrand (1983).

disruptive role of public unemployment compensation, or the influence of anticipations of the future can explain stagflation, even though the phenomenon has been common since the late 1960s. In addition, this line of analysis often, though not inevitably, leads to the recommendation of almost complete 'laissez-faire', since surely market economies would be structurally sound, were it not for ill-advised and always belated intervention on the part of governments?

Both the history of capitalism and theoretical research make it perfectly obvious that such a miraculous property derives more from an assumption or belief than from 'scientific' results.

3.1. Some basic definitions and concepts

There is room, it seems, for another theory, which differs from the above in that the gradual transformation of social relations leads in time to a change in the laws governing the operation of particular economic systems. This is the premise that underlies the *regulation* approach. To stay with the question of labour relations, it is the concept of *wage/labour relations* that enables these changes in the functioning of the labour market to be analysed. Similarly, it is important to describe the breakdown in the process of growth by distinguishing between the concept of recession (or cyclical crisis) and that of *structural crisis* (or 'major crisis'). This approach has been the subject of a series of studies. Here, I shall merely give a few brief definitions: the interested reader may refer to the works cited.[3]

The basic hypothesis is that the economic, political, and legal features of social relations may take various forms, the configuration of which must be specified. Such is the purpose of the concepts of *structural (or institutional) form*. The consequence of each of these forms, which span the social and economic spheres, is both to define the place of individuals and groups in society and to produce principles of adjustment, and hence an element of regularity, in the economic order.

The term *regulation* as used here will signify the dynamic process by which production and social demand adapt. It occurs when economic adjustments encounter a given configuration of institutional forms. In a system dominated by the logic of the market and by capitalist relations, the success of regulation is gauged by its ability to guide and channel the process of capital accumulation, and to contain the imbalances that this tends constantly to generate. What may then appear is a *system of accumulation* marked by relative compatibility between the dynamic of

[3] See Cassiers (1986); Chavance (1984); Drache (1984); Gutierrez Garza (1983); Haussmann (1981); Leborgne (1982); Letourneau (1984).

income distribution on the one hand, and the growth of the means of
production and consumption on the other. The term *mode of development*
will sometimes be applied to the symbiosis between a method of
regulation and a viable system of accumulation.

These definitions attribute a central role to *institutions*, which unite the
legal and social spheres, since they generate the rules of the game and the
conventions determining collective and individual behaviour. In this
sense, it is generally meaningless to refer to 'pure' economics if we wish to
analyse a specific economic situation, and even more if we wish to analyse
the transformation of economic processes over a long period of time or
during a structural crisis.

It is consequently not enough to refer to the most general, abstract
features of social relations that lie behind every economic system,
although their precise nature, i.e. the structural forms on which they rest
in a given society and at a given time, must be explained. Similarly,
unlike the idea of equilibrium, the concept of regulation stresses the
dynamic of the links in the economic process (which normally generate
fluctuations) and not so much a timeless point of equilibrium. Furthermore, there can be extremely *diverse methods of regulation* and not just one
single principle of equilibrium: 'economic laws' are ideally related to a
combination of structural forms. They are therefore likely to alter in the
long term. Research has thus shown that over two centuries the
traditional method of regulation has been succeeded by competitive and
finally monopolistic methods of regulation; it has also demonstrated that
the 'scarcity' method of regulation of Eastern European economies is
original and distinct from that of other countries.

3.2. An analytical approach to long-term changes and structural crises

It is inherent in the very definition of regulation that imbalances are a
permanent feature of every economic system, particularly when the
system is largely activated by decisions regarding capital investment.
Some kind of more or less periodic crisis is thus the consequence of any
given method of regulation. It can in fact be demonstrated that the
nature of cyclical crises has radically altered since the late eighteenth
century. But not all crises take this form: during certain periods in
history, a downturn in economic activity is insufficient to compensate for
the imbalances that have accumulated.

A distinction must hence be drawn between 'minor crises' and
structural or 'major crises', as the two are qualitatively (and quantitatively)
different. I shall designate as a major crisis an episode in which the
dynamic of the system itself, and/or the form taken by social and political

struggles, conflicts with the network of structural forms on which the system of accumulation and method of regulation are based. An easy way of pinpointing such a period is to observe the destruction, bypassing, or decay of the most fundamental institutional forms. But a breakdown in some of the previous regularities may also be identified. This affects capital investment in particular, but also unemployment, inflation, and interest rates. The current period thus has all the characteristics of a structural crisis.

Finally, one of the many structural forms emerges as being especially important: *wage/labour relations*. We shall use this general term to designate the process of socialization of productive activity under capitalism: wage-earning. This may be organized in one of several ways. The network of legal and institutional conditions governing the use and reproduction of the work-force will be called the *form of wage/labour relations*. These terms define the way in which wage-earners fit into society and the economic system. The different forms of wage/labour relations therefore result *a priori* from the combination of a method of labour organization and, more generally, of production norms and a life-style defined by the equivalent of a series of consumption norms.

On a more analytical level, wage/labour relations can conveniently be disaggregated into their five components:

- organization of the work process;
- the stratification of skills;
- worker mobility (within and between firms);
- the principle of direct and indirect wage formation;
- use of wage income.

This definition calls for three comments. First, wage/labour relations assume special relevance when one studies mature capitalist societies, where the proportion of waged work is considerable and dominates other forms of economic activity. This has been precisely the case with European economies over the past decade. Second, this concept is sufficiently broad for us to be able to anticipate *a priori* close linkages between the form of wage/labour relations and the method of regulation, which have in fact been confirmed by long-term historical research covering the United States and France. So readers will not be surprised to learn, from the national studies, the extent to which economic crisis and change in wage/labour relations determine one another. Finally, there is evidence of changes in labour organization, wage formation, and life-styles in the history of industrial capitalism. This makes possible extremely diverse forms of wage/labour relations, which is the point I shall now stress, in returning to my initial question: why was there exceptional growth after 1945?

4. From Taylorism to Fordism: A Fundamental Change in Wage/Labour Relations and Methods of Regulation

By way of illustration, I propose to label as *Taylorian* the wage/labour relations that gradually emerged in industry from the late nineteenth century onwards: fragmentation, then reconsolidation of the organization of labour, generated a new method of obtaining productivity gains on the one hand plus a slight change in life-style, while maintaining the competitive determination of wages on the other. Conversely, since 1950 the dominant pattern of wage/labour relations has been of the Fordist type: on the one hand a prolongation of the Taylorian phase by mechanization, and on the other a shift in consumption norms, mainly as a result of nominal wages rising to keep pace with anticipated gains in productivity. Of course, this is only one of a series of changes that have recurred; others include changes in the form of competition, in state intervention, in currency policy, and in the system of international relations. Nevertheless, previous research has attempted to show that what was new about the period 1945–73 had mainly to do with changes in work relations, or more precisely in wage/labour relations, to use our terminology.

The shift from Taylorism to Fordism, from competition-based to wage-orientated methods of regulation, was no transitory phenomenon but a radical change in the way in which labour markets functioned, and, even more, in their role in the process of growth and in determining economic activity. So we can summarize very succinctly some of the factors that facilitated the transition from stagnation and the perverse linkages of the 1930s to sustained growth and the virtuous circle of the 1960s (Fig. 1.1). The postwar employer/employee compromise (workers' acceptance of modernization in return for an assurance that their standard of living would benefit from the resultant productivity gains) is what lent momentum to the gradual consolidation of the Fordist wage/labour relations and to the decline in the competitive logic that made 'downward' adjustments (bankruptcies, lay-offs, price wars) the primary methods of regulation. This is, moreover, the basis of the efficiency of Keynesian global demand management policies and of their acknowledged success during the mid-1960s. There is no guaranteeing, for example, that they could have rescued the United States from the 1929 crisis without significant changes to wage/labour relations, to government intervention in production, or to currency management. One might be tempted to say that 'the combination of the New Deal and Keynesianism' was what halted the highly unfavourable trends of the interwar period.

This over-concise historical review is not without relevance for the analysis of the transformations that occurred a decade ago with respect to wage/labour relations and economic policy in European countries. Two points spring to mind:

1. The accelerator (the Keynesian stimulus to demand via the multiplier process) must not be confused with the motor (the postwar mode of development, which focused on mass production and consumption).

2. It is no accident that those responsible for economic policy insist on referring to the functioning of the labour market as being of central importance, but that is merely the expression of a hitherto hidden dialectic between the success of Keynesianism and a specific form of labour relations.

First, however, let us elaborate on the above analysis and ask whether it corresponds to experience in the various countries: have Fordist wage/labour relations been homogeneous, or have they, on the contrary, differed significantly between countries according to their history, socio-economic structures, and political leanings?

5. The Diversity in Fordist Wage/Labour Relations in Different European Countries

The specific nature of each of the European economies can be seen in Table 1.1, which summarizes, in a succinct and somewhat oversimplified manner, the aspects explored by the national reports, to which readers may refer for a fuller and more detailed analysis. This national diversity affects all components of wage/labour relations.

5.1. *Various configurations of trade union–employer–government relations*

Labour market institutions are in fact strikingly heterogeneous in the various countries considered (see Table 1.1), so that postwar wage/labour relations sometimes derive from significantly different configurations of social and economic factors.

In some cases, *trade unions* exercise their main influence at the level of the firm, not only as regards labour organization and working conditions but also as regards wage bargaining. This seems to be the case in the United Kingdom, Ireland, and, apparently, Italy. But in other cases the structures and strategies of unions are defined at sectoral level, through the negotiation of agreements fixing minimum levels of wage rates or pay rises, for example. This second configuration applies to West Germany and, to a lesser extent, France. In still other countries, wage norms and certain general conventions affecting all wage-earners are directly determined at national level between occupational groups. This category includes Franco's Spain, France after the 1968 Grenelle *accords*, and most European countries during the 1970s.

There is just as much diversity as regards employer organizations between European countries. In West Germany, for example, these are highly structured, possess financial resources, and are able both to represent an entire industry and to guarantee the application of agreements reached. Elsewhere (Ireland, United Kingdom), employers do not appear to have any unified or centralized power, whether because of the role of multinationals or because of a long tradition dating from the early days of industrialization. But there are also intermediate cases (France, Italy) where employer organizations take part in national agreements, although they have little power over individual firms; nor are they always able to represent interests that often conflict (small versus large firms).

The *role of the state itself* in labour relations varies greatly between countries and is determined largely by political history. In some cases the state is omnipresent, and acted as the catalyst, or even the driving force, in the emergence of Fordism, as seems to have been the case in France and Belgium — and indeed in Franco's Spain, where 'fascist paternalism' meant that the state almost totally dominated industrial relations. In other countries, history and tradition dictate that negotiations are the prerogative of the 'social partners' (West Germany), although the state sometimes finds itself obliged to intervene when the system seizes up (as in the United Kingdom since the 1960s, and Ireland in the 1970s).

Consequently, the conventional Fordist doctrine of wages being based on the cost of living and anticipated productivity gains may be determined by very different socioeconomic circumstances. At one extreme, local trade union representatives might negotiate this type of contract in the most dynamic firms or sectors, where they are in a strong position; then, in a bid for parity, national unions might demand that the results achieved be extended to the whole system. That is exactly what happened in the United States after the Second World War (with the spread of the Fordist conventions originating in the automobile industry). The same process also exists in European countries such as the United Kingdom (with shop stewards having the power to negotiate for improvements over national pay agreements), Ireland, and even Italy or France (with firms such as Fiat and Renault playing a central role in the dynamic of wage movements in the 1950s).

At the other extreme, there are successful income policies resulting from an agreement between employers, unions, and the government about a general formula relating to wage formation. A principle, rather than an explicit, binding norm, prevailed in most European countries (Belgium, West Germany, France) during the 1960s. As we have seen,

TABLE 1.1. *A summary comparison of methods of organizing wage/labour relations in seven European countries*

	France	UK	Ireland	Belgium	Spain	Italy	W. Germany
Trade union movement	Very low unionization; competition between rival unions; fairly loose organization	Very high unionization of blue- and, to a lesser extent, white-collar workers; proliferation of trades and industrial unions	Very high unionization; claims generally wage-related; labour disputes extensive	High rate of unionization; pluralist, competing unions	Workers operate under corporatist system; unions illegal until 1977	Periods of union strength and unity alternate with others of division and decline	Average rate of unionization; well structured; unions extremely united
Employers' organizations	Split into various trends and bodies; not much structure or power	Fairly weakly organized	Significance of 'small' multinationals	Relatively unified	Obligation under Franco to belong to vertical sectoral unions	Frequent oppositions; public holdings/private companies	Powerful, well organized, with certain binding powers
Government intervention	Massive intervention; almost all national accords tripartite; historically, change initiated by the law or public settlements	Principle of voluntary negotiations between firms and unions; from 1960s periodic tripartite agreements negotiated and wage norms fixed	Legislative system similar to UK: principle of non-intervention by government, but growing involvement in the 1970s	Significant government mediation in labour relations and especially wage formation; sophisticated network of social consultations at all levels	Heavy involvement in management of labour relations before and after 1977; less so in the 1980s	Major legislative interventions in response to worker struggles (*Statuto dei lavoratori*, 1970)	Government excluded from contractual relations between social partners
Types of collective agreement							
Level of negotiations	Dominant role of agreements within or between sectors; little bargaining in firms until Auroux laws	Originally mainly between firms, or even plants, but trend towards centralization since 1960s	Centralized until 1970s and additional local negotiations	Minimum conditions set at sectoral level, then negotiations to improve them within firms	Quite heavily centralized despite recent changes	Centralization at confederal level in 1950s, then an upsurge in decentralized contracts after 1969	Sector or large firms
Frequency of agreements	Usually annual	Annual	Annual	Annual/pluri-annual	Annual	Annual	Annual

Role in wage formation of:

Productivity	Government announced principle of distributing 'dividends of progress' in 1961; consequently, minimum wage and public sector pay policy	General principle of distribution accepted; various examples of efficiency bonuses; generally no explicit clauses	Agreement with a view to boosting productivity; productivity clauses in some wage agreements	Distribution principle accepted since 1954, but few explicit agreements	Few implicit references to any distribution	Not explicitly provided for, either by government policy or in collective agreements	Exists implicitly at national level
Cost of living	Indexation illegal but practised increasingly from late 1960	No indexation clause as such, but increases often backdated	Explicit clauses fixed in 1970 and 1972; proportional in 1974 and 1975	Explicit indexation procedures	Revision clauses based on inflation, past and predicted	Indexation clauses have become widespread and comprehensive	In theory, all indexation prohibited
Labour market	Little direct effect on average wages, but some effect in certain sectors (e.g. public works)	Little influence until early 1970s	Major role of migration in adjustment of job market	Significant in the past and for certain competitive sectors	Initially, political pressure; after 1980, suspension clauses where firms might go out of business	Particularly sensitive during boom periods and when job market is tight	General economic situation, especially abroad, taken into account
Social security							
Extent	In line with EEC average	Significantly lower than EEC average	Initially poor, but growth in the 1960s	Widespread	Patchy	Initially poor and regressive	Widespread
Level of benefits	In line with EEC average	Significantly lower than EEC average	Lower than in UK, but higher than in comparable countries	Close to EEC average	Well below that of other European countries	Always below EEC average	About EEC average, except for unemployment benefit
Finance	Mainly by employers, but also the insured and the state	Predominantly financed from national budget; small contribution by employers and insured	Social welfare by government; social insurance by employers and employees	Employers and government; small contributions by the insured	Overwhelmingly by employers	Mainly by employers, the state, and, marginally, the insured	Especially by employers, plus roughly equal contributions from the insured and public funds

these two methods may succeed each other over time in one and the same country, so that the initiative may shift from an individual firm to a sector to the government, or vice versa.

These differences become even more marked when we compare *social security systems*, an important, if not essential, element together with direct wages in the dynamism and regularity of the macroeconomic process of development. Every nation combines, in variable proportions, insurance and relief, financial contributions by beneficiaries and by the state through taxation and budgetary measures, and the distribution of welfare costs between firms and wage-earners. Furthermore, depending on the history of the union movement and the nature and the stage of industrialization, the social security systems tend to be more or less complete and well integrated.

A key lesson to be drawn here is that 'importing the American model' has by no means meant a gradual convergence of institutional forms of wage/labour relations. In fact, each European country seems to have introduced it by adapting its national traditions, to such an extent that it is clearly wrong to claim that Fordist wage/labour relations can have only one configuration. In one sense, the regulation-based approach is confronted with the same difficulty as were theories of corporatism:[4] such an extreme variety of these forms emerges from international comparisons that the concept itself requires further elaboration, or at least amendment.

5.2. *Differing degrees of compatibility with the virtuous circle of Fordist growth*

If we now measure how close each country comes to the typical Fordist model, the heterogeneity is equally striking. Yet some countries represent clear exceptions.

Pre-eminence of state intervention and a marked tendency towards the formal institutionalization of wage/labour relations: France. The weakness of union organizations in France, the divisions between them, the resolve of employers to resist social progress, and the inadequacy of negotiations within firms undoubtedly explain why the state plays such a role, more so perhaps than in any other of the seven European countries considered. Not only does it intervene in tripartite agreements of the kind found in the United Kingdom and Belgium, but it extends the results of individual agreements to the national level by means of legislation. Further, it has sometimes initiated major changes in labour law in response to particularly bitter social conflicts (e.g. May 1968, after 1936, and 1945). It is tempting to see the French government as the leading actor in the

---

[4] See in particular the analyses by Schmitter (1974), and Panitch (1980). An analysis of various European countries has been edited by Berger (1980).

arena of labour relations. The consequence of this characteristic is that wage/labour relations have become institutionalized and legalized to a high degree. Inasmuch as workers and union organizations have accepted that modernization is justifiable and imperative, these advances towards sharing the fruits of economic progress have contributed to economic dynamism, making France an outstanding example of the successful adaptation of the Fordist model — at least in the 1960s.

Fordist wage/labour relations with neither industrial modernization nor increased growth: the United Kingdom. Because of the specific form of union organization and occupational traditions in the United Kingdom, skills and remuneration are linked to the holding of a job whose description is fixed by collective bargaining. This is a major break with Fordism. On the one hand, British wage-earners obtain early recognition of their social rights, and wage disputes are often bitter. But on the other hand, the usual safety valve of constant job reorganization and industrial modernization is partially blocked. Consequently, there has been no productivity boom equivalent to that in other countries. The difficulty of restoring industrial competitiveness has led to the famous 'stop–go' cycle, encompassing a very unfavourable trend in the rate of industrial profit and early de-industrialization. It is no surprise, therefore, that reform of industrial relations has been on the political agenda for almost twenty-five years.

The aim of the eternal quest for productivity agreements has surely been to restore the basis for virtuous growth. The United Kingdom is therefore unique in that it exemplifies a premature crisis in somewhat atypical Fordist wage/labour relations.

Institutional similarities and externally orientated growth: Ireland. Ireland, no doubt owing to its size and belated industrialization, seems to conform to a model in which labour, and subsequently industrial products manufactured by subsidiaries of multinationals, are exported, rather than to one of growth hampered by the simultaneous extension of production and consumption norms. The paradox may ultimately be that wage/labour relations have so many characteristics of Fordism (wage indexation, apportionment of productivity gains, a huge increase in the admittedly very low social security levels), whereas the dynamic of economic growth is externally orientated. In addition, for historical reasons, legislation relating to labour relations is very similar to that of the United Kingdom. This cannot fail to cause problems in that the industrial and social structures of the two countries are so different.

A high foreign trade propensity, with institutionalization of wage/labour relations: Belgium. Perhaps one of the most striking characteristics of the Belgian model is that relations between employers, unions, and government at all levels (firm, sectoral, national) are extraordinarily close-knit. In a context where workers do not put forward demands of a structural kind, disputes relate first and foremost to improvements in real wages. Remarkably, throughout the 1960s, although the bargaining process was distinctively Belgian, it proved to be quite compatible with continued competitiveness. Belgium even won larger market shares and improved its position in the international division of labour. Recent years have witnessed a sharp contrast: the former codification of wage/labour relations has had an adverse effect on the foreign trade balance.

Wage/labour relations based on 'fascist paternalism' rather than Fordism: Spain.   Until 1977, the Franco regime banned all official union activity, both local and national, and in effect imposed corporatism in the strict sense of the term, a rare phenomenon. And yet, beneath their legal veneer, practices within firms tended to resemble those in democratic countries.

In any event, in the 1960s industrial modernization took two forms: an upswing in typically Fordist sectors, and mass consumption of durable goods. The implantation of a mode of development hinging on mass production and consumption, with no explicit compromise as to how productivity gains were to be distributed, is undoubtedly paradoxical.

An upsurge in mass consumption before Fordist wage/labour relations are established: Italy.   The paradox is hardly any less blatant in Italy. It would seem that mass consumption began to emerge between 1958 and 1965 — while the socio-political situation was such that trade unions were excluded from economic life. A second surprise is that the rapid spread of Fordist methods took place long after the changes in life-style. Moreover, social security cover remained embryonic and inadequate before undergoing a massive expansion from 1969 to 1975. Finally, it was only in 1970 that a form of wage/labour relations that goes beyond strict Fordist logic was legalized and formally institutionalized, affecting worker mobility and labour organization in the work-place. Also, as Enrico Wolleb puts it (Chapter 7), a period of unregulated labour relations was followed by a plethora of reforms. Having lagged behind, Italy found itself in the lead in the 1970s, just when the deepening of the international crisis caused employers to view the guarantees inherent in Fordist wage/labour relations as a source of 'rigidity'.

Decentralized negotiations and a continual search for flexibility within wage/labour relations: West Germany.   West Germany is unique in that employer–trade union negotiations are very decentralized and the state's role, a very minor one, is generally limited to suggesting the broad direction to follow without intervening in individual agreements. This lack of institutionalized government involvement no doubt partially explains the considerable degree of flexibility in labour relations. Moreover, in contrast to the state of affairs in the United Kingdom, job mobility and technological progress are usually more readily accepted than in most other European countries. Not all the productive processes are predominantly Taylorian, but they rest on particular skills and versatility: only in the late 1960s did Fordist logic take a firm hold (especially in the automobile industry, when resort was made to immigrant manpower).

West Germany thus seems to be midway between Fordist wage/labour relations and pre- (or post-?) Fordist mechanisms which are relatively competitive as compared with other European countries.

5.3. Divergences in macroeconomic performance

Finally, what consequences do these configurations have for the pace of modernization and hence the behaviour of the main indicators constituting the circular process of productivity–wages–consumption–investment–growth? Table 1.2 presents some results from the seven European countries considered during the period 1960–73, i.e. before the crisis.
Spain, Italy, Ireland, and *France* all experienced rapid productivity growth, leading in turn to a rise in output. Since the institutional systems of these four countries are quite different, it is tempting to see the similarity of their economic performance as the consequence of catching-up. Industrialization in these countries had been belated and incomplete. Their growth rate accelerated after the Second World War and continued to do so until the 1960s and 1970s.

At the other extreme, in the *United Kingdom* productivity gains were comparatively small, both in relative terms and from an historical perspective. This poor performance cannot be explained, in the 1960s any more than in previous years, by the lead taken by British industry in terms of productivity and specialization: during this period most other European countries outstripped Britain. Its endemic crisis in industrial relations, which hampers the modernization process, was probably not unrelated to this outcome.

West Germany and *Belgium* fell between these two extremes. Productivity growth was considerable: more moderate than in the first group of countries but more rapid than in the United Kingdom. It should be stressed that in terms of levels of productivity the results would be different, as the surveys show a convergence during the 1960s *before* the disparities became pronounced (see e.g. Boyer and Petit, 1980; Guinchard, 1984).

TABLE 1.2. *Success indicators of Fordist growth, 1960–1973*
Annual average rate for the whole period

	France	UK	Ireland	Belgium	Spain*	Italy	W. Germany
GDP growth	5.6	3.1	4.4	4.9	6.6	5.3	4.5
Productivity (output per head)	4.9	2.9	4.3	4.2	5.4	5.6	4.2
Real wages	5.0	3.3	5.4	5.0	6.4	6.5	5.3
Employment	0.7	0.2	0.1	0.7	1.1	−0.3	0.3
Unemployment	1.0	2.1	4.7	2.3	2.1	5.2	0.8
Current balance of payments as % of GDP	0.2	0	−2.4	1.3	—	1.7	0.7
Ability to finance public services: Net government lending or borrowing as % of GDP	0.5	−0.3	−3.6	−1.8	—	−2.6	0.3
Inflation rate (consumer prices)	4.7	4.9	5.9	3.7	—	4.8	3.7

* Long-term data not available. These figures are for the years 1964–73.

Sources: *Economie européenne*, November 1984, pp. 225–7; July 1984, Table 2, p. 11; for Spain, Toharia (1984, pp. 81–124).

This virtuous circle is a remarkable phenomenon. It results, in all countries except Italy, in the net creation of jobs that, even if their number does not match the increase in the working population, are none the less sufficient to keep unemployment largely in check. Need we recall that between 1960 and 1973 average unemployment was in the region of 1 per cent in France and West Germany, and about 2 per cent in the United Kingdom, Spain, and Belgium? Two countries were exceptional: Italy, which experienced chronic unemployment arising in particular from the imbalance between North and South, and Ireland, where unemployment has long been a major problem which industrialization in the 1960s and 1970s seems somewhat to have alleviated.

Three other features are of interest because of the contrast they provide with the situation between 1973 and 1984. Throughout the earlier period, trade, capital movements, and production became increasingly international, yet growth and national independence were not adversely affected. There was no obvious correlation, either for the seven European countries or for a larger group, between macroeconomic performance and the degree of openness to foreign trade (see Boyer and Ralle, 1986a). Measures to stimulate and stabilize the economy tend to be used alternatively to balance national budgets in countries such as France, the United Kingdom, and West Germany. Italy, Ireland, and Belgium were exceptions to this rule (see Table 1.2). Further, the pace of growth in productivity gains made it relatively easy to finance social security increases. In short, financial policy was not hampered by any public debt constraints. From the late 1960s, however, inflation began to soar and to pose problems of monetary stability at both national and international levels. And the grounds for this phenomenon were the subject of the first challenges to 'Fordist–Keynesian' logic and economic policies.[5] In the late 1970s, moreover, the difficulty of balancing foreign trade and the persistence of public deficits were factors that handicapped the pursuit of former growth patterns.

More fundamentally, from the late 1960s onwards, productivity and real wages fell out of step, owing to the effect of both social struggles and imbalances. The average data for the period 1960–73 reflect this advance in wages (Table 1.2). The phenomenon appears to be significant in almost all the countries apart from France and, to a lesser extent, the United Kingdom. This change served to depress profitability and hence to reduce investment potential, a fact that was concealed for a while by the vigour of the temporary boom in 1969–73.

Returning to the period 1960–73, we see that all seven countries experienced growth, although to varying degrees. It is not the object of this book to conduct a comparative analysis of the relationship between the nature of industrial relations on the one hand and macroeconomic performance on the other. The national surveys use a different method to examine these links: a *chronological* analysis, often going back beyond the 1960s. But, in essence, their authors address themselves to one key question: why was growth halted and the former institutional environment challenged?

[5] It was also the subject of the first analyses in terms of regulation: Aglietta (1976), Boyer and Mistral (1978), Lipietz (1978).

6. An Analysis of Changes in Wage/Labour Relations during the Crisis: A Brief Presentation of the Volume

Any classification is somewhat arbitrary, and the national reports in this comparative study could have been presented in a quite different order. It is up to readers to select their own ordering of the seven countries examined. It nevertheless seemed appropriate to arrange them in a particular order, the criteria for which will now be explained briefly.

It seemed natural to begin by examining the case of *France*, since it has already been the subject of several studies which have greatly contributed to theoretical work on the concept of wage/labour relations. This does not mean that Chapter 2 merely recapitulates previous analyses: its author, Pascal Petit, begins by offering his own views on a number of issues. He questions the role of government in the great success and then breakdown of Fordist wage/labour relations, and he distinguishes between various alternatives where the state takes the lead and where, on the other hand, it follows and legitimizes trends set by individual agreements. Next, and most importantly, he conducts his analysis with reference to the results of the ·other national reports, which puts into perspective the initial approach to Fordist wage/labour relations: he feels that omnipresent public intervention constitutes more of a specific than a general feature. Lastly, now that sufficient time has elapsed to make this possible, Petit considers the significance of the policy conducted since May 1981.

Chapter 3, which is by Terry Ward and deals with the *United Kingdom*, is both similar and contrasting to the previous chapter. In the United Kingdom, too, wage/labour relations have become highly contractualized because of bi- and tripartite bargaining and significant government intervention in social protection. But there are major dissimilarities. On the one hand, trade union structures are very different. They are such that pay depends very much upon the post held within a firm. The fragmentation of British unions contrasts with the unity that derives in France from a proliferation of agreements between sectors or even occupations. On the other hand, whereas trade union representatives have some control of the organization of work in the United Kingdom, French unions tend to accept the *de facto* situation. The consequences of these differences are reflected in the macroeconomic performance of the two countries, both in the 1960s and in the 1980s. It is thus useful to study wage/labour relations in the United Kingdom so as to highlight certain limits of Fordism by describing historical experience long before 1973.

It is logical to move next to *Ireland* (Chapter 4), in that Miceal Ross shows to what extent the institutional system of labour relations has been determined by reference to the UK model. The general conception of collective bargaining is similar. But here, paradoxically, the structure of production and the international dimension are quite different: the model of development owes more to expert dynamism triggered by the setting-up of plants belonging to multinationals than it does to the mass production/consumption link in the domestic market. A second feature is that the imbalance between the working population and the work available tends to give rise to major waves of migration, in a way reminiscent of the competition-based method of regulation that prevailed in the nineteenth century in Ireland as elsewhere. This contrast between apparently Fordist institutional forms and a non-Fordist system of accumulation ought hopefully to stimulate fresh theoretical activity. In the past, certain scholars have tended to infer the significance of the latter from the existence of the former. It is clearly important to describe and compare these sets of circumstances — institutional and economic.

In one sense, Chapter 5 continues this line of thought. *Belgium* is also a country with a small domestic market, wide open to multinational capital and to foreign trade. This structural characteristic should *a priori* imply the persistence of a method of regulation of employment and wages based mainly on competition. But the historical analysis by Geert Dancet demonstrates that the procedures institutionalizing wage/labour relations are extremely sophisticated. They appear to have succeeded in rec-onciling two objectives often considered to be conflicting: growth in real wages and social security, and a stable foreign trade balance. But this compatibility seems to have been shattered in the early 1980s, when foreign trade failed to recover and the structural nature of the present crisis became apparent. Geert Dancet's analysis is thus also of relevance to countries with larger domestic markets faced with the same dilemma: can the maintenance of a high standard of living and an extensive social security system be reconciled with an improved international position?

The following two chapters carry the analysis further by presenting an equally paradoxical configuration: a quick march towards Fordist growth, while labour relations remain governed by a legal system and power structure that are pre- and even anti-Fordist.

The study of *Spain* by Luis Toharia (Chapter 6), exemplifies this. The productive system was modernized under the mantle of wage/labour relations inspired by corporatism in the strict sense of the term, as practised by fascist regimes. It would be futile to search for the slightest reference to notions of distributing productivity gains under this system, since the aim, at least in principle, was to guarantee employment stability to wage-earners. However, within firms, circumstances were often quite different in practice, and this gave some impetus to growth in Spain at the time. In short, throughout this period the institutions lagged behind industrial and economic change. But, after the fall of Franco, the pace of institutional modernization quickened so markedly that, in less than ten years, the legal system registered a shift to explicit Fordism (explicit indexation clause, negotiation of a nationwide social contract, etc.), followed by a search for employment and wage flexibility, under the formidable pressure of a dramatic slow-down in growth and an unprecedented spurt in unemployment. There could be no better example of the extreme complexity of the relations linking political and social history with economic logic over both the medium and the long term.

The lesson we learn from Enrico Wolleb's study of *Italian* growth (Chapter 7) is broadly similar. At the end of the Second World War, there were numerous obstacles to a compromise between union and employers' leaders: the political and ideological isolation of the Left in a system dominated by the Christian Democrats, the relative newness of industrialization, the geographical heterogeneity characterized by surplus manpower in the Mezzogiorno, and so on. And yet in northern Italy the basis for mass production was laid, and mass consumption began to soar. Only in the early 1970s, however, after the worker struggles of 1968 and 1969, did the legal and contractual system record a shift to explicit Fordism. But this transformation was so radical and so extensive that it jeopardized the pursuit of growth and productivity gains even in large plants using Fordist production methods. Consequently, managers began much earlier than in the rest of Europe to explore alternatives (robotics and automation on the shop-floor) or means of circumventing the bastions of worker power (by the use of moonlighting or illicit labour, the development of smaller companies, and, more generally, the decentralization of production). Ultimately, the attempt to over-institutionalize Fordist relations has had the opposite effect: a proliferation of forms of flexible employment.

As for *West Germany*, that country seems for many years to have been exploring totally different ways of making labour more adaptable. This is the main theme developed by Gerhard Leithäuser in Chapter 8. First of all, the fragmentation and division of tasks accompanying the move towards Taylorism was less pronounced here than in other countries, so that there is less polarization of skills and less conflict over the acceptance of technical innovation. Second, foreign manpower is traditionally used as a means of adjusting to short-term fluctuations and aberrations; thus, in the labour market certain competitive forms of adjustment persist. Finally, acceptance of the principles of a social market economy have led to great flexibility in the rules governing the participation of wage-earners in general economic progress. Furthermore, collective agreements, which are largely decentralized, result from confrontation between employer and union organizations without any government interference. Here we have a striking contrast with the tripartite agreements customary in France and the United Kingdom. We might be tempted to coin the somewhat crude term 'flexi-Fordism' to depict the institutional framework and economic dynamic prevailing in West Germany since the Second World War. This historical legacy explains the specific way in which flexibility has been sought since the late 1970s: a *de facto* if not *de jure* incorporation of the need for large firms to adapt to the new technology, and negotiations over the redistribution of working time, taking the form of discussions about a 35-hour week or manpower swaps between companies. In short, the German model contrasts strongly with both Italy (since the need for adaptation is more readily accepted by large firms) and France (because the government has a very limited role in initiating new forms of wage/labour relations).

The second part of this book weighs up the similiarities and divergences in the trends prevailing in Europe. It first explores in particular those factors that might explain the general challenge to Fordist institutions: the pace of technological and industrial change at international level, management strategies to improve the profitability of firms, and the role of the fear of unemployment in conditioning trade union demands. There follows a discussion of the concept of flexibility, which today is so widely regarded as one of the best ways out of the crisis. There are in fact as many forms of flexibility as there are components of wage/labour relations, and their social and economic consequences, in the short and the long term, may be extremely diverse. By way of illustration, it is possible to imagine an *offensive* strategy, combining technological modernization with social progress (both within firms and globally), as opposed to a purely *defensive* flexibility, where an improvement in competitiveness takes the form of retrograde measures likely to jeopardize the chances of achieving an enhanced position in the international division of labour and, thus, a lasting recovery. Various possible scenarios are presented, arrived at by combining hypotheses about the reconstitution of wage/labour relations, the dynamic of the international system, and the orientation of national economic policies.

This initial comparison of the different national studies clearly necessitates an elaboration of the simplified model of Fordism, from both a theoretical and empirical standpoint. Finally, and above all, the changes that have occurred since the crisis struck lead us to reiterate the questions referred to above, three of which may serve to guide us through this book:

- Have reactions to the crisis been more homogeneous than divergent?
- How have the different countries coped with the rise in unemployment and the crisis of Fordism?
- Does the general quest for flexibility signal the decline of the old wage/labour relations?

Problems of the State in Dealing with the System of Wage/Labour Relations: The Case of France

Pascal Petit

1. The Influence of Recession

The crisis that broke in 1974 has led to fundamental and far-reaching changes in the system of wage/labour relations in France. Growth, which had averaged 5.7 per cent per annum between 1959 and 1973, fell to an annual average of 3.1 per cent between 1973 and 1979, and to just 1.1 per cent between 1979 and 1983.

Between 1974 and 1982, unemployment rose steadily and rapidly: the percentage of unemployed among the working population increased fourfold, from 1.8 per cent in 1973 to 8.3 per cent in 1982. The rise in the number of unemployed, which had for a time held steady around the 2 million mark, picked up again at the end of 1983.

The share of wages in value added jumped from 50 to 55 per cent between 1974 and 1976, and by 1983 was around 56 per cent. In the period 1969–73, however, this share had remained in the 48–50 per cent range. This shift, to a new distribution between wages and profits which has been maintained since 1979, is largely the result of an increase in the level of indirect labour costs. From 1978 onwards, direct pay accounted for roughly the same proportion of GDP as it did in 1974.

Recession has increased the demands on social security (both for unemployment pay and to finance pensions and other family income supplements), with the result that social security deductions have had to rise, adding to labour costs. At the same time, the growth of expenditure on health care has continued at a rate similar to that in the pre-crisis period.

The changes that have occurred cannot be explained simply in terms of shifts in relative prices. There have also been marked changes in the sectoral composition of GDP. Social security, which is financed mainly by employee and employer contributions, placed a heavy burden on labour costs, with the drop in growth making it necessary to call on the guarantees of financial support (mainly unemployment benefit, but also old-age pensions and family allowances), while exogenous factors have encouraged growth in health expenditure, which has now reached a rate similar to that of the pre-crisis period.

Furthermore, these long-lasting changes in expenditure cannot be attributed merely to changes in the relative prices of GDP and consumer goods: they are also linked to changes in volume. The most striking of these is the relatively steady growth in household consumer demand, at a ...ne when expenditure has reflected the slow-down of economic growth:

- from 1959 to 1974, gross fixed capital investment increased at an annual rate of 7.1 per cent; consumer demand increased at annual rate of 5.4 per cent;
- from 1974 to 1983, the average annual growth of investment was no higher than 0.5 per cent, while consumer demand continued to grow by 3.1 per cent per annum.

The growth in disposable income, relative to GDP, coupled with a falling savings rate, has ensured that the growth of consumers' expenditure has remained relatively stable.

This buoyancy of consumer demand has been more beneficial to imports than to domestic production. A striking example of this is the automobile market, where import penetration of the domestic market rose from 22 per cent in 1979 to 32.7 per cent in 1983. In an economy where growth is restricted because of difficulties in ensuring an equilibrium in the balance of payments, this propensity to import consumer goods leads to the introduction of policies favouring invest-ment, which are possibly more expensive in terms of imports but are considered more capable of restoring a competitive edge to the economy. If the principal determining factor in private investment remains the prospect of expanding markets, these policies can only be deflationary.

It is against this background that we should assess the development of labour productivity in industry. Numerous factors (trends in technical development, rapid depreciation of machinery owing to increased competition in markets with lower growth rates) have meant that the drop in productivity growth has been less than the decline of growth in output. This differential has brought about a marked decrease in the number of jobs in industry, where a total of 1 million jobs have been shed over a period of 10 years (from 5.9 million in 1974 to 4.9 million in 1983), while in the same period of time the number of people employed in the service sector increased by 1.3 million.

This shift of jobs to the tertiary sector has radically altered the dynamics of industrial relations. The recent decline in employment in the industrial sector has diminished that sector's former leading role as an employer in the labour market, particularly of young people entering the labour market.

All these changes in the macroeconomic characteristics of the system of wage/labour relations have had an influence on the various forms of social organization (institutions, customs and practice) that govern labour practices and condition their continuation and development (Table 2.1). Sectoral wage freezes and local unemployment have a cumulative effect, which in turn has a tendency to change completely the fabric of industrial relations that ensured a prolonged period of growth during the 'thirty glorious years' (1945–75).

TABLE 2.1. *Productivity, growth, and employment in France, 1960–1983**

	Employment, 1960		1960–73		Employment, 1973		1973–79		1979–83		Employment, 1983	
	000	%	Q	P	000	%	Q	P	Q	P	000	%
Industry	5 182	27	7.3	6.4	5 764	27	2.9	4.1	0.2	2.6	4 375	20
Market services	5 462	28	5.9	3.5	7 307	34	4.3	2.0	1.9	0.8	8 679	41
All sectors	19 581	100	5.6	4.9	21 303	100	3.1	2.8	1.2	1.5	21 348	100

* Average annual rates: Q, value added; P, productivity (%).

Thus, the crisis has opened the way to changes in social institutions and practices, in line with prevailing political philosophies. The political change of direction in France that came in 1981 shows the scope for policy choice, in a crisis that for the most part goes beyond the economic and social environment of France alone. In order to go into this point in more detail, I propose first to sketch a brief outline of the wage-earning sector of the population at the beginning of the 1980s (Section 2), and then to put into perspective the great evolution undergone by this sector over the last thirty years (Section 3), before going on to assess the direction being followed by current developments (Sections 4–6).

2. General and Specific Features of the Wage-earning Sector in 1984

Wage- and salary-earners make up more than 80 per cent of the working population in France; thus, the organization of paid labour, its implementation, and its reproduction have affected all aspects of society. Before outlining the trends that developed and the various points of deadlock that were reached during this crisis in the system of wage/labour relations, I shall set out the position in 1984. This shows how previous characteristics combine with new features which have either come to the fore during the crisis or are the result of long-term trends and developments. A long view of the subject is needed for full understanding.

2.1. The shift of labour to the tertiary sector, the increase in the number of women employed, and the pressures of unemployment

Of a working population in France of 21.4 million people (in 1983), 83 per cent were employees.[1] This wage-earning sector has a predictable structure. Sixty per cent were male, for the most part aged between 25 and 60. In this age group the activity rate was about 90 per cent among men and 60 per cent among women. The blue-collar category was in the majority among men (51 per cent), while more than half the women were employed as white-collar workers (55 per cent). This reflects employment by sectors, with 62 per cent of jobs in the service sector. Industry, in the strictest sense of the term, employed only 29 per cent of the total number of employees. It is noteworthy that, out of the 10.9 million employed in the tertiary sector, 4.5 million were employed by the state or by local authorities. On the other hand, 98 per cent of jobs in industry were in the market sector of the economy, incuding jobs in the nationalized industries. This category of employees was mostly an urban group: four out of five lived in towns with a population of more than 2000, two out of five in towns or cities with populations of more than 200 000. Regional variations in activity rates underline the importance of this link between the expansion of the number of people employed and urbanization: in the Paris region the activity rate among women between the age of 25 and 55 was nearly 70 per cent.

Possibly more unexpected are the effects on the working population of demographic change and variations in activity rates. The activity rates of young and old people provide one example. Although school attendance is compulsory only up to the age of 16, a mere 20 per cent of men and 15 per cent of women started work before the age of 20. Likewise, two-thirds of men between the ages of 60 and 65 retired early, even though the official retirement age remains 65.

These trends in starting work and retirement are influenced by the situation on the labour market and by measures taken to promote employment (expansion of vocational training schemes and development of early retirement schemes). The extent of unemployment among young people is worrying. Although the rate of unemployment for the whole of the working population was 7.9 per cent in March 1983, the percentage among young people between the age of 15 and 25 was actually 21 per cent. Likewise, the long periods of time involved in looking for work could

[1] These and the following statistics are taken from the Labour Force Survey carried out in March 1983.

discourage older people: the average length of time for a person to be unemployed was 13.9 months (in March 1983); for persons above the age of 50, the length of time increased to 21.7 months.

Difficulties on the labour market have not, however, hindered a steady increase in the activity rate of women aged between 25 and 55 from the end of the 1960s onwards. The rate of unemployment among women is nevertheless higher at all ages than that of men; in March 1983 unemployment among men amounted to 6.1 per cent, whereas among women this figure rose to 10.5 per cent.

This change in women's attitudes, in which a higher level of education and a gradual change in social values have played an important role, has been accompanied by a drop in the birth rate: the average number of children born fell from 2.9 in 1965 to 1.8 in 1975. However, a favourable age structure enabled the natural high ratio of births to deaths to ensure a population growth rate of above 0.6 per cent per annum up to 1973. This demographic increase explains most of the steady growth of the working population up to 1983 (+180 000 workers per annum on average, after 1963), as net immigration (which had been as high as +120 000 foreign workers per annum between 1963 and 1973) had been halted since 1974.

After making allowances for cyclical economic effects (+387 000 employees in 1982, and −6500 in 1983 following measures promoting early retirement), it is estimated that demographic changes will lead to an average increase in the working population of 130 000 per annum between the years 1985 and 1990.

2.2. *Industrial relations: the role of contracts*

Collective bargaining essentially comes within the framework of a 1950 law on collective agreements, which institutionalized relations between employers' organizations and trade unions. Such bargaining can be carried out at various levels: from the most centralized national inter-industry level to that of the branch of the industry concerned (1950 law); from the industry at the regional level to, more recently (1971 law, then 1982 law), the level of the individual firm. The state can initiate central negotiations, but it can also, by means of an extension procedure, make a collective agreement subject to common law. This procedure ensures a certain homogeneity in the development of labour relations, particularly with regard to those activities not subject to agreements. (In 1981, 1 out of 10 employees in firms employing more than 10 people was not covered by any collective agreement.) Certain jobs in special categories were not covered by such collective agreements; these include jobs in public services and in firms in the public sector that have a special status. These agreements cover, *a priori*, all aspects of the conditions of employment and labour organization, but until 1982 negotiations on wage levels were generally not included. This exclusion, and the unspecified period covered by the agreements, explain the relatively poor results obtained by collective bargaining. The 1982 law, which legally requires annual negotiations on wage levels, tried to remedy this situation.

The low level of trade union membership among employees is the main reason for the weakness of collective bargaining. Thus, it was calculated that in 1981 only 23 per cent of employees were trade union members. Trade unionism in France is essentially divided into five confederations. In 1982 their titles (in abbreviated form) and membership numbers were as follows: CGT, 1 900 000; FO, 1 000 000; CFDT, 979 000; FEN, 500 000; CFTC, 250 000.[2]

Work-place union branches (recognized in 1968) have given some impetus to trade union activity, and have encouraged the election of staff delegates and works committees (in firms employing more than 50 people). Moreover, a body of civil servants, work inspectors, and a joint elective court — the industrial tribunal — ensure control and arbitration in the application of labour law (legally binding obligations) and in the interpretation of collective agreements (contractual agreements). In particular, any proposed redundancies are subject to the assessment of the work inspection department.

An important statutory restraint is provided by the existence of a minimum wage (inter-industry minimum growth wage, or SMIC). In 1982 around 1 million employees, that is 6 per cent of the total, received this minimum wage. Increases in the SMIC beyond the rate of inflation are decided by the government. In January 1984 the SMIC was at Ffr 3850, having increased in real terms since 1983 by 0.7 per cent, i.e. more than average real wages.

Various legal statutes distinguish employees according to their conditions of employment: temporary workers, apprentices, workers with a limited-term contract (one year), employees on training courses, etc. In 1983, out of 12.5 million employed in the private sector, 2 per cent were working under a one-year contract, 0.9 per cent were temporary, 0.4 per cent were on training courses, and 1.4 per cent were apprentices. Within the public sector, 82 per cent have security of tenure while only 18 per cent do not. Only very few people were employed part-time: 3.1 per cent of blue-collar workers, and 13.1 per cent of white-collar workers (especially women, among whom 17 per cent were employed for less than 30 hours per week). These statistics underline the predominance of full-time workers with an unspecified term of contract, under which the right to redundancy is subject to authorization by the public authorities, and

---

[2] According to estimates made by the European Trades Union Institute (Brussels).

negotiations on wages and working conditions tend to be carried out by means of collective bargaining.

An historical perspective moderates this image of a monolithic body of wage-earners. A look at how wages are determined and the socialization of income highlights a clear diversity in the situations of different groups of employees.

2.3. *Wages: negotiated structures and conflictual pay rises*

The diversity is less apparent in the methods of payment (the basic wages of workers with contracts of unspecified lengths have been paid on a monthly basis since 1980) than in the composition of monthly salaries. On top of basic pay, there are various seniority bonuses, plus transport, holiday, or thirteenth-month (holiday) allowances, which are most often defined in the collective agreements. In firms with more than 10 employees (according to the 1981 EUROSTAT survey on the structure of wage costs), these bonuses amount on average to 10 per cent of the basic salary, varying to a considerable extent according to the sector involved (20 per cent in banking and insurance, 5 per cent in consumer goods industries).

Blue-collar workers, on the other hand, tend to receive higher payments for days absent in firms with more than 10 employees (see INSEE, 1984, p. 104). Taking account of these factors (bonuses, absenteeism, etc.), the range of annual salaries by broad socio-industrial category in 1982 is on a scale stretching from 1 (Ffr 54 100 in 1982) for blue-collar workers to 3.16 (Ffr 171 200) for management (1.05 for white-collar workers).

The structure of wages is thus based on a series of complex rules (qualifications, bonuses, allowances), negotiated mainly at industry level. There are, however, no hard and fast rules governing how wage rises are negotiated. The annual obligation to negotiate wage levels (which does not include any obligation to conclude the negotiations) introduced by the 1982 Auroux laws is still too recent for us to be able to judge what effect they will have on previous practices.

The minimum wage level and price indexing constitute two important determining factors in wage rises. Recommendations for wage rises put forward by the industry's employers' organizations serve as a reference for the firms concerned. The lack of agreed procedures for negotiations on pay increases explains why so many industrial disputes arise from pay claims.

On top of wages (70 per cent of labour costs, according to EUROSTAT in 1981), we can add the social security contributions paid by employers to finance social security benefits. These indirect wages accounted for three-quarters of the legal obligations (74 per cent). Employees also contribute directly to social security expenditure by means of deductions at source from their earnings; their contributions amount to between one-third and one-quarter of the employers' contributions, according to the wage level.

The social security system financed by these deductions is divided into a certain number of funds, each corresponding to a particular type of 'guarantee' of financial support: sickness benefits, old age pensions, family allowances. These make up the social security funds in the strictest sense of the term, and to these we could add a supplementary retirement fund and an employment fund. Each of the separate funds that provide financial support is managed autonomously by representatives elected by employees and employers under the supervision of government officials. In this way they set the level of contributions separately for employers and employees, as a percentage of gross wages, and with a ceiling for contributions in respect of the retirement, family, and unemployment funds.

We can obtain an overall view of the relative importance of the direct and indirect shares of the wages by relating them to GDP. In 1983 total labour costs were 55 per cent of GDP, split up as follows (shares of GDP):

- 36.9 per cent for net salaries;
- 5.4 per cent for employees' contributions;
- 12.7 per cent for employers' contributions.

These contributions, however, finance only a part (79 per cent in 1980) of social security expenditute (Ffr 754.5 billion in 1980). Public funds pay for certain supplementary benefits, such as special welfare schemes (these special schemes cost the state Ffr 74.8 billion in 1980), and make good the deficits of certain schemes (including the agricultural scheme) (Ffr 51.4 billion in 1980).

2.4. Social security: largely autonomous growth

The social security system, which absorbs one-quarter of GDP (that is, more or less the average for funds channelled into this area in the countries of the European Community), has a very complex system of benefits, particularly those relating to retirement pensions and unemployment benefits.

Sickness benefits and pensions together accounted for almost 60 per cent of all benefits in 1984 (25.5 and 34.4 per cent respectively of total expenditure); family allowances absorbed 11.9 per cent of the total. Tax allowances linked to the size of the family explain the fact that the percentage of these family allowances in France is much higher than in the countries of its European neighbours.

Unemployment benefit constitutes a rapidly increasing percentage of other social benefits. It rose from Ffr 32.8 billion in 1980, i.e. 4.2 per cent of all expenditure on social security, to 8.5 per cent, i.e. Ffr 98.2 billion by 1984.

Growth in benefits can be induced either by a new agreement or policy measure, or by a change in demographic or economic conditions. The number of people benefiting from sickness insurance schemes and retirement and family allowances is largely dependent on the demographic situation. On the other hand, the number of recipients of unemployment benefits or social welfare schemes depends on economic activity. The autonomy of insurance funds and the interrelation between the gradual increase in benefits and the surrounding economic and demographic environment implies the need for a frequent review of regulations to define the field of beneficiaries covered and the amount of benefits granted.

Sickness benefits (Ffr 293.8 billion in 1984) provide an example of 10 years of largely 'autonomous' growth linked to the increase in the number and quality of medical services provided to each beneficiary: an expansion of the 'client group' of those insured under social security, and an increase in the level of reimbursement of medical costs, have contributed only 0.6 and 0.3 per cent, respectively, to an average annual growth in sickness benefits of 4 per cent per annum in real terms between 1975 and 1982.

The value of the financial support provided by unemployment benefit and old age pensions is best seen in relation to wages. In 1983, 65 per cent of unemployed people received benefit. For a worker in his or her first year of unemployment, this payment was the equivalent of 64 per cent of wages.[3] The rate of payment was increased to 74 per cent in cases of redundancy (one-third of unemployed men, one-quarter of unemployed women). Recent efforts to encourage early retirement at the age of 55 and above led in 1983 to the payment of 505 000 early retirement bonuses costing roughly the same as a first year's unemployment benefit.

Old age pensions kept pace with changes in wage levels, but the minimum guaranteed pension, like the SMIC, could be subject to discretionary increases — as was the case in 1981 (+10.4 per cent) and in 1982 (+20.6 per cent). The minimum old age pension reached Ffr 76.85 per day on 1 January 1984, i.e. the equivalent of 3.25 hours payment of the SMIC.

Family allowances (Ffr 137.1 billion in 1984) have not been linked to either price or wage indices. At this level, these benefits have a

---

[3] According to CERC (1982), the percentage of previous wages paid as unemployment benefit was much higher in France than in Britain (between 21 and 39%) or West Germany (53%).

redistributive effect on household incomes of the same order of magnitude as income tax (Ffr 198.9 billion in 1984). Thus, in a household with two children, where there are two people earning average wages, receiving a combined annual income of Ffr 149 770, the family allowances received would amount to Ffr 10 830, and the taxes paid on income would be Ffr 9 410.

Finally, growth in benefits follows wage changes, imbalances on the labour market, and 'internal' developments in the benefits situation (health insurance). Certain key rates are used by policy-makers to contain or accelerate expenditure in relation to wages and prices. In this context, the minimum old age pension and the base family allowance play an important role.

A look at the past development of the social security system enables us to assess further the scope for further changes in social security.

2.5. *The state as employer*

All personnel in public office, and established employees of nationalized industries, i.e. a third of all employees, enjoy good job security and a high level of welfare benefits, particularly old age pensions and sickness benefits. On the other hand, wages in the public sector tend to be lower than those in the private sector.[4] This is evident only at management level: the salaries of top and middle level civil servants amount to 63 and 81 per cent, respectively, of those paid to their counterparts in the private sector (INSEE, 1984, p. 114). The rise in unemployment and a stagnating economy have enhanced the value of any existing job security and regular wage rises.

This assessment of the situation explains why public sector wages have been restrained since 1977, and it also accounts for the establishment in 1982 of a 1 per cent levy to provide for unemployment benefit.

Employees in the public sector and those in the private sector are quite distinct; people enter into jobs in the public sector early, often after vocationally orientated academic training. The semi-public sector (public firms in the competitive sector) is often better able to provide the impetus for change in industrial relations in the economy as a whole.

The key role played in the past by public corporations such as Renault underlines the importance of the recent nationalization of nine industrial groups and commercial banks (which brought the size of the work-force in the nationalized sector up from 1.09 million to 1.76 million employees), which was accompanied by a series of laws on the

---

[4] This qualification does not, however, apply to jobs in state-owned enterprises such as EDF (French Electricity Board), Air France, etc.

democratization of the public sector. This was done to ensure that the enlarged public sector maintained its leading role in social policy.

In some ways, the procedure followed is quite characteristic of the way industrial relations in France have evolved. Following a social or political event or change of national importance (a national strike or a change in government), statutory measures or new regulations provide the impetus for lasting changes in industrial relations, depending on the local or sectoral context. However, some measures do still go unheeded.

2.6. *The crisis in the system of wage/labour relations*

Pinpointing and explaining the structural and institutional characteristics of wage-earners does not account for the level of tension in industrial relations. Workers no longer pin their hopes of social integration in a meritocracy on paid work alone. Unemployment is seen no longer as a breach of contract, but rather as a protected risk. Stagnation of the average wage level no longer leaves a question mark hanging over careers. An understanding of the pressures imposed on the system of wage/labour relations by the need for employment, demands for flexibility in production, a reduction in the difference between the highest and lowest wage levels, and growth in the level of deductions from wages is possible only by taking a longer view. This might allow us to relate changes in the statutory and legislative framework to changes in practice. The crisis has upset relations between actual labour practices and written laws. The political change of direction that came about in 1981 illustrates the scope allowed to the politicians to influence changes in the system of wage/labour relations in a period of crisis. Past experience shows the extent to which policy has been responsible for change.

3. The Main Periods of Change in Wage/Labour Relations since 1950

On the basis of numerous factors, three periods in the development of the system of wage/labour relations can be distinguished (see also Table 2.2). The character of industrial relations, the composition of the working population, the opening of the economy to foreign markets, the mode of development of social security, the pressure of wage increases, etc., are all involved. The crisis that took hold in 1973 had, by 1977, called into question the system of wage/labour relations that had prevailed from the end of the 1960s. This would suggest division into the following periods:

- *1950–68*. This was a period of transition towards a wage-earning society. The state played a central role in this change, in the absence of a developed system of collective bargaining between employees and employers.

- *1968–77.* Here we can observe an extension in the formalization of the system of wage/labour relations, with the development of collective bargaining at all levels and the 'positive' expansion of social security.

- *1977–81 and after.* This period can be seen as a time in which certain previous tendencies are called into question. The outcome of this period is uncertain, and depends on the scope allowed to changes in policy after 1981. It is generally acknowledged that since 1977 there has been a deep-seated crisis in capital/labour relations, but the diversity — indeed, the disparity — of the various changes means that this period has remained transitional in character so far. This will continue to be the case until reforms brought about by political change intersect with macroeconomic circumstances to bring about definitive changes in practice.

The precision in defining these periods is misleading. A number of authors (e.g. Reynaud, 1978; Jobert, 1974) agree that that the beginning of the new era in industrial relations should be situated around 1967–8. Dating the appearance of the crisis as a lasting phenomenon in the system of wage/labour relations can be less exact. The first austerity plan of Raymond Barre dates back to September 1976, but the implementation of a wage policy did not occur until 1978. According to several authors (Colin *et al.*, 1984; Boyer, 1981), the change in emphasis and direction in labour relations occurred around 1977. In the transitional phase that began then, the change of government in 1981 is an event of major significance. The outcome — that is, the form that industrial relations will have taken following the legislative changes of 1982 — remains uncertain.

There are two sides to the question here: one concerns the link between legislative changes and practical developments, the other, the challenge posed to policy-makers in coping with problems of growth and employment. History points the way to an answer, as much with regard to the development of practices as to the effectiveness of economic policies.

3.1. 1950–68: a period of transition

We shall focus primarily on the period between 1950 and 1968 — which, because of the key role played by the state, provides a useful parallel with developments taking place in the 1980s (Delorme and André, 1983).

From 1950 onwards, there was a fairly well developed institutional framework governing industrial relations. The law on collective agreements detailed the conditions to be laid down in collective bargaining. Discussion on wage levels (previously fixed by the Parodi system of

TABLE 2.2 *Development of wage/labour relations over a fifteen-year period: a few reference points*

Components of the wage/labour relation	1967	1968	1969	1970	1971	1972	1973	1974	1975	1976	1977	1978	1979	1980	1981	1982	1983
Wages Effect of economic conditions on wages		Guaranteed minimum wage +35%					Price indexing became general practice, 1973-6				Price freeze: the Barre plan	Min. wage rose more slowly than av. wage, 1977-81			Buying power of min. wage greater than av. wage, 1981-3	Min. wage +5.5%	Prices and wages freeze
Social welfare contributions				Introduction of min. wage indexed to internat. min. wage			1968-76: min. wage rose faster than av. wage		Partial abolition of ceiling levels	Reductions for young people; employment pact			Growth in contributions for unemployment and sickness insurance, 1978-81				
Type of wage formation		Worker participation in profits		Progress contracts in all sectors	Declaration in principle in favour of monthly wage payments			Agreements on monthly wage payments, reorganization of qualifications, end of production-linked wages (1975)				Monthly payments general practice; increase in low wages				Mandatory annual negotiations—the Auroux laws	
Employment and organization of labour Employment conditions			Redundancy notice and compensation			Collective bargaining for temporary employees		Immigration stopped	Authorization to dismiss now required		Agreements limiting the employment of temporary staff, 1977-9		Law on fixed-term contracts		Law on part-time work	Law on the use of temporary staff	
Supervision and organization of labour		Recognition of the trade union sector						Social plans for works' councils	Agreement on improvements to working conditions						Health and safety committees	Mandatory annual negotiations—the Auroux laws	
Working time			Fourth week of paid holiday					Agreements on reductions to the working week, 1975-9							Transition to 39-hour week; fifth week of paid holiday		

	1	2	3	4	5	6	7	8	9	10	11
Social protection Unemployment benefits	Compensation for part-time unemployment				90% compensation for redundancies due to economic factors			First flat-rate compensation; end of 90% system			Second change; different benefits merged
Social security and pensions	**Reform of social security**		Maternity benefit	Agreement on early retirements 70%		Agreement on early retirement for all employees 60 yrs and over			Solidarity contracts	Early retirement: system extended	
Training			Law on leave for in-service training courses			First pact on youth employment		Second pact on youth, women	Third pact	Plan for the futures of young people, 1981–3	
Political and social climate Social conflicts		May '68 strikes	Particularly intensive series of strikes	LIP affair	Radio strike	Oct '76, May '77, Dec '77 — national strike days		Conflicts and Manufrance violence in the steel industry and in immigrant hostels		Conflicts in the car mfg sector involving immigrant workers	Lowest level of strikes since 1965
Political events		Election of Pompidou	Union of the left		Election of Giscard	Chirac plan for economic revival	Arrival of Barre	Austerity plan	Breakup of the left-wing union	Election of Mitterand; moderate revival	Austerity measures

classification in 1945) could now be carried out freely. A guaranteed inter-industry minimum wage, the SMIG (created in 1950 — forerunner of the SMIC), was linked to a price index; the aim of this was to maintain a minimal buying power for all wage-earners. Labour regulations continuing the social progress instigated in 1936 (40-hour working week, paid holidays, etc.) and the liberating intentions shown by the Conseil National de la Résistance (control of redundancies) completed this institutional framework. The social security system, a mutualist insurance system created in 1945 guaranteeing everyone a minimum in social security, was managed by representatives elected by the workers.

This institutional framework was under the overall financial supervision of the state. In fact, the *anomie*[5] of industrial relations, notably, the absence of any direct contact between employers' representatives and employees, meant that such a framework did not work well. Custom-and-practice rules were rare, and regulations (40-hour working week, control of redundancies, etc.) were not applied. Industrial relations were broadly adversary, with employers reluctant to recognize trade unions and trade unions maintaining a resistance to change. Strikes or arbitration carried out by the government (which appointed experts) often constituted the only way in which wage recommendations put forward by employers' organizations could be disputed.

These conflicts, and the upheavals caused by the decline in the non-waged sectors of the population (guaranteed outlets and prices for agriculture, the reactionary attitude of small traders to socioeconomic development), were reflected in the persistence of a relatively high rate of inflation (4.8 per cent per annum on average between 1950 and 1968).

Against this background, the determination of the system of wage/labour relations in the long period of growth between 1950 and 1968 implied, directly or indirectly, a central role for the state and the public sector. At that time the government five-year Plan played a leading part in reconciling different industries and sectors.

With the 2nd, 3rd, and 4th Plans, the guidelines for the modernization and development of industry were drawn up. These guidelines were heavily dependent on a dynamic nationalized sector (EDF, SNCF, Renault). The aim of adding on social planning was abandoned in the middle of the 1960s. Instead, it was the nationalized sector (the SNCF, EDF, and Renault, successively), combining productivity gains and social advances, that gave a considerable boost to the rate at which improvements in labour conditions took hold. In retrospect, the limitations of such a 'system' of industrial relations appear to be many.

---

[5] This was the term used by Cellier (1981).

3.2. The limits of state management, 1950–68

First of all, worsening pay disputes acted as a brake on industrial growth and on the possibilities for restructuring industry. The serious strikes of 1967, which followed the pressure put on wages by the stabilization plan of 1963, highlighted the archaic method of distributing value added. Moreover, the increase in the percentage of women working, the growth in immigration, and the effect on the labour market of the postwar bulge in the birth rate brought about a steady growth in the working population which was not offset by a parallel growth in jobs available. Unemployment began to rise from 1967/8 onwards. It is quite significant that the development of collective bargaining was marked in 1967 by the inter-industry, intersectoral agreement on benefits paid for partial unemployment. By 1968 the minimum wage (SMIG) lagged well behind wages. This heightened inequalities by maintaining zones of low wages; however, the May 1968 events led to an increase of 40 per cent in the SMIG.

Plans for the administration of social security by workers themselves were frustrated by problems of finance. The steady growth in expenditure for sickness benefit and old age pensions gave rise to a need for increased contributions, which employers refused to make. (A 1967 reform led to a joint system in which employers, workers, and the state all helped administer the different social security funds.)

In addition to these signs of impasse, it became clear that certain gradual social changes towards a wage-earning society were reaching the point of completion: 70 per cent of the population were now living in urban areas; 77 per cent of the working population were already wage-earners. Consumption of durable goods in well-off households had reached saturation levels. In addition, the creation of the Common Market, by then in its eleventh year, heavily restricted interventionist actions by the state. This led to a decline in the indicative planning process which had so characterized the 1950s and 1960s.

It is against this background of seeking to overcome the difficulties facing a mature wage-earning society that the development of collective bargaining between workers, employers, and the state after 1968 needs to be seen. And it is a result of this background that industrial relations in France came to resemble more closely those in economies that had undergone earlier industrialization.

3.3. 1968–77: an extension of the management of wage/labour relations

In broad outline, an initial characterization of how industrial relations developed from 1967/8 onwards can be attempted. One of the most salient features of the period was an extension of collective bargaining, through industry-wide negotiations on terms and conditions of pay (change-over to a system of monthly paid salaries, abolition of low pay, reduction of the working week), but also through agreements made by large firms, following the extension of the law on collective bargaining (1971). These changes were accompanied by the recognition of trade unions. (Trade union representation in firms was made legal in 1968.) Another significant point about this 'modernization' of the system of wage/labour relations was the change-over from the minimum wage known as the SMIG to the SMIC (minimum inter-industry growth wage) in 1970; instead of being indexed only to prices, the new minimum wage was designed to ensure that the lowest paid shared in the general growth of the economy.

The payment of 90 per cent of former wages where workers had been made redundant, a measure introduced in 1974, was part of the same movement. (The sharp rise in unemployment was, on the other hand, considered by the Chirac government and by employers to be a cyclical phenomenon.) However, these developments in industrial relations had a limited effect on the level of wages. Collective agreements only covered indexation clauses (which, incidentally, were officially forbidden), while the minimum wages negotiated bore little relation to actual wage levels. Negotiations on wages were, on the whole, not conducted at the industry level, so as to allow each firm its own room for manoeuvre.

The related need for flexibility in the management of the labour force explains the increased use of less secure forms of employment (temporary, limited-term contracts, etc.) (see Germe and Michon, 1979), at the same time as contracts of employment became more favourable to workers.

The development of collective bargaining diminished the influence of the public sector in shaping industrial relations, especially after the limited success of Jacques Chaban-Delmas (and Jacques Delors) in establishing long-term bargains, trading off guaranteed pay rises for industrial peace. No-strike clauses proved an early obstacle to the signing of such agreements by the trade unions (e.g. the EDF contract).

In matters of social security, however, state intervention appears to have been more direct and far-reaching than in the past. Although the 1967 reform established joint management, the state then had to intervene in order to ensure the proper working of the system (1974 reform). In 1972 all employees were required to belong to private schemes (on top of social security), and guarantees of financial support for the unemployed (state aid) were extended; they were later extended to the whole population (waged or unwaged) under the 1978 law. These interventions show a characteristic French tendency towards excessive legislative control. Nevertheless, the independence of many benefit schemes raised questions about their financial viability, made acute in a period when the crisis had become entrenched.

3.4. 1977–81: the system of wage/labour relations under scrutiny

In France, the deceleration of economic activity that followed the oil crisis of the last quarter of 1973 came both late, because the effects were felt only in the second half of 1974, and rapidly, since the trough in economic activity came at the beginning of 1975. This explains why most commentators at the time took the view that the recession that began in 1974 was cyclical in character. However, the brevity of the recovery in 1976, not only in France, but also in the majority of the developed industrial countries, even before the second oil crisis of 1980, showed quite clearly the long-lasting nature of the crisis. Continuing high unemployment and the difficulties in financing welfare schemes (social security, unemployment) and budgetary expenditure signalled to the state the start of a new era. Moreover, the share of wages in GDP, which up to that point had been quite stable, increased from 1974–5 onwards; with the propensity of households to save remaining unchanged, and even falling after 1979, this shift was reflected in a trend towards higher consumption, to the detriment of investment. This is seen by some as the root of the problem of poor growth. The reorientation of policies that accompanied the arrival in power of the Barre government in the summer of 1976 clearly illustrates this new awareness. Since the inflation of the mid-1970s favoured wage-earners, breaking down inflationary mechanisms (all the more important since the composition of wages was still little subject to collective agreements) became the main objective of a policy aimed at re-establishing previous shares of GDP.

After 1977, incomes policy became the touchstone for these policies. However, these firm intentions were not backed up by adequate means. The means were constrained by the extension of collective bargaining but also by a certain gap between the professed ideology and the real strategy of the Barre government. The price control policy aimed to contain wage inflation, but without going as far as formal pay restraint. Moderation in wage increases was strongly recommended to the private sector. The minimum wage continued to rise in real terms (1.8 per cent between January 1977 and January 1981), but at a slower rate than average pay (2.0 per cent). Full-scale wage austerity was applied to the public services. The buying power of civil servants levelled out before starting to decline in 1979, and by 1983 was down to its 1975 level. Against this background, increased collective bargaining in the private sector became a less significant issue.[6] Furthermore, the movement towards collective

---

[6] The Sudreau Report (1975) was not to be followed up, except in some clauses of the 1982 Auroux laws.

44   *Pascal Petit*

bargaining appeared to be running out of steam. From 1977 to 1981, collective bargaining at the industry level was ineffective (length of working week), or succeeded only with great difficulty (hygiene and safety committees). The agreements reached were essentially defensive in nature, e.g. restrictions on the amount of temporary employment in some industries, and the 1979 inter-industry agreement on the reform of unemployment benefit.

Positive action to promote employment, such as the 1977 agreement on early retirement schemes (for all employees over the age of 60) and the Youth Employment Pacts[7] (apprenticeships, exemption from employers' contributions, practical and vocational training periods paid for by the state), constituted little more than modest measures towards the establishment of a new way of sharing work in order to decrease unemployment. The slow-down in economic growth and the limited scale of employment creation policies offered little prospect of bringing down the total of 2 million unemployed reached by 1981.

Low employment combined with a growth in health expenditure to put added pressure on the financing of social security. Measures intended to contain expenditure, such as the reform of unemployment benefit (January 1979), did bring the regulations a little further into line with one another (with the abolition of the 90 per cent payment of previous wages introduced in 1974), and began a movement towards a reduction in the guarantees of financial support, even though these were in any case too low. In 1980 pressure to reduce wages and growth in the rate of deductions from wages led to a drop in the disposable incomes of households, a phenomenon unknown since the 1950s. This drop led to a fall in household savings (from 17.5 per cent in 1978 to 14.1 per cent in 1980), while consumption continued to grow. Policy seemed to be precariously balanced, with industrial relations and wage negotiations in deadlock and a chronic crisis in social security, which seemed to call into question the existing state guarantees of welfare support.

All of these factors contributed to the creation of conditions for political change in 1981. The new Socialist government responded by deciding to give top priority to the search for a solution to the impasse.

4. After 1981: The Pursuit of a New Basis for the System of Wage/Labour Relations

The Socialist government quickly set up a series of extensive legislative and institutional reforms. I shall not list these in full here, but shall limit

---

[7] These 'pacts' offer young people work experience, but have no medium-term effect on employment (see Gaspard and Frank, 1981).

myself to a brief outline of the programme before focusing on three key issues in Section 5: flexibility, wage structures, and the new concept of work-sharing.

This intense government activity highlights clearly the two types of constraint limiting its impact on the system of wage/labour relations. One could be described as being of an economic nature — a Keynesian macroeconomic policy, however modest in scale, is soon faced with problems arising from the scale of the foreign trade deficit that it engenders. The other constraint, more social in nature, highlights the necessity for consensus as a basis for changes of a legislative and statutory nature. Since Keynesian policy, however cautious, had demonstrated its limitations within the space of one year, the question of the social basis required to move from the stage of legislative changes to actual changes in the system of wage/labour relations became quite a worrying problem.

This leads us to the following timetable for each series of measures:

1. Keynesian policies, in the broad sense of the term, affecting disposable incomes of households (benefits, wage structures, deductions) in the first year;

2. direct action to promote employment (length of the working week, solidarity contracts, state employment) in 1982–3;

3. questions raised by the implementation in 1983 and 1984 of changes to labour law, introduced by the 1982 Auroux laws.

4.1. *From economic recovery to economic austerity*

The first measures taken to benefit households were reflected in an increased share of disposable income in GDP, which rose from 74 to 76 per cent. This development came about mainly because of increased social benefits, following the sharp rise in the real value of the basic family allowance (+10.7 per cent in 1982) and old age pensions (+10.4 per cent in 1981, +20.6 per cent in 1982). The strong growth in social security deductions in 1981 and 1982 (+36.7 and +17.2 per cent, respectively, in real terms) was linked less to the rise in unemployment, which had stabilized since the summer of 1981, than to a sustained policy for the promotion of employment (training expenditure, early retirement schemes).

From 1981 onwards, minimum wages rose more rapidly than average wages (the differential was of the order of 5.6 per cent in 1981 and 2.3 per cent in 1982), narrowing the difference between the highest and lowest wages. A rise in the minimum wage, an increase in basic allowances, and an extension of growth in direct tax pressure all gave the 1981 and 1982 recovery an important redistributive dimension, but the scale of the recovery remained quite moderate. (The public budget in 1981 and 1982 amounted to only 1.5 and 2.6 per cent of GDP.) This did not, however, prevent the recovery from coming up against a rapid deterioration in the foreign trade balance. (The trade deficit reached 3.9 per cent of GDP in 1982.)

The austerity policy introduced in mid-1982 led to a price and wage freeze from July–November onwards. The struggle against inflation once again took priority, as it had in the late 1970s. Improvement in the trade balance, which had been expected to result from improved price competitiveness, was instead largely the result of the fall in domestic demand. Overall, the stance of policy in 1983 contrasted clearly with the first two years. The income available to households decreased slightly (-0.3 per cent in real terms). The growth in social benefits — much more limited than in the past ($+2.5$ per cent in real terms) — was for the most part stimulated by several measures taken in 1982 to encourage early retirement (early retirement schemes, solidarity contracts). The real growth in the SMIC was itself quite modest ($+0.7$ per cent). Finally, an increase in tax rates (from 7.82 to 8.43 per cent between 1982 and 1983) completed this change of emphasis towards an austerity policy. The rise in unemployment towards the end of 1983, as a consequence of stagnation, also reflected the move away from the priority previously attached to employment and other measures taken in this sphere in 1981 and 1982.

4.2. *An extensive and varied employment policy*

The policy of actively encouraging work-sharing appears to have had impressive results when one tries to explain the stabilization of the number of unemployed around the 2 million mark from 1981 to 1983, at a time when the total number of jobs decreased by 138 000 and the potential working population (at a constant activity rate) increased by 640 000. Measures to reduce labour supply, either by the encouragement of vocational training or by early retirement, were also of considerable importance in this respect.

These measures are less striking for their innovative character ('Young Peoples' Future' Plans replacing the Barre Government Pacts and early retirement schemes) than for their scale. Thus, at the end of 1983, 700 000 people were benefiting from early retirement schemes. The measures to cut labour supply had the effect of reducing unemployment by 100 000 in 1981 and 1982, and by 200 000 in 1983 (Colin *et al.*, 1984; Levy, 1984).

When employment is falling, such measures cannot contain unemployment in the long run unless they are steadily increased in scope; but from

1983 onwards the austerity policy had a contrary effect. The solidarity contracts (a rather innovative policy) placed the financial burden of early retirement schemes (for those aged above 55 years) on the state, as long as the firm concerned kept up the level of employment for one year; these contracts were abolished on January 1984 with the exception of a few in areas of acute industrial crisis.

The provision of public sector jobs illustrates the reversal in another way. In 1981 and 1982, 200 000 public service jobs were created in education, health, post and telecommunications, and above all by local authorities. There were plans to create only 16 000 posts in 1983, and none at all in 1984.

Measures to encourage work-sharing were essentially of a legislative or statutory nature (such as a reduction in the working week); these were not directly limited by budgetary constraints, since the costs were borne either by employers or employees. However, the effectiveness of these measures depended on the state of industrial relations. This uncertainty regarding the effects of the practical content of measures was a common feature of all reforms in labour law introduced after 1981.

The reduction in the number of hours in a working week provides us with an interesting example of this. Although collective bargaining on this matter at a national level had not met with success for two years, the government decided, from February 1982 onwards, to reduce the number of hours legally worked from 40 to 39, and to introduce a fifth week of paid holiday (applicable from the year beginning May 1982). The methods of application (wage compensation for the hour abolished and seasonal adjustment for the reduction) were to be freely negotiated. To put an end to the difficulties surrounding these negotiations, the government recommended that no reduction in wage should accompany this reduction in hours worked.

The length of the working week was effectively reduced from 40.6 hours in 1981 to 39.2 hours in 1983, but the effects of this on employment remained very modest: the latter was increased by 30 000 jobs according to INSEE, and by 65 000 jobs according to Frank and Kergoat (1983).

This modest impact on unemployment, and the deadlock in collective bargaining on the terms of the reduction, led the government to postpone indefinitely the initial objective of reaching a 35-hour week by 1985, other than by means of solidarity contracts on the reduction of hours worked in a week (this had little impact: +7000 jobs in 1982 and 1983 according to Levy, 1984). This difficult change-over from one limit (40 hours) to another (39 hours) illustrates the breakdown in the cohesion of collective bargaining — a breakdown that was capable of holding up the application of a whole series of modifications in labour laws introduced in 1982.

4.3. Labour laws: a new deal

The Auroux laws of 1982 specified a whole series of new rights for workers, extending the long-term trend towards the institutionalization of bargaining at increasingly decentralized levels. Application of these new rights in practice, however, depended on the scope for their inclusion in negotiations.

The obligation to negotiate wage levels annually in all firms employing more than 10 people has been the most important of these initiatives. Even so, its effect has not been binding, since there is no obligation to conclude these negotiations. The extension of negotiations has therefore continued to depend on local conditions. Nevertheless, against the background of economic crisis, this institutionalization of wage negotiation in firms has encountered opposition, both on the part of the employers, unwilling to cede any of their powers (which in the case of wage levels have remained discretionary: see Eyraud and Tchobanian, 1984), and on the part of the trade unions, worried about the isolation of negotiations with firms in difficulties, who for this reason would prefer that negotiations at company level were more firmly anchored in industry-wide agreements.

The exercise of individual rights by workers (which are directly recognized by the 1982 laws) was expected to lead to an improved legal standing for workers within firms. However, the status of the employee continued to be subject to constraints from other laws (property, commercial, international, etc.).

Thus, the new rights did not establish even indirect forms of employee co-management, since there was no obligation to conclude negotiations. Labour law and commercial law have remained distinct. Violations of the former do not rule out judicial actions under the latter. However, certain procedures in commercial law, such as compulsory liquidation, can contravene workers' rights (Verdier, 1984). Restrictions on the use of short-term or temporary contracts under the 1982 laws cannot prevent the use of other means of achieving flexibility, such as subcontracting, or the creation of subsidiary companies. In addition, the 1982 laws, by extending the framework of negotiations at firm level, leave open the possibility of agreements that remove common law rights.

This remaining scope for adjusting to the effects of the crisis continued to be double-edged, and thus was able to contribute to the appearance of a new system of wage/labour relations characterized by negotiation:

- flexibility of employment;
- wage bargaining;
- management of labour and leisure time.

In the long term, this scope could also undermine the objectives of the legislation by strengthening the tendency for diminished job security to be seen as a necessary condition for economic recovery. It is the uncertainty of the outcome for the system of wage/labour relations that identifies the period beginning in 1981 as transitional.

5. Key Questions for the Development of Wage/Labour Relations

Since 1977, two governments with contrasting outlooks have tried to affect the outcome of the current upheavals in the system of wage/labour relations. In some ways, their respective policies have come up against similar problems. I have chosen to divide them into three types of question. The first concerns flexibility of employment. This point covers many very different considerations. We shall look at only a limited number of the main points, dealing with changes in employment as output varies. Other related aspects will be taken up in the discussions of wage determination and work-sharing.

5.1. Flexibility of employment: how to balance adaptability and social regression

Stagnation in the world economy and the resulting intensification of international competition have a twofold effect on levels of output of national economies. They lead to fluctuations in demand, and to pressure for structural change. In general terms, flexibility of employment is the ability of the system to adapt to these short-, medium-, and long-term developments. Ease of adjustment depends critically on the terms and conditions of employment. These include the hiring and firing of employees, as well as subcontracting, scope for special forms of employment, and short-time working.

The dilemma is therefore quite simple: greater flexibility in conditions of employment reduces obstacles to the hiring of employees and increases sectoral mobility, but in a weak labour market ease of dismissal can set off a deflationary spiral as household incomes fall. Neither growth in the foreign demand nor renewed investment, in view of the stagnation on the markets, would be able in the long term to stop a depressive cycle being triggered off, similar to that observed in the interwar years. Only a policy geared to maintaining household incomes could counteract this process.

Employers, trade unions, and governments each attach different weights to the costs and benefits involved in increased flexibility. Employers believed that a relaxing of the redundancy regulations, even if only limited to new jobs created, would provide an extra 400 000 jobs in 1984.[8] Trade unions have criticized both the increased segmentation of

[8] Declaration made by the CNPF, *Le Monde*, 5 July 1984.

the labour market and the general worsening of employment conditions caused by the introduction of measures to increase flexibility. While acknowledging the arguments of both sides, the government hesitates to combine measures to reduce restrictions with other measures to maintain the level of household demand, having seen a modest Keynesian reflation fall foul of the balance of payments constraint.

Up to 1977, the development of the system of wage/labour relations was marked by a growth in the use of permanent contracts. The recent change-over in the payments of workers' wages to a monthly salary basis, and the effective control of redundancies, show that this movement continues. Parallel to this, there was increased institutional support for victims of employment flexibility, such as payment for partial technical unemployment (1967), an undertaking to finance continuous training (1971), an encouragement to mobility, extensive payments for unemployment caused by redundancy (1975), the regulation of special forms of employment (temporary employment 1972, short-term contracts 1979), the relaxing of working conditions for part-time employees, and so on.

However, as soon as the crisis began to put a strain on the smooth running of the employment system, this 'well ordered' flexibility came under attack from two sides. On the one hand, a large number of people accepted less secure forms of employment. This was socially 'acceptable' because the jobs were in any case marginal. On the other hand, agreements ceased to be respected. Collective agreements and legislative measures could quite quickly eliminate the first distortion by, for example, restricting recourse to special forms of employment.

Thus, the 1982 Auroux laws limited the employment of workers on a temporary basis, or on the basis of short-term contracts. These laws also limited the annual amount of overtime that could be worked (beyond the legally established 39-hour week).

It is much more difficult, however, to limit the undermining of agreements. An example of this is the use of indefinite lay-offs instead of redundancies. Older examples include restricting the size of firms to get round the obligation to negotiate collective agreements, or other devices used to avoid an over-restrictive industry-wide agreement. The use of Youth Employment Pacts to hire cheap labour on short-term contracts is one of the more pernicious practices. Finally, an increase in the black economy clearly sets a limit to the extension of collective bargaining against a background of economic crisis (see Conseil Économique et Social, 1983).

Seen from this standpoint, negotiations on achieving increased flexibility in employment can hardly be avoided. The issue becomes one of controlling the direction taken by the trend towards flexibility, to ensure that neither increased dualism nor the above-mentioned recessionary effects are created on the labour market. In the light of past experience both at home and abroad, we can chart two directions to be followed by 'progressive' flexibility.

One is to aim to absorb short- to medium-term changes in output by greater use of technical unemployment. By combining methods tried by the Italian Integration Fund and the trade union management of labour in the Parisian publishing industry, a formula involving both employers' and employees' representatives would, for example, yield reductions in manning levels (the dismissal of surplus work-force), while reaffirming employers' responsibilities towards their employees (payment of some of the cost of unemployment benefits, training schemes to facilitate redeployment, participation in activities carried out by trade associations or other firms). The various solidarity contracts (reduction in weekly hours worked, investment in job training) work to this end.

Looking at medium-term objectives, the other trend tries to supplement the above by encouraging sectoral mobility, relying on policies promoting training and employment subsidies for workers coming from sectors facing structural change. Such policies, based on a common interest in maintaining employment both locally and at the national level, could involve direct financial aid from one firm to another. We can see various elements of this logic in the policies of 'reconversion zones' established during the cyclical downturn at the beginning of 1984.

The local employment committees created in 1981 highlight the importance of tripartite action in local labour markets even though it consists mainly of the local application of central measures.

5.2. Determination of wages and income: distributing the fruits of weak economic growth

At the beginning of the crisis in 1974, there was a shift in final demand for goods and services towards consumption, and away from investment, while the share of wages in GDP increased. The re-establishment, at least, of the share of investment appeared to the two governments that came to power after 1977 to be a prerequisite for the restoration of a basis for economic growth. However, the means applied to achieve this objective differed vastly. For the Barre government, a revival in investment could be achieved only by restoring profits, and therefore by reducing the share of wages in GDP. This was the justification for seeking to fight inflation by means of slowing down wage increases.

For the Socialist government in 1981–2, much of the revival in investment was to come from public investment, as private capital was much more concerned with obtaining short-term profits from abroad.

The funding of this investment (above all in the enlarged nationalized sector) consequently also involved the problem of redistribution. The policy proposed by Pierre Mauroy and Jaques Delors from 1982 onwards can be characterized as follows:

- it had to avoid any further fall in the share of profits;
- it had to ensure the availability of sufficient funds to permit an increase in public investment.

To meet the first point, wage rises were not to exceed in total the rate allowed by productivity growth; wages were not to follow pay rises in the sectors with the fastest productivity growth.

Consequences of the second objective were that, in order to meet the capital needs of the public sector, a strict control of public expenditure and an increase in revenue were necessary (if the fear of inflation and the burden of the public debt were to limit the budget deficit — in this case, to below 3 per cent of GDP). However, the establishment of new forms of wage determination, and the financing of more investment, must be seen against a background of considerable change owing to economic stagnation and measures of social justice, most of which introduced after 1981. The scope allowed to the government to promote another type of wage structure appeared to be greatly reduced.

The formula put forward by Delors (1984) had three elements:

1. wage parity levels close to the level of SMIC;
2. wage specificity to depend on firms' profits;
3. wage promotion based on individual merit.

These three elements clarified the objectives, but it was still necessary to determine the macroeconomic consequences on the distribution (between wages and profits) and social consequences (difference between the highest and the lowest wages).

In a period of slow growth, there is only a narrow margin available to introduce differentiated wage rises that depend on the firms involved and individual merit. Significant differences are likely to increase the share of wages in value added. The net reduction in the difference between highest wages and lowest wages, which was brought about by a slightly more rapid growth in the average minimum wage from 1981 onwards, underlines the small amount of scope allowed for new wage policies. The type of wage structure sought was aimed at substituting the sectoral dynamic force of wage rises, which had provided the impulse for the system of sharing pre-crisis high productivity gains, with another type of wage structure, negotiated in the fairest way so as to share reduced productivity gains. The formula allowing such adjustments to be implemented involved a finely adjusted incomes policy similar to the control of wage increases unsuccessfully introduced in 1975.[9]

This wage policy could not be dissociated from redistribution policies. The increase in deductions that resulted from a growth (whether independent of or increased by the crisis) in social service benefits made the adjustment to new wage structures much more difficult. Changes in the deduction system and in the wage structure are linked, and the opposition encountered by consequent changes in the deduction system has remained sufficiently strong to postpone indefinitely any major plans to reshape the tax system. This lack of flexibility accordingly limited any innovations in incomes policy; moreover, it was just as important for a policy that aimed at restoring the basis for growth to ensure the ways in which wages were spent as to ensure the process by which they were determined.

Now, parallel to the crisis, there came a shift towards increased consumer demand in the pattern of use made of income available to households. To counteract this tendency, numerous measures have been introduced to try to give consumers greater incentives to save (apart from saving for housing). Formulae for advantageous investment conditions were substituted for other forms of investment but did not result in notable recovery in the rate of savings. Compulsory savings schemes, such as save-as-you-earn, either have not got off the ground or have had only limited success.

The aim of policies to boost household savings is to influence the way in which capital accumulation is financed. Boosting the contribution of the personal sector appears to be all the more desirable, since other sources of funds (profits, public funds, foreign finance) have been limited by debt accumulated during ten years of slow growth. Systems such as wage funds, which earmark a part of salaries for the direct financing of a firm's investments, could then give some firms access to finance that would otherwise be unavailable. The advantages of such a process which eliminated the need for a financial intermediary are, *a priori*, considerable for small- and medium-sized firms (although they are insufficient in a situation of rapid growth, and do little for firms whose prospects are poor). One attraction of such systems for employers is that there would be an incentive that might lead to more meaningful negotiations at the level of the firm.

Work-sharing and increased leisure time are two further points that have emerged as issues in negotiations between employers and employees.

5.3. A new way to organize time and share work

Since 1974, unemployment and recession have called for a continual

---

[9] An index-linked deduction on income was aimed at the taxation of wage rises that were too high in relation to the growth of value added.

redefinition of work and leisure time. According to some authors,[10] this redefinition could herald a way of life completely different from the present, even the coming of a new type of society. We are far from being able to describe, or even outline, possible changes in society that would provide an immediate alternative to the 'consumer society'. The social status conferred by consumption patterns, however, is not the only issue. A whole series of links between production methods and the pattern of consumption are affected. The division of time between work and non-work in the course of the crisis owes as much to the continuation of trends already apparent in the period of expansion of the wage-earning sector, and of sustained growth prior to 1974, as it does to pointers towards a fundamental reorganization of life-styles. Recognition of this indicates that profound changes in society are unlikely to occur soon.

If we consider, first of all, trends in starting and stopping work, we can see that the crisis prolongs long-term tendencies rather than changing them. This is clear in the measures introduced to raise the school-leaving age, where slow growth and unemployment have led to more school education and training in much the same way as do strong growth and sharp rises in living standards.

That this trend persists could appear paradoxical at a time when the activity rate of women aged 25–55 years is rising. However, uncertainty about job security, and the increased necessity — owing to wage austerity — for a second salary to help with the household budget, combines with a new understanding of women's role in society to explain in large part the increase in the number of women working. The effects of early retirement, however, are more ambivalent. Retirement, or early retirement, can be both a compensation and a rejection. The lowering of the retirement age can be understood as social regression if it means a marked decline in disposable income (as is shown by the example of Japan). The threshold of 'acceptability', however, remains quite high, if we are to judge by the early retirement schemes in use at present.

The rise in unemployment has had only limited effects on behaviour as regards work. The adverse effects of unemployment, however, can be considerably softened, as was shown in the experiment where people made redundant were paid 90 per cent of their previous wages in unemployment benefit (or 110 per cent in cases of training) — at a price. But the steady rise in unemployment has tended to cut short such experiments.[11] In other words, people's attachment to work, to the social status that it represents, and to the income that is thus gained remains a

---

[10] Cf. the report by the group studying the long-term effects of the 9th Plan, Commissariat Général du Plan, La Documentation française, 1983.

[11] Payment of 90% of previous wages in unemployment benefit was abolished in 1979.

predominant feature in their attitudes; and the payment required to induce people to stop working early is, on the whole, too great.

The experience of the recent change-over to a 39-hour week confirms this tendency. Maintenance of full wages, even though the number of hours worked fell, appeared to be a principal priority for the great majority of workers, who in return accepted changes in working practices sought by their employers (see Pépin and Tonneau, 1982). However, drastic changes in employment in 1975 caused workers in some firms that went over to short-time work to adjust to life-styles that combined working time and time at home in a new and popular manner.

The change-over to the 39-hour week teaches us other lessons. The large majority of employees apparently would have preferred a block reduction in their working time, such as one Monday or one Friday off per month, to the more staggered reduction in their working time that, at the instigation of the trade unions, is the most usual solution. The preference shown by employees for a system clearly separating their time at work and not at work is perhaps the mark of an urban life, where an important no-man's-land between work and non-work mitigates 'marginal' variations in working time.

These preferences bring to mind the still essentially urban character of wage-earning groups. The halt in the shift towards urban concentration, which was highlighted in the report on life-styles drawn up under the 9th Plan, only opens up possibilities for the dispersal of wage-earning groups from urban areas in the long term. Although a shift of production centres out of the large cities has been made possible by the development of computer communications and improvements in production techniques, it is a possibility that has little bearing on the worries caused by the steady rise in unemployment in the 1980s. Work-sharing and a redefinition of working habits are unlikely to diminish expectations of a continuing development in consumer trends, partly because the crisis slows down any such trend. (The same thing holds for any trend in population dispersal.)

Ten years after the start of the crisis, the ways of choosing between work and non-work seem if anything to have become less flexible, after the initial move in this direction of the years 1968–73.

6. Conclusions

An historical approach has shown how long-term developments in the system of wage/labour relations have been called into question as the crisis has worn on, and has also indicated the scope allowed for changes in policies so as to give direction to these new developments. Stagnation in the economy has slowed the extension of collective bargaining that took place in an economic climate marked by relatively full employment, sustained growth in real wages, and a 'positive' expansion in the social security system.

From 1981 onwards, the left-wing government tried to stem a downward trend in employment, social security, and income from employment, plus a worsening of industrial relations, a trend that the policy of the previous government, which had liberal leanings, had not been able to halt. This new policy relied on:

- a 'Keynesian' recovery plan, moderate enough not to entail too high a trade deficit, but sufficiently strong to revive growth in employment, wages, and social security;
- an active pursuit of a new concept of job-sharing, allowing a net reduction in the volume of existing unemployment;
- extensive changes in labour law, encouraging both the continuation of the earlier trend towards an increased emphasis on the use of negotiated agreements in industrial relations and the shift towards greater 'industrial democracy' at the level of the firm.

From the very first year it was applied, the Keynesian recovery was faced with a much larger foreign trade deficit than had been foreseen; this led to an austerity policy following a cycle similar to the 'stop–go' policies of Labour governments in the United Kingdom.

The policy of actively pursuing a new concept of work-sharing succeeded in stabilizing the level of unemployment, but without doing anything to reduce existing unemployment, as had been hoped in visions of a new social order. During the crisis, life-styles seem to have become more inflexible, rather than opening up to the extensive changes hoped for in a new distribution of time between work and leisure.

Faced with budgetary austerity, the reformed labour laws seem to bear the seeds of innovations to come. The new laws are capable of greatly influencing flexibility of employment and wage determination. Their impact depends on whether circumstances allow changes in the law to change practices themselves.

The discrepancy between legal innovations and the inertia in practices is surprising when it seems that the areas of deadlock caused by the crisis ought to promote far-reaching changes in a system of wage/labour relations that is no longer capable of ensuring full employment or maintaining growth in real wages (cf. Boyer, 1982). This raises questions about the conditions under which social pressure for change in the law are likely. Several hypotheses could contribute to an explanation of the relative inertia of society, which enable changes in the law to precede changes in practice.

The first hypothesis notes the absence of large-scale social changes similar to those of June 1936 or May 1968 (which confirms the relatively modest impact of the general strikes in 1976 and 1977). If a change of any importance and scale is taking place in France at the moment, then it is being carried out in an historically new manner. The existence of a relatively extensive social security system could explain why deadlock in the system of wage/labour relations does not have as profound an effect as in the past.

A second hypothesis is that social groups, or institutions capable of implementing government initiatives, have little impact within firms or in the local labour markets at the level of the firms themselves, which are most affected by the new laws. The trade unions, which could play a part, have seen their activities hampered by a loss of influence and only a limited foothold in small- and medium-sized firms.

Within the framework of the decentralization programme, the government has set up institutions designed eventually to improve contacts at the local level between civil servants, employers, and workers. Local employment committees, which offer such a tripartite structure, are now only at the stage of taking their first hesitant steps (see Ginsbourger, 1985).

A third hypothesis emphasizes the development of workers' behaviour towards greater autonomy. With the benefit of an extensive social security system and a higher average level of education than in the past, workers are better able to exert control over their working lives and to defend their own interests (Cellier, 1981).

The three lines of argument put forward all lead to the same conclusion: the opening up of the way to new rights, at a time when the system of wage/labour relations has reached deadlock, could, in the long term, lead to important changes in industrial relations. For the most part, however, this remains a gamble.

The ability to render employment more flexible, to invent new wage formulae, and to redefine the rate of work involves the creation of new social alliances, giving shape to the right to work and to income. The application of such creative capacities remains an audacious objective for the institutions whose responsibility it is to give stimulus to these changes.

3

From Mounting Tension to Open Confrontation: The Case of the UK

Terry Ward

1. Industrial Relations: A Major Long-term Issue

The institutional framework within which the distribution of income has been determined in the UK over the postwar years was largely already in place by 1950. The system of industrial relations, based on voluntary collective bargaining, much of it conducted at the shop-floor level, and on informal agreements rather than on legally enforceable contracts, had long since been established over much of industry. In 1948 almost 60 per cent of male manual workers in industry, and around 45 per cent of employees generally, belonged to one of the many hundreds of different unions that had been formed at various times from the latter part of the nineteenth century onwards. These were variously craft-, industry-, or general-based. Unlike in many other countries, there was no attempt to create a more logical structure in the immediate postwar years. Employers' organizations were similarly numerous and fragmented, with little co-ordination between them. The war and the period of planned reconstruction that followed, however, gave an impetus to central organization and to union and management involvement in national economic affairs.

The immediate postwar years saw the development of a universal system of social security and a free national health service, together with a commitment to full employment through the management of domestic demand.[1] These policies were espoused by both main political parties in a conscious effort to avoid the social deprivations of the interwar years and to ensure that no one fell below a minimum acceptable standard of living. The political consensus extended to industrial relations as well,

The author would like to thank the Economic and Social Research Council for financial support during the preparation of this chapter.

[1] The principles were outlined in Beveridge (1942, 1944).

with a general, if tacit, agreement to keep politics out of collective bargaining between employers and unions over pay and conditions of employment, and to limit government interference.

This institutional framework laid the basis for the same kind of 'Fordist' mode of development that occurred in most other industrialized economies in the 25 years after the war and under which the growth of mass consumption was financed by significant and almost continuous gains in real wages made possible by rapidly expanding output and productivity. In the UK, however, growth proved less rapid and less continuous than in other countries, and therefore less capable of reconciling the competing claims on national income. As a result, the circular and cumulative process of Fordist development was less coherent and more unstable than elsewhere.

The institutional framework and political consensus came under increasing strain as the postwar period developed. In the full-employment years of the 1950s, there was an increase in the strength of trade unions at the local level in the form of shop stewards (shop-floor representatives), and a rise in the number of disputes, almost all of an unofficial nature. By the early 1960s there was growing unease about the allegedly anarchic state of industrial relations, the power of shop stewards, and the apparent inability of trade union leaders to control their members.

Concern also began to be expressed about the performance of the UK economy, particularly in comparison with that of other countries. Periodic balance of payments crises concentrated attention on the competitive weakness of British industry and the excessive tendency towards inflation, with the virtual commitment to a fixed exchange rate (encouraged by the reserve currency status of sterling) narrowing the policy options available. From the early 1960s onwards, a succession of income policies of various kinds were imposed in an attempt to moderate wage inflation, while Labour and Conservative governments alike began seriously to consider ways of reforming industrial relations through legislation. At the same time, attempts to engender greater co-operation between labour and management were made for similar reasons, and the machinery of tripartitite negotiation between government, industry, and the trade unions was established at the national level.

By 1970 the fragile political consensus on industrial relations had broken down completely, and growing economic problems were making it increasingly difficult to reconcile conflicts between the interests of workers and business. Since then, industrial relations have been a central political issue for much of the time. Increasingly, the power of organized labour to resist change and bid up wages has been presented as the major weakness of the economy. Legislation has been introduced, and ardently resisted, to curb this power under two administrations, and successive governments have continued to intervene in the process of pay determination.

From 1973 onwards, global recession has compounded the special problems of the British economy, aggravating conflicts within society and giving a sense of urgency to the implementation of measures intended to strengthen economic performance.

The virtual stagnation of the past decade has also led to the breakdown of consensus on social welfare. The near unanimity on the desirability of improving and extending welfare services has begun to break down, as the costs to taxpayers have risen and the prospects for future funding have deteriorated.

These points are discussed in detail below.

2. The Years before 1973

2.1. De-industrialization and the growth of service employment

The shift of output and employment from agriculture into manufacturing and services, which has been an important feature of many European economies over the postwar period, had already taken place in the UK well before 1945.

In the years up to 1973, the main structural trend was the growth of employment in services and the progressive contraction of jobs in manufacturing, although output as measured grew faster in manufacturing than in services (Table 3.1b). Indeed, the evidence suggests that there was no substantial shift in final demand from manufactures to services, but instead a growing 'tertiarization' of production as an increasing proportion of activities previously carried out in the manufacturing sector was transferred to specialist concerns located in the service sector. Between 1960 and 1973, employment in both private and public services grew by 16 per cent, while jobs in manufacturing declined by 7 per cent (Table 3.1a). Many of the additional jobs created in services were taken by women as a rising proportion of these joined the labour force (Table 3.1c), many working part-time rather than full-time. (Two-thirds of the extra jobs in services created over this period were part-time, and by 1973 around 40 per cent of women employed in services worked part-time.) In 1973 just over a third of the total labour force was employed in manufacturing and over half was in services; 20 per cent was employed in central and local government, 8 per cent in public enterprises.

These trends had potential implications for trade union membership (since this had traditionally been concentrated among manual workers in the primary and secondary sectors, as well as in the public sector), and for the strength of organized labour. However, the effects were more than outweighed by a growing tendency for union membership to increase among three overlapping groups: non-manual employees, service sector workers, and women. By 1973, therefore, membership had risen to half the labour force, and although there were still some 500 independent unions in existence, most members belonged to a few very large unions.

Unemployment was low throughout the period, at around 2 per cent or

TABLE 3.1 *Employment, value added, activity rates, and unemployment in the UK, 1960–1983*

(a) *Employment*

	% of total employment			Growth rates (% p.a.)	
	1960	1973	1983	1960–73	1973–83
Agriculture	4.7	2.8	2.8	−3.6	−1.0
Energy	4.3	2.5	2.6	−3.8	−0.6
Manufacturing	33.1	29.8	23.2	−0.6	−3.4
Construction	6.9	7.5	6.3	0.9	−2.1
Private services	33.5	37.6	42.0	1.1	0.2
Public services	17.5	19.7	23.2	1.2	0.7
Total employment	100.0	100.0	100.0	0.2	−0.9

(b) *Value added*

	% of value added			Growth rates at constant prices	
	1960	1973	1983	1960–73	1973–83
Energy	8.3	5.7	12.0	1.8	7.6
Manufacturing	34.1	28.0	20.6	3.1	−1.8
Private services	37.8	43.4	42.8	2.9	1.1
Public services	11.1	12.8	16.4	1.1	0.7

(c) *Activity rates*

	Working population % of 15–64 age group		
	1960	1973	1983
Men	98.1	93.1	87.1
Women	46.1	53.3	57.6
Total	71.1	73.1	72.3

TABLE 3.1 cont.

(*d*) *Unemployment*

	1965	1973	1978	1983
Total rate (% of working population)	2.0	3.2	6.3	13.2
Unemployed women (% of total)	23.2	14.5	26.6	28.5
Unemployed young people (% of total)	24.2	24.9	44.9	39.6
Duration of employment (% of total registered):				
over 6 ms.	36.7	43.8	40.5	57.7
over 1 yr	20.5	28.8	24.4	40.4

Source: EUROSTAT, OECD, UK Central Statistical Office, and UK Department of Employment.

below in most years, but it reached a peak of 4 per cent or so in 1971/2 as restrictive policies introduced to combat balance of payments problems slowed down growth. There were, however, significant regional variations, with rates three times the national average in Northern Ireland and almost twice the national average in Scotland, Wales, and the North of England. As officially recorded, unemployment among women in all years was extremely low (only around 15 per cent of the total number registered as unemployed). But the rules governing eligibility for social security benefits gave little incentive to register, and many married women actively seeking jobs were not counted as unemployed. Youth unemployment was never a serious problem (Table 3.1d).

2.2. Pay bargaining and the organization of work: the compromise between employers and workers

Wages and working conditions in the UK have traditionally been determined through a process of voluntary collective bargaining between representatives of labour and management, largely outside the framework of the legal system. Unlike in most other countries, the trade union movement had developed from the shop-floor up rather than from the top down, and its bargaining strength was located primarily at the plant level (see e.g. Crouch, 1979). This was altered to a major extent by the interwar recession and by the war itself, which encouraged centralization and national negotiation. The effect of full employment and sustained growth after the war was to tilt the balance of power back towards the shop-floor. As a result, in many concerns, especially large companies in industries such as engineering, shop-floor representatives — or shop stewards — were able to exercise sufficient power to have a measure of control over the organization of production (see Kilpatrick and Lawson, 1980). In most cases, this power was a negative one of being able to prevent, or at least hinder, changes in the productive process or in working methods proposed by management, rather than a positive one of being able to push through changes favourable to labour.

There was a clear division of responsibilities: the function of management was to pursue policies that would maximize the profits of the enterprise; the function of employee representatives was to oppose any managerial initiatives that might worsen working conditions or reduce real wages in pursuit of profits. The prevailing attitude among trade unionists was to favour such a confrontational approach, largely because their role was then clearly defined, rather than to push for more involvement in decision-making (see e.g. Elliott, 1978).

This attitude began to change in the 1960s, partly in response to the increasing complexity of industry and the growing importance of multinational production, which made simple resistance to change less effective and the outcome less predictable. But even in 1977, when the Bullock *Report on Industrial Democracy* was published, union support for the proposed participation of labour in the decision-making process was by no means universal.

The situation was on the whole different in small companies and in much of the service sector, where unions were either non-existent or in a weaker position. Here workers were partly reliant on government intervention through wages councils and general legislation to maintain minimum levels of pay and conditions of employment, although the maintenance of near full employment throughout most of the period up to 1973 strengthened their position.

Overall, the rates of pay and conditions of employment that generally prevailed over this period were influenced only very little by the economic forces of supply and demand. Social and political factors were far more important. The concept of a 'just' wage for a particular job, especially relative to that paid for comparable work in other parts of the economy, seems to have been widely accepted. There is evidence of a stable hierarchy of rates of pay as between different groups in the labour market (Tarling and Wilkinson, 1982; Lawson, 1982), and although indexation was rarely incorporated explicitly into a wage agreement, wages did tend to be closely related to the prevailing rate of inflation as measured by the retail price index (see Coutts *et al.*, 1976; Henry *et al.*, 1976). It was also generally accepted that wages could justifiably increase

at the same rate as productivity, and that they should bear some
relationship to profits.

In most cases these links operated indirectly and with a lag, so that,
whereas real wages in the long term tended to increase at a similar rate to
productivity, no clear short-term relationship between the two is evident.
At the same time, successive income policies to moderate wage increases
were introduced from the early 1960s onwards, and these had an almost
continuous effect on the observed behaviour of wages.

In addition to the widely accepted notion of a 'just' wage and the
institutionalized nature of the wage-fixing process, the relative unimport-
ance for wage movements of demand and supply in the labour market
can be explained by two factors: the segmented nature of the labour
market, which limited effective competition for work, and the policy of
most large companies of offering attractive rates of pay together with
secure prospects of employment in order to maintain a stable work-force
and minimize the cost of training and assimilating new workers.

The rates of pay of men and women rose more or less in parallel in the
years up to 1973 (Table 3.1). Normal hours of work over most of industry
were reduced by stages, from 48 to 44 to 40 hours per week, although
actual hours worked fell more gradually (by only 6 per cent between 1960
and 1973) as overtime working at enhanced rates of pay was increased.
In many cases such bonuses were an essential part of weekly earnings,
necessary to bring them up to a tolerable level.

*2.3. Growing state intervention: wage restraint and the 1971 Industrial Relations
Act*

Up to 1971, there were no legal rights entitling workers to join a union or
go on strike. Instead, trade unions were protected by immunities against
legal action for any damage to business caused by a trade dispute. Apart
from legal restrictions on the employment of women and children and
health and safety rules (incorporated in various Factory Acts from the
early nineteenth century onwards), contracts of employment were treated
as voluntary agreements between employers and employees, enforceable
under common rather than civil law.

Similarly, there were no universal legally enforceable minimum wages
or conditions of work. There was, however, partial coverage to safeguard
the weakest groups in the labour market through a system of Wages
Councils which fixed statutory minimum rates of pay and working
conditions in certain trades (such as retailing, catering, clothing, and
agriculture). In addition, statutory rights were introduced in the 1960s
entitling all workers who had been employed for a certain length of time

to a period of notice before dismissal and to redundancy payments (payment financed by the government through a levy on all employers). In 1968 racial discrimination in employment was outlawed, in 1970 equal pay legislation was introduced to narrow wage differentials between men and women, and in 1971 workers were given protection against unfair dismissal, with the onus of proof on employers.

In 1971, legislation aimed at curbing the power of trade unions and restricting their activities in pursuit of grievances and disputes was introduced for the first time. Well before then, concern in political quarters had been growing over the apparent ease with which organized labour could disrupt production, and in particular over the seeming inability of union leaders to control their membership, especially their shop stewards. This concern was accentuated by the relatively poor performance of British industry in home and overseas markets. In the 1960s the political consensus of the 1950s on industrial relations — on the desirability of leaving the two sides to sort out their own differences and reach acceptable compromises — began to break down rapidly as the number of unofficial disputes increased (see Donovan, 1968). The trade unions themselves appeared to be doing little to remedy things. In 1968 the Labour government put forward proposals for legislation (*In Place of Strife*), but these were withdrawn because of opposition within the party.

The purpose of the 1971 Industrial Relations Act was to establish a legal framework of control by confining legal immunities to officially registered trade unions and to genuine trade disputes. In addition, however, the Act gave positive legal rights to trade union members for the first time, by requiring employers to recognize unions once they had majority support in a place of work.

The passing of the Act led to widespread protest and to the mass refusal of unions to register and comply with its provisions. This made the Act difficult to enforce since the courts found themselves dealing not with a few maverick shop stewards but with the national leadership of unions with hundreds of thousands of members. Moreover, most employers refused to bring legal proceedings, in order to avoid prolonged industrial unrest. As the economy began to grow rapidly in 1972, this reluctance to take action was reinforced and was matched by a similar desire on the part of the government to avoid confrontation. By 1973 the Act was virtually a dead letter, and the attempt to regulate collective bargaining had effectively collapsed.

In place of legislative controls on industrial relations, the government in 1972 imposed compulsory wage restraint to achieve much the same end of moderating wage inflation. Indeed, by then this had become the customary means of curbing trade union bargaining strength and tackling the problem of competitiveness and a tendency towards excessive inflation. From the early 1960s onwards, there were few years when wages were left to be determined by free collective bargaining. Nevertheless, although pay restraint was successful in depressing wages for a year or two at a time, it proved unable to contain the pent-up pressure for wage increases and the restoration of traditional differentials over the long term (see Tarling and Wilkinson, 1977; Cambridge Economic Policy Group, 1980, p. 26; and Henry and Ormerod, 1978). The imposition of compulsory pay restraint in 1972 in fact provoked as much if not more industrial unrest than the Industrial Relations Act and led to a number of bitter disputes, including two prolonged miners' strikes, the second of which precipitated the fall of the Heath government.

2.4. The social welfare system

The social security system that developed in the early postwar years had two main elements: fixed-rate benefits for those qualifying by virtue of national insurance contributions, and means-tested benefits (called 'supplementary benefits') for those not in full-time employment who were either ineligible for fixed-rate benefits or whose income from all sources fell below a certain level. Fixed-rate unemployment benefits were payable for the first year out of work, after which a person became reliant on supplementary benefit (unless his accumulated savings made him ineligible). From 1967 onwards, an earnings-related supplement was payable for the first six months of unemployment, with the intention of encouraging job search and improving the efficiency of the labour market. In practice, however, the rules were formulated in such a way that only a relatively small proportion of the unemployed were eligible (20 per cent or so of men, 15 per cent of women on average).

Up to 1973, pensions and employment benefit were raised broadly in line with the growth of real wages, or slightly above, although the increases were somewhat erratic and in some years the real value of benefits declined. There was no formal or statutory linking of benefits to inflation or real wages, although all governments tended to accept an informal obligation to preserve or improve the relative position of social benefit recipients.

The significant growth of social expenditure that occurred between 1945 and 1973 was financed for much of the period by a gradual reduction in military spending following the Second World War and then the Korean War. By the mid-1960s, however, the scope for continued reduction in military spending in relation to national income was regarded as limited, and from then on further growth of social expenditure necessitated a rising tax burden.

3. Developments since 1973

3.1. Accelerated de-industrialization and rising part-time employment

The main structural change that has occurred since 1973 has been the relative decline in the importance of manufacturing in respect of both value added and employment. In 1973 manufacturing industry accounted for 28 per cent of value added in the UK and for 30 per cent of employment; by 1983 these proportions had fallen to 20 and 23 per cent respectively. By contrast, value added in services (market and non-market) rose from 56 to 60 per cent of the total, while employment in services increased from 57 to 64 per cent (Table 3.1). This reflects a fall in manufacturing jobs of over 2 million over the period and a growth in service jobs of around 600 000, much less than the rate of increase experienced before 1973.

The decline in employment in manufacturing is largely the result of a contraction in demand for the products of British industry as its international competitiveness has continued to deteriorate and its share of home and overseas markets has continued to fall (see e.g. Begg and Rhodes, 1982). Since 1980, however, it has also been partly the result of de-manning, plant closures, and the rationalization of production as companies have been put under intense pressure to keep down costs and raise productivity, not only because of the global recession but also because of the restrictive financial policies pursued by the Thatcher government. Attitudes in industry have therefore hardened against maintaining employment and preserving jobs, objectives that were features of the 1970s. Whereas labour productivity in manufacturing rose by an average of only 1 per cent a year between 1973 and 1979, in the five years after 1980 it grew by 5 per cent a year. However, the productivity of the available work-force, which is arguably the most relevant concept, remained almost constant (Table 3.2). The substantial and well publicized gains in productivity, therefore, were achieved not by getting more output out of available resources, but by making relatively fewer productive resources permanently idle.

Although the recession has hit manufacturing in particular, services have by no means escaped. The policy of successive governments since the mid-1970s has contributed greatly to this. The public provision of services has been deliberately held down to ease financial strains and to shift the balance of economic activity to the private sector.[2] In

[2] See, for example, H.M. Treasury (1976), which was very much based on the arguments in Bacon and Eltis (1976), and H.M. Treasury (1979) for an initial statement of the Thatcher government's objectives.

TABLE 3.2　*Average earnings, hours worked, productivity growth, and real income in the UK, 1960–1983*

	Growth rates (% p.a.)				
	1960–73	1973–5	1975–9	1979–80	1980–3
Average real hourly earnings					
Men	3.1	1.7	−2.3	3.4	1.5
Women	3.4	5.7	1.0	2.0	1.3
Hours worked					
Men	−0.4	−2.2	0.2	−2.3	0.2
Women	−0.5	−0.9	0.3	0.3	0.6
Average real weekly earnings					
Men	2.7	−0.5	−2.1	1.0	1.7
Women	2.9	4.8	1.3	2.2	1.9
GDP per employee	2.9	−1.9	2.2	−2.7	4.0
GDP per member of working population	3.1	−1.9	2.0	−3.9	0.7
Real post-tax income per employee	2.2	0.6	0.6	0.1	1.0

Source: UK Department of Employment.

consequence, employment in the public sector has remained virtually unchanged since 1976, whereas in the ten years before that it increased by 1 million.

Just as before 1973, a large proportion of the additional jobs created in the service sector over the past decade have been part-time ones, taken mainly by women, an increasing number of whom have joined the labour market — at least before 1980. By 1983 around 44 per cent of women in employment worked part-time, predominantly in the service sector, as opposed to 36 per cent ten years earlier. The trend towards part-time work had therefore continued unabated, although it has shown no sign of accelerating, despite the search for greater flexibility in working practices which the recession has supposedly encouraged. Nor is there much indication of any significant reduction in average weekly hours worked in industry, which might have been expected in such circumstances:

between 1973 and 1983 the average hours of male manual workers in industry fell by only around 5 per cent, whereas for women average hours have actually increased slightly (Table 3.2).

3.2. Changes in pay bargaining and the organization of work

So far as industrial relations are concerned, it is tempting to divide the period since 1973 into two main parts: the years of Labour government (1974–9), which initially saw the restoration of industrial peace through the Social Contract with trade unions and a change in legislation in their favour, and the years since 1979, which have seen the Thatcher government's attempt to make the labour market work according to the laws of supply and demand. Although such a division has some validity, the latter part of the Labour government's period in office saw a renewed outbreak of industrial unrest as real wages were squeezed to an unprecedented extent by Labour's own income policy, introduced to tackle familiar problems of inflation and lack of competitiveness.

What is unquestionably true is that government intervention in the form of wage restraint, legislative action, and macroeconomic policy, combined with economic recession, has had a major effect on collective bargaining and the relations between employers and workers. Before 1973, there were signs of a change in attitude on the part of trade unions in favour of greater worker participation in decision-making and away from the traditional confrontational approach to management. This led to the Bullock Committee Inquiry on Industrial Democracy, which recommended a genuine power-sharing structure in industry, a recommendation bitterly opposed by industrialists. Subsequently, the deepening recession and a hardening of attitude towards trade unions under the Thatcher government has reversed any slight trend towards greater participation and has reinforced the already powerful confrontational tendencies in UK industrial relations.

It is confrontation, however, with the balance of power firmly on the side of management, as high unemployment and job insecurity have severely weakened the bargaining position of unions. Faced with considerable uncertainty about future developments and market prospects, companies have downgraded the benefits of maintaining a stable work-force and avoiding industrial unrest and have been far more prepared to close plants and announce redundancies. Trade unions have had little to bargain with, and have usually been unable to count on support from workers in other plants or other industries, who tend to be reluctant to do anything that might jeopardize their own continued employment.

The economic context within which wage bargaining has taken place has therefore been dramatically different during the years of the Thatcher government. But even before then, the policy of wage restraint pursued by the Labour government from 1975 onwards greatly limited the potential influence of the social and institutional factors that had been important determinants of pay movements over much of the postwar period up to 1973. For the first time since the war, wage increases have fallen significantly short of the rate of price inflation for more than brief periods of time, and the principle of wage indexation has increasingly come under attack. Nevertheless, over the long term, pay settlements have continued to exceed price rises despite prolonged recession and government efforts to depress wages (Table 3.2).

Over the two years 1975–7, real earnings fell by around 7 per cent before tax and by slightly more after tax, as the Labour government imposed a ceiling on wage settlements well below the rate of price increases in an attempt to bring down inflation (which in 1975 had reached 25 per cent) and improve international competitiveness. (The balance of payments had been in substantial deficit in 1974 and 1975.) By 1978, the pressure for the restoration of real income lost over the preceding two years and of traditional differentials, especially from workers in the public sector who had been squeezed hardest, had built up to such an extent that it could no longer be contained. Even though a general election was imminent and industrial peace was important to Labour's chances of being returned, a series of public sector strikes in the winter of 1978–9 led to the breakdown of the policy, open confrontation between unions and the government, and escalating wage increases.

Since then, the Thatcher government has sought to depress real wages by austerity measures rather than income policies. In fact, in 1980 and 1981, when industrial output and business profits fell most sharply and unemployment increased most rapidly (at a rate of ½ per cent of the labour force per month at one stage), average pay settlements declined by almost the same amount (relative to the rate of inflation) as four years earlier. Since then, however, as output has begun to rise slowly and unemployment to increase less rapidly, pay settlements have risen once more in real terms, although at a less dramatic rate than after the collapse of the income policy.

A somewhat different picture emerges if movements in total wages, including all the various supplements for overtime working and so on, are examined instead of basic, nationally agreed settlements (which tend to be the minimum rates paid for a particular job). Thus, although total average earnings fell slightly in real terms in 1981, since then they have risen by around 2 or 3 per cent per year. Since 1979, therefore, over the Thatcher government's period in office they have gone up rather than down, despite the creation of enormous surpluses of labour. In relation to the scale of economic contraction and lost jobs (almost 2 million, or 25 per cent of the total, in manufacturing), wage moderation has been modest. Nevertheless, the share of wages in national income was depressed by 1–2 per cent per year between 1980 and 1983, largely because of the fewer numbers employed.

On the other hand, it does appear that pay bargaining has changed over this period. Social factors — the concept of a 'just' wage, comparability with wages in similar activities, etc. — seem to have played a less important role, and economic factors, especially the financial position of the company or industry concerned, seem to have increased in significance. Wage rises in manufacturing, for example, have lagged behind the recent abnormally high growth in productivity, and profits have gained to a greater extent than might have been expected on past behaviour.

The change in behaviour has been most marked in those sectors exposed to international competition or hit hardest by declining markets, and there have even been a few well publicized instances where workers have accepted cuts not just in real but in nominal wages. Such instances have occurred where jobs have been most at risk and where any other course of action might have meant plant or company closure. It is difficult to judge how widespread changes in behaviour have been — certainly, pay settlements in less exposed parts of the service sector seem to have been less affected — and how permanent they will prove. If there is any significant economic recovery and job insecurity diminishes substantially, then wage behaviour could well revert to its familiar historical pattern. There are already signs of this happening as economic conditions deteriorate at a less rapid rate, with pay claims in many areas far exceeding the prevailing rate of inflation. At the same time, to realize these claims, trade union negotiators have often been forced to accept some deterioration in conditions of employment and reductions in manning levels.

One feature of the deterioration in economic climate that could persist for some time is the reversal of the effect of equal pay legislation in narrowing differentials between male and female wages. Between 1972 and 1977 average hourly earnings of women went up by around 15 per cent in real terms (before tax), while average real earnings of men actually went down. (The hourly pay of women rose by 10 per cent between 1973 and 1977, while that of men fell by 5 per cent.) Since 1977, however, the earnings of men have consistently risen more rapidly than those of women, despite the marked disparity between levels of pay for similar work which still seems to exist. In the present economic climate, therefore, the equal pay legislation appears to have lost its effectiveness. So long as unemployment remains high and married women have no entitlement to unemployment benefit, and so long as the financial pressure on them to look for scarce jobs remains, the relative pay of women is unlikely to improve.

Under such conditions, it is also likely to prove difficult to bring about the significant reduction in hours of work for which the trade unions are pressing in order to combat unemployment (see e.g. Trades Union Congress, 1983). Although the standard working week was reduced from 40 to 39 hours over much of industry in the early 1980s, further moves in this direction have been resisted by employers and the government, on the grounds that they would only add to business costs and would adversely affect industrial competitiveness. The recent reduction in hours seems in practice to have had little effect on employment. Instead of taking on additional workers, firms appear to have increased productivity by minor changes in the production process (see Department of Employment *Gazette*, 1983; White, 1982). The growth in demand that has occurred since 1981 has been met by a similar response, with employers proving reluctant to add to their workforce, partly perhaps because of uncertainties about longer-term prospects.

4. The Role of Government since 1973: The Breakdown of the Social Contract and the Rehabilitation of Market Forces

In its first two years in office, the 1974–9 Labour government abolished most of the provisions of the 1971 Industrial Relations Act and restored to trade unions the immunities against legal action that had existed before then. Employers were obliged to recognize trade unions that had a sufficient number of members, and new arbitration and conciliation machinery, independent of government, was established with the power to impose terms and conditions of employment on companies. The Equal Pay Act became fully operational, and further legislation was introduced to outlaw sex discrimination in employment, education, and training.

These reforms were implemented immediately the Labour government came to power and before the scale of economic problems was fully realized. They formed an important element in Labour's Social Contract, an agreement with trade unions designed to secure pay moderation in return for social and economic policies favourable to workers (see Tarling and Wilkinson, 1977).

By mid-1975, however, the Social Contract was in disarray, under the strain of economic recession and mounting financial difficulties on the one hand, and high and increasing wage inflation on the other. Taxes on wages had already been raised significantly in two Budgets (in March 1974 and April 1975), cutbacks in public expenditure plans were beginning to be made, and the interventionist industrial policy (with its

proposals for extended public ownership of companies, planning agreements, and a state investment fund — the National Enterprise Board)
was in the process of being considerably diluted. From mid-1975
onwards, the policies followed by the Labour government were significantly less favourable to workers, with the emphasis firmly on containing
inflation, restoring competitiveness by depressing real-wage costs, and
avoiding financial crisis — an objective that became overriding after the
sterling crisis of 1976 and the forced resort to IMF support.

From 1975 onwards, the government imposed controls on prices and
progressively tighter limits on pay rises in order to bring down inflation.
This led to growing labour unrest, particularly among workers in the
public sector, whose wages were reduced considerably in relation to
employees elsewhere in the economy, and culminated in open confrontation
with the government.

The protracted strikes that occurred, particularly in refuse collection
and sewage disposal, were exploited by the Conservatives both for
electoral purposes and to galvanize support for proposals to limit the
power of trade unions. Since 1979, the Thatcher government has largely
reversed the measures taken in 1974–5. The legal immunities enjoyed by
trade unions have been greatly diminished, the right to belong to a union
has been weakened, and the right not to belong has been strengthened.
The only industrial action clearly immune from legal action now is that
between workers and their immediate employers over wages and
conditions of work, and then only so long as such action has been
sanctioned by secret ballot. Procedures for establishing trade union
recognition and for enforcing recognized terms and conditions of
employment on low-paying employers have been abolished and the
creation of a closed shop made more difficult. Protection against unfair
dismissal has been lessened, by extending the period of employment
necessary to qualify for compensation and redundancy pay (from six
months to two years).

In addition, the Fair Wages Resolution of 1890, under which
government contractors are required to pay the 'going rate' for labour,
has been abolished, and the government may well renounce the ILO
convention on minimum wages, which at present acts as some safeguard
against the complete abolition of Wages Councils. The number of
Councils has already been significantly reduced, and the size of the
inspectorate scaled down to wholly inadequate proportions.

The legislative changes restricting trade union activities have encountered the same kind of opposition from the labour movement as the
earlier and similar provisions of the 1971 Act. However, it has been less
widespread, less vigorously pursued, and less effective in mobilizing
support, not only from the public at large, but also from union members,

owing in part to the very different economic situation and in part to a dramatic weakening in public sympathy for workers who appear to put scarce jobs in jeopardy. Through its hard line and resolute refusal to intervene in trade disputes, irrespective of the damage to industry and hardship to the public, the government has reinforced the reluctance of workers to take strike action even in defence of their own interests. (Despite the fact that the 1984–5 miners' strike lasted a year, added around £3 billion to public expenditure — around 1 per cent of GDP — and caused great damage to the economy, the government effectively blocked all attempts to secure a compromise settlement.)

Nevertheless, the government has so far been reluctant to make full use of the provisions of its own legislation and has as yet failed to take action against public sector employees engaged in illegal disputes. The same is generally true of large companies, which, as after the 1971 Act, seem to have attached greater importance to restricting the long-term damage to industrial relations than to securing compensation for immediate damage to profits. As before, it has been left to small employers to use the Act to strengthen their hand against unions.

The workers most affected by the legislation therefore have been those employed in small firms who tend to be most weakly organized and on the lowest pay scales. The progressive abolition of Wages Councils has had a similar effect, while the government policy of contracting out to private enterprise activities previously performed by public sector employees has further worsened the position of the low paid. The effect of this policy in practice has often been to force workers previously employed as, say, cleaners or refuse collectors in central or local government to seek employment in non-union firms undertaking the same service but offering lower wages and worse conditions of employment so as to achieve savings in cost. There are numerous examples, for instance, where hospital cleaners have suffered wage reductions of 30–40 per cent once the contract passed to a private company.

This is the kind of exploitation that 90 years ago the Fair Wage Resolution was designed to deter, but which the government now not only tacitly approves but actively encourages. Thus, wage reductions are seen and are presented as an essential way of expanding employment among people who have been priced out of the labour market by well-meaning but misguided attempts by government and trade unions alike to protect their interests.

This philosophy also underlies the approach that the government has pursued towards youth unemployment. The training and work experience programmes introduced have deliberately been set up at minimal rates of pay (about half the average wage obtaining in the job market for people of similar age). The effect has been not only to safeguard the position of low-wage employers in the private sector, but also to put general downward pressure on pay scales by creating a cheap source of labour.

5. Social Welfare: Cut-backs but Continued Cost Escalation

Over the past decade, a social welfare system that was developed in the immediate postwar years, explicitly in conjunction with a policy of demand management to maintain full employment, has had to cope with high and rising unemployment. Between the end of 1973 and the end of 1975, the period when the world economy was hit by the first oil price shock, unemployment rose from 0.5 million to over 1 million (5 per cent of the work-force) as output fell. It remained at this level up to 1980, when industrial output collapsed in response to declining domestic demand and a grossly overvalued exchange rate. By the end of 1980, unemployment as officially measured had increased rapidly to 2 million (8½ per cent of the work-force), and it rose almost continuously through most of the 1980s. The official figure in 1985 stood at over 3 million (13 per cent of the work-force), but this includes only those receiving social security benefits: the true figure, including the many married women who are ineligible for benefit, is almost certainly over 4 million. Since an increasing proportion of those unemployed have been out of work more than a year, the people concerned have accordingly exhausted their entitlement to unemployment benefit and have become reliant on the system of mean-tested supplementary benefits. A system that had been intended purely as a safety net to catch what was expected to be a very small minority who happened not to qualify for the main benefits has therefore come to play an extensive role in the relief of poverty, a role for which it was never designed.

The response of the Thatcher government to the increasing importance of supplementary benefits has been to tighten the administration of what is essentially a discretionary system by encouraging officials to interpret the regulations governing payment more strictly and to employ more investigators to uncover cases of abuse. This, however, is only part of the effort that has been made to limit the size of the social welfare budget as high and rising unemployment has added significantly to expenditure — an effort that, although greatly intensified under the present government, can be traced back to the measures taken by the Labour government in the mid-1970s.

Thus, in an attempt to reduce government borrowing and appease financial markets, growth in social expenditure (on the health service in particular) has been cut back dramatically. Although, at the same time, the government committed itself to protecting the real income of those in receipt of welfare benefits, it effectively meant the abandonment of the long-established policy aim of progressively extending the welfare state and improving the relative position of benefit recipients.

Although benefit scales have continued to be raised broadly in line with inflation since 1979, significant reductions in real terms have been mooted from time to time; so far they have been resisted by moderate forces in the Conservative Party. Already, however, the earnings-related supplement has been abolished (in 1982) and benefits have been made liable to tax for the first time.

Such cut-backs are presented not only as necessary to limit escalating costs but also as positively desirable to improve the efficiency of the economic system and combat unemployment. High benefits, it is claimed, merely encourage workers to demand excessive wages and prevent firms from being able to offer the low-paid jobs that the unemployed are capable of carrying out. Moreover, they foster work-shyness and offer insufficient incentives for workers to hang on to their jobs. Whereas in the past the unemployed were commonly regarded as victims of society and its failure to provide sufficient work, they are now represented as being largely responsible for their own predicament.

Cut-backs in benefits have been accompanied by attempts to limit expenditure in other parts of the public sector, particularly on the education and health services. In the former case, opportunity has been taken of falling school rolls to reduce spending rather than improve and extend provision, while in the latter case, real expenditure has barely kept pace with the demands imposed on the system by an ageing population. Those able to afford it have opted in increasing numbers for the private provision of services.

Increased unemployment has also been accompanied by various kinds of job creation measures to supplement the social security system. These measures were intended initially as short-term means of moderating the effects of declining employment, which was at first thought to be temporary. In the last three years of the Labour government, 1976–9, an average of around 300 000 people were supported by such schemes. The Thatcher government, despite its philosophy, supported 875 000 people in 1981 under the temporary short-time working scheme alone. Since then, expenditure has been directed increasingly towards the young, the most conspicuous victims of the recession. In 1982–3, almost 550 000 young people were given temporary places under the Youth Opportunity Programme, although at minimal rates of pay. In mid-1983 the total cost of special employment measures of one kind or another amounted to almost £1 billion, equivalent to around 15 per cent of the total expenditure on social welfare benefits to the unemployed.

6. The Costs of Recession: A Widening of Inequalities

It is clear that the burden of recession has not fallen uniformly. The hardest hit have been those who have lost their jobs and become dependent on social welfare benefits, which in most cases fall far short of wages when in work.

Unemployment has been particularly concentrated in certain groups and in certain regions. About 40 per cent of the total officially recorded as unemployed are at present under 25 years of age, and in the absence of special government measures the proportion would be close to 50 per cent. (Before 1973, only around 25 per cent of the unemployed were under 25.) Moreover, 40 per cent of the total unemployed in 1983 had been out of work for a year or more (well over 1 million people), and nearly 60 per cent had been out of work for at least six months (Table 3.1d). In Northern Ireland the unemployment rate now exceeds 20 per cent, and in the North of England it is over 16 per cent. In the South-east unemployment is still below 10 per cent. In particular areas within the worst affected regions, as well as in inner cities, unemployment has reached 30 per cent or more, whereas there are still towns in the South and East of England where the figure is less than 5 per cent. The chance of a school-leaver finding genuine employment is still quite high in these places, but it is almost non-existent in areas such as Merseyside, Tyneside, or inner London.

Although the official figures show that men rather than women have borne the brunt of increased unemployment, this presents a grossly misleading picture. In reality, the proportion of the total number out of work who are women is far in excess of the 30 per cent that is recorded, since this figure includes only those drawing benefit, and therefore excludes most married women. The actual proportion is probably around half of the total, as in other European countries with different benefit schemes and different methods of counting unemployment. Many more households formerly reliant on the wife's earnings to bring their income up to a reasonable level have been hit by the recession therefore than is reflected in the official figures.

When postwar growth first came to an end in 1974, there was some attempt on the part of the then Labour government to offset the effects of recession and spread the costs of expanding public expenditure and increasing taxes. Between 1973 and 1975, the average burden of taxation rose by 3 per cent of GDP, and public spending in real terms grew by more than at any other time in the postwar years. Thereafter, however, the emphasis switched to holding down taxes, and major cuts were made in social expenditure programmes.

Since the Thatcher government came to power, the cost of financing the increased social welfare expenditure that has accompanied rising unemployment has been borne to an important extent by North Sea oil. Between 1977 and 1984 government receipts from North Sea oil grew from virtually nothing to £12 billion, almost 4 per cent of national income and around 12 per cent of total tax revenue. Since the cost to the state of each person unemployed, taking account of forgone tax revenue as well as of welfare benefits, is estimated to have been around £5000 in 1983, the growth in oil revenue was just about enough to cover the cost of the increase in unemployment of about 2 million that occurred over this period. Although the tax burden has increased on average during the recession (Table 3.2), the rise has therefore been much less than would have been required without oil — assuming that similar policies had been followed — and those in work have been able to enjoy some growth of real income even after tax, despite the fall in economic activity (Table 3.2). Oil revenue has similarly helped the government to keep down taxes on business, which in other countries have funded a large part of additional social expenditure.

Nevertheless, one effect of the way in which oil revenue has been used in the UK has been to widen inequalities in income distribution. Taxes on the very rich were cut considerably as soon as Mrs Thatcher took office (the top rate of income tax being reduced from 83 to 60 per cent) and have been gradually reduced further since then (by cutting progressively the effective rate of tax on capital gains and unearned income). At the same time, the tax burden on the poorer members of the community has been raised. Indeed, the lower the level of income, the greater has been the increase in tax. (The average tax on a married couple with average earnings is officially estimated to have increased by £5.50 per week at 1983/4 prices between 1979/80 and 1983/4: the average tax on a couple earning five times the average was *reduced* by £71 per week: see H.M. Treasury, 1983a; *Hansard*, 1983.)

At the same time, partly as a result of the other government policies discussed earlier, the wages of the lowest paid have increased the least rapidly. For example, between April 1979 and April 1983 the earnings of male manual workers in the lowest decile of the earnings distribution increased on average by 51 per cent, as compared with a rise of 65 per cent for those on average earnings and a rise of no less than 78 per cent for those in the highest deciles of white-collar workers.[3] Added to this, the maintenance of high interest rates throughout the period and the abolition of foreign exchange controls have further boosted the income of the wealthiest in society.

[3] Department of Employment *Gazette*, 1979–83; figures calculated by C. Pond of the Low Pay Unit.

Overall, therefore, the 1975–85 decade, and the period of Thatcher government in particular, has witnessed a significantly regressive shift in distribution, with the burden of recession falling predominantly and increasingly on the weakest and poorest members of society.

7. Future Prospects: Growing Tensions and the Difficulties of Compromise

Perhaps the most important change that has occurred over the past ten years has been the breakdown of social consensus on a number of central issues. Before 1973, the widespread view was that reducing conflict between the various forces in society and pursuing greater equality were important not only for their own sake but also for improving economic performance and achieving higher rates of growth. It was commonly accepted, moreover, that the state had a responsibility for managing the economy to maintain full employment and acceptable rates of growth, and for ensuring that the gains from economic expansion were equitably distributed.

Events since 1973 have shaken the foundation of these beliefs. Successive governments have proved incapable of sustaining growth and preventing high unemployment. Obvious conflicts have opened up between social groups which seem impossible to reconcile in the context of stagnation. Policies of redistribution and social welfare seem to be incompatible with improving economic performance, which more and more is presented as being dependent on increasing individual incentives and widening inequalities.

The Thatcher government, with its free market philosophy and its emphasis on individual enterprise, has clearly played an important part in undermining consensus. But it was under the preceding Labour government from the mid-1970s onwards that the commitment to full employment was first abandoned, or at least suspended, that social aims were sacrificed to the achievement of financial objectives, that public expenditure was cut back to relieve the burden on taxpayers and to increase incentives, and that real wages were reduced significantly both to combat inflation and to favour profits. These policies were all justified at the time as being a necessary response to the global recession and the UK's lack of competitiveness. It was not that social goals were being completely abandoned, but just that their achievement was being postponed until economic performance was strong enough to support it.

This is not so different from Mrs Thatcher's philosophy, except that it was perhaps less vigorously pursued. Moreover, there is little doubt that, as economic conditions have worsened further and prospects of a rapid recovery have receded, the appeal of such a philosophy and the policies that it implies has become ever stronger. The recession has created an environment in which it is only too apparent that individual success depends on the failure of others and that the dictates of market forces have to be respected. So long as the recession persists, it is hard to see why this philosophy and the cult of the individual that it promotes should not become even more firmly entrenched. Although it may involve open confrontation between social forces, such confrontation could well result in further strengthening the position of those in power and accelerating the development of a more authoritarian regime.

4

Standard European-type Institutions in a Developing Economy: The Case of Ireland

Miceal Ross

1. Introduction

The system of institutions and practices that governs wage/labour relations in Ireland has its roots in the British system of social security arrangements and labour institutions which the newly independent state inherited in 1922. This heritage was often added to by imitation of British innovations in succeeding decades, and it is only in comparatively recent times that a distinctively Irish set of institutions has evolved.

While the institutional arrangements were developed in a general British environment, the Irish economy in which they operated in the post-independence era was by no means typical of Britain. This is due to the predominance of agriculture based on family farming and, to a lesser extent, to self-employment in trades, such as retailing, in a widely dispersed and not heavily populated landscape. As agriculture shed labour, the share of employees in the labour force rose from its 1926 level of 47 per cent to 62 per cent in 1961 and 76 per cent in 1981, when agriculture still claimed 17 per cent of the total work-force.

The extent of the exodus from agriculture could have created a salaried class sooner had it not been for high levels of emigration. In these regards the Republic of Ireland has its closest EEC parallel in the Mezzogiorno region of Italy. The heavy industries of northern Italy are similar to those in the Belfast area, which remains within the United Kingdom. This meant that the fledgling state took on the character of a developing economy rather than the industrial society so typical of northern Europe in general. Even today, it is difficult to pinpoint industries of a scale and character where a 'Fordist' ethos would be found.

In discussing the development of the system of wage/labour relations in Ireland, it is appropriate to concentrate on the period beginning in the late 1950s, when new industrial policies and the extension of social security services marked the beginnings of modern Ireland. This watershed, coinciding with a demographic turnaround, promoted a general rise in the total population for the first time in over a century.

2. The Period 1959–1973

2.1. A developing economy

Political independence did not alter Ireland's economic dependence on the British market. Ireland remained part of the British labour market, and there were few cultural obstacles to hinder the flow of workers to Britain from the Irish countryside. In the post-independence period unemployment has never dropped below 5–6 per cent of the work-force. However, unemployment has not traditionally been regarded as the major indicator of economic failure in Ireland. Before 1960, that indicator was the scale of emigration. Abundant research has shown the links between participation rates, unemployment levels, wage rates, and emigration from Ireland and labour market conditions in Britain. Convergence in relative prosperity and employment levels can reduce or reverse outflows from Ireland just as the opposite can stimulate them. Irish policy had to take this mobility into consideration in any attempt to industrialize, and Irish programmes frequently had to be more generous because of it.

2.2. Industrial and economic policies

Immediately after the war, a large programme of public investment financed by borrowing sought to remedy some of the major deficiencies in Irish social and infrastructural facilities. This was brought to an end in 1952 by a massive balance of payments deficit, which highlighted the exporting weakness of the small-scale industry that had developed. A combination of industrial parochialism and domestic deflation plunged the country into the greatest depression since the war and launched a downward spiral of falling employment and rising emigration, producing falls in population and in demand.

Deep Irish economic stagnation in a booming Europe encouraged a rethinking of industrial policy which led to tax relief on export profits, an Export Board to promote Irish sales overseas, and the repeal of the Control of Manufactures Act in 1956 to facilitate foreign investment.

In 1959 the first Programme for Economic Expansion was launched as part of a concerted attempt at economic development. The renewal of expansionary policies was accompanied by population growth as emigration slowed down significantly and eventually became negative after 1969, for the first time in centuries. At the same time, there was a marked increase in the exceptionally low Irish marriage rate as the high average age of marrying declined, so that, although average family size fell, the formation of more families maintained the birth rate at a very high level. Irish youth dependency ratios were much higher than the EEC generally — 54.2 as against 36.8 in 1975 — and, despite relatively low age dependency ratios — 18.9 as against 21.1 in the EEC as a whole — there were more social security claimants to be catered for out of a lower national income than in most other European countries. The longer-term effect was to deliver large numbers of young people on to the labour market from the mid-1970s onwards, just as employment opportunities were becoming more difficult.

It is estimated that an additional 23 000 (2 per cent of the population in 1981) will enter the labour market each year up to the year 2000. That is in contrast to the general situation in Europe, where the rise in the labour force is expected to come to a halt by then. There will be progressively fewer people retiring, so the problem will be to absorb the new entrants, the unemployed, and those leaving agriculture. The challenge which that represents goes far beyond what has been achieved in the past.

The much bolder approach to demand management as Keynesian ideas became assimilated, and the changes begun in the 1950s in industrial policy, led to a high and steady growth in aggregate demand as the serious structural problems of the 1950s were alleviated. By the end of the 1960s, however, the growth of output and employment was beginning to slow down as tourism suffered from the outbreak of civil war in Northern Ireland; the rate of inflation increased considerably, bringing with it an increase in industrial disputes, and reduced growth in public social investment led to a decline in building and construction. One response to this situation in 1969 was to revamp the powers of the Industrial Development Authority (IDA), which had a growing reputation as a successful canvasser of footloose foreign firms whose output in the 1970s was to form the greater part of the export expansion of the decade.

2.3. Political ideology and trade unions

Trade union organization began with the decentralized activities of craft unions; this was followed much later by industrial unions and finally in the twentieth century by general unions. As in Britain, Irish labour sought first to develop a strong industrial power base from the shop-floor up, and then to become independent of Parliament and the courts by overcoming the legal obstacles of legitimacy. The development of industrial countervailing power preceded any development of political countervailing power. Irish unions are thus different from many continental unions, which were launched by and were subsidiary to left-wing or social democratic parties. Attitudes to regulatory legislation are also different. Irish unions vehemently resist such legislation, whereas on the continent the unions operate within a developing framework of statute law. Irish law was identical to that of the UK up to 1970, and industrial relations, attitudes, and practices still conform to the British pattern of that period. Apart from legislation fixing statutory minimum wages in certain trades and guarding against abuses in relation to working conditions, contracts of employment were voluntary agreements. The law did not intervene, except to provide unions with immunity against claims of damage caused by trade disputes. This freedom from state involvement, apart from where facilitating machinery was provided, is designated the 'auxiliary' role of the state and is central to the Anglo-Irish tradition of free collective bargaining. At all times, compliance with agreements and income policy has been voluntary and Irish trade unions have never had to face mandatory compliance.

The political climate under which Irish income policy has operated has been a favourable one. Stable governments without strong class leanings have mirrored the general absence of major class cleavages in society in general. Since 1931 one party, Fianna Fail, retained power for two long periods of 16–17 years each and represented a broad coalition of interests, including those of the major trade union. In years when Fianna Fail was not in power a coalition of Fine Gael and the Labour Party continued to be responsive to both employer and employee interests. At no time has there been a government in power that was hostile to organized labour.

In part, this state of affairs can be traced to the orientation of Irish trade unions along a 'economistic–solidaristic' continuum. 'Economism' focuses on bread-and-butter issues relating to pay and disposable income and aims at maximizing the immediate advantage to the members in these areas, to the exclusion of long-term objectives. A 'solidaristic' orientation would typify Austria or Scandinavia, and is likely to prevail where a long and strong tradition of left-wing politics exists and where feelings of class solidarity are resilient enough to supplant sectional interests on the part of individual unions as the overriding guiding principle in negotiations. Thus, organized labour is willing to abstain from using its full bargaining power in wage negotiations in return for influence in overall economic policy, and perceives the potential for an advantageous trade-off between short-term income maximization and a more long-term acquisition of power. In this respect, Irish unions have been very much towards the economistic end of the spectrum. This was shown in the unwillingness of craft unions to admit new members in the depressed 1950s. It is seen in the split between the Congress of Irish Unions and the Irish Trade Union Congress, which lasted from 1944 to 1959 and which arose from the idea of the smaller CIU that all Irish workers should belong to Irish-based unions. It is also seen in the inter-union rivalries that continued after the Irish Congress of Trade Unions (ICTU) was formed. On the political front, the nearest trade unions have come to exercising influence has been to organize a few marches demanding taxation of farmers. Political strikes are virtually unknown.

Equally, Irish society did not experience the concomitants of 'orthodox' liberal capital development. This may be explained in part by the historical development of Ireland. The Republic has never experienced a high level of class formation along industrial lines and expressed in class politics; nor were there concentrated industrial units served by more or less independent organizations of rank-and-file trade unionists. When growth came in the 1930s, the Irish industrial labour force was rapidly assimilated from rural areas, which were natural constituencies for nationalist rather than class politics.

Irish governments of all political complexions have shown an extraordinary ability to adapt to the changing needs of society represented in a broad coalition of interest groups. The conservatism of the Irish Labour Party has meant that it has never developed policies on industrial relations different from those adopted by Fianna Fail in the 1960s. The absence of left-wing radicalism has inhibited any polarization within Irish society such as might have produced a backlash to trade unionism.

2.4. The rise in joint employer/employee institutions

A number of new institutions were set up following the launch of the First Programme for Economic Expansion in 1959. In furtherance of its economic programme, the government set out to entice trade union representatives to join a number of primarily consultative bodies established in the context of the planning of industrial development. This led to a gradual redefinition of their role, although the principle of collective bargaining remained inviolate. The bodies involved were the Irish National Productivity Committee (1959), which tried jointly with the employer's body to promote growth in productivity and therefore growth of incomes in industry; the Committee on Industrial Organization (1961), which sought to prepare industries for the dismantling of tariff protection; and the National Industrial and Economic Council, which was the main consultative body on economic planning and included in its brief the monitoring of pay and price trends. In much the same spirit, and in the belief that a 'new era in industrial relations' was dawning, unions and employers in 1962 established the bipartite National Employer Labour Conference (EL), a body that was to become central to industrial bargaining in the 1970s.

Against the background of general buoyancy, unions achieved unprecedented gains in real income during this period, but it became increasingly evident that expansion *per se* was not contributing to the reform of collective bargaining required for economic planning.

2.5. *Social expenditure and relative poverty*

In European terms, Ireland is a relatively poor country. In 1973 Irish GDP per capita was 53 per cent of the EEC average and 42 per cent of that of Denmark. In addition, dependency ratios are high, and Ireland is less able to meet higher social expenditure needs than most other parts of Europe.

The basic social security system was inherited from Britain at the time of independence. It is fundamentally a dual system, comprising 14 schemes of social insurance and 12 schemes of social 'assistance'. Entitlement to insurance benefits is determined by the insurance record and the occupational category of the applicant. Three-quarters of the labour force are insured for all those benefits as a package. Social assistance schemes, mostly means-tested, cater for those who, for one reason or another, are not entitled to a benefit under the social insurance system.

The Social Welfare Act, which established the legal basis for the modern social security system, was passed in 1952, although this was just when the postwar expansionary period was ending so progress in introducing new measures was slow.

Significant growth in social spending (and public employment) was delayed until the 1960s, when its share of GNP increased rapidly. According to Kennedy (1975), the expansion in public social expenditure in the years 1963–74 happened 'initially on an *ad hoc* basis but with a gradual development towards a cohesive social policy'. Social benefits were extended considerably in terms of the amount paid and coverage. Redundancy payments and an industrial training authority were launched in 1967 to expedite structural change. In health, a series of reforms led ultimately to the setting up of Regional Health Boards with enhanced funding. In this process of change, an important departure was the shift away from selectivity, or provision on a means-tested basis, towards universalism, or general provision without reference to means.

Although Irish social expenditure was only slightly lower in 1970 as a proportion of GNP as compared with the UK (19.2 per cent as against

20.5 per cent), in absolute terms the level of service provided was very much lower because of lower income per capita and higher levels of dependency and unemployment. Nevertheless, while expenditure may be low compared with other European countries generally, it is high compared with countries with similar per capita income.

3. Major Changes since 1973

3.1. *Economic policy*

The expansion in expenditure during the 1960s was undertaken with a balanced budget on current account, the finance being provided by real growth of the economy and inflation which brought more people into the tax net. Tax rates themselves changed little. Such borrowing as occurred was for capital purposes and mainly from domestic sources. All this changed after the 1973 oil shock.

At that time, the Irish remedy for declining world markets was to boost domestic demand by a combination of budget deficits and increased capital expenditure on construction. Exchequer borrowing for current and capital purposes in 1974 doubled (compared with the average of the previous four years), to 12 per cent of GNP. Such a development was counter-cyclical in that it offset a collapse in agriculture income and the world recession. But it was insufficient to prevent output growth in 1975 and 1976 falling to 2 per cent from the 4.5 per cent average rate of the previous decade. Exchequer borrowing in 1975 increased to 15 per cent of GNP, and the current deficit rose from £95 million to £259 million, or from 3.1 to 6.9 per cent of GNP. At this point the Coalition, elected in 1973, became alarmed and instituted a policy of retrenchment. One of the most visible of these cuts was a ban on recruitment to the public service, which had been growing rapidly. By these means Exchequer borrowing was reduced to 10 per cent of GNP by 1977 and the current deficit was reduced to almost half its 1975 level, to 3.7 per cent of GNP.

In late 1977 a new Fianna Fail government was elected, pledged to a policy of full employment and abolition of taxes on housing, cars, and other consumer durables. Public employment was expanded, with, in some cases, considerable pay increases. The borrowing requirement also rose. The underlying growth rate of the economy was pushed up by 2 per cent in both 1978 and 1979. Employment grew rapidly, by 2.5 per cent a year in the three years 1977–9, and unemployment fell from its 1976 peak of 9.5 per cent to 7.4 per cent by 1979. The cost was a deficit on current account of 7 per cent of GNP and a public sector borrowing requirement of almost 17 per cent of GNP. These developments left the public finances in a poor way to sustain domestic demand in the face of a renewed downturn in the world economy following the second oil shock in 1979/80.

At the international level, the general policy response to the second oil shock was to introduce restrictive policies aimed at containing inflation. Irish policy, however, remained expansionary in 1980 and 1981, when the current deficit was 8 per cent of GNP and the borrowing requirement 21.5 per cent. At this point a coalition was re-elected which gave priority to eliminating deficit spending for current purposes by 1987, an aim that is now being pursued largely by cutting public expenditure, but also by some increases in taxation.

Government expenditure has increased as a share of GNP. Having risen from 25 to 33.5 per cent between 1969 and 1971, it was pushed up to 41 per cent between 1973 and 1975. After a pause of three years it rose again, to 54.5 per cent in 1982. However, as yet there has been no widespread demand for less government, even though the need to finance this expansion and bring down borrowing has produced a rapid rise in taxation including contributions to social security, which rose from 10.3 per cent of GDP in 1973 to 17.5 per cent in 1981.

3.2. The 1979 watershed

Such developments can significantly distort wage-earners' and employers' respective perceptions of wages as income on the one hand and costs on the other. The trends since 1973 are set out in Table 4.1. Real after-tax incomes of employees in 1983 were only 5 per cent higher than in 1973, and were significantly lower than in 1979, since when they have declined continuously. Labour costs, on the other hand, have shown no similar downward trend and were almost 32 per cent higher in 1983 than a decade earlier. This rise in costs was not matched by a proportionate rise in productivity, so that unit labour costs rose by 12 per cent in real terms. Real after-tax income of employees, on the other hand, was no higher in 1983 than in 1975 and significantly lower than in 1979. Even so, Irish labour still had the lowest hourly cost in the EEC in 1979 and was 5 per cent below that of Italy. Since additional social costs per hour were the lowest in·Europe, Irish total labour costs were by far the lowest in Europe — for example, 40 per cent below those of Italy, where social security costs are high.

3.3. Job losses and rising unemployment

In recent years, the rate at which new firms have been added to the modern sector by the Industrial Development Authority (IDA) has not

TABLE 4.1 *Divergence between the growth of productivity and the drop in real income in Ireland, 1973–1983 (1975 = 100)* *

	Productivity real GDP/ employment	Terms of trade	Productivity adjusted by terms of trade	Real cost of labour	Real disposable income	Relative cost of labour†
				Per non-agricultural worker		
	(1)	(2)	(3)	(4)	(5)	(6)
1973	95.1	119.9	104.4	90.5	95.1	100.0
1974	97.6	101.6	98.4	98.4	98.4	97.5
1975	100.0	100.0	100.0	100.0	100.0	100.0
1976	103.0	103.7	104.8	102.5	96.4	95.3
1977	108.1	101.8	109.5	99.9	96.4	93.4
1978	111.7	103.7	114.5	103.2	106.3	94.7
1979	114.9	99.6	114.8	108.9	111.1	95.8
1980	117.0	92.8	110.4	114.6	108.6	102.8
1981	121.2	91.4	112.4	118.6	106.4	98.9
1982	123.7	93.8	119.0	117.5	103.1	102.7
1983	129.5	95.3	126.2	119.1	100.1	n.a.

*In 1975 the terms of trade were representative of the long-term situation: 1973 was a great exception.

†Relative cost of Irish labour compared with the weighted average in 19 other countries.

kept pace with closures and shake-outs (mainly in 1982 and 1983), so that manufacturing employment peaked in 1979 and declined by 13.3 per cent in the four years to 1983. Output continued to rise and productivity increased by 14 per cent in 1983 — owing largely to a structural shift in favour of electronics. At the same time, unemployment more than doubled — from under 90 000 — and reached 215 000 in the first quarter of 1984, 16 per cent of the labour force.

A major contribution to this increase was the 23 000 newcomers entering the labour force each year as a result of the population boom. The halting of the public employment programme, which had reduced unemployment between 1977 and 1979, and the industrial shake-outs left young people leaving school major victims of the recession, alongside workers made redundant. In 1979, 9.2 per cent of those under 25 years were unemployed or seeking their first job; two years later, the figure was 14.1 per cent; in 1983, 25.5 per cent of those leaving school were unable to find employment. In 1979, 10.5 per cent of school-leavers were still

without work after six months; in 1982 this proportion had increased to
37.8 per cent. Some of these young people were engaged in training
programmes, on which average participation rose from 2 per cent in 1981
to over 4 per cent in 1983.

Between 1975 and 1981, the participation rate for women rose from 34
to 35.7 per cent, while for men it declined from 89.2 to 87.5 per cent. In
the same period, the proportion of women working part-time decreased
from 10 to 8 per cent and among men from 1.8 to 1.3 per cent. These
trends are contrary to those in Britain and many other countries. The
unemployment rate for men in 1983 was 16.1 per cent as against 13.1 per
cent for women, but unemployment among women was growing more
rapidly than that among men. (In 1976 the rates had been 10.5 and 6.7
per cent, respectively.) In contrast, the rate for women unemployed for
more than a year has been falling steadily in recent years, while that for
men has been unchanged and is twice as high.

Increasing unemployment has led to a growing reluctance on the part
of industrial workers to take strike action. This is especially true in
manufacturing, where real wages in 1982 even before tax had fallen back
to the 1977 level. In manufacturing, multinationals in general have been
relatively strike-free. In the older Irish industries cuts in nominal wages
have been accepted in some cases to keep factories open, although it is often
not clear whether talk of closure is fact or blackmail. This threat is less
plausible in the protected sector, both public and private, and it is here
that much of the industrial action has occurred, keeping the number of
days lost through strikes at a relatively high level.

3.4. Increased state intervention in industrial relations

As noted earlier, the 1970s saw a trend towards increased centralization
in wage bargaining and growing government intervention. Although the
trade unions were hostile to such a development, the first state
encroachment on industrial relations was presented as part of a process of
national building which required real consultation between government
and interest groups in the formation of public policy. The unions went
along with the proposals because of the possibilities (for their members)
inherent in economic development.

Centralized bargaining remained based on free collective bargaining,
in which two parties now predominated. Unlike some other countries, it
did not progress to the point where the central organizations of the two
sides of industry were responsible for the enforcement of the terms of
particular agreements. This enabled a 'two-tier' system to develop,
involving, in addition to the basic terms of agreements, local bargaining
for further increases, often falling within the broad terms of national

settlements but sometimes lying outside them. The voluntary nature of the agreements was underlined by the continuous difficulty during the 1970s of getting ICTU approval for the terms. In this, there was frequently a clash between ICTU strategy and the ambitions of individual unions.

Employer acceptance of centralized bargaining was based on the belief that such an arrangement was superior to the outcome of inter-union rivalries pushing up demands, as was demonstrated by the maintenance men's strike of the late 1960s. Within an agreed and stable set of relativities, opportunities were expected to occur for negotiation on new technology, etc. Employer research indicated that, where there were agreements, disputes were substantially reduced. Some unrest, however, was almost inevitable, as a result of the changing structure of Irish industry brought about by the activities of the Industrial Development Authority. By 1982, half of the jobs existing in 1970 had been replaced by new ones.

Government support for centralized bargaining owed much to the enhanced role of the state in the economy in the early 1970s. This afforded it the scope to entice worker co-operation over wage restraint in return for real influence over a range of policy measures including tax rates. This course, it was hoped, would provide the tighter control needed for economic planning.

The national agreements reveal a growing tendency to impose tighter, but still not complete, control on second-tier pay adjustments allowable under 'anomaly' and 'productivity' clauses. This peaked in an embargo on 'special claims' in the public services in 1976. A more rigorous procedure was devised by the state for restraining industrial action, exemplified by the legislation enforced to prevent the non-ITCU Irish Bank Officials Association from settling above the norm. The ICTU too increased its authority, by greater control over picketing and by a judicial role in inter-union disputes. The agreements forced the Labour Court to develop a code of law, or 'a certain consistency regarding interpretation and decision'. The possibility of 'rights–obligations' actions had been rejected in the formative years of the Court. Thus, there was a pragmatic acknowledgement that, within the prevailing political economy, pay restraint was a requisite of economic expansion, and further, that it required the imposition of controls on pay determination.

3.5. The introduction and problems of national wage agreements

The 1970 and 1972 national wage agreements had contained an element of fixed indexation (i.e. a fixed cash increase per percentage point rise in the price index). The 1974 national wage agreement, however, was difficult to negotiate against the background of rising inflation and falling growth rates. Since in that year the termination of many agreements happened to coincide, the opportunity to introduce proportional indexation was taken to facilitate the orderly development of wages in a context of accelerating inflation. Indexation was repeated in 1975 in an attempt to ignore the consequences of the adverse shift in the terms of trade. Faced with rapid inflation and a deterioration in competitiveness, the government abandoned its position of neutrality and intervened actively. It demanded downward re-negotiation of the 1975 agreement and offered in return a wide range of subsidies to moderate prices. This brought budgetary policy to the bargaining table, where it remained for the rest of the 1970s. For its own part, the government banned further public service recruitment and the payment of any special awards to civil servants. This ban remained while the Coalition fought to reduce the borrowing requirement.

Once actively involved, the government followed up its initiative in 1976 by getting employers and unions to focus on the economic and social policy to be pursued over the following two years. A Tripartite Conference on resources, employment, welfare, prices, and public finances proved abortive, but sowed the seed that eventually flowered in the National Understandings of 1979 and 1980. In the period 1976–8 the accent was on costs, and the national wage agreement contained no indexation clauses. During this period manufactured exports increased by 20 per cent annually as new firms began to export. Indexation had earlier increased the share of non-agricultural wages and salaries in GNP. The new approach led to a considerable recovery in the share of profits and professional earnings between 1976 and 1978. Benefits from membership of the EEC and changes in the terms of trade led to a recovery in agricultural incomes from their low level in 1976.

Late 1977 saw the return to power of a Fianna Fail government pledged to a programme of full employment. A new Department of Economic Planning and Development formalized further the process of tripartite consultation. Under its aegis, tripartite working parties were set up and a series of programmes for economic development were produced.

The First National Understanding was launched in 1979 against the background of a PAYE strike by employees who resented the negligible taxes paid by farmers. The Understanding sought to provide an integrated programme covering employment, pay, taxation, and social expenditure. The 1979 Budget continued the expansionary stance of 1978 and dissipated the attempts to secure financial stability of the last years of the Coalition (1976 and 1977). Net external liabilities increased although European Monetary System (EMS) membership increased borrowing facilities. The second oil shock and worsening terms of trade, in addition to expanding demand, caused the balance of payments deficit to jump from £200 million to £725 million.

The National Understanding contained an explicit recognition of the link between pay and employment on the part of all involved. For its part, the government proposed to set up a National Hire Agency and a National Enterprise Agency, and to provide a more equitable tax structure. Employers undertook to resolve industrial relations problems in collaboration with the unions, which in turn agreed to deal with inter-union disputes. In 1980, however, the period of employment creation was nearing its end and unemployment was beginning to rise.

The year 1981 saw the return to power of the Coalition, which had to cope with the consequences of the large borrowing of the previous four years and the generous settlements made to certain categories of civil servant. The Coalition, which included the Labour Party, accepted the constraints on policy so long as repayments remained high, and set about reducing the size of the debt.

The centralized bargaining of the 1970s is now in suspension, partly because of the inability of the government to offer any inducements. Debt repayment, often to foreign creditors, has eliminated room for manoeuvre and jeopardized the chances of maintaining the social progress already achieved, although the suspension was due partly to the feeling that the opportunity costs of preserving consensus in the past have been too high. National wage agreements fixed rates in excess of the terms sought by the state, and these rates were exceeded in practice by the use of bogus productivity deals.[1]

A further reason for suspension is that the ICTU has been faced with a coalition of interests — mainly craft unions — which finally succeeded in imposing their opposition to centralized bargaining.

All three parties, however, have perceived that the others are not in a position to deliver what they promise. Government is hindered from offering tax concessions and further public sector employment. Unions are unable to guarantee industrial peace or wage restraint. Wage restraint in itself does not ensure profits, investment, or jobs. Even if profits increased, employers could not guarantee that these would lead ultimately to jobs.[2]

It is questionable whether these attitudes will persist. In part, they go against the conventional trade union wisdom, which favours national wage agreements in difficult times and decentralized bargaining in times of economic buoyancy. It is possible that, when tripartite talks eventually

---

[1] For example, in the public sector in 1979 and 1980, 'special' pay increases over the norm exceeded the cost of the national wage agreement increases.

[2] Between 1975 and 1983, although real compensation per employee in Ireland rose less than in the EEC generally, this was not reflected in a better employment performance.

resume, bargaining will be more realistic and more shrewdly evaluated. But a new institutional framework will be required if income policy is to be used for stabilization purposes. Here, a common framework for analysis would be a first step. A convincing and highly visible industrial development policy is also essential to ensure that any resources freed by tax concessions, wage restraint, and so on would produce jobs. A mechanism is needed to face up to breaches of the agreements that could be forthcoming if other reforms are pursued vigorously. As a first step, the scope for wage drift should be reduced by abolishing phoney productivity deals. Wage restraint needs also to be married to restraint on other sources of income. Such non-wage restraint has not proved easy to police in the past.

3.6. Present trends in social expenditure

With the return of a Coalition government committed to tackling poverty, the share of social expenditure in GNP rose rapidly, from 21.8 per cent in 1973 to 26.5 per cent in 1974 and 28.8 per cent in 1975. Subsequently retrenchment pulled the share back to 1974 levels by 1977, but the 1975 peak was regained in 1979. By 1980 social expenditure had reached 31.4 per cent of GNP, more than 50 per cent higher than eight years previously, reflecting the development of the National Under-standings. Although comparable figures are not available for more recent years, it is clear that expenditure has continued to grow.

Between 1953 and 1973, income maintenance payments in Ireland rose by 1.6 times the rise in GNP. Since 1973, the rate of increase has accelerated and new schemes have been introduced. These include pay-related benefits, introduced in 1974, a gradual reduction in pensionable age, and allowances to unmarried mothers. Despite the effect that these improvements have had on taxation, until recently there was little evidence of any widespread desire to concentrate the costs of recession on those who have been its main victims through losing their jobs. The most recent increase in social benefits, which does not fully compensate for inflation, may denote a new trend.

In summary, the recent past has seen a breakdown in centralized wage bargaining, an apparent shift in bargaining power towards employers, especially in exposed sectors, and a sharp decline in real post-tax wages. Considerable and continuous borrowing by the government in support of employment has pre-empted discretionary revenue for interest payments abroad and has set in train the reluctant beginnings of a trend to cut government expenditure, to which even social welfare payments have begun to be exposed. Virtually unanimous opinion holds that unemploy-ment is the major problem taking precedence over all others including inflation. Low wages, however, are not deemed sufficient to ensure growth and jobs, so that concern is increasingly focused on the possibilities of international reflation as the best means of getting out of the crisis.

5

From a Workable Social Compromise to Conflict: The Case of Belgium

Geert Dancet

1. Introduction

The late 1970s and early 1980s produced a radical change in the economic thinking of the academic élite in many industrialized countries. Their starting point was the notion that the current economic depression, which had already persisted for a decade, could not be remedied by traditional policy instruments. This was not because the policy mix was fundamentally wrong but because the economic and social structure showed so much rigidity that any fine-tuning had little effect. What was needed was a restoration of the economic rationality of the market as a pre-condition for renewed economic growth. Private industry could be relied upon to renovate or restructure itself if output and factor markets were sufficiently flexible. The consequences of such thinking are far-reaching and drastic. They include a cut-back in government involvement in the economy, the abolition of the labour monopoly of trade unions, and the liberalization of capital markets, all pre-conditions of a supply-oriented, neo-liberal economic policy.

Wherever a centre–right government took office in a Western country in the 1980s, this strategy became popular and was in varying degrees implemented. In Belgium, since December 1981, the elected centre–right government led by Mr Martens has been receptive to the arguments of the advocates of neo-liberalism and has progressively introduced elements of it. The more radical sections of the employers' association are not satisfied with the poor results achieved so far and want to go much further. They dream of a new system of work-place relations which would facilitate the application of new technologies in individual firms. This offensive on the part of the employers, who happen to be most strongly

The author is grateful to Frank Vandenbroucke, Toon Colpaert, and Chris Serroyen for the many useful suggestions and comments on earlier drafts.

placed at present, is making it difficult for trade unions to defend their position.

In order to understand present circumstances, it is necessary to review the history of the old system of labour relations and consider its rationale, its structure, and its limitations.

After the war, the European economies tried to attain a higher level of productivity by modernizing their industries and improving living standards in imitation of the American model of mass consumption. With this new model of consumption and production went a new system of wage/labour relations, generally referred to as 'Fordism'. Fordism implied a co-operative structure of industrial relations and an equitable division of productivity gains between profits and wages. There was also a broad acceptance of the government's playing a leading role in social and economic affairs, as had begun to happen in the late 1930s and during the war. President Roosevelt gave the modern governments of industrialized countries a new task. They were to be responsible for ensuring 'freedom from want' through better labour conditions, economic progress, and a system of social security. A new economic theory, Keynesianism, provided the instruments for governments to manipulate aggregate demand so as to attain full employment and economic prosperity.

In Belgium, over the postwar period up to the mid-1970s and the beginning of a new structural crisis, a complete institutional framework was developed to formalize the collective relations between the three major actors in the economy: the government, the employers' associations (first two, later unified into a single body), and the trade unions (first two organizations, later three corresponding to the three political parties in Belgium: Socialists, Christian Democrats, and Liberals). In order to minimize labour conflict, collective relations were institutionalized along two lines: 'negotiation' and 'consultation'. Trade unions and employers were also invited to co-operate with government in developing a complete social security system as well as a system for economic planning.

In the 1970s, the fragile social consensus between the three parties over collective relations gradually broke down as recession highlighted the weaknesses of the industrial and social structure. Economic growth slowed, and with it the possibility of financing large public expenditure programmes. Unemployment became the major problem. The whole system of wage/labour relations and its many institutional elements ceased to produce satisfactory results, giving the Belgian government an opportunity to pursue a more authoritarian policy.

These points are elaborated below. In Section 2, the Fordist system of wage/labour relations as it operated up to the mid-1970s is described, with the focus on pay bargaining, conditions of employment, the extent and form of government intervention, and the nature of the social security system. In Section 3 the breakdown of this system is analysed, beginning with the problems of pay bargaining which created the conditions for strong government intervention. Emphasis is also put on fundamental divergences of interest which prevented an easy return to normality. Finally, the current offensive of the employers' organization for a new system of wage/labour relations is described.

2. The Constitution and Functioning of Typical Fordist Wage/Labour Relations, 1944–1975

For analytic purposes, the postwar years up to 1975 are divided into four sub-periods: 1944–51, 1952–9, 1960–9, and 1970–5.

2.1. The foundations of a complete system of wage/labour relations, 1944–1951

At their regular informal meetings during the war, the representatives of the government, the employers, and the trade unions (Catholic and Socialist) emphasized the need for solidarity and a mutual acceptance of each other's role as a necessary condition for postwar reconstruction and the development of a social welfare system. This resulted in 1944 in the so-called agreement on social unity (Projet d'Accord de Solidarité Sociale), which was generally referred to as the 'Social Pact' (or 'Cease-fire'), although it was never officially agreed by any of the three parties. The Pact included the acceptance of the principles of a generalized system of social security as well as of a system of consultation between employers and employees, but it also stipulated that the government could impose temporary control on wages as part of a policy to contain postwar inflation.

Soon after the liberation of Belgium, the first government, with the participation of Socialists and Communists, put the Pact into practice, starting with a general scheme for social security. Although the spirit of Roosevelt and Beveridge was present, the social security system set up in December 1944 was intended to cover only salaried workers. The basic innovation was the centralization of the contributions (fixed by law) of both employers and employees in one single public institution managed by the two sides. The private institutions that already existed concentrated on the payment of social security benefits.

In 1944 the government also organized a National Labour Conference (Conférence National du Travail), which became the crucial 'consultation and negotiation' body at national level for that period. The first postwar conference fixed wages at a level 40 per cent higher than 1940 in nominal terms while at the same time granting a 20 per cent subsidy on food and other basic needs. It also fixed minimum hourly wage rates. How these resolutions were to be translated so far as any individual worker was concerned was entrusted to the sectoral 'comparability commissions' (*commissions paritaires*) which had existed before the war and began operating again in 1944. In a brief space of time, Belgium was transformed from a low-wage to a high-wage economy.

In 1945 the comparability commissions even acquired a legal structure and the right to negotiate wages through collective agreements (*conventions collectives*), although to begin with the scope for pay bargaining at sectoral or enterprise level was limited. It should, however, be emphasized that the social climate in 1944 was extremely favourable for the establishment of a new system of wage/labour relations. The principle of consultation was accepted by the two sides of industry as well as by government and all political parties. Wages were fixed at a level that would stimulate industrial demand, and the principles of social welfare were established, at least for salaried workers. From 1945 until 1948, the government tried to control inflation using its special powers. During the Labour Conferences that followed, the government convinced employers and employees of the need for wage moderation. Indexation of salaries such as had existed before the war could not be restored. But prices kept rising, so a reduction in the purchasing power of the working classes seemed unavoidable. Only minimum wages were allowed to increase. Nevertheless, in several sectors, after severe strikes, employees and employers agreed upon the introduction of several kinds of bonus payment, which in reality were disguised pay rises. In 1948 the government gradually withdrew its control over wages. Inflation was much lower, the black market had disappeared, and the re-emergence of unemployment was also expected to temper pay rises. In order to encourage a return to a more normal system of wage formation, the government restored automatic indexation for public sector employees and prepared legislation on collective bargaining.

The Law of 20 September 1948 established a complete system of social consultation at three levels: at the enterprise level (the works councils — Conseils d'Entreprise — and councils for health, safety, and work-place improvements — Conseils de Sécurité, d'Hygiène, et d'Embellissement des lieux de Travail), the sectoral level (trade councils — Conseils Professionnels), and the national level (the central economic council — Conseil Centrale de l'Economie) advisory bodies were created, with a fifty–fifty representation of trade unions and employers. Worker membership of these bodies was reserved for union members elected in the *elections sociales*. Wages were discussed not in these bodies but in the sectoral *commissions paritaires*, and in some sectors there were further pay negotiations at enterprise level, between management and union delegates, whose rights were recognized by law in 1947. All agreements were included in the *conventions collectives de travail* (collective labour agreements).

What was important and new in this law was the elaboration of a social structure for the enterprise, something that had already been accepted in principle by the Social Pact of 1944. Together with the acceptance of union representatives (*délégués syndicaux*), it formed the basis for negotiation over labour conditions at the enterprise level. This was the preferred sphere of action for socialist trade union officials, who saw the *conseils d'enterprise* as the key to structural reform. Once the government withdrew, a structure existed for firm-by-firm negotiations, and this was the important forum in the 1950s.

The general application of automatic indexation of wages to consumer prices in 1950 and 1951 meant the disappearance of the last vestige of government control over wages. Wage formation, which was centralized in the early postwar years, ended up being completely decentralized. Some wages were agreed at a sectoral level, others at enterprise or regional level, with the system of indexation varying from sector to sector.

Economic conditions in Belgium soon after the war were comparatively favourable. Although the war left industry and infrastructure damaged, the situation in 1945 was not as disastrous as in neighbouring countries. Most of the country's industrial capacity was intact, and by 1947 the prewar level of industrial output was achieved without much new investment. The Marshall Plan (1947–51), which financed the reconstruction of industrial capacity in Western Europe, was therefore less important for Belgium than for other countries. In 1949 the Belgian franc even appreciated. As a result, Belgium entered the 1950s with comparatively obsolete productive capacity, an overvalued exchange rate, and a renewed problem of unemployment.

2.2. The division of productivity gains, 1952–1959

Since 1952, wages and working conditions have been fixed through a process of free bargaining between employer and trade unions, firm by firm or sector by sector.

Because of the government's desire to maintain a certain degree of centralization, a 'National Labour Council' (Conseil National du Travail) was established in 1952 to advise on wages and working conditions at national and occupational level. In practice, however, the Council concentrated its activities in the 1950s more on working conditions than on wages. National consultation served mostly to avoid strikes or to solve labour disputes.

In Wallonia, in the south of Belgium, labour relations were generally more confrontational. Collective pay bargaining was often accompanied by strikes. Collective agreements were mostly agreed by firm or by region, while in Flanders sectoral agreements prevailed.

The crucial issue in the early 1950s was not the adjustment of wages to prices but the way in which the relatively high profits of industrial enterprises should be divided. Trade unions were not prepared to accept wage reductions (in line with price falls) while profits were rising. Workers in metal industries were the first to demand a productivity bonus in 1952, thereby establishing a direct link between profits and wages. (Because profits tend to fluctuate a great deal, productivity gains are possibly a more stable and better basis for determining wage increases.)

In the early 1950s, both employers' organizations and trade unions recognized that the Belgian economy was backward, particularly in terms of low industrial productivity, as compared with neighbouring countries. The revival of international competition that followed the period of reconstruction highlighted the fact that only an increase in productivity could restore the competitiveness of the Belgian economy, reduce unemployment, and justify relatively high wages. This resulted in 'The Common Declaration on Productivity' (La Déclaration Commune sur la Productivité) of 1954, which was revised in 1959.

This agreement stated that productivity gains should be divided in a fair way between enterprises, employees, and consumers. However, it was not specified how productivity gains should be measured, on what basis they should be divided between the three parties, or by what means employees should get their share. In the light of the present debate, it is remarkable that international competitiveness was not then identified as a factor influencing the division of productivity gains between profits and wages. Both texts also specified that the employees' representatives would collaborate in trying to achieve productivity gains, which in practice amounted to trade unions adopting a 'responsible' attitude to the need for rationalizing weak enterprises.

In accordance with this common interest in productivity growth, productivity bonuses were introduced in many industries in the 1950s and early 1960s. Although employers originally insisted that these bonuses should be related exclusively to the physical productivity of labour, and therefore should be an effective means of securing pro-ductivity improvements, in practice there were very few genuine productivity bonuses (i.e. individual incentives). Most bonuses were collective and were linked to the profits of the enterprise instead of to labour productivity. For the trade unions, this meant the acceptance of a link between productivity and wages. For the employers, it also expressed the need for a more centralized system of wage formation which could be linked to social peace.

Meanwhile, the trade unions gradually improved their organizational structure and increased their strength at both enterprise and industry level. Apart from a substantial increase in wages and purchasing power, a reduction of the working week (to 45 hours in 1955) and some improvement in social security were achieved. The elaboration of complementary social security schemes, sector by sector or firm by firm, reaffirmed the traditional insurance principle for salaried labour, and participation in such schemes continued to be a condition for obtaining social protection.

The decentralized system of negotiation and consultation that prevailed in the 1950s failed to reduce social unrest. The number of strikes was high, culminating in 'the strike of the century' in December 1960, which ended in disillusion for the Socialist trade union, since it underlined the internal disagreement between its Flemish and Walloon factions.

2.3. *The Golden Age of social planning and growth, 1960–1969*

From 1960 onwards, every two years the employers' associations and the trade unions concluded an 'inter-trade [i.e. national] agreement' followed by sectoral agreements, a practice known as *programmation sociale*. Through these agreements, certain minimum conditions were established at the national level. Thereafter, in the 'comparability commissions' actual wages and working conditions were fixed at sectoral level through sectoral collective bargaining, in the light of the recommendations contained in the national agreement. The translation of all labour benefits into wages was also new, and it meant that only those elements that could be so translated were discussed in the negotiation round.

Employers had a preference for greater centralization of wage negotiations over bargaining firm by firm, since it enabled them to plan labour costs over a longer period and to avoid expensive strikes. Because wages increased more rapidly than labour productivity in some sectors in the late 1950s, their desire was to link labour costs more closely to industrial performance and more precisely to productivity improvements. At the same time, a commitment to 'social peace', which was explicitly included in sectoral agreements from 1960 onwards, was for them the best way of controlling social unrest. For the trade unions, more centralized pay bargaining was a potential way of reducing the enormous disparities that existed in wages and other working conditions. It also gave them more power at the national level to influence government. More importantly, the Flemish Catholic trade union, which was becoming the strongest in number and influence (after the débacle of the

1960 strike), had traditionally been in favour of a *modus vivendi* with employers based on consultation.

The consequences of the *programmation sociale* for both sides were not negligible. Trade unions developed rapidly in the 1960s, particularly at the sectoral level, with a corresponding demise in the strength of union officials at the enterprise level. Gradually the distance between union members and their leadership widened. On the other side, employers were forced to organize more tightly. In negotiations, employers could no longer address the problems of each firm individually. Both sides seemed to find a common interest in sharing out the ever-increasing gains from growth in a way that benefited the most organized members of society.

The key to *programmation sociale* was its link with the policy of economic expansion, based on attracting multinational investors, which was pursued by the government of Gaston Eyskens. In the 1950s the Belgian economy lagged behind the economies of neighbouring countries. While Belgium grew on average at 2.8 per cent a year, the average growth rate of other members of the European Coal and Steel Community was twice as high, at 5.6 per cent a year. The foundation of the Common Market in 1957 was a unique opportunity for the Eyskens government, which introduced a series of measures in 1959 aimed at economic expansion. These involved subsidizing new investment and supporting it by government guarantees. The consensus at the time was that government intervention and planning was the way to modernize the Belgian economy. Between 1960 and 1970, 37 per cent of gross capital formation on average was subsidized by government. It was, however, foreign firms (and in particular, US multinationals) that benefited most from government support. Of all investment in new plants receiving government subsidy, two-thirds was accounted for by multinationals. At the same time, industrial concentration was increasing rapidly as Belgian and foreign companies collaborated in investment projects.

The link between economic expansion and an effective system of consultation between the two sides of industry is obvious. Long-term economic expansion requires social peace, which can be assured only by regular agreements between employers and employees at national or sectoral level. Acceptance of the 'peace clause' meant a corresponding acceptance of all points in the agreement for the period that it covered.

The emphasis of *programmation sociale* was on collective bargaining at the sectoral rather than the firm level. Within each sector, differences in wages and working conditions were reduced dramatically. As a form of compensation for social peace, employers started to pay a trade union bonus (*prime syndicale*) to union members, making membership attractive to all workers. Non-monetary issues and proposals for structural reform disappeared from the agenda of trade unions. What counted was the improvement in the real disposable income of each employee in the sector concerned.

A consequence of *programmation sociale* was a narrowing of regional and intra-sectoral wage differentials as well as a lessening of disparities between men and women. On the other hand, wage differences between sectors widened rather than narrowed. The net effect of these tendencies was to cause an overall increase in labour costs. This was not so much of a problem in the 1960s, as the Belgian economy was expanding rapidly. There were also other effects. The two major trade unions, which in the early 1960s had very different strategies and priorities, agreed in 1965 to present common demands and establish permanent contacts in order to formulate a common strategy and strengthen their bargaining power.

At the end of the 1960s social consultation became more difficult, as the interests of trade unions and employers' associations began to diverge. Government policy, however, was to centralize pay bargaining even further by giving greater authority to the National Labour Council, which, as a result of the law of 5 December 1968, was able to conclude inter-trade collective agreements, binding on all industries by royal decree. This law also gave official trade unions and employers' organizations sole authority to engage in collective bargaining, as well as authorizing the government to mediate in the bargaining process and to translate the outcomes into decrees. The use of this authority was the main change in the process of collective bargaining in the 1970s, a period of social unrest and economic crisis.

During the 1960s the economy grew rapidly; unemployment was low, there were few labour conflicts, and the real income of workers increased rapidly. It was possible to widen the coverage of the social security system by extending social welfare to all those not participating in the labour process. Health insurance was extended between 1964 and 1969, followed by child and unemployment benefits, while pension funds were revised and centralized in 1967. A system of scholarships was established to improve access to education for all classes. At the same time, there was a concern gradually to raise the minimum level of benefits. The social system not only brought about a more equitable division of economic growth directly, but also had wider consequences. For salaried workers it meant stable real income growth, complete protection against risks of unemployment and ill-health, and access to education. For employers it meant a stable growth of demand, greater social peace, and the possibility of increased flexibility of labour inasmuch as it was easier to lay off workers temporarily. For the government· it meant more responsibility and power, but also a permanent obligation to provide finance for social security, which added to public expenditure.

During the 1960s it also proved possible to reduce the average working week to 42 hours, to increase annual holidays, and substantially to revise the system of price indexation which from 1968 was based upon a full inquiry into household budgets.

Between 1960 and 1970, the structure of employment and value added changed substantially. (The proportion of total employment in agriculture fell from 10 to 5 per cent and its share of value added from 6 to 4 per cent.) Manufacturing industry increased its share of value added significantly, from 22 to 26 per cent, while it continued to account for around 30 per cent of employment. Employment in services rose rapidly from 49 to 54 per cent, while its share of value added declined marginally to 57 per cent. Energy and construction both experienced a gradual reduction in their share of employment and value added.

Inflation was low throughout the period and substantially lower than wage increases, with the result that real-wage growth varied between 2½ and 6½ per cent a year. For the economy as a whole, there was a relatively constant and stable relationship between real wages and productivity, with salaried workers gaining slightly (Table 5.1). The proportion of salaried labour in the total working population increased rapidly in the 1960s, and the number rose by almost half a million while the number of non-salaried employees fell significantly. In total, although more people joined the labour force, they were absorbed by the economy without great difficulty, and the unemployment rate was lower in 1970 than in 1960.

2.4. Social conflicts and tensions in wage/labour relations, 1970–1975

1970 was a key year. It began with a lengthy conflict in the Limburg coal mines and strikes in other sectors. At the request of trade unions, the government organized an Economic and Social Conference. The Conference ended in important concessions to the unions, and these were implemented through the collective pay agreements approved in the National Labour Council. In the same year, the government attempted to reactivate the system of advisory bodies at sectoral level; at regional level, it created regional development agencies as advisory bodies on regional economic policy. In order to reduce social unrest, the government intervened again in wage bargaining. However, by organizing national labour conferences outside the *programmation sociale*, it undermined the bipartite procedure of consultation, which dissatisfied the unions. In these conferences, pressing issues such as structural reform and employment measures, which had been carefully kept off the agenda of consultation in the 1960s, were open for discussion. Trade unions under pressure from their members emphasized the need for structural reform inside companies (workers' control), and this was a theme discussed in special conferences organized by each of the two major unions.

Although economic conditions improved in 1972, unemployment continued rising towards 100 000. Accordingly, the government initiated another Employment Conference. Since an active employment policy was not yet on the political agenda, the main focus was on improving the position of individual workers, which meant a considerable wage increase (and an even greater rise in labour costs, as a result of a reduction in working time to 40 hours a week), the introduction of automatic indexation, and an increase in employers' social security contributions.

Agreements between the now unified employers' association and the two major trade unions became more and more difficult to achieve as the crisis intensified in 1974 and 1975. Wages continued to rise — in real as well as nominal terms — as did prices, unemployment, and the number of bankruptcies. A last *accord de programmation sociale* ('social agreement') was signed in February 1975. This agreement was reached surprisingly quickly, although employers found the package of union requests hard to take. Some employers were unable to support the agreement because they felt the cost was too high, especially that of the minimum wage, which for the first time was fixed through an inter-trade agreement. Some members of the employers' association called for the abandonment of *programmation sociale* because it was no longer able to reduce social unrest and it both increased wage costs and strengthened the position and unity of trade unions.

In general, in the first half of the 1970s the trade union movement was politically and socially in a very strong position, despite the fact that from 1974 a centre–right coalition government was in power. This was reflected in rapid pay increases, although not in the meeting of union demands for structural reform. The reforms that were secured at the beginning of the 1970s — a new and comprehensive law on economic planning in 1970 and legislation on economic democracy in 1973 — did not in fact achieve very much.

Inflation increased rapidly, from 4 per cent in 1970 to nearly 13 per cent in 1975, and nominal wage rises went up even more markedly, from 12 per cent in 1970 to 20 per cent in 1975. At the same time, hourly wages increased in real terms at unprecedented rates varying between 7½ and 9 per cent a year during this period. Despite accelerating inflation, the real income of salaried workers therefore went up, as did their share of total national income. The growth in the numbers of salaried workers in employment, however, slowed down significantly. Instead, unemployment rose rapidly, reaching levels in 1975 as high as those of the early 1950s. Most disturbingly, perhaps, youth unemployment increased to 44 per cent of the youth labour force as against only 25 per cent in 1970.

Moreover, between 1970 and 1975 there were enormous variations in wages and other working conditions both between and within sectors. The 'inter-trade' agreements, which established uniform principles, were modified sector by sector, or even enterprise by enterprise, according to the relative strengths of unions and employers as well as the economic situation prevailing in the sector or enterprise concerned — the more open the sector, the greater the variation. Thus, in construction there were negotiations only at sectoral level, while in most manufacturing industries there tended to be negotiations at enterprise or sub-regional level, and multinationals mostly negotiated individually. In general, the procedure was that unions presented requests for changes in wages and working conditions after taking formal or informal soundings among their members. The employers responded by outlining the concessions they were prepared to make given the financial and economic state of the enterprise, sector, or economy, depending on the level of negotiation. In open sectors, regard was paid to the competitive position of the firm. The outcome depended on the relative strength of the two sides. In case of conflict, a 'social mediator' from the Ministry of Labour actively intervened to secure a compromise.

No single company consistently took the lead in setting the scale of pay settlements. Negotiations over wages were opened whenever the old agreement terminated, and this could be at any time of the year (with two peak periods in April and December). But if more than one agreement terminated at the same time, trade unions attempted to begin negotiating in the sector or enterprise where their position was strongest. Unions in succeeding negotiations then usually attempted to match the settlement reached in the first case. In those sectors where negotiations were held at enterprise level, big companies tended to take the initiative, with one leading company (e.g. F.N. for the metals sector) making the running and smaller ones following closely behind.

The basis of wage/labour relations in Belgium was a bipartite system of collective bargaining which concentrated on the division of growth between profits and labour. The effect of introducing a system of automatic indexation to protect employees against the erosion of real wages was to focus bargaining on the real growth of the economy, industry, or enterprise. Real wages were able to rise roughly in line with labour productivity, and while in reality there was no precise formula to ensure that economic growth was distributed in this way, such a tendency is apparent over the long run (Table 5.1). Before 1970, increases in real wages per hour moved closely in line with productivity gains. Between 1970 and 1975, however, real wages rose more rapidly than productivity, especially in 1974 and 1975, which were the last years of free bargaining and the first years of economic crisis. The early 1970s

TABLE 5.1 *Average changes in real wages and productivity per hour and unemployment in Belgium (% per year)*

	Real wage per hour[a]	Productivity per hour [b]	Unemployment rate[c]
1954–59	3.6	3.9	5.9
1960–69	4.6	5.1	3.7
1970–75	9.2	7.0	4.0
1976–81	3.7	3.8	10.9
1982–84	−1.2	3.4	18.4

[a] Constructed by dividing the deflated total wage bill (using national income statistics) by the total number of hours worked.
[b] Total value added divided by total number of hours worked.
[c] The number of unemployed receiving unemployment benefit as % of the number of wage-earners insured against unemployment.

Source: The Planning Bureau and the National Bank statistics, plus author's calculations.

showed a rapid increase in labour productivity without any creation of new jobs. It is, however, hard to discern any relationship between real-wage growth and the unemployment rate.

A central question is why employers should have agreed to real wages growing faster than productivity. A possible answer is that a strong and unified trade union movement was able to benefit from the preceding boom and the short-sighted optimism of employers. In the same years, costs also increased rapidly for other reasons: the working week was reduced in many sectors from 42 to 40 hours, employers' social security contributions increased once more, and a national guaranteed minimum wage was introduced. Moreover, in a number of sectors (especially metal industries) sectoral pay bargaining was abandoned in favour of bargaining by enterprise or region, which also tended to push up real-wage increases since the threat of strike action became more potent. Furthermore, the development of the social security system reached its peak in the early 1970s. Total expenditure on social security rose from 17 per cent of GDP in 1970 to 22 per cent in 1975, an expansion that imposed an increasing burden on both government finances and employers' contributions, and which necessitated continuing rapid growth of the economy if it were not to become intolerable.

All of these are symptoms of a weakening of the old system of wage/labour relations. But what caused this to happen? In the first place, mention should be made of widespread working-class protest against the welfare society which began in Europe around 1968. Quantitative growth failed to satisfy the qualitative needs of workers. Such aspirations as an interesting job, respect from the employer, identification with the products of labour, or participation in decision-making had not been achieved through rapid increases in industrial production. The call for structural reforms at both firm and national level should be seen as part of this phenomenon. In Belgium, however, such pressure only resulted in real-wage increases, the traditional response to more fundamental demands.

Second, the economic recession that was initiated by the increase in oil prices brought the motor of postwar growth to a halt, and productivity growth slowed down markedly after 1975. From 1970 onwards, both inflation and unemployment went up steeply, an occurrence that was hard to explain in terms of the so-called Phillips Curve. The government decided that these economic policies could no longer be resolved through bipartite collective bargaining: only a strong hand could restore the old equilibrium.

3. The Period since 1975: The Disintegration of the Fordist System of Wage/Labour Relations

3.1. The end of the Social Compromise and the emergence of an experimental policy, 1976–1981

The motor of the Fordist system of wage/labour relations, namely rapid growth of labour productivity, slowed down markedly after 1975. Between 1976 and 1981 productivity grew no faster than in the 1950s (Table 5.1). At the same time, employment declined, especially in the industrial sector, and many industrial enterprises closed down, while others were forced to rationalize and abandon old production techniques. Unemployment became a critical problem and, unlike the 1950s, was out of control. The numbers out of work and the cost of supporting them reached a level such that they began to affect all other economic aggregates, including wages.

In 1976 the wage drift experienced in previous years represented a central problem for pay negotiations. The government refused to take a passive role any longer and proposed a modification of the wage indexation mechanism in order to control inflation. Profits and other income were also to be frozen. At the same time, the government wished to stimulate economic activity and employment. The result was the 'recovery' laws (*lois de redressement*) of 1976. Free wage bargaining was still possible, but only within well defined limits. Automatic wage indexation above a certain limit was suspended by law for nine months, a fact that is not detectable in the statistics since, immediately after the nine months were up, wages increased to compensate for the loss in disposable income.

The growing centralization of pay bargaining of the 1960s and early 1970s came to an end as unemployment rose and enterprises began to make losses. Employers preferred instead to negotiate at the enterprise level so as to emphasize the link between wage moderation and business solvency. Their position became stronger, and trade unions were forced on to the defensive, concentrating their efforts on reducing working time nationally and putting pressure on the government to bring down unemployment.

In spite of the introduction of training and early retirement schemes and alternative job programmes, however, unemployment continued to rise. The unions' campaign from 1976 onwards for an overall reduction in working time to 36 hours a week ran into opposition from employers, who argued that a reduction in labour costs was the only solution, that wages should be reduced through collective bargaining at the enterprise level, and that employees should accept lower wages or risk losing their jobs. Agreement was not possible, and the *programmation sociale* broke down. In most industries some shortening of working time was agreed on in place of real-wage increases, although in historical terms there was no overall acceleration in the pace of reduction in working time.

The modest economic revival of 1976–9 ended abruptly in 1980. By then, it was commonly accepted that the crisis was having a serious effect on traditional industries and that these could survive only through large-scale reconversion which required government support. Steel, textiles, mining, glass, and shipbuilding industries were declared 'sectors of national interest', while all other sectors were entrusted to the newly created regional administrations. The government, in consultation with the EEC, initiated massive reconversion plans for the five national sectors, starting with textiles. In 1981 the government introduced a direct link between subsidies and wage cuts, 5 per cent for employees and 10 per cent for executives and directors, although only in the case of certain loss-making enterprises. The general formation of wages in these sectors, however, became a matter of government concern.

From 1980 onwards there was renewed recession, accompanied by rapidly growing unemployment. In two years, both the Budget and the trade deficit more than doubled, a situation that could not go on for long. For the Union of Belgian Enterprises (the employers' association), only an overall reduction in wage income could remedy the so-called 'Belgian sickness', and the Union began to press the government to implement the necessary measures. In October 1980 the government organized a National Labour Conference focusing on wage moderation and, in particular, on automatic indexation, which was to be an abiding theme from then on. The system of wage indexation had even been improved in the 1970s in many sectors, including the public sector. At the Conference the government threatened a complete wage freeze, but employers and unions agreed upon wage moderation by national agreement, thereby retaining the system of indexation but reducing working time and restricting real-wage increases to those sectors that already had a 38-hour week or less. The agreement, enforced by law, was to last until the end of 1981 but was extended until the end of 1982. By this means wage formation was controlled nationally, but bargaining continued at sectoral level.

Pay negotiations sought to restore the old state of affairs where real wages could grow so long as they remained in line with productivity increases. This, however, was not sufficient to restore the old system of wage determination, in part because collective pay negotiations were no longer free. Agreement between both sides of industry on how the crisis could be resolved was not possible.

The other axis of wage/labour relations, the social security system, could hardly bear the cost of unemployment. Expenditure on unemployment benefit (mainly financed by government) rose from 2 per cent of GNP in 1975 to more than 5 per cent in 1981. By then, total social security expenditure had reached 28 per cent of GNP, and government subsidies to support the system were still increasing, despite the fact that the public sector deficit had risen to an all-time high of 11½ per cent of GNP. Since the mid-1970s, the employers' association had been arguing that any further rise in the social security contributions of both employers and the government would damage the economy in a number of ways. An increase in their contributions would push up wage costs and lead to greater shedding of labour, an argument that seems to have met with some success, since employers' contributions have remained constant in relation to GNP since 1976. Increases in the government subsidy to social security were identified as the main cause of public expenditure growth, which in the long run led to a 'crowding-out' of private spending by the public sector.

There were other structural changes that occurred between 1975 and 1981 to influence wage/labour relations. While the industrial sector maintained its share of total value added (at 25 per cent), its share of total employment declined from 28 to 23 per cent, a fact that worried trade unions who recruited their members mainly from industry. (In Belgium, almost 90 per cent of industrial workers belong to a union.) The service sector increased its share in total employment and value added significantly. By 1981, two-thirds of employees worked in services, mainly in white-collar jobs (and only half of such jobs were held by union members). Over a period of 20 years, the industrial sector changed from being labour-intensive to being capital-intensive, while in services, and especially in non-tradable services, labour intensity increased continuously.

Inflation, which was the main problem of the early 1970s, moderated in the latter part of the decade though it proved impossible to control completely, and in the early 1980s began to rise again. Nominal wages increased more rapidly than prices between 1975 and 1981 because of the automatic indexation of wages. What was of concern to both sides of industry and government alike was that it was not possible to create new jobs. Since the active population and participation rates were both increasing, total unemployment rose to more than 10 per cent of the labour force. This was accompanied by a very high rate of youth unemployment, a long average duration of unemployment, and a high rate of female unemployment. It is small wonder that the 1981 election campaign concentrated on possible solutions to the structural problems of the Belgian economy.

3.2. *State control of wage/labour relations during the years of bitterness (1982–1985)*

The state of the Belgian economy deteriorated further in 1981, and the once strong Belgian franc became the subject of speculation. Other member governments of the European Community, worried about this sudden change, advised the Belgian government in strong terms to modify its 'prejudicial' system of wage indexation. After the 1981 elections, there was a political majority to initiate a neo-liberal policy of severe deflation. The new government (Martens's fifth) decided it could not work with the network of consultation bodies, which existed not only in the economic sphere but also in the political, and demanded 'special powers'. In February 1982 the Belgian franc was devalued by 8.5 per cent and the link between wages and consumer prices was broken, except so far as minimum wages were concerned (Decree 11). From February until June wages were frozen, while for the rest of the year a system of *indexation forfaitaire* was implemented. This meant that every time the consumer price index increased by two percentage points, all wage-earners received only the nominal increase in the minimum wage, or Bfr 536. While the 'moderation laws' of 1976 and 1980–1 had attempted to limit real-wage increases and restrict wage bargaining, the Royal Decree of 29 February 1982 completely controlled all possible bargaining and dictated how much of his disposable income every wage-earner had to give up.

The government remained unprepared to free wage bargaining in 1983. Facing unemployment, which was still rising, it first launched the

'5–3–3 formula' as a norm for negotiations between employers and employees. The formula signified that a 5 per cent reduction of working time could be allowed and a 3 per cent increase of jobs could be financed if real wages were reduced by 3 per cent. As before, this reduction in real wages was implemented by means of a change in the wage indexation system (*indexation forfaitaire* plus a smoothing cut). In practice, the 5–3–3 formula was introduced through sectoral agreements, but these failed overall to achieve the job-creating objective of the exercise. Nevertheless, those enterprises that did not create new jobs with the money saved on wages were obliged to transfer this money to a special employment fund. How that money is to be used remains an open question.

In April 1983, the government forced through a highly important innovation in Belgian collective bargaining. It stipulated that by law average nominal wage costs in Belgium should not increase more rapidly than the weighted average of nominal wage costs in the seven major trading partners. The 'index of competitiveness' has accordingly become a constraint on collective bargaining. By the Law of April 1983, the government was empowered to impose such a 'norm of competitiveness' if employers and trade unions could not agree.

This clearly has important implications. It means that the traditional notion of rewarding productivity gains by real-wage increases has been discarded, since Belgian wages are effectively determined by pay increases in its trading partners. (According to the government, productivity gains are caused largely by labour-shedding and the demise of marginal firms rather than by workers' efforts.)

In September 1983, the system of wage indexation was restored, on the basis of not an ordinary monthly index but a weighted index of the last four months, implying a slower adjustment of wages to prices. In 1984, the critical state of the budget was used by the government as an argument for constraining wage bargaining. The proposal was that wage-earners and social benefit recipients should transfer 2 per cent of their income to the government over the following three years. This was to be achieved in practice by forgoing one indexation round each year and paying the proceeds into a special fund — which is tantamount to levying a special tax. At the same time, employers and unions attempted to negotiate a new national agreement on wages, employment, and labour time for the following two years — under constraint, however, of 'the norm of competitiveness'. The government made it clear that productivity increases would not be a relevant factor in collective bargaining if the profitability of the firm or sector were in danger. Under such constraints, it was not possible to reach agreement (opposition coming from the Socialist trade union). Consequently, the government formulated norms for sectoral negotiations, allowing a maximum increase in the real wage bill of 1½ per cent for 1985 and 1986, to be used for reductions in working time, additional employees, or wage increases.

In short, government policy since 1982 has forced real wages down and has substantially improved the cost competitiveness of the Belgian economy. Trade unions have accepted the policy only in exchange for an obligation on the part of employers to provide information in each enterprise on what has happened as a result of the money saved on the wage bill, promises of job creation, moderation of other forms of income (which has been far less than in respect of wages), and stricter price control. Up until now, these forms of compensation have been realized only to a very minor extent.

It should be clear that the Fordist system of wage/labour relations based on an equitable distribution of the gains from growth cannot be restored. Between 1982 and 1984 real wages fell substantially, while productivity increased only slowly. In a few years, the share of profits in national income was restored to what it was before 1970 and the period of wage drift that followed. Moreover, the share of profits in national income has continued to rise because of the depressing effect on wages of unemployment. The unusual coincidence of increasing productivity and declining real wages cannot therefore be explained solely in terms of a reversal of what happened in the early 1970s.

The economic consequences of a reduction in the purchasing power of wage-earners are important. Private consumption has fallen since 1981, causing a fall in demand for industrial products, which explains a large part of the increase in unemployment and the decline in industrial activity.

How have large sections of public opinion become convinced that real wages had to fall, even though productivity was continuing to grow? Two fundamental reasons can be identified. In the first place, as already indicated, unemployment became more than a 'normal' problem. The economic crisis that stimulated labour-saving technologies was translated into more unemployment, but this reached a level that the government was no longer capable of handling. Initially, the government started to employ as many people as possible in the public sector. Between 1974 and 1981 the government created some 150 000 new jobs in the public sector, but at the same time more than 200 000 jobs were lost in the private sector. Then the government introduced special employment and early retirement schemes; the number of people involved in these in 1974 amounted to only 10 509 but in 1981 reached 186 194. Although the wages of such people, and the transfers to them, were kept down as much as possible, these policies constituted an increasing burden on the government budget. Most importantly, the number of unemployed receiving normal benefits quadrupled between 1974 and 1981, reaching

391 785. This trend could not continue without raising public debt to an unsustainable level. So Martens's fifth government introduced measures to reduce the burden on the budget deficit in the form of a freeze on public sector recruitment, the introduction of more part-time working, and an increase in the importance of 'non-paid unemployment'. The biggest impact on the budget, however, is likely to come from the announced reduction of real wages and social transfers (the 'Saving Plan').

The second main reason for cutting real wages relates to the need to compete in international markets. In Europe, all major countries initiated a policy in the 1980s of lowering labour costs in order to improve competitiveness. This international bidding down of labour costs was associated with a reduction in demand, an increase in protectionism, and an attack on conditions of employment. It is clear that governments were attempting to push up the share of profits in the economy in the expectation that this would be converted into the development of new products and processes. But the outflow of capital and the process of de-industrialization in Europe has continued.

Whereas before 1982 the government only attempted to influence bipartite negotiations, since then it has suspended free collective bargaining. It has also tried effectively to discourage negotiations at the sectoral level, which traditionally were the most important, in favour of centralized negotiations at the national level and highly decentralized negotiations at the firm level.

To keep consultation going, the government has also delegated part of its responsibilities to the national consultation bodies: the Central Economic Council and the National Labour Council. But it has not yet restructured the whole system of collective labour relations, and the question remains as to whether the present scale of government centralization of collective bargaining and consultation will continue.

Present government policy is also to restructure the social security system in a fundamental way, the objectives being to alleviate financing problems and to create a system that encourages employment, takes care of the family, and is also more uniform and therefore easier to administer. Consultation has already started on the basis of a plan drawn up by the Minister of Social Security.

4. Segmentation, Flexibility, and Government Disengagement: A New System of Wage/Labour Relations

There is no discussion at present between employers, unions, and the government in Belgium about the need for and the possible shape of a new system of wage/labour relations. Nevertheless, extreme factions of the employers' association began as early as the late 1970s to present proposals for fundamental changes in labour relations which could eventually add up to a complete new system. On many issues they found the present government, which seems to share the employers' vision, prepared to co-operate. It is important to mention, as background, that most enterprises in Belgium are facing stronger competition, and in order to survive are seeking to adapt as quickly as possible to new technology. Automation and the use of robots are not only destroying jobs but are also changing labour relations within the firm. The nature of jobs is being altered at every level as a result of new production techniques, the introduction of which is often taken as a pretext by management to force trade unions and the government to change the rules of game.

What are the targets of the employers' offensive? First, there is the difference between gross and net wages. The real concern here is the marginal tax rate, which is claimed to be too high to encourage employment. The current tax system adversely affects incentives to work and stimulates a 'brain drain' of highly skilled labour. The short-term strategy of employers is to avoid paying taxes by giving special benefits. In the long run, direct taxes and social security contributions should be reduced significantly.

Second, there is a focus on the segmentation of the labour market. By increasing the number of types of employment (part-time work, temporary jobs, and so on), the job security of employees is undermined. At the same time, it makes it more difficult for trade unions to recruit members from among such workers because the demands put forward for full-time employees are of no concern to them. For example, a general reduction in hours of work cannot interest people who already work part-time.

Third, there is an attack on the role of trade unions as representatives of labour in individual firms. The intention is to reduce the protection given to union officials, to open up elections to non-union candidates, to offer separate representation to high-ranking employees, and to allow collective agreements in smaller firms to be signed by employees who are not necessarily union members. More subtly, there is also an attempt to replace union functions by management initiatives such as quality circles, employee referenda, the provision of certain social services by personnel departments, company newspapers, and so on. In this way, the aim is to create a sort of Japanese model of trade unionism, with a different union for each company. There is also a concern to increase the flexibility of labour and pay. In many cases workers are obliged to take on a new job in the production process, after going on a training course. Employers wish to see an increase in labour mobility without this implying any particular change in pay. A further aim is to revise the social security system. The employers' association favours a complete dismantling of the system, so that it covers only a 'reasonable' proportion of the unemployed. Unemployment benefit should be reduced to increase incentives to work. Insurance against sickness, accidents, and old age should be privatized as much as possible. In the short run the social security system is being undermined by the promotion of group insurance for employees, which is fiscally attractive for employers but destroys the wish of employees for a universal system.

Moreover, it is possible to avoid union representation and the advantage this gives to labour through the creation of new small firms. Large firms seem to prefer to rely on such independent firms for the development of new technology, research, and risky business ventures. Here, working conditions are not controlled by trade unions and legislation is more favourable as regards employment, social security, and subsidies.

Other aims can also be identified, such as the deregulation of consumer standards, changes in company structure, and the search for a new principle to govern wage increases. In the latter respect, it is important to stress that the employers' association has no interest in a new productivity agreement, as proposed by the unions. Instead, it wishes to decouple wages from productivity and would prefer a general agreement on the introduction of new technology.

The need for industrial modernization is a central objective of government policy. It is not surprising that many of the employers' proposals are reflected in the so-called 'Hansenne experiment'. Under this experiment, the government exempts from labour legislation companies that introduce new technology requiring an increase in production time, so long as it is accompanied by a reduction in working time and the creation of new jobs. Under the experiment, union representation is discouraged, flexibility of wages and working conditions is encouraged, and so on.

It should be clear that the success of the current offensive by the employers' association is partly a result of the deficiencies in the old system of wage/labour relations. The alienation of workers from, on the one hand, union representation and, on the other, the production process is implied in certain proposals put forward by employers. This is reminiscent of the Japanese way of informally linking employees to the companies in which they work. At the same time, the old dream of the welfare state, the notion of solidarity through social security, and the idea of increasing efficiency through government involvement in the economy have faded in the eyes of workers. In a clever way, the extreme proposals exploit the lack of trust of the small man in big complex state systems.

The new-technology type of reasoning presents a prospect of a much more attractive future for the young, and flexibility is increasingly accepted as a necessary condition for this.

As for the trade unions, which happen to be on the defensive, little time is left for them to restore communication between the leadership and the grass roots and to formulate an alternative strategy capable of convincing the great majority of social and political groups. Much will depend on the degree of unanimity between the two largest trade unions in their analysis of the situation and in their proposals regarding the system of wage/labour relations.

6

Partial Fordism: Spain between Political Transition and Economic Crisis

Luis Toharia

1. A Review of the Franco Regime, 1939–1975

The system of wage/labour relations in Spain during the Franco regime must be seen in terms of two main features: the legal ban on the working-class trade union movement, with no right to strike, and the very high degree of government intervention, which combined a paternalistic belief in class co-operation rather than class confrontation and an open clamp-down on any transgressions of established norms. The main institution in labour relations was the Trade Union Organization (OS), made up of 20 vertical branch unions, to which all workers and all firms were forced to belong under state supervision.

The Franco era should be divided into two periods: before and after 1958, when the government set up a controlled system of collective bargaining through the Trade Union Organization. In the first period the government used labour regulations to control working conditions in the various sectors, including the minimum wage which roughly reflected the growth of overall wages. The law that ratified the 1958 collective agreements marked the beginning of a new system to meet the needs of the economic liberalization which the new technocrats in ministerial office planned for the Spanish economy. This process called for a new, more flexible method of determining wages. The result was a very special system, under the firm control of both the government and the Trade Union Organization; the latter was limited in what it could do, however, since the political system could not cope with real collective bargaining, which would have required truly representative workers' organizations.

The author wishes to thank Professor Lluis Fina of the Universitat Autonoma de Barcelona for his many comments and suggestions. Any remaining errors cannot of course in any way be attributed to him.

1.1. Beyond paternalistic, repressive institutions

One of the most firmly established characteristics of the Franco era was that the workers were protected by a high degree of rigidity, produced by a system originally paternalistic and fascist in nature, but only so long as they were disciplined in their work and accepted the 'rules of the game' — in other words, so long as there were no freely elected political or trade union representatives. In theory, therefore, the system was characterized by a high degree of state protection against 'arbitrary' dismissals. In fact, the interpretation of the term 'arbitrary' excluded dismissals for disciplinary reasons, which were regarded as 'just' by the law, making it possible to dismiss any worker involved in union, or even political, activities. If employees were protected by the state, it was only in exchange for total silence on union rights, working conditions, etc.

It should also be pointed out that collective dismissals were possible only through the Expedientes de Regulaçion de Empleo (ERE) (certificates on labour adjustments), which were administered by the government, but for which the fixing of redundancy compensation was under the jurisdiction of the labour tribunals. This meant that the tribunals had a considerable leeway in deciding whether to award compensation and, if so, how much. This system allowed the workers to exert quasi-legal pressure (although strongly challenged by the administration) and to present arguments counter to their bosses against reductions in employment. In practice, collective bargaining was used primarily as an instrument for mobilizing the workers. This was particularly true during the last years of the Franco regime, when the workers' position was relatively strong, although limited by the constraints of the political system.

On the other hand, there was no norm established by law on the duration of contracts of employment. It was the judges' interpretation of that law that temporary labour could be used only when the nature of the work was also temporary. In industries that were typically seasonal, this mechanism for adjusting employment could be used freely. But eventually, workers' resistance to this type of contract forced a considerable reduction in temporary employment. At the beginning of the 1960s, the proportion of temporary workers in businesses with at least 10 employees was 48.4 per cent in construction and 32.2 per cent in food, drink, and tobacco. By 1976 the proportion for both was down to around 15 per cent.

Collective agreements became increasingly important in the 1960s and were the main instrument for determining the level of wages. Two features of the system of collective bargaining of that time should be noted:

1. the dichotomy between agreements at *industry* level and agreements at *enterprise* level: in fact, the former, which were more numerous (68 per cent of agreements signed, representing 89 per cent of workers over the period 1958–72), were abandoned much more frequently than the latter, which were closer to being free negotiations. Hence the importance attached by the trade unions, illegal at the time, to enterprise agreements, which were regarded as an instrument not only of economic negotiation but also of worker mobilization and political struggle;

2. the emergence during wage negotiations of numerous 'complements' linked particularly to productivity, which made up the variable part of the wage and remained under entrepreneurial control: this variable component of the wage, which could on occasion amount to as much as 50 per cent of the total wage paid, introduced a high degree of flexibility in pay and made it possible to introduce large pay differences without, however, entailing an excessive rise in labour costs, since wages and productivity tended to vary together and social contributions were fixed by reference to basic wages, which were considerably lower and less variable than the wages actually paid.

As for state intervention, its general hold on the system has already been noted. It operated particularly through legal dispositions, which stipulated that collective agreements had to be validated by approval of the relevant government authority. But the state also intervened directly in the process of collective bargaining. When no agreement was possible, or when the agreement signed was deemed inadequate, the government could impose a compulsory ruling. These rulings became an important instrument of wage policy and were used especially often during the last years of the Franco regime when workers' demands became more pressing.

The state used two other means to intervene in the process of wage fixing: one was the minimum guaranteed wage (SMIG) introduced in 1963, and the other, the various decrees passed from 1965 onwards, the aim of which was to fix maximum growth rates for money wages.

Some authors regard the SMIG as the fundamental element of the government's wage policy, although this is debatable. Fixed by statutory order, it was always more symbolic than real since its level was kept low enough for its direct effect not to be important. But its influence was felt in two ways. First, it served as a guide for the growth of basic wages and collective pay settlements, enabling, and indeed encouraging, differences between the contractual and the actual wage. The SMIG also formed the minimum basic level for fixing social security contributions. Variations in SMIG, therefore, had an indirect effect on the labour costs paid by firms through contributions.

1.2. A pseudo-Fordism characterized by parallel changes in productivity and real wages

In 1965 the government started to set maximum growth rates for money wages which had to be respected in signed collective agreements. These measures were fairly effective, especially before 1973; for example, the wage freeze imposed until the end of 1968, as part of the stability measures following the devaluation of the peseta in November 1967, had to be lifted at the end of summer 1968 — it had proved so effective that there was a risk of excessively prolonging the contraction of the economy.

The year 1973 saw a change in the criteria used for setting the maximum growth rate for wages. In earlier years the government had fixed the rate for money wages without any apparent reference to the rate of inflation, but the decree of November 1973 fixed the wage increase for 1974 at or below the inflation rate of the previous year (measured by the cost of living index), with the possibility of it exceeding 5 per cent only in exceptional circumstances. As in 1968, wage restraints were lifted some months later (in August 1974), but this time not because of their success but because of their ineffectiveness. Wage restraints were reimposed in April 1975, but with 'exceptional' increases over and above the cost of living being reduced to 3 per cent. This decree was extended until 31 December 1976.

The main feature of the way in which income policy developed after 1973 was the inability of the Franco regime to control a system that, despite all its constraints, had allowed a certain degree of worker organization (secret but none the less effective because of its strategy of entry into the official trade union organization). That is how it became the rule, in most signed collective agreements, for wages to increase by a few points more than the cost of living, which theoretically was supposed to happen only in exceptional cases. In practice, the government rates became merely the minimum acceptable to the illegal unions, which adopted the tactic of systematically breaking down wage barriers. This stand should be seen not only as a demand for improved living conditions, but also, and more especially, as a political gesture in defiance of the government. The government could react only through compulsory arbitration, but its ability to hold down wages was limited unless it was willing to accept the liberalization of the trade union and political system, which was obviously not the case. Consequently, it was forced to adopt a monetary policy aimed at mitigating the growth of wage costs indirectly through controlling inflation.

It should be emphasized that during the Franco era, especially from 1960 onwards, Spanish society experienced a very marked process of economic growth and modernization. The annual growth of GDP averaged 6–7 per cent and durable consumer goods (cars, TVs, household electric appliances) began to be widely acquired. It is therefore in this sense that we can talk of the beginning of a Fordist process of development, albeit with important specific features, namely, the existence of a repressive paternalistic system of labour relations, the lack of social protection or a developed tax system, and strong state intervention in the economy, especially in the form of customs barriers to protect national industry from foreign competition. The best empirical proof of this relationship is given in Table 6.1, which shows the average annual growth rate of productivity and real wages per capita for various periods between 1964 and 1984.

In the period 1964–75, the change in the series under consideration was remarkably similar, which shows that the Franco system, for all its peculiarities and constraints, was able to establish a pseudo-Fordism where salaries and productivity tended to vary in similar ways in the short and medium term — which was undoubtedly one of the main reasons for the strong growth of the Spanish economy during that period.

The last few years of the Franco period coincided with the start of the economic crisis triggered off by the increase in the price of oil, the effects of which were not felt until 1975, when GDP increased by only 1.3 per cent, compared with 5.9 and 8.1 per cent in 1974 and 1973, respectively. At the outset, however, the crisis passed almost unnoticed in a society that enjoyed full employment (partly owing to the 'export' of workers to other European countries), and was apparently more concerned with the political future of the country. And so, perhaps more than elsewhere, the economic crisis was considered in Spain to be temporary and not serious.

2. The Period after 1975: The System of Wage/Labour Relations between Political Transition and Economic Crisis

The death of Franco in November 1975 signalled the start of the political transition and of the complete breakdown of the system of wage/labour relations established by the Franco regime, a breakdown that had already begun some years earlier. The economic crisis was to play a fundamental role in ensuing events. The first governments of the transition, overwhelmed by innumerable political problems and enor-mous social demands, were to prove incapable of implementing a policy to overcome the crisis and therefore simply followed a completely permissive monetary policy. The resulting inflation served to postpone the problems of the Spanish economy. Later adjustments were to prove extremely harsh and to produce one of the highest rates of unemployment in the OECD (over 20 per cent of the active population in 1985).

TABLE 6.1 *Real wages and productivity: first similar rates of change, then a change in the pattern in the 1980s*

| | Average annual rate of growth (%) | | | |
	Productivity[a]	Direct and indirect wages[b]	Direct wages	Labour cost[c]
1964–68	5.25	6.29	7.20	0.99
1968–72	6.18	6.68	6.11	0.47
1972–75	4.66	4.37	3.71	−0.27
1964–75	5.42	5.90	5.84	0.46
1975–78	4.54	4.74	3.45	0.13
1978–81	3.39	2.93	1.34	−0.44
1981–84	2.96	0.35	0.51[d]	−2.53

[a] Gross domestic product at factor cost per person employed (constant prices).
[b] Direct wages plus total social contributions.
[c] Ratio of direct and indirect wages/productivity.
[d] Estimate for 1984 based on wage increases negotiated in collective agreements adjusted for wage drift and expressed in real terms by using the consumer price index.

Sources: INE, *Contabilidad Nacional de España*; *Encuesta de Población Activa*, various years.

This worsening economic crisis, combined with the object of consolidating the new political order, had two main effects. First, it forced both sides of industry to negotiate an income policy aimed at keeping a check on wage growth, in both money and real terms, and especially in relation to the growth of productivity. The success of this policy is undoubtedly one of the significant features of the democratic era which began in 1978. As is seen in Table 6.1, the close parallel between wage and productivity movements came to an abrupt end in that year. It should also be noted that this new policy was not restricted to wages but, as we shall see, also affected labour market flexibility and employment in particular.

On the other hand, it filled the institutional vacuum in labour relations following the breakdown in the system of wage/labour relations established under Franco. The second important feature of the period that started in 1975, and especially from 1977 onwards, was the process of redefining the system of wage/labour relations — a process that was to prove fraught with difficulties and is still not complete today.

To study this period, we shall first of all review general economic developments and the economic and wage policies followed before examining changes in the system of wage/labour relations as such (see also Table 6.2).

TABLE 6.2 *Principal statistics of the Spanish economy, 1964–1984*

	Growth rate of GDP (%)	Growth rate of employment[a]	Unemployment rate[a]	Activity rate[a]	Inflation rate (CPI)[b]	% of wages in value added[c]	Budget deficit (% GDP)
1964–74	6.6	0.91	2.03	52.1[d]	—	54.75	—
1974–77	2.6	−1.21	4.86	52.9[e]	18.72	55.48	−0.18
1977–80	1.2	−2.41	8.14	50.3[f]	16.98	55.43	−1.53
1981	0.2	−3.15	14.36	48.2	14.60	55.4	−3
1982	1.2	−1.22	16.29	48.2	14.40	55.4	−5.6
1983	2.3	−0.88	17.80	48.1	12.13	53.8	−5.9
1984	2.2	−2.91[g]	20.59[h]	47.8	10.51	51.3	−5.1

[a] Data on activity, employment, and unemployment refer to those of 14 and over before 1977 and those of 16 and over after 1977.

[b] Annual averages: figure corresponding to the change in the consumer price index between December 1983 and December 1984 was 9.0%.

[c] Corrected to reflect increase in number of people incorporated into wage structure.

[d] Refers to 1964.

[e] Refers to 1974.

[f] Refers to 1977.

[g] About half of this drop is due to the change in definition of the population in employment which no longer includes beneficiaries of 'community employment' (system to protect against unemployment in agriculture and the building industry abolished in 1983), now included in the unemployment figures.

[h] If we were to adjust for the change referred to in note a, the rate would be about 1 point lower.

Sources: INE, *Contabiladad Nacional de España; Encuesta de Población Activa,* various years; Banco de España (1984).

2.1. Reduced growth and sharply rising unemployment in a context of structural change

The growth of value added fell dramatically from 1975 until 1981, when it was negative (−0.35 per cent); it then recovered slightly, to 1.2 per cent in 1982, 2.0 per cent in 1983, and 2.2 per cent in 1984. At the sector level, construction was worst hit, with value added declining continuously after 1974 (1982 was the only exception); the sector experienced an overall loss of 20 per cent during the period 1974–84. In manufacturing, up until 1978 the growth rate was lower than before but still above 2 per cent per annum, but after 1978 there was no growth at all, and value added fell considerably in the metal industry (by nearly 2 per cent per annum between 1978 and 1981). It was the service sector that was responsible for the rise in value added in the economy as a whole during the crisis. The importance of non-traded services, as reflected in the employment figures, should not be overlooked. To sum up, there was a definite slowing down of economic growth, but value added in 1984 was about 13 per cent above what it was in 1976.

As for employment, which is probably a better indicator of the crisis than unemployment since it does not include new arrivals on the job market, the economy lost over 1.7 million jobs, or more than 14 per cent, between 1977 and 1984. But this big overall loss conceals major disparities which are revealed if disaggregated figures are examined.

1. If one considers the proportion of salaried workers in the active population, then the growth rate observed since the 1960s comes to a stop and even goes into reverse, especially in some sectors, such as construction. In other words, salaried employment is affected by the crisis rather more than self-employment (with certain implications, explained below).

2. So far as salaried employment is concerned, one must not overlook the high growth of employment in the public sector, probably associated with the late development of the 'welfare state', or the policy of maintaining employment in unproductive and loss-making public enterprises (a policy that the Socialist government promised to change when it came to power in October 1982). Between 1977 and 1984, the proportion of public employees in total employment rose from 9.4 to 16.2 per cent, whereas that of private employees fell from 59.4 to 52.8 per cent.

3. As for self-employment, there was a relatively slight fall of 5.6 per cent in the number of individual businesses and self-employed workers, compared with a bigger fall of 11.2 per cent in employees, which meant that the proportion of self-employed persons in total employment rose from 17.9 to 19 per cent. But this rise, although reflected in all sectors, was not uniform; it was twice as high (from 8 to 16 per cent) in construction, but less spectacular in industry over all (from 5 to 6 per cent) and the service sector (from 15 to 16 per cent).

4. To sum up, there was a steep fall in employment in all sectors except services, where there was a slight rise over the period as a whole. In agriculture and construction, this fall has continued since 1977; in industry, it started one year later. Statistics show that the economic crisis hit the private sector especially hard, as the maintenance of jobs in services was linked to the significant growth already noted of non-traded services and social protection. The sharp decline in jobs in agriculture may seem paradoxical in a period where job opportunities have clearly worsened. But a detailed analysis of the statistics indicates that this decline in employment was due to the increasing number of people retiring, itself the result of the ageing of the agriculture population and the rural exodus of previous years.

The analysis in Section 1 shows an important structural change in the Spanish economy since the beginning of the 1970s. There has been a fall in both value added and employment in industry compared with services, but this fall in quantity goes hand in hand with an improvement in quality, in the form of a rise in productivity. So, whereas the increase in productivity between 1976 and 1983 was about 25 per cent for the economy as a whole, the increase for industry was 35 per cent. There is no explanation beyond simple arithmetic for this growth, which is undoubtedly one of the main features of Spanish development over the last few years; in other words, the explanation generally given is that productivity has increased *because* employment has decreased (which is of course far from being a substantive explanation).

Inflation had reached record levels in 1977 and 1978 (over 20 per cent), but the income policy adopted in 1978 has managed to check it. There was a slow reduction in inflation between 1979 and 1982, but then it fell by more than two points a year in 1983 and 1984 to reach 9 per cent for the period December 1983–December 1984. So the Socialist government has had the greatest success in reducing inflation, which has become one of its priorities. The government aimed at a target of 7 per cent in 1985 and 6 per cent in 1986; however, experts estimate inflation for 1985 at around 8.5–9 per cent.

2.2. *Economic policies: reconstructing profits, but not recreating jobs*

The economic policy of successive governments has been constrained markedly by the process of political transition, by political weakness, and by the internal problems of the UCD, the party founded by Adolfo Suarez in 1977, which won the 1977 and 1979 elections although it did not gain a parliamentary majority. From this first electoral victory onwards, Suarez seemed set on imposing a stringent and effective economic policy, which he entrusted to a prestigious academic. (The latter resigned a little later, apparently convinced of the impossibility of attaining the proposed objectives because of political compromise; however, he retained considerable influence.) That was to remain the situation until the elections in October 1982: good intentions constantly frustrated by internal squabbles of the party in power, which was to lead to Suarez being abandoned just before the abortive *coup d'état* of 23 February 1981.

Despite this weakness, however, successive UCD governments followed a fairly determined line in economic policy. The 'excessive' growth of wages was always blamed as the main reason for the worsening of the crisis and the obstacle to economic recovery in Spain. Parliamentary debates on the economy centred on whether the top priority was inflation (favoured by the right) or unemployment (favoured by the left); gradually, there came to be general agreement that the basic problem was unemployment, but differences remained on the most suitable remedy. The government advocated reducing wage increases in order to 'rebuild' business profits, in other words reducing not only money wages but also real wages, to which the response of the left was that this would only aggravate the crisis in demand.

In practice, the government view seemed to win the day. 1978 saw the start of a slight fall in the proportion of gross wages in value added, adjusted for variations in the proportion of wage-earners which had been more or less constant from 1967 to 1977. This development again demonstrates the break in the tendency for wages and productivity to grow at similar rates, observed in the last ten years of the Franco regime (cf. Table 6.1). But the result the government was hoping for failed to materialize; even though there was a rise in the share of profits in value added, private investment did not respond, perhaps because of uncertainty over market outlets for the products produced and because of the institutional framework of the labour market, although this probably became less important, as we shall see later.

The share of wages did not fall any further because of the increasing importance of social contributions in relation to direct wages earned by workers, which shows again how much more important the welfare state was becoming, even in the last few years of the Franco period.

Two consequences follow from this. First, the share of direct wages in value added tended to decline considerably, which implies that, while there is no direct, automatic link between wages and productivity gains, there is an aggregate effect, i.e. if direct or indirect dependents of employees (families, retired persons, unemployed, etc.) are included. The second, not unconnected, consequence is the increasingly important role of the state in income distribution.

This phenomenon is reflected in taxation and social expenditure. Here, a distinction should be made between income from employment and income from capital, and between salaried workers and recipients of social expenditure, mainly retired people. On the first point, changes in taxation and successive fiscal reforms (especially the reform of personal income tax, introduced in 1978) tended to fall on income from employment more heavily than on capital income, with 85 per cent of tax revenue coming from the former, according to official estimates. On the second point, developments since 1970 are fairly clear: overall social expenditure doubled compared with GDP as a result of the greater weight of pensions and unemployment insurance, although coverage of the latter is far from complete, as we shall see later.

To sum up, the tax–wages spiral was not a decisive factor in the development of wages and the distribution of income, especially in recent years after the welfare state had increased in importance. One result of the dual action of social protection and incomplete taxation is the growth of the budget deficit, which rose from 2.0 per cent of GDP in 1980 to 5.9 per cent in 1983.

The coming to power of the Socialist Party (PSOE) in October 1982 was to mark a significant change in economic policy, not so much with regard to new ideas, but because it was a strong government with a considerable parliamentary majority. After the initial measures taken by the new government (especially the devaluation of the peseta), it became increasingly clear during the course of 1983 that the PSOE in power was set on an economic policy of reducing inflation significantly, with redistribution both to encourage private investment and to improve external competitiveness. At the same time, employment policy amounted to a revival of the 1981 programme to make employment more flexible, and in particular to encourage the taking on of people on short-term contracts. This hard-line policy, imposed by the realities of the crisis, was accompanied by measures to reduce the public sector deficit (rationalization of public enterprises, industrial reconversion, reform of the administration, and measures to combat fiscal fraud) and to counter the worst effects of unemployment (increasing unemployment insurance, the coverage of which had diminished markedly since 1980).

The policy of the Socialist government has met with a certain degree of success, even though the election promises of creating 800 000 jobs and maintaining purchasing power have not been kept. Inflation dropped below 10 per cent in 1984 for the first time since 1972. Furthermore, wage growth has been slowed down considerably; this has led to a significant redistribution of income, which, according to the Minister for Economic Affairs, should trigger off economic recovery in accordance with the well-worn maxim, 'today's profits are tomorrow's investment and the day after tomorrow's employment'. Similarly, the external sector is 'pulling' the Spanish economy, enabling it to grow (cf. Table 6.2), despite internal demand increasing only slightly as a result of the afore-mentioned redistribution. Finally, the budget deficit is being gradually reduced through the reduction in public investment (considered 'socially unprofitable'). However, the problem continues, and experts from the Bank of Spain warn against serious effects on inflation in the medium term.

The result of this economic policy of so-called 'adjustment' has been a sharp rise in unemployment. In fact, everything points to the first Socialist term of office running the risk of finishing with 800 000 *fewer* rather than more jobs. In turn, the PSOE government has finally faced up to the problems that have beset the Spanish economy since the political transition. Some believe it has done so by betraying both its electoral programme and the social class it claims to represent. Others consider that it has acted courageously in view of the situation it inherited from the past, especially from the weakness of the UCD governments. Nevertheless, the electorate seems to have accepted this hard-line economic policy, to judge from the opinion polls, which do not reveal any significant erosion of support for the Socialists, certainly nothing on the scale of that in France, for example.

2.3. Rapid changes in labour legislation

Having analysed the general economic situation, we can now examine institutional changes which may help to identify trends towards a new system of wage/labour relations.

The period beginning in 1975 can be divided into three parts. The first goes up to the general elections in June 1977. On the one hand, it is characterized by an explosion in wage demands, with a sharp rise in industrial disputes and in nominal wages. On the other hand, this period saw the final break with the Franco system, with the legalization of free trade unions in April 1977. This happened after a certain number of decrees were passed to facilitate dismissals, to eliminate the scope for action that labour tribunals previously had for settling disputes and issuing ERE (certificates on labour adjustments), and effectively to legalize the right to strike.

The second period goes up to January 1980, with the passing of the Estatuto de los Trabajadores (Workers' Statute), and is characterized by the consensus (marked by the Pactos de la Moncloa, signed in October 1977 by the government and the political parties), which guaranteed a certain 'social peace', and by the drafting of the above-mentioned statute, which was to establish the definitive basis for the *new institutional order* as regards labour relations.

Finally, the third period dates from 1980 to the present day, and is characterized mainly by the operation of a new system amidst a deeply worsening economic crisis, particularly in unemployment, which has risen to more than 20 per cent of the active population. This is the period in which state intervention now receded in order to let the two sides negotiate freely, which they do within the framework of annual global agreements signed jointly by the employers' organizations and trade unions. There has generally been some weakening in the position of trade unions, a trend that, perhaps paradoxically, seems more pronounced during the period of Socialist government (1982–5).

Before analysing in greater detail how the various components of the system of wage/labour relations have developed, it is of interest to look at the general trends during the transitional years from the Franco regime to the present democracy, which can be summarized as follows.

1. *free trade unions legalized,* and consequently Franco's vertical unions eliminated; at the same time, employers' organizations set up;

2. *a tendency to establish agreements through collective bargaining* (especially on wage increases) at the highest level, between groups of affiliated trade unions and employers' organizations and eventually the government, although the government's intention is more and more to keep out of collective bargaining;

3. *wage increases on forecasts of inflation* rather than past rates: generally, the wage 'band' agreed is based on this inflation forecast; an indexation clause is included in global agreements renegotiated each year and generally fixed with provision for a mid-year wage review if the consumer price index exceeds a certain level;

4. *the scope for appropriate or fair dismissals for 'objective' reasons widened,* with a general reduction in the compensation paid, the amount of which is left to the judges' discretion;

5. *the system of recruiting people under short-term contracts made more flexible* and more open to both normal and 'encouraged' usage;

6. *a tendency for certain forms of state intervention to disappear* (e.g., compulsory arbitration was banned under the Estatuto de los Trabajadores and later even declared unconstitutional);

7. *strong growth of the black economy* and, more generally, more uncertain labour market conditions.

Table 6.3 sets out the concrete effects of these general trends concerning the institutional development of the system of wage/labour relations in Spain since 1973. In order to explain the comments in this table, we shall concentrate on three basic aspects: collective bargaining, flexibility of employment, and protection against unemployment.

2.4. A new direction for collective bargaining

Collective bargaining took on a new dimension in Spain with the democratic period that began in 1977; during the Franco period it was used as a very flexible instrument of wage control, and as the only possible legal mechanism to mobilize the working masses. The new system would obviously depend on the conditions prevailing in the Spanish economy in society: an economic crisis that was beginning to make itself felt, an explosion of all kinds of claims (political, economic, and trade union), and a period of the drafting of the new Spanish Constitution. All points of view converge on the need for a major social agreement: it is the period of the constituent consensus, marked by the Pactos de la Moncloa signed at the end of 1977 by all political parties. From the point of view of the economy, and especially of collective bargaining, the Pactos contain three important features.

TABLE 6.3 *Institutional development of wage/labour relations in Spain since 1973*

Components of wage/labour relation	1973–76	1976–78	1978–80	1980–82	1982–85
Wages Indexation	Wage review in the light of past inflation plus several points in exceptional cases		Clause on mid-year review in the light of the index included in collective agreements (inflation forecast)		AES: review clause at end of year
Sharing of profits from productivity	Not directly planned; pressure for equal sharing or sharing in favour of workers			Open to negotiation in collective agreements but priority to re-establishing firms' profits (little influence in practice of collective bargaining)	
Effect of economic conditions on wages	Political pressure on wages			Safeguard clause in relation to agreed wage-band for loss-making firms (little used) ANE: agreed wage-band lower than inflation forecast	
Employment; organization of Labour Rights of dismissal	*April 1976*: Law on labour relations, re-employment compulsory if dismissal declared not relevant (this clause abolished several months later) Statutory order *March 1977*: reduction in job security; recognition of right to strike *April 1977*: trade unions legalized		*Dec. 1979*: creation of IMAC: steps can be taken in cases of individual dismissal with pre-agreed allowance *Jan 1980*: Estatuto de los Trabajadores; objective reasons for 'relevant' dismissal extended; judges' discretion reduced		AES: promise to adapt to EEC directives (i.e. allow collective dismissals)
Control of organization of labour				AMI: organization of labour to be negotiated (little influence in practice)	
Legal extent of working	Left to legal interpretation; in practice, most contracts indefinite 48 hrs max. (1931 law), duration negotiated in collective agreements since c.1970. LRT: 48 hr week max.		Moncloa Pacts: first steps to making work more flexible through use of temporary labour	ET: normal duration unlimited, but existence recognized for the temporary labour ET: 42/3 hr week max.	ANE: measure to promote employment; temporary and part-time work. Increase in temporary work; attempt at rationalization; 40 hr week max.

Indirect wages **Unemployment benefit**	Max. period 18 mons; entitled to benefit after 3 mons. contributions; amount fixed in light of contribution basis (generally lower than actual wage) Only in cases of 'non-relevant' dismissal	*Oct 1980*: LBE duration in light of contribution period, 18 mons. max. (Min. contribution period 6 mos.); introduction of complementary allowance independent of contributions	Max. duration lengthened; small reduction in contributions; complementary allowances increased. Increase in 'relevant' dismissals
Youth training	Moncloa Pacts: temporary work programmes for young people aged 16–26 (reduction in social contributions and subsidized training	Work promotion programmes 'training scheme contracts' (reduction in social contributions) for 16–18 yr-olds	
Retirement and early retirement	**Retirement age: 65 with 100% of contribution base with 35 yrs. of contributions; lower amount on earlier retirement (min. age 60) or if contribution period shorter (min. 10 yrs. which entitles person to 50% of base at age 65). Possibility of early retirement with 100% subsidized by National Fund for Protection of Labour**	ANE: early retirement with 100% at age 61 if worker replaced by young unemployed person	Reform of pension system (15 yrs. contribution min.) guaranteed annual review in light of inflation
General political situation	*Nov. 1975*: death of Franco *June 1977*: elections	*Dec. 1978*: Constitution *June 1979–Oct 1982*: UCD (centre) government *23 Feb. 1981*: abortive *coup d'état*	*Oct. 1982*: PSOE (Socialist) government

1. The signatories fix a 'band' for wage increases, which must be adhered to in any collective agreements signed. The aim was to guarantee limited wage increases while simultaneously assuring a 'social peace' conducive to bringing the crisis to an end. This aim was achieved, and the need to establish a general agreement as a guide for collective bargaining was retained as one of the main features of the new system. This consensus was breached, however, in 1984, despite the government's insistence on the need for a major social agreement.

2. The wage band was based on the inflation forecast for 1978 (22 per cent), and not on the inflation figure for the previous year (which had risen above 25 per cent). Furthermore, there was a clause whereby wages could be revised if inflation exceeded 11.5 per cent by 30 June. This was, therefore, a semi-indexation system, which was, as it turned out, the system to be adopted in the future.

3. At least 50 per cent of the increase of total wages was to be distributed in a uniform way. This was in response to an old trade union demand to correct the large wage disparities that the Franco system had allowed and even encouraged. This measure was fairly successful because the percentage distributed in a uniform way was in fact well above 50 per cent, and the statistics gathered by the *Wages Survey* show a compression of the wage structure in 1978, a trend that had been apparent as early as 1976 and 1977. Since 1979, however, there has been a return to the criterion of proportionality and a great discretion in defining the reference wage, which has led to another increase in wage disparities.

The Pactos therefore established a new approach to the system of collective bargaining. At the end of 1978, the Minister for Economic Affairs, fearing a return to the previous situation, convened a symposium for employers and trade unions. This resulted in the statutory order of 26 December 1978, which stipulates the wage band to be adhered to in collective bargaining. The wage band was established on the basis of the same criteria as in the Pactos de la Moncloa. The statutory order relating to it was to be the government's last active intervention in wage negotiations, and followed consultation with the interested parties.

The results of this statutory order are rather interesting. The wage band fixed serves as a general reference point. However, the *Wages Survey* indicates a much higher average increase in wages — 22.5 per cent as compared with the average increase laid down in collective agreements of 14.1 per cent. This disparity is sometimes interpreted as arising from an error on the part of the *Wages Survey*, the methodology of which was changed in 1977; but it can also be interpreted as proof of the existence of a wage drift arising from the disparity between wages officially declared to the administration (which had to respect the band in the statutory order, or else the government would declare the collective agreements signed to be invalid) and wages actually paid. This experience so interpreted indicates, as has been clearly proved in Spain, that a negotiated income policy is much more effective than one directly imposed by the government, even after consultation with both sides of industry.

The year 1979 is marked by discussions on the draft workers' statute (Estatuto de los Trabajadores, hereafter referred to as ET), which revealed major differences between the two main trade union organiz-ations, the Socialist UGT and the Communist Workers' Commissions CCOO. It was because of those differences that the CCOO refused to join in the inter-confederate agreement (AMI). The aim of this agreement, signed for 1980 by the UGT and the CEOE (the largest employers' organization), was to establish the effective basis for a modern system of collective bargaining in which trade union involvement would extend beyond the simple defence of workers' purchasing power. For example, the AMI acknowledged the importance of work-place relations for the smooth running of productive activites, and recommended negotiations on such important issues as productivity, absenteeism, and technological innovation. Despite the refusal of the CCOOs to partici-pate, the AMI fulfilled its objective of establishing a general reference for collective bargaining, respected by most agreements signed.

The AMI was extended into 1981, the only change being in the wage band, which was now centred on the forecast rate of inflation instead of being fixed around a higher level, as in 1980. The abortive *coup d'état* of 23 February 1981 was to have a decisive effect on the government and both sides of industry, as it emphasized the need for a major national agreement on employment (ANE). The main feature of the ANE is that the wage band is lower than the inflation forecast; in other words, for the first time, the unions accepted a *reduction* in real wages. In return, the government promised to create 350 000 new jobs. However, the terms of this promise remained vague and the objective was not met.

Two other points should be made about the ANE. The agreement included a certain number of programmes to make employment more flexible (cf. Section 3.1 below); and furthermore, like all earlier agreements or statutory orders from 1977 onwards, it incorporated a mid-year wage review clause.

The practical effect of this clause might be discussed before the ANE: a limited number (about 40 per cent) of signed agreements contained a clause of this type, and inflation had never exceeded the limits necessary to trigger off the review. In 1982, however, the minimum inflation rate of 6.09 per cent (excluding the price of energy) was exceeded, and the unions immediately raised the question of wage revision; they wanted it to apply to all collective agreements and not only to those specifically including a review clause, as the employers maintained. The final ruling granted by the Central Labour Tribunal — which experts claim is debatable from a legal point of view — was in favour of the union position, which demonstrates the practical importance of the established system of semi-indexation.

The year 1983 saw the return to agreements between employers and unions without government intervention. The most significant innovation of the new inter-union agreement (AI) was the wage review clause, which, in view of the argument that the 1982 review had been triggered off by seasonal factors, was held back and became operational only on 30 September. And although the overall annual rate of inflation was a little higher than forecast, the rate of 30 September was only 7.9 per cent, considerably below the rate of 9 per cent decided as the threshold for the wage review.

For the first time since the ET came into being, no central agreement was signed in 1984. At the same time, wage rises fell considerably, so that 1984 became the 'year of wage adjustment'. We should, however, be wary of establishing a link between the absence of a central agreement and wage restraint. Collective bargaining in 1984 was still based on the model instigated by the Pactos de la Moncloa and especially the AMI. And government action is an important factor because it fixes a fairly low inflation rate (8 per cent), which is considered realistic, and also a very low rate for wage increases (6.5 per cent) in the public sector.

In mid-1984 the government, the Socialist union UGT, and the employers' CEOE signed the economic and social agreement (AES) for 1985/6. It contained a number of tripartite agreements on economic and social policy (on taxes, reform of social security and the right to work, inflation, etc), plus a general union–employer agreement on collective bargaining similar to the AMI, of which the main point is that for the first time the wage review clause is fixed for the end of the year.

To sum up, the collective bargaining system established during the Spanish political transition fixes agreements at the highest level while at the same time allowing a certain degree of flexibility in specific agreements. This system was acceptable to the employers' organization, for under it they could keep wage rises under control and considerably reduce the number of working days lost through strikes. Another important, though little used, element of wage flexibility was the 'adjustment clause' introduced with the ANE, under which a loss-making firm was not obliged to adhere to the general agreements. For the unions, the centralized system is a rather effective measure, as they have had great difficulty in becoming established in firms, and union membership has dropped dramatically in the last few years to between 10 and 20 per cent. This drop seems to be the logical outcome of a system where collective bargaining, carried out by committees elected by the workers, is legally applied to all workers, irrespective of whether or not they belong to a trade union.

3. The 1980s: A Race to Make Jobs Flexible

As we have already seen, one of the main features of the system of wage/ labour relations in Franco's time was the rigidity of employment, although there were important exceptions. Dismissals at any rate were possible as long as compensation was paid to the worker. The first government under the monarchy, under pressure from the workers' movement at the beginning of 1976, passed a law on labour relations that prohibited compensation from being paid to a worker whose dismissal had been declared unwarranted by the courts, and that demanded instead his reinstatement. This was strongly condemned by the employers, and the clause in question was scrapped several months later. That law marked the start of a slow but persistent tendency towards an *erosion of job security*, which the unions wanted to preserve at all costs, especially in view of the economic crisis, but which the leading employers' organizations doggedly fought against, arguing that rigidity of employment (i.e. the inability to dimiss at will and without compensation) could be justified only where workers did not have the instruments of free representation at their disposal.

3.1. Widening the scope for dismissals and temporary work

This process of erosion took place on two fronts; first, as regards the possibility of dismissal, by reducing its cost and widening its scope, and second, as regards new jobs, by encouraging temporary employment.

On the first point, although the first steps for increasing the possibilities of dismssal were laid down in the statutory order of 4 March 1977, they were finalized in the ET, which spelled out cases of warranted dismissal for 'objective' reasons. Furthermore, the government created the Instituto de Mediación, Arbitraje y Conciliación (IMAC) (Institute for Mediation, Arbitration, and Conciliation), the aim of which was to make it easier to go through the steps necessary to dismiss individuals. Where there was preliminary agreement between the firm and the worker, it would no longer be necessary to go to court. Of the 1 300 000 dismissals of individuals between 1980 and 1984, two-thirds went through IMAC. For collective dismissals (ERE), administrative authorization must still be sought from the Ministry of Labour, even if there is a preliminary agreement between the firm and the workers (which usually happens in about two-thirds of the ERE cases). Although such authorization is granted in more than 90 per cent of cases, the employers believe that this step should be abolished. They argue that the government compromise, included in the AES, to adapt Spanish labour laws to EEC directives in fact implies its abolition, although the UGT interprets it differently. If it is abolished, and all the indications point to the government interpreting it in the same way as employers, then it will almost complete the process of liberalizing dismissals (although of course not without cost.)

On the second point, the first steps to promote temporary jobs were taken in the 1977 agreements, the Pactos de la Moncloa. The workers' statute of 1980 gave a legal form to temporary work, which was authorized in a certain number of 'normal' instances as well as in the special cases that the government could determine as part of its policy of promoting employment. The orders under the national agreement on employment, signed in 1981, were the main stimulus behind these special programmes, the scope of which, in terms of the maximum percentage of workers employed, was later reduced on several occasions. The Socialist government introduced a reform of the ET in 1984 to eliminate the maximum percentages laid down in previous orders, and to establish a new case of 'normal' temporary work, namely the creation of a new activity. This reform therefore made recruitment more flexible. In practice, however, there was already a certain degree of flexibility; although there are no official statistics available, the unofficial picture is that most of the 1.5 million people annually registered as taking up a new job by employment offices (about 20 per cent of wage-earners) are on short-term contracts, either normal or special ones.

Thus, the broad tendency is fairly clear: to encourage any kind of work as much as possible, since (it is argued) temporary employment is better than none at all. The segmentation resulting from these measures could well aggravate existing differences in a society with a flourishing black economy (which is therefore beyond any control); although it could also be argued that, by making recruitment more flexible, it could contribute (although no one knows to what extent) to the disappearance of the black economy, especially to the extent that the black economy was a response to the rigidity of employment.

3.2. *Constraints imposed by extending unemployment protection*

The last important point to be made concerns unemployment protection. Unemployment benefit was very low during the Franco regime, both as a percentage of GDP and as a proportion of wages, since it was calculated in relation to the basic wage only. But the gradual rise in the unemployment figures especially at the end of the 1970s, raised the overall cost of benefits to the state. And so in 1980 the government passed the Ley Basica de Empleo (LBE) (Basic Law on Employment), which stipulated, among other things, that a longer period of contributions was necessary before a worker was entitled to unemployment benefit, and which established a link between the period of receiving benefit and that of contributing towards it. By way of compensation, the LBE created complementary allowances irrespective of the period of contribution, which basically amount to maintaining sickness insurance once the period of receiving unemployment insurance has passed. The effect of this is obvious at a time when long-term unemployment is on the increase: the gross rate of coverage of unemployment insurance (defined as the total number of recipients compared with the number of unemployed persons registered) dropped from 61.5 per cent in 1980 to 37.8 per cent in 1984.

The tendency is to increase protection for the unemployed, a palliative used by the Socialist government to counteract its harsh economic policy. Extension of the benefit period and increased complementary allowances under the LBE are therefore included in the same programme as warranted dismissals. The aim of the AES for 1985 and 1986 is to reach a gross rate of coverage of unemployment insurance of 43 and 48 per cent, respectively. Increasing and rationalizing the indirect wage in this way, both to achieve a fairer distribution and to control the budget deficit, may be one of the main elements in a new system of wage/labour relations, in so far as it is an attempt to counter the redistributive effects of macroeonomic policies and wage restraint.

7

Belated Industrialization:
The Case of Italy

Enrico Wolleb

1. Introduction

Italian industrial relations since the end of the war have been
characterized by considerable conflict. There was no 'Fordist' stability in
industrial relations (see Aglietta, 1976; Boyer and Mistral, 1983a;
Salvati, 1975, 1978). One of the main reasons for this is the way in which
politics are organized in the country and, in particular, the consequences
for social and institutional behaviour of the system of 'imperfect
democracy', i.e. the fact that power has not alternated between political
parties — the main labour party, the second-largest, has always been
kept out of government coalitions.

Even though in recent years it has looked as if this anomaly might
cease, the unequal political representation of the various social groups
has had a profoundly negative effect upon the development of industrial
relations. It has exacerbated the class war and encouraged a markedly
ideological interpretation of industrial relations, which the protagonists
have seen rather as part of a general political confrontational situation
than in terms of contracts.[1]

From another angle, by guaranteeing executive power to part of the
electorate, and in particular to certain parties, this 'imperfect' system has
saved the party leaders from any risk of political change. Their incentive
to rush through the reforms that the country needed, and to seek the
compromises necessary for the development of more modern and
egalitarian industrial relations, was thus reduced.

In Italy, a Fordist system of industrial relations, based on Taylorism
— on the development of mass consumption in a context of consensus
over income distribution, with wages growing along with productivity
and an all-embracing social security system — appeared late in the day,
and then only gradually, as compared with the other major European

---

[1] These components are not mutually exclusive, but it is a question of relative weight and,
above all, of political culture.

countries. When the system of regulation did develop into a 'Fordist' one, the country was already caught up in the general international crisis; it did not therefore provide or guarantee the stability in industrial relations that had by then emerged in other European countries. In fact, the various components of the Fordist system of regulation took almost 20 years to become established.

Mass production and consumption materialized as early as the mid-1950s and flourished especially between 1958 and 1965, with Taylorian organization being particularly evident from 1964 to 1969. The creation of a social service system and the institutionalization of industrial relations began in the mid–1960s, but the period of significant development came between 1969 and 1975.

The delay in the reform of the welfare state, despite the years of rapid growth, and the continuation up until 1969 of a less institutionalized system of industrial relations, unfavourable to workers as regards working relations and income distribution, explains the high level of worker demands that exploded between 1969 and 1973, the reverberations of which were felt until the end of the 1970s. This delay in terms of expectations and needs resulted in an excess of reforms — so much so that today analysts, whatever their views, call for 'a reform of the reforms'.

Reforms were 'excessive' in at least three senses: first, in relation to the growth potential of an economy in rapid decline; second, because they were too sudden; and third, because they came at a time of particular trade union strength, which made the effects of these changes difficult for firms to bear. Reforms in industrial relations, social services, and the organization of the state which in other countries had taken 20 years to accomplish were carried through in a few years.

Italy arrived at a Fordist system of regulation too late to absorb its repercussions, while worker maturity, partly the fruit of the unfinished Fordist experiment of the 1960s, was already too advanced to accept an intensification of Taylorian organization and to finance its cost through higher productivity. Finally, it was too late for the system of production, centred on large firms, to adapt, in unfavourable international conditions, to a major change in costs and above all in labour relations on the shop-floor.

2. Industrial Relations in the 1960s: The Delay in the Development of a Fordist System of Regulation

2.1. *Economic policy*

The period following postwar reconstruction (1945–55), from the 'economic miracle' (1956–63) to the growth that lasted until 1969, was not characterized in Italy, as it was in other European countries, by a rapid development of industrial relations. The major growth years (1953–63) were marked by *laissez-faire* policies, an expansion of trade, monetary stabilization, and the exclusion of trade unions from economic and political life. This was the basis for extremely rapid growth in productivity (the 'economic miracle'), but it succeeded only in accentuating economic, social, and geographical imbalances.

The most evident and significant example of imbalance was that of the Mezzogiorno (see Graziani, 1979). The influence of an underdeveloped South on the country's socioeconomic development since 1945 (which I shall not dwell upon here) is the background to the study. Southern voters determine the composition of government coalitions because of the comfortable majority that they give to the largest party. Furthermore, the South's social and productive structure has acted as an economic and political counterweight to the spread of industrialization; and the decision to transfer existing resources to the Mezzogiorno rather than create the conditions for autonomous development, which would have profoundly changed the social structure there, affected the size and composition of the national Budget. The fact that public funds are allocated on a largely discretionary basis has slowed down social development, by tending to go for consensus and dependence.

Dualism, emigration, inequality of income distribution, the burgeoning and inefficiency of the tertiary sector, and public administration in the South — such was the burden inherited by centre–left governments[2] at the end of the 'economic miracle' in 1963. Mass consumption, which in other countries had acted as a powerful social catalyst, promoting an unprecedented equality of living standards and consumer habits, occurred in Italy in a context of persistent economic and social inequality. The exclusion of left-wing parties from government and of trade unions from decision-making processes, notwithstanding the advent of an era of mass consumption, was the essential condition for the high productivity increases and low wages that sparked off the virtuous circle of growth and rebalancing of foreign trade accounts in the 1950s. It was no coincidence, therefore, that in the 1960s Italy experienced an insufficient expansion of aggregate demand, combined with a level of investment very much lower than that of savings and an increase in wages lower than that of productivity.

In these circumstances, it is not surprising that there was an upsurge in the consumption of durable goods, and in particular of vehicles, at a rate of 11 per cent a year from 1958 to 1963. Consumer spending continued to

---

[2] See 'Rapporto Saraceno 3 squilibri' in Graziani (1979).

gather pace throughout the 1960s, while public consumption rose more slowly than incomes (3.7 per cent) and remained lower than other items of public expenditure, even during the period under investigation (see Table 7.1).

TABLE 7.1   *Public and private consumption in Italy, 1955–1981*

	Average annual growth rate at constant prices (%)				
	1955–60	1960–65	1966–69	1970–73	1974–81
Durables	10.9	11.8	7.0	6.1	5.4
Semi-durables	5.2	6.6	5.4	3.6	2.3
Non-durables	4.5	5.5	4.3	2.7	1.8
Services	6.9	4.8	4.9	2.9	2.3
TOTAL (private)	5.2	7.4	4.9	3.1	2.3
TOTAL (public)	4.0	3.7	4.3	3.4	2.0

Source: ISTAT.

A glance at trends in economic policy during these years may provide some explanation of the period following the 'economic miracle'. From 1964 onwards, economic policy, and monetary policy in particular, was characterized by creeping deflation and a current account surplus — rather unusual for a country experiencing rapid development, desperately in need of investment in order to adjust capital stock to the supply of labour, continuously in excess of demand, and meeting competition from older and more strongly industrialized countries. This can be explained by the Bank of Italy's 'philosophy' on income distribution and its attempt to maintain the virtuous economic circle of the 1950s, which was suddenly interrupted in 1963 because of the first significant wave of wage increases.

The unexpected rise in wages during the boom of 1962–3, which marked the end of the 'economic miracle', caused the first shock to income distribution in the postwar period, and drove the Bank of Italy to bring about a brief cyclical downturn with the object of halting the process. The success of this manoeuvre induced the monetary authorities to cool down the economy still further, in order to sustain a pattern of development based on low wages and led by exports. 'Export-led' growth had already been initiated, with explicit strategic objectives as regards specialization and income distribution.

A by-product of this strategy was insufficient investment in industry and the social infrastructure. In fact, the period of growth was brought to an end by capital flights, associated with the balance of payments surplus and intended to avoid a revaluation of the lira.

This development was also the result of political factors. The investment 'strike' was partly a reflection of an unstable system of industrial relations, whereby confrontational attitudes, rooted in strong ideological beliefs, prevented a process of negotiaton from being established. Governments, unstable for similar reasons, were incapable of implementing a Fordist-type consensus, even though this did occasionally manifest itself, in embryonic form, throughout the decade. The deficit on capital account of the balance of payments was also the result of a flight of speculative capital induced by the nationalization agreements of that period (electricity, Montedison), which, partly because of the lack of negotiations between management and workers, similarly allowed important sources of national savings to be diverted. If there had been a stable and harmonious system of industrial relations, the outcome would probably have been different.

The Social Contract, which was the main pillar of Keynesian polices in other countries, was not yet completely formed in Italy; the welfare state and industrial relations were underdeveloped; and full employment was still a long way off. Economic, social, and political history combine to explain this delay.

The political and social climate in Italy immediately after the Second World War, together with the long delay in industrialization, was the major reason for the weak position of the working class during the early years of rapid development. The political division within the working class between Catholics and Marxists, and the marginalization of the latter, prevented the growth of a strong and authoritative trade union movement which would have provided a counterbalance in the Fordist system. The marginalization of the principal workers' party, moreover, removed one of the essential protagonists in the Fordist system, which in other European countries had taken place under the aegis of social democratic and labour parties.

These political elements are an important part of the explanation of the state of industrial relations in that period, but other aspects of the socioeconomic environment should not be overlooked. The most important of these was without doubt the rural exodus, a process in which, from 1951 to 1971, more than 5 million workers moved out from agriculture and away from their homes and places of work. In the Mezzogiorno alone, the ratio of agricultural to industrial employment went from 3:1 to less than 1:1 in the course of 20 years. But this process was not insignificant in the North, either, where it affected more than 70 per cent of agricultural employment.

It was a social transformation of enormous proportions, which saw the birth of large concentrations of industry in the North and of services in the South, and the abandonment of the fields and inland regions in favour of the coastal regions and cities. The following figures, pertaining to net emigration between 1952 and 1971, bear this out:

1952–61	
South	−1755
Centre–North	+ 720
1962–71	
South	−2230
Centre–North	+1145

A second factor instrumental in delaying the introduction of the Fordist system was the unpreparedness of the state apparatus to assume responsibility for controlling the economic system and administering the welfare state. The teething troubles of Keynesian policies in the 1960s not only were attributable to the postwar *laissez-faire* policy, which was in fact perfectly compatible with the growth of public holdings (IRI and ENI), but were deeply rooted in the inefficiency of public administration.

Governments, which after the war inherited from Fascism an extremely backward public administration (see Daneo, 1975), did not change the system sufficiently to enable it to carry out the new tasks that the growing role of the state in the economy created for it. On the contrary, the existing apparatus was used as the principal source of new employment especially in the South, so as to achieve consensus there. It was this inefficiency of public administration, which was due as much to the backwardness of administrative practices (Reviglio, 1975) as to the role that was accorded to it, that prevented the use of Keynesian techniques of controlling and manipulating public spending in order to stabilize economic activity, to stimulate private investment, redistribute income, and increase public consumption.

2.2. *Industrial relations*

All aspects of industrial relations reflected trade union weakness and a low degree of institutionalization of negotiating procedures. In spite of the late development of Fordism, however, the changes that occurred during the 1958–64 period of growth and the years that followed were considerable. The shortcomings, as compared with mature Fordism in the rest of Western Europe, and the chaos and ineffectiveness of the embryonic reforms initiated in the second half of the decade, if nothing else, made all those involved aware of the institutional changes necessary at the political level.

Collective bargaining in the 1950s had remained centralized; union representation at the firm level was limited and sporadic. The first step towards decentralization got off to a difficult start with the sectoral bargaining of 1956, which became established throughout the industrial sector only in 1962–3, when the economic miracle was drawing to a close.

Because of the 'economic miracle', certain sectors of the labour market for the first time felt the strain of full employment. This must be the only example in recent trade union history when worker demands — in this case for wage rises and union rights — coincided with an appropriate phase of the economic cycle. Employers during this period maintained an attitude of passive resistance to the development of relations with unions on the shop-floor. There were public sector holding companies and a few large industrial concerns that did accept these initial changes, although the majority within the Association of Industrialists were opposed to them (Baglioni, 1982).

In the 1960s, national bargaining became institutionalized and regularized (every three years) and took on a normative and unifying role (as against bargaining within firms, which remained weak). Nevertheless, as early as 1966, along with the joint technical committees on piece-work and the conditions and organization of work, there developed the system of having a 'firm's delegate', which was to become more important in the decentralized bargaining of the period 1969–73.

Over these years, trade union representation increased in line with the development of an anti-Taylorian feeling.[3] Unionization, after the postwar explosion when the rate increased to over 50 per cent by 1950, fell to 22 per cent in 1959 and stayed at that level for almost 10 years. Seen in a long-term perspective, the involvement of the grass roots was therefore the catalyst for the profound institutional changes that occurred during these years. This 'participation' is the third distinctive feature of the development of industrial relations, which were neither constructed around a table by the heads of state institutions and political representatives, nor the outcome of political compromise: rather, they were 'snatched' from amid the conflict.

3. Industrial Relations in the 1970s: 'A Surfeit of Reforms'

3.1. The reformist parabola of the 1970s

The institutionalization of industrial relations and the reform of the social security system both took place between 1968 and 1975. The fact that industrial relations were reformed during a period of exceptional worker strength meant that the institutional framework created was particularly favourable to them. This upset the relations that previously existed

[3] It was at the end of this period that the first law (1.604, 1966) was passed guaranteeing trade union freedoms and regulating the sacking of individuals by employers..

between workers and firms, and was judged responsible for the recession and for the constant disputes that marked industrial relations in the 1970s.

The reforms, confronted with insufficient pragmatism, became 'excessive' in relation to the capacity for political and administrative adaptation on the part of public institutions. In spite of the 1948 Constitution (Art. 39), which presaged trade union freedom, it was the Workers' Statute (20 May 1970) that brought a long period of 'anomie' in industrial relations to an end through extensive legislation regulating in detail the relations between unions and workers on the one hand and enterprises on the other.

Paradoxically, this statute marked the beginning of an institutionalized system of industrial relations and, at the same time, that of its progressive crisis. Since its adoption, there have been no years when the distribution of income has been relatively stable in the 'Fordist' sense. Whereas in other European countries, from the 1960s until 1973, new industrial relations were an element of stability in the economic system, in the case of Italy economic history took quite a different path.

Fordist development, which began in the period 1958–63 (the 'economic miracle') and lasted until 1969, was founded on a system of industrial relations that was badly organized institutionally and generally unfavourable to the working class. Once the system had been reformed by the Workers' Statute, and once works councils began to develop spontaneously and inevitably, marking the dawn of worker involvement in Italy's economic and social life, a crisis began to loom in industrial relations. Its explosion was delayed until the end of the decade, for two important reasons. The first was the period of national consensus (the agreement between Communist and Christian Democratic Parties). This political agreement made it possible to maintain what had been won in the period 1969–73 in terms of wage guarantees, jobs, and indexation. In exchange, there were to be no further demands; i.e., claims would be moderate with respect to both wages and the organization of work. The implicit consequence was that industrial relations came once more under centralized (federal or confederal) union control after the brief, exciting, but 'dangerous' episode of works councils. The unions and the left were conscious, at the end of 1975, of having achieved as much as was possible from the pont of view of remuneration and organization of work at plant level. The strategy of co-operation under which unions assumed responsibility for overall management of the economic system is known as the 'EUR' line.

The second factor was of an 'institutional' nature and lay in the legislative strength of the provisions of the Workers' Statute, in the guarantees contained in it, in its socially progressive tenor, and in the

Enrico Wolleb

difficulty for governments of intervening overtly in industrial relations.

The serious and long delays in instituting reform of many aspects of industrial relations, and the changes that occurred in the 1970s, were tolerated and 'mediated' by governments, rather than foreseen and managed by them. Only in 1976 did a brief period of greater co-operation begin, with governments intervening directly in industrial relations in order to contain the escalating cost of labour and social services. These direct interventions, initially based on consensus, became unilaterally imposed from 1980 onwards.

3.2. The irresistible growth of worker demands, 1969–1973

A movement for reform emerged on the shop-floor out of rising opposition to a management policy of low wages and high unemployment, a policy that was supported by the Central Bank in the period 1964–9. This revitalized trade unions from the point of view of both the claims made and recruitment and organization. The explosion occurred in the autumn of 1969 (see Table 7.2).

TABLE 7.2   *Union membership in Italy and rates of unionization, 1950–1984*

	Union membership (000)				Rates of unionization
	CGIL	CISL	UIL	Independent	
1950	4641	1190	—	—	50.814
1955	4194	1342	—	—	43.926
1960	2583	1324	—	—	28.489
1965	2543	1468	—	—	28.498
1969	2626	1641	—	—	29.416
1970	2943	1808	780	—	38.478
1971	3138	1973	825	—	41.121
1975	4018	2594	1033	—	48.736
1976	4313	2824	1105	310	51.332
1977	4475	2810	1160	316	52.250
1978	4528	2869	1285	322	51.801
1979	4583	2906	1327	346	50.857
1980	4599	3058	1347	370	49.827
1981					48.89
1982					47.47
1983					45.43
1984					43.75

The common nature of the objectives of this grass-roots movement led to the merging of the three central trade union organizations, which strengthened their bargaining power and institutional weight. The master of the new system of wage/labour relations was the shop-floor delegate, who was the counterpart of the works council at the firm level. The rate of unionization remained at around 2 per cent for a decade, then spiralled upwards from 1968 to 1977, when it reached 52 per cent, a record level in the history of Italian trade unions. It was left-wing unionism, largely Communist, that benefited particularly from this explosion, with an increase in membership from 2.4 to 4.6 million in 1980. The other unions also increased in size, although on a smaller scale.

The growth in recruitment was accompanied by the progressive institutionalization of the unions' role in the administration of the social security system. There was a real failure on the part of the state to provide individual benefits to certain sectors. The rate of unionization in the agricultural sector and among pensioners was therefore nearly 100 per cent, and was a unique phenomenon of welfare unionization — quite different from, although complementary to, the confrontational pay bargaining activities of works councils, which were hardly institutionalized at all.

The factory delegate, who emerged spontaneously in large firms as early as the mid-1960s, institutionally provided for and protected by the Workers' Statute, rapidly became widespread in small- and medium-sized firms. His function, at first limited to negotiating the speed of assembly lines, protecting the position of individuals, and monitoring the rate of production, grew to the point where he effectively represented the workers' side in the Fordist organization of production, with a bargaining power and an impact beyond anything achieved in the preceding decade. Bargaining was at its most decentralized in 1969–73.

For management, these demands from the grass roots and in the work-place meant a breakdown in the system of organization and in the control of production and the labour force within the firm. With this new balance in power relations on the shop-floor, but also in society, a practice of continuous detailed bargaining became 'institutionalized', backed up by widespread and effective means of enforcement, which first affected the growth of wages but later affected every aspect of work with a bearing on productivity (see Table 7.3)

In the majority of cases, the outcomes of the claims made were so innovative in terms of industrial relations that they served as a guide to subsequent collective agreements. Trade union leaders often found themselves lagging behind what was happening at the grass roots, and they therefore concentrated on consolidating the gains made in collective agreements.

TABLE 7.3   *Number of disputes, workers taking part, and hours lost in Italy (average), 1954–1984*

	Disputes	Workers taking part	Working hours lost
1954–59	1453	1003	21 097
1960–68	2233	1697	57 451
1969–75	2619	4108	107 086
1976–82	1386	6843	73 602
1983–84	1601	—	78 126

Source: ISTAT.

In spite of the multiple claims put forward by unions at the grass-roots level, the overall results of reforming efforts, whether as regards wages and the organization of production or the social security system, were an increase in benefits and a reduction in the differences within and between the various categories of worker.

During this period, central union activity in both national sectoral negotiations and confederal agreements was aimed principally at reducing wage differentials and qualifications, so as to standardize benefits between different workers and extend them from large to small firms. The institutional measure that triggered off these numerous reforms in industrial relations was the 'Workers' Statute' (Statuto dei Lavoratori). This established rights on freedom in the work-place, on working conditions, on professional practice, on trade union freedoms, and on relations between employee and employer, granting the workers specific rights and powers which did a good deal to promote unionism within firms. Support for union activity was indirectly strengthened by the possibility of taking immediate action through magistrates' courts against anti-union conduct on the part of employers.[4]

The effects of this Statute had enormous repercussions on power relations, and encouraged a proliferation of claims regarding remuneration, organization, and the pace and hours of work, as well as the beginnings of participation in company decision-making. Between 1969 and 1975, fundamental rules were laid down on all these aspects of industrial relations.

The political significance of these demands, in terms of the organization of production and economic policy, was that they gave rise to the principle that wage claims need to be limited because they are rapidly

---

[4] The 'Work Law Reform' of 1973 set up procedures for the rapid resolution of work-place conflicts and thus made possible the effective implementation of the rules of the Workers' Statue.

swallowed up by inflation; any action, therefore, must provide for control of the supply of labour as well as of wage increases. The experience of the years 1962–3 was adverse because increases were rapidly 'swallowed up' (see Foa, 1983).

The demands that had the greatest effect on production were:

- reduction of the working week to 40 hours, with an eight-hour day, and increased holidays;
- quantitive restrictions and other means of discouraging overtime;
- negotiations on the pace of work and on mobility inside the factory;
- protection of jobs in the event of sickness;
- monitoring of the working environment;
- progressive reduction in piece-work;
- narrowing of the range of qualifications and wages;
- abolition of the distinction between blue- and white-collar workers (limited to a few sectors).

3.3 The attempt at consolidation, 1974–1979

Between 1969 and 1976, major attempts were made to consolidate collective agreements. They gave rise to two institutional changes which largely determined the growth of labour costs and expenditure on unemployment during the second half of the decade: the laws on wage guarantees (20 May 1975, no. 164), and reform of the indexation mechanism, with the 'single point' on the cost of living scale.

The law on wage guarantees was intended to be a short-term measure, enacted with the aim of introducing flexibility in industrial production and speeding up and facilitating the process of restructuring and retraining. The aim of union action, therefore, was to guarantee wages against the stoppage of casual employment in the event of company reorganization. The principle emerged that the cost of such reorganization should not be met by the industrial wage-earner, while employers were encouraged to proceed with necessary adaptation without fear of labour disputes, and with considerable financial relief.

The effectiveness of this law in terms of mobility and redundancies was reinforced by various procedures contained in other rulings on industrial policy, with regard to restructuring and employment. For several years, therefore, political pressure for the use of the CIG (Cassa Integrazione Guadagno — 'Earnings Compensation Fund') and the complexity of administrative procedures regarding redundancies meant that employment levels were frozen — for new entrants as well as for those leaving the work-force.

Labour turnover (see Table 7.4) halved in the period 1973–80. However, from 1980 onwards almost twice as many left as entered the

TABLE 7.4   *Turnover rates per 1000 workers, manufacturing and construction companies (annual average)**

	Manufacturing		Construction	
	E	L	E	L
1965–72	28.773	262.67	939.92	925.45
1973–80	154.67	155.33	414.99	486.46
1981–84	85	141	258	362

* E, entering; L, leaving the work-force.

Source: *Confindustria* (Economic Situation Report) (various years).

work-force, which confirms that the reversal of trend was already evident in 1979.

The new mechanism of wage indexation, agreed in 1975 following the explosion in inflation in 1973–4, provided for an across-the-board increment of L2,389 for all grades of wages and salaries for every percentage point increase in consumer prices, taking effect on the date of negotiation of the agreement. The effect of this reform, apart from raising the inflation cover for wages and salaries in general, as compared with the past, was to even out discrepancies in wage levels.

With these measures, which ended the phase of labour domination in industrial relations, the impression is that, in view of the inevitability of recession, claims (which in the meantime had returned to the control of the central bodies) concentrated on the 'defence' of what had been achieved in terms of income, the organization of work, rules on dismissals, and wage security. If we construct a picture of the institutional patchwork of the system of wage/labour relations at the end of the decade, we see that, in the space of a few years, a complete system for protecting and controlling employment had been constructed, during a period when the fear was beginning to spread that the recession would last and labour-saving reorganization, especially in industry, would proliferate.

Labour demands in these years were loudest in the industrial sector, which consequently experienced the most widespread and complete institutionalization of wage/labour relations. There was tight legislation on work contracts; where positions are permanent, individual dismissals are now allowed only for a 'just cause' or 'justifiable reason', i.e. the proven and serious inadequacy of the worker. Part-time and seasonal contracts are strictly limited to a few sectors and specific cases. The provisions of the Statute with which employers must comply, in the case of irregular dismissals and illegal contracts, are strictly and swiftly applied; they include not only a fine but also the re-employment of the worker.

The provisions concerning the power to control the organization of work at plant level are effective, as are the results achieved in successive phases of bargaining within firms (mobility, piece work, the pace of work, hours, etc.) Wage levels, negotiated from a position of strength, are effectively defended by indexation (*la scala mobile*), even though it has been clear since 1973 that the monetary authorities tend to 'favour' price rises.

The unemployment benefit fund (la Cassa Integrazione Guadagni — CIG) completes the system of protection in the new industrial relations, restricting the possibility of redundancy in the event of business crises, and freeing workers from the effects of the widespread move towards the reorganization of production.

Once the Fordist system of relations was in place, there was, in theory, a formidable system for monitoring and guaranteeing employment, virtually eliminating the possibility of dismissal in return for less and less say in the organization of work and productivity.

This system rapidly showed several weak points, partly because of an incorrect evaluation of external factors and partly because of the way reforms were made. In the first place, it was never regarded by employers as a permanent solution but was tolerated only as the least unfavourable in their position of political, cultural, and strategic weakness. As soon as power relations altered, the 'agreements' would be dissolved. Second, this system was based on the 'incorrect' hypothesis (although one shared by governments and unions in other industrialized countries) that the recession would be temporary and recovery was imminent.

Political debate focused on the oil crisis and the recycling of the OPEC surplus; what failed to be appreciated was the complex relationship between the movement opposed to Fordist wage/labour relations and the domestic and international situation. The effects of the impressive rise in the power of financial capital and its mobility, of the rise in interest rates, of the spread of the trend towards manpower savings, and of the social divisions created by rapidly increasing employment were not yet clear. The stability of this institutional framework rested on assumptions that failed to materialize. Moving from an overall strategy to the actual management of industrial relations, it seemed evident at that time that the rigid job protection enjoyed by employees gave rise to widespread avoidance of the system, with a rise in unregulated work and the search for 'flexibility'.

154   *Enrico Wolleb*

4. The Social Security System

The development of welfare services came about simultaneously with the
power of workers as regards pay and working conditions. It erupted into
being in the same rapid, chaotic fashion, between the end of the 1960s
and the beginning of the 1970s. The necessary investment in social
infrastructure and the finance for pensions, unemployment pay, health,
education, and housing reform (during a phase of fierce international
competition and financial difficulties for firms), burdened the state with
budget deficits — although it also weighed heavily on labour costs and
taxation (see Table 7.5).

TABLE 7.5   *Tax burden as a percentage of GDP at market prices*

	Indirect taxes	Direct taxes	Social security contributions		Total taxes
			Employer*	Employee*	
1965	11.5	6.1	7.7	2.0	27.3
1973	9.8	6.0	9.0	2.4	27.2
1978	10.9	10.0	10.2	2.3	32.6
1980	10.1	11.1	9.4	3.2	33.8
1982	10.1	14.0 (13.2)†	9.9	3.4	37.3 (36.5)†
1984	11.3	14.7	9.9	3.3	39.2

* Excluding extra taxes (rebates and surtax).
† Income from public sector only.

Source: EEC *National Accounts 1964–1981* and *Income Statistics of Community Countries, 1965–1982.*

These reforms necessitated the formation of complex local administrative structures during a phase in the country's institutional history
when, in addition, considerable political and administrative decentralization was taking place, stemming from the setting-up of the regions.

The 'surfeit' of reforms, their lateness, and the unfulfilled demands
that had accumulated showed up the backwardness of central and local
administration, on which these reforms had to be based, with considerable cost, wastage, and frustration.

The long cycle of reforms that began in the early 1960s reached its peak
between 1968 and 1975. Then, because the institutional, administrative,
and financial structures failed to adapt, it proceeded by fits and starts

towards a general trend of reduction in expenditure and revision of the principles behind the reforms. The reform of the social security system took shape as a result of a strong push towards egalitarianism, in a spirit of extending benefits and providing equal services for all. Once these objectives were attained, demands were concentrated on the defence of all benefits against inflation, especially at the lowest levels.

Pensions represent the most important and dynamic part of national insurance spending. From 1970 to 1983 an increase of more than 6 points in the GDP was recorded, almost one-third of the increase in total public expenditure. The weight of pensions within social security expenditure grew rapidly, from 54 per cent in 1970 to 81 per cent in 1983. This development was due to several causes: the ageing of the population, the extension of benefits to various groups, a more rapid adjustment to inflation, the increase in the lowest pensions by more than the inflation rate, and, finally, the incorrect use of some pensions as a substitute for the guaranteed minimum wage (SMIG).

The intervention of the welfare state to guarantee an income for the unemployed was reinforced and extended during the 1970s, with numerous measures for raising the level of aid and adding new categories of beneficiary. After 1979, with the worsening of the recession, such intervention became the key point of the system of wage/labour relations; particular pressure was exerted on it by both unions and employers, in order to burden the state with the cost of changes in labour organization. Intervention by the CIG avoids dismissals by entrusting the state with the salary burden of surplus employees with a minimal contribution from employers. Its protective function, at least theoretically, is twofold, because on the one hand it guarantees wages and on the other it impels the firms to reduce or suspend working hours, rather than dismissing employees. But in most cases this is an illusion. Since the links between wage compensation and reorientation projects (where they existed) were very tenuous, the institutionalized consultation procedures have not turned to participation in company decision-making regarding either innovation or restructuring.

Given the limitations of intervention, expenditure on wage guarantees has grown as a proportion of GDP (from 0.4 to 0.8 per cent between 1975 and 1983), but it remains less than that in other European countries, despite the fact that the unemployment rate has been consistently higher.

The use of the CIG concealed a wide array of dismissals in the manufacturing sector, resulting from insufficient orders, restructuring and reconversion for 'labour-saving' purposes, decentralization, or the withdrawal of capital from production. In reality, the main objective of these reorganizations of production was, in almost all cases, a significant reduction in manpower. Consequently, the CIG has acted as an unofficial SMIG, restricted to industrial workers; it has nurtured the illusion of the future return of laid-off workers to the company, and, inasmuch as this has not occurred, has increased disputes and frustrations.

In conclusion, with the extension of the use of uncontrolled labour, with improper use of the CIG, and the collapse of agreements on economic policy, the unions have not succeeded in recent years in acquiring control of the restructuring process, despite their initial position of strength, while the costs, financed by the state budget, finish up being paid by the employees themselves.

5. The 1980s: The Search for Flexibility

From the explosion of the old wage/labour relations to the longest postwar recession (1981–3), industrialists reacted to the increased power of the trade unions by pursuing various strategies, united by a common, relentless drive for flexibility.

Such was the premise for regaining control of the organization of work and for reviving profits. Flexibility, which became the official objective even of economic policy, with the aim of 'adapting' production to foreign competition and to the heightened cyclical instability of demand, had an unequivocal effect on power relations in the work-place in terms of productivity, dismissals, and wages.

During these years there have been three main routes to flexibility, each with a different emphasis in relation to domestic and international conditions: 'arbitration through inflation', decentralization and restructuring, and the regaining of power in the work-place.

5.1. 'Arbitration through inflation'

The absence of a system of industrial relations capable of guaranteeing a steady distribution of GDP means that the Italian economy was in a state of continuous conflict over income distribution as far back as the 1960s. The result was cyclical fluctuations in GDP of the 'stop–go' variety and higher average inflation than in other countries.

Inflation was a necessary means of 'arbitration' to limit wage rises in the years when employment increased significantly and other routes to flexibility were blocked. The state played the role of 'mediator' between the various social groups, by accepting demands incompatible with budgetary constraints and then making them consistent by means of inflation. These were the years when the state smoothed over conflicts concerning distribution, pushing the costs of all reform on to the welfare

system, nationalizing numerous crisis-torn companies, and raising production subsidies and incentives. Such action met with the agreement of
both unions and employers — the disappearance of firms and problems
of unemployment were apparently taken care of. But such arbitration is a
short-term phenomenon, and devalues the economic function of public
enterprises. The employers were successful on two counts: they shifted
the costs of the crisis, and they threw public enterprises into a 'financial'
and 'political' crisis, which became synonymous with 'inefficient'
management and the 'wastage' of resources, so that the public sector lost
its role as an alternative to private capital in the growth process, and the
initiative returned to private enterprise.

An essential component of this policy was the adjustment of monetary
and exchange rate policy to increases in prices of industrial products and
services. This policy mix led to a marked slow-down in economic growth,
which was nevertheless still higher than what would have been attainable
without inflation and with bitter social conflict instead. It entailed the
monetary authority's triggering an inflationary spiral (inflation–devaluation–deflation), which intensified as time went on.

This policy had a twofold effect on distribution. First, inflation allowed
prices to recover, and in some cases to overtake wages, while devaluation
from February 1973 onwards relaxed the constraint imposed by foreign
competition. Second, deflation was aimed at controlling the rising trend
of wages through a reduction in the demand for labour. What lay behind
this combination of measures was the assumption that the relationship
between wages and unemployment was of the Phillips Curve type; this
seemed to be valid for 1960s, above all during the 1964 depression and
the subsequent creeping deflation (1964–9), when profits were growing
continuously in relation to GDP.

In addition, the aim had been to hold down domestic demand in line
with external constraints, and to promote export-based growth. The
latter proved an obstacle to the development of Fordism and to the
stability of industrial relations. It did not necessitate a rise in domestic
demand and wages in line with productivity: on the contrary, the more
the latter exceeded wages, the more foreign competitiveness increased, as
did the possibility of exporting the difference between domestic production
and demand. In terms of distribution, the low level of domestic demand
weakened trade unions, slowed down wage rises, and therefore triggered
a virtuous circle whereby development was based on the need for a
harmonious distribution of GDP between wages and profits.

It is understandable that the central bank, immediately after the wage
increases of 1969/70, declared that 'the economy has been wounded' and
that it considered the recovery of profits a necessary prerequisite for
getting back to sustained growth. This strategy of 'arbitration through

inflation', already complicated enough because of the increasing bar-gaining power of the workers, was pursued during a period of international crisis and a succession of significant changes in the conditions of international competition.

Initially, the fall of the dollar and the collapse of the fixed exchange rate system facilitated devaluation, while the growth of international trade that followed the recycling of the OPEC surplus allowed an increase in exports. Subsequently, the gamble of export-led growth, pursued by all the major nations (domestic deflation combined with measures to stimulate exports), failed, which further reduced the margin for growth.

'Arbitration through inflation' began after the major wage rises of 1969/70 with a dramatic fall in domestic demand, from 7 per cent a year to virtually nil, while exports grew by over 6 per cent — effecting a 'correction to the economy', as the Bank of Italy report modestly put it. However, although wage increases were contained, profits failed to recover substantially during the upturn in the economy (see Figs. 7.1–7.3).

Economic adjustments took place at the cost of profits for two main reasons: the fall in productivity, and the coincidence of expenditure growth in 1973 with a new wage round, where the unions' position of strength allowed them to appropriate the productivity gains that were slowly materializing. The recovery was extremely brief, and there was a new deflationary shock in 1974/5: wages stopped rising in 1974, but so did productivity; the few resources that were released did not turn into profits, which continued to fall, although they served to compensate to some extent for the loss of trade in 1974 (−18 per cent).

In 1975 the economy fell into the deepest recession since the war, with GDP declining by 3.5 per cent, the loss of trade continued (−22 per cent), and its initial impact was again on profits, while real wages began to rise once more despite the adverse economic situation.

Why were policies only partially effective?

5.2. *Changes in the relationship between productivity and the business cycle*

The effect of cyclical variations in economic activity and distribution is linked to three basic relationships, themselves interconnected, which in the period 1969–75 were modified by a change in industrial relations. The first relationship is that between the level of economic activity and employment: the fall in employment was the primary cause of the change in the attitude of unions to wages and the organization of work. It was learned in the postwar years that, when faced with a significant decline in jobs, the unions tend to prefer constant or increased employment to pay rises. The second relationship is therefore between the recession and the slowing-up of wage increases. The third, which derives from the second, is between productivity growth and GDP growth, the former exceeding the latter during recessions. This, together with the easing-off of wages, produces recovery in the rate of profit.

The stimulus to economic activity derives from the temporary occurrence of a kind of 'entrepreneur's dilemma'. For the entrepreneur, the high rate of profit in the final phases of the depression has a limited effect on the volume of profits if the rate of plant utilization remains low. He is thus encouraged to increase production. In macroeconomic terms, once a trend favourable to profit forms in the low phase of the cycle, recovery is essential. During the recovery, the volume and the share of profits will rise until there is a demand for labour sufficient to increase wages more rapidly than productivity.

The two deflations in Italy of 1970–1 and 1974–5 initially depressed profits — an inevitable consequence, given that it takes longer for employment and wages to react. The mechanisms designed to reverse the change in distribution were 'blocked' on account of the institutional changes regulating redundancies, the organization of work, and wage bargaining (see Fig. 7.1). In the recession of 1963–4, employment and wages were 'flexible', while movements in productivity were a mirror image of production. However, during the two recessions of 1971–2 and 1974–5, productivity growth became pro-cyclical and fell as production declined. A decline in average hours worked per employee was, in fact, what absorbed the reduction in economic activity, while employment, partly protected by the CIG (Earnings Compensation Fund), remained almost constant during both recessions (see Fig. 7.1).

The trade unions were able to 'control' productivity by means of hours worked, with overtime responding flexibly to the amount of work. They were also in a position to resist redundancies during the recessions, while wage settlements, by then annual, followed hard on the heels of productivity growth in 1973, in the upturn, and preceded it in 1975, restricting the recovery of profits (see Fig. 7.2).

5.3. *Shifts of power on the shop-floor*

During the 1976 recovery, the first effects of this strategy became apparent, with entrepreneurs progressively regaining power on the shop-floor. The overall effects were clearly distinguishable from the sudden change in the elasticity of employment in manufacturing with respect to variations in economic activity: during the growth (+5.9 per cent) of 1976, in fact, the demand for labour paradoxically declined (−1.3 per cent), and continued to do so for another two years. This confirmed the dichotomy not only

Enrico Wolleb

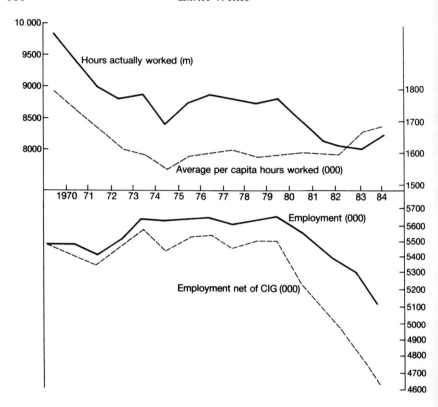

Fig. 7.1. Hours worked (total and per capita) and industrial employment in Italy, 1970–1984. (*Source*: Bank of Italy data)

between production and employment, but also between employment and investment. The moderate increase in per capita working hours did not explain the reduced demand for labour, which implies that investment had rationalization and labour-saving effects.

The second sign of weakness was the sudden rise in unemployment, which, owing to demographic factors, rose by almost 1 point in a year when income increased by about 6 per cent, as a result of immigration and greater female participation.

The extension of indexation to the majority of those on fixed incomes (pensions, etc.) was whittling away the groups on to which the state could unload the cost of inflation (because of 'money illusion'[5]) and

[5] i.e. the propensity to respond to changes in money magnitudes as if they represented changes in real magnitudes.

reducing the potential of arbitration through inflation. Apart from industrial profits, which because of permanent devaluation were effectively indexed in line with wages, there remained only unindexed savings to pay the cost of arbitration through inflation: real income from savings declined between 1974 and 1976 by an average of 6 per cent, at the same time as interest rates were beginning to rise.

This was also a sign that the limits of arbitration (1970–6) had by then been reached. The disappearance of money illusion, in a fully indexed economy where more is demanded than is available, made even devaluation impracticable, since prices and wages had begun to recover with considerable alacrity. While inflation and the public deficit chased each other's tails, the export-led rates of growth declined even more as a result of the speed with which balance of payments constraints checked domestic demand in the absence of devaluation.

The period 1977–84 was therefore characterized by a total reversal of trends that had been, in general, favourable to wages. Profits began to recover at the same time as wage rises progressively diminished in relation to preceding years. The most significant shifts in wealth, however, were not between profits and wages, but between financial

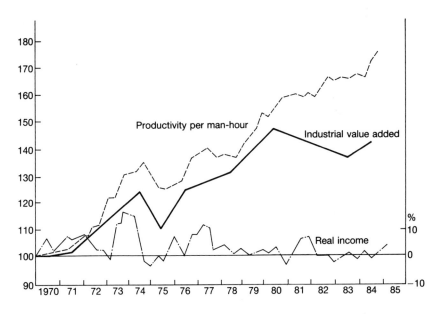

FIG. 7.2. Productivity per man-hour, industrial value added, and real income in Italy, 1970–1985 (1970=100). (*Source*: ISTAT and Bank of Italy)

income on the one hand and profits and wages on the other. The proportion of national revenue paid to families in the form of unearned income rose from 7 to 15 per cent between 1975 and 1984. More than half of this was paid by the state, which from 1977 onwards progressively financed its deficit by issuing Treasury bonds, indexed at high rates of return and non-taxable, while controlling the money supply. The cost of this redistribution was borne by the most highly taxed groups (employees) and by firms that had obtained their finance on the credit market at rates competitive with those on Treasury bonds.

Thus, industrial capital did not wholly benefit from the fall in real wages, while investment and the level of economic activity failed to recover, leaving the labour market in a position of increasing weakness. The recovery of industrial profits was insufficient, at a time of international recession and high interest rates, to bring about a recovery in economic activity and employment. In these circumstances, other aspects of economic behaviour began to operate after 1977 as they had prior to 1971.

Productivity followed a pro-cyclical path and grew continuously from 1977 until 1984, as both employment and GDP fell. Average hours per worker per month declined by less than total hours, allowing hourly productivity to remain constant during the 1977 recession and to rise during that of 1982/3. In terms of both employment and hours worked, the labour market regained 'flexibility'. There was a parallel fall in real earnings and effective employment on a scale unprecedented in the previous 20 years.

Various other factors have contributed to the fall in wages since 1980. First, wage claims and collective bargaining progressively declined throughout 1982. Second, the sliding scale of wage indexation was cut in January 1984 in the face of rampant inflation. Over this period, bargaining concentrated on the cover afforded by the sliding scale, and the growth in other components of wages became negligible. In conclusion, the monetary strategy of financing the public deficit by issuing Treasury bonds at positive real interest rates made it impossible to come to terms with inflation and produced a distribution shock that favoured financial capital and, to a lesser extent, industrial profits.

Nowadays, inflation upsets the distribution of income but does not release sufficient resources to make the economy's accounts balance. Nevertheless, the fall in real wages is limited; unearned income has increased at an unprecedented rate; the rise in profits has been restrained. The conflict in distribution, in the absence of devaluation, has been transferred to the issue of indexation of the various sources of income and to their differing rates of taxation (see Fig. 7.3). The state budget has become highly regressive in terms of both tax and

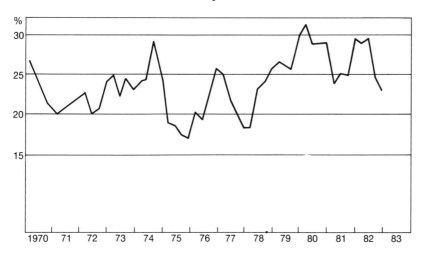

Fig. 7.3. Share of gross profits in value added in industry, 1970–1983. (*Source*: Bank of Italy data)

expenditure. In the case of taxation, extensive evasion is important, as is the exemption of unearned income, which amounts to more than 15 per cent of GDP. In the case of expenditure, there has been a progressive increase in transfers to industry since the end of the 1970s.

The third element that depressed real wages was the increase in direct taxation. Because of inflation, from 1975 onwards average wages were hit by rising effective tax rates which increased from 3.6–6.4 per cent in 1975 to 8.9–10.6 per cent in 1980/1. Fiscal drag thus reduced nominal earnings by approximately 5 per cent over this period. The re-emergence of flexibility was demonstrated by agreements on hours, the introduction of part-time work, and the control of absenteeism, while the power of the unions to control organization within factories weakened progressively as jobs were lost.

5.4. *Flexibility regained, 1981–1985*

The search for flexibility on the part of management and policy-makers was concentrated on manufacturing industry and the labour market. More than a decade after the beginning of this process, several effects are clear.

While the structure of firms has shown a great capacity for adaptation, the consequences for the labour market of firms' flexibility have generally been adverse, and have taken the form of mass unemployment. Since there is a negative correlation between flexibility of firms and the maintenance of high 'employment, there is no doubt that any concrete improvements in flexibility were paid for by job losses. This took place, despite the profound changes in the labour market, in response to a demand by firms for a 'flexible' labour force.

It is doubtful whether the industrial system could be described as being in crisis in the 1970s. It would be even more questionable to attribute the need for change in large industries exclusively to industrial relations and labour costs. Large companies, vertically integrated and linked to the patchwork of small local firms and to Italian society, made their fortunes in the postwar period by carrying out public contracts for reconstruction. Subsequently, the rapid development of private consumption and a limited amount of competition in the rapidly growing domestic market made it possible for them to develop without much investment. In the 1970s the growth of the domestic market slowed down and became unstable; consumer habits changed, consumption goods became more differentiated, and foreign competition increased even in labour-intensive, low-wage sectors, while it became essential to export more and more because of the rise in the price of oil and raw materials. The rigid organizational structure of large firms came up against the problems of a more complex capitalist society, open to the outside world, with 'European' costs, facing difficult international conditions.

5.5. *Decentralization*

'Adaptation' to changes in production conditions and in market outlets affected not only private enterprises, but the whole of society. Even though more flexible attitudes on the part of labour derived from the need to comply with external constraints, the process of decentralization undoubtedly did not meet with the type of rejection of and resistance to the outside environment that had prevailed in large firms in the 1960s. The reason for this convergence towards flexibility is twofold: first, the extension of the services and guarantees of the welfare state has created living and working conditions more consistent with an 'unstable' system of wage/labour relations.

Decentralization, based on self-employed labour, family firms, new services, and regional integration, rested heavily on both the services of the welfare state and an economic policy of adaptation and inflation: it is therefore wrong to consider it a factor of rigidity in the system. The industries with the highest productivity increases — mechanical engineering for example — were those that made the greatest use of the CIG. The emergence of new industries, self-employment, and family businesses came about partly thanks to tax evasion and exemption. The north-western regions in which small industry prospered were those in which the network of public services was best organized and most extensive.

The second reason has to do with the relationship between businesses and their environment which characterizes decentralization. The decentralization of large firms was based on the exploitation of local features as regards both the labour force and productive relations with local industry. New decentralized plants were therefore integrated into the production process at all stages, thereby realizing the advantages of size. At the same time, the fact that they were autonomous enabled them to specialize in a particular stage of the production process while differentiating their final product, having several outlets, and using the capital invested more intensively.

Decentralization and other forms of restructuring thus had regional implications, causing the growth of some regions and the decline of others; it also led to developments at the sectoral level, with numerous methods of adapting to changing circumstances. Large firms became a central means of co-ordinating independent and decentralized stages in the process of production, with the object of increasing productivity at the cost of employment. This important change in the nature of investment, aimed at achieving substantial economies in the use of labour and affecting mature industries as well as the most dynamic ones, emerged in 1976 and persisted until 1984, during which time manufacturing grew by 3.9 per cent in real terms while employment fell by 270 000 (see Table 7.6)

Faced with a rapid, sustained rise in productivity, employment continued to decrease more and more markedly over these eight years — even when growth of production was significant (as in 1984). This creates the impression that a strong inverse structural correlation has been established between the two variables which is destined to rule out any recovery in employment, even if there were to be steady growth over the next five years.

Sectors that began to restructure at an early stage (food, textiles, and clothing) do not seem to have achieved a more balanced relationship between productivity and employment. The changes in the size of firms from this process of decentralization were not unambiguous. The most labour-intensive industries (textiles, clothing, footwear) and those using 'mature' technology, which are an integral part of the structure of production, have displayed a tendency towards consolidation; this derives from the concentration of employment in small- and medium-sized firms at the expense of large firms, which have vanished completely — as have most of the very small firms. The fall in employment is negligible, even though this is a period when change has affected firms of all sizes (see Table 7.7).

TABLE 7.6   *Increase in the number of employees per category of firm for the entire sector in Italy, 1971–1981 (%)*

	0–9	10–49	50–99	100–499	500–999	1000 and over
1. Food	+0.4	−0.6	−0.5	+2.3	−0.6	−1.1
2. Textiles	+7.7	+6.9	−0.2	−4.4	−5.7	−4.2
3. Clothing	−3.9	+14.2	−0.5	−6.16	−2.8	−1.8
4. Footwear	−7.7	+11.1	−0.2	−3.0	−0.3	—
5. Iron & steel	—	+3.6	−2.0	−2.4	+3.7	+0.7
6. Mechanical eng.	+3.0	+5.4	—	−3.8	−2.6	−2.0
7. Motor vehicles	+0.8	+1.7	−0.1	+3.0	−1.0	−4.4
8. Other transport equipment	+1.6	+1.4	−0.7	−1.4	+7.2	−10.0
9. Electric eng.	+0.2	+3.6	−0.2	+1.4	+2.7	−6.7
10. Rubber	+3.0	+6.8	+3.3	−1.3	−2.9	−10.0
11. Chemicals	+1.6	+1.6	+0.3	+1.9	+3.4	−9.0

Source:compiled on the basis of ISTAT data, 1981 census.

The dynamic sectors are undergoing a more intense process of decentralization: on the one hand, new small firms (10–50 workers) have emerged, and on the other, the restructuring of employment in large firms (+1000 employees) has led to a greater concentration of employment in medium-sized firms, in an overall context of relative employment growth.

The size of firm towards which all industries seem to have converged is one of 10–49 employees — which seem compatible with the types of activity ascribed to the decentralized firm, combining the advantages of being less bound by legislation and trade union agreements with those of lower taxes.

5.6. *Regional effects*

The crucial difference between a strong economic and social structure and a weak one lies in the capacity to adapt. Such a capacity acquires greater importance in periods of crisis than in periods of steady growth. It is for this reason that, despite the considerable efforts made towards redistribution, and despite the crisis in the highly industrialized areas, the divergences between North and South during the period under examination were accentuated, the more so as the process of change developed.

The changes that took place in the structure of production and

TABLE 7.7 *Social security payments[a] made by the public sector administration[b] as a percentage of current total welfare spending (CS) and GNP at current rate for each year, 1960–1981*

Year	Pensions and income[c]		Unemployment benefit plus CIG		Family allowance		Sickness maternity accident		Total current spending	
	% CS	% GNP	% CS	% GNP	% CS	%GNP	% CS	% GNP	% GNP	% GNP/ per capita
1960	54.4	4.7	2.4	0.2	41.2	1.1	4.8	0.4	8.6	8.0
1965	61.7	7.2	2.9	0.3	20.9	2.4	4.9	0.9	11.2	10.5
1970	68.3	7.6	1.7	0.2	14.0	1.7	9.4	0.6	11.1	10.3
1975	69.0	9.2	4.4	0.1	13.6	1.8	6.3	0.8	11.3	13.1
1980	70.5	10.8	4.2	0.4	7.2	0.9	4.2	0.6	13.7	13.8
1981	81.6	11.6	4.8	0.8	6.1	1.0	5.0	0.8	16.6	16.6

[a] Excluding health and medical care.
[b] Excluding the rest of the economy.
[c] Including invalidity, industrial accidents, old age, and survivors.

Source: compiled on the basis of ISTAT data and the *Report on the State of the Economy.*

employment had significant regional consequences, altering the geographical distribution of employment, in line with the changes observed in methods of production.

The recession has especially affected large industrial firms and social services, the latter as regards both costs and demand. Consequently, even regions containing large conurbations with an industrial base have been particularly hit by the fall in employment and by the unavoidable pressure on social services that resulted from it. For the first time since the war, there was a considerable fall in employment in the regions in the industrial triangle. The structure of employment shifted in favour of the service sector. The crisis, however, was confined to employment and did not extend to industrial production, so that the effect on regional income was limited.

The decentralization of large firms and the increase in importance of small firms in both the industrial and the tertiary sectors has spread to the north-western and central regions. These were regions devoid of large urban and industrial centres, characterized by a highly homogeneous, stable social structure and reinforced by an extensive network of social services. The economic structure of these areas was quite diverse, with a high degree of integration between sectors and a productive organization that facilitated shifts of seasonal labour between sectors.

These central and northern regions, from Venetia to the Marches, have gained from the process of industrial change and growth in services: they have enhanced their share of production in these sectors, have avoided job losses, and enjoy a higher growth rate. The growth of these areas extends as far as the two eastern coastal regions of the Mezzogiorno which are without large conurbations, along a geographical line that goes from Venetia and Emilia to the extreme South, covering about a quarter of the Mezzogiorno.

The most dramatic effects of the crisis are concentrated in the most densely populated regions of the Mezzogiorno, such as the large urban centres of Naples and Palermo, and above all in the mountainous rural areas (with poor agriculture and sheep farming). There are several reasons for this:

- the concentration in these regions of large crisis-torn primary industries — chemical and metals;
- the lack of an industrial restructuring process (see Table 7.8);
- the highest growth rate in the working population: approximately 200 000 new workers each year;
- the growth of underemployment in agriculture, and the resulting contraction of this sector's productivity;
- the freeze on emigration abroad and the slowing-down of internal emigration.

TABLE 7.8 *Increases in productivity (P) and employment (E) in some manufacturing sectors in Italy, 1970–1984 (average annual rates of increase)*

Sector	1970–75		1976–81		1982–84	
	P	E	P	E	P	E
Chemicals	3.2	3.6	8.5	−1.2	+11.5	−7.3
Metal products	−0.8	1.1	3.4	0.2		
Industrial machinery	0.6	1.8	2.6	0.3	+0.1*	−2.4*
Vehicles	0.6	2.0	5.4	1.0	+13.4	−8.2
Foodstuffs	3.4	0	4.7	−0.1	+2.5	−1.5
Textiles clothing, leather goods	2.3	−1.4	6.0	−0.5	−6.7	−2.1

* For these years only aggregate data are available, which also include the items 'office machinery, precision tools' and 'electrical material and supplies'.

The adverse development of those factors that determine the size of the work-force — demography and emigration — meant that the Mezzogiorno accounted for almost 70 per cent of the new supply of labour, with an unemployment rate twice that of the rest of Italy, concentrated in the large overpopulated cities, with production less and less well adapted to demand.

5.7. Those in employment and those without — a growing disparity

Up until 1981, the changes described took place within an overall framework of stable employment. Major job losses were small and occurred in the textile industry, where there was a great deal of unregistered labour, and in the iron and steel industry, which probably felt the effects of energy-saving. On the whole, up until 1981, output in manufacturing increased (+2.1 per cent), even though employment fell; while in services employment rose more than output (+5 per cent as against +2.8 per cent).

Export-led growth, in a context where devaluation was impracticable, accentuated a growing divergence between protected sectors and those exposed to competition. The relative growth of employment in services therefore was not only the effect of the 'third technological revolution' but, more mundanely, also the result of the fact that service industries

were able to alter prices and thus employment levels, while manufacturing industry was less and less able to do so. Therefore it was not the
irresistible drive for productivity growth that shifted relative value added
to services, but their own lower sensitivity to competition.

The 1981–4 recession seems to have shattered the somewhat precarious
and inadequate employment equilibrium and to have hit industrial
employment and real income. Over 450 000 jobs were lost, and the share
of manufacturing in total value added declined by 4 percentage points.
There was a net increase in jobs between 1973 and 1984 (+1.3 million),
but it was way below the increase in the work-force (+2.5 million) (see
Fig. 7.1).

There were very marked changes in the labour market during this
period, reflecting the tenacious defence of jobs by middle-aged employees
and the flexibility introduced by the increased importance of women
workers and the self-employed. The rate of unemployment, stationary at
around 4.5–5 per cent up until 1974, suddenly began to rise, and by the
end of 1984 had risen to over 10 per cent of the work-force.

The most serious aspect concerns the structure of unemployment; even
in 1973, 60 per cent of the unemployed were less than 25 years of age; at
the end of 1984, 76 per cent of the unemployed were under 30 and 52 per
cent of them were women. The concentration of employment in the
central age bands means that 70 per cent of the unemployed are people
seeking their first job, and that the turnover between employment and
unemployment is at an all-time low and has declined throughout the
decade. Voluntary redundancy is almost non-existent, while in other
European countries it is normal practice.

Second, this has in its turn produced a reversal of the historical trend
in the ratio of employees to the self-employed. At the same time, while
self-employment fell by over 2.8 million between 1960 and 1973,
predominantly in agriculture, between 1973 and 1984 self-employment
rose by about 1 million, mainly in services. If it is borne in mind that
employed labour in Italy is about two-thirds the average of the European
countries, and that self-employment is more than double, this trend
appears even more extraordinary.

The spread of self-employment also has social and political implications of enormous relevance for industrial relations. It is synonymous
with a change in the social role of the family, which, from being a
spending unit, has now also become a production unit: this has brought
considerable changes in labour organization; it provides a response to the
demand for flexibility that other production units cannot match in terms
of part-time, seasonal, and freelance work.

171 - 88

W. GERMANY

8220 8320
8240 8242
8300 8250
9150 8760
8750

8

Crisis Despite Flexibility: The Case of West Germany

Gerhard Leithäuser

1. A System Undermined by the Crisis

In West Germany, the key institutional feature around which wage/labour relations are organized is the highly developed system of collective agreements. Compared with other European countries, collective agreements in West Germany seem very sophisticated in the way in which they operate and in terms of the well tried arbitration procedure they incorporate. This institutional system of collective agreements has allowed the growth of both productivity and real wages to be efficiently controlled. The social costs of such control have been relatively low if we take the number of working days lost through strikes as a yardstick. The system has always been a solid basis for industrial consensus in West Germany. It has not, however, been able to prevent falling growth rates of both value added and productivity.

Productivity growth was remarkably constant up until 1974, but since then the growth rate has declined, increasingly so after 1979. This change in productivity growth was preceded by a fall in the growth of value added in 1973. The two phenomena are linked, although the nature of the link is controversial.

The system of wage/labour relations, therefore, was an efficient institution and mechanism up until 1973. From that date, the crisis began progressively to undermine both the way in which the system functions and the way in which it is organized. The fall in productivity was accompanied by a slow-down in growth and even a fall in real wages. The decline in domestic demand that ensued could not be counteracted.

A more traditional point of view is that crises are synonymous with a falling rate of profit. In the long run, there is certainly a downward trend which follows rather closely what has happened to economic activity (see Schmidt *et al.*, 1984). The crisis that began in 1973 was clearly responsible for accelerating the decline in profitability, which fell below 10 per cent at the beginning of the 1980s, although only for two years.

Studies show a close link between profitability and the rate of investment (defined as the ratio of capital investment to gross value added), although the latter falls more steeply than profitability. A fall in investment is accompanied by an underutilization of capacity. Low productivity growth and low investment are therefore two marked features of the recession. The third is the growth of unemployment.

It is growth of unemployment that is the most prominent consequence of the crisis in West Germany: only 0.7 per cent in 1970, it reached 4.8 per cent in 1975–6 and then declined to 3.8 per cent in 1980. From 1980 onwards it increased rapidly and continuously, reaching 9.5 per cent in 1983. However, unemployment has received scant attention from politicians, who have been more concerned with balancing the budget and bringing down inflation. In particular, the recession of the early 1980s was accompanied by a pro-cyclical policy which reinforced it.

On the whole, the country has not faced up to the crisis very well as far as the basic institutions of the system of wage/labour relations are concerned. Falling internal demand could not be counteracted. Management procedures have not been seriously affected by joint management or works councils. Although working time is included in collective agreements, the unions are too weak to gain any further reduction in the working week (see Fig. 8.1).

Unemployment has permanently weakened union bargaining power. In fact, it seems to have been the catalyst to transform wage/labour relations. This change is part of a process of bypassing existing institutions. A large proportion of the decisions affecting wage/labour relations are not covered by collective agreements. This process is aimed at increasing the flexibility of the economy, in the face of changes in the world economy and technology. By flexibility we mean the ability of the German economy to adjust quickly to domestic and external fluctuations. West Germany is a country in a state of evolution; changes in wage/labour relations are taking place very gradually and are difficult to recognize and interpret. The consequences of these changes have not yet shown up clearly in any statistics.

In short, in West Germany it can be said that the process of change in the system of wage/labour relations is as follows. During the crisis, management and government have increasingly questioned certain aspects of the system. Because of this, the ability of the system to withstand the crisis has been diminished. The system has not collapsed — either it has been modified, or existing institutions have been bypassed.

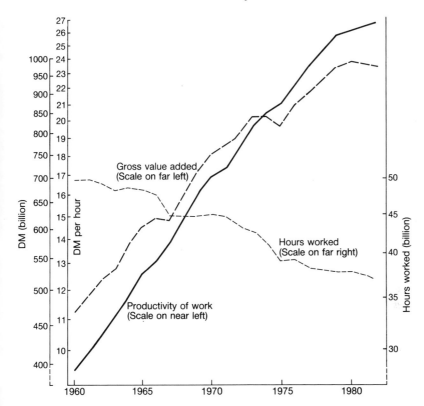

Fig. 8.1. Production, hours worked, and productivity of firms in West Germany. (*Source*: Klodt, 1984, p. 13)

2. The 1960s — Sophisticated Collective Bargaining Procedures with No State Involvement

Industrial relations in West Germany are the result of laws passed during the Weimar Republic. A brief résumé of the system of collective agreements in force in West Germany will help in understanding the ritual of negotiation. Collective agreements are based on a legal framework, the foundation of which was laid in 1949 and amended in 1974. The rich experience of more than 30 years of practice, plus substantial legislation, have helped make the German system of collective agreements a sophisticated industrial procedure capable of solving industrial disputes.

The main objectives of collective agreements are:

- to protect individual workers from all-powerful employers;
- to organize industrial relations over a specified period of time;
- to prevent industrial disputes and to promote harmonious industrial relations.

Basic collective agreements exist that determine general questions such as working conditions as well as, in many cases, the length of the working week, but are concerned above all with questions of pay. Basic collective agreements usually last several years, whereas normal collective agreements currently last for one year.

Although collective agreements are drawn up between unions and employers' organizations, they also benefit workers who do not belong to unions. The two parties try to resolve their disputes without state involvement; the two sides of industry therefore work together to ensure industrial peace, helped by the 40 000 or so collective agreements currently in force.

West German unions exert an important moderating influence on economic and social conflict. There are 17 unions within the confederation of German unions (DGB), organized according to industrial sector. On the other hand, there is also an employer's organization (DAG), which is not organized by industrial sector but follows the same collective bargaining procedures. There are also a few small unions that are not affiliated to the DGB, but these are relatively unimportant. The degree of union membership is not known exactly, although it is estimated at around 40 per cent of the work-force. At the beginning of the 1970s union membership seemed to be diminishing slightly, but currently it seems to be increasing.

There are many more employers' organizations representing particular activities within a given sector. These are organized regionally at the *Land* level as well as the national level. The two most important are the Confederation of German Industry (DBI) and the Confederation of German Employers' Associatons (BDA), the latter representing all the employers' associations. Approximate 80 per cent of all employers belong to an association. Although the organizational structures of their professional bodies are more complicated than those of trade unions, their decision-making structures are remarkably efficient. The employers' associations possess a bureaucratic structure with an unknown number of employees. They are capable of organizing well timed lock-outs at regional or national level and are able to exclude members who express internal dissent.

The state plays virtually no role in the collective bargaining process, with the exception of public services, where it merely adopts the role of employer. Fig. 8.2 depicts the rules of the game of an industrial dispute.

After a collective agreement has expired, employees and management

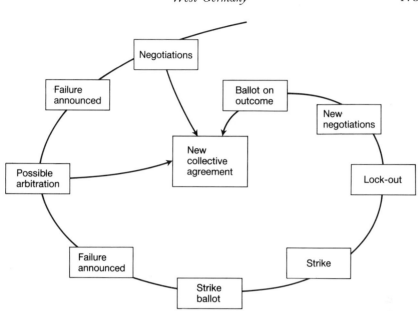

Fig. 8.2. The collective bargaining process in West Germany.

confront each other and a negotiation procedure takes places as depicted in Fig. 8.2. The unions make their claims. The employers' association rejects them and makes counter-proposals, which are sometimes followed by a warning strike. In general, a new collective agreement results from this procedure. If a compromise cannot be found, one of the sides declares the negotiation to have failed. At this stage the two sides might agree on an arbitration procedure and an arbitrator, which then might lead to a new agreement. On the other hand, if no compromise can be reached, then one of the sides can declare the arbitration procedure to have failed. This declaration is followed by a strike ballot. A strike begins if the workers vote in favour (a 75 per cent majority is usually necessary). Often management hits back with a lock-out. Fresh negotiations then begin, on the basis of which a ballot on ending the strike takes place, which is successful if 25 per cent of the workers vote in favour. The result of this procedure serves as a basis for a new collective agreement.

As a general rule, collective agreements are concluded at regional level, that is within 'collective agreement regions'. Negotiations begin and industrial disputes are settled at this level. The other regions often copy, with minor changes, what has been achieved in the key region. Union statutes make provision for a referendum or a vote by the 'grand commission responsible for collective agreements'. Rejection is very rare.

The apparatus of the unions has a tight authoritative hold on the organization and proceeds with quite remarkable efficiency.

Unions have only a very limited influence on management procedures through collective agreements. In some collective agreements, usually the basic ones, there are clauses protecting elderly workers from dismissal, guarantees against the effects of rationalization, declarations of intent on improving the working environment, and agreements on social plans in the event of dismissal or the closing down of a company.

Nevertheless, it seems that management and unions need to pit themselves against each other from time to time in order to reassure their own organizations and members, as well as to prove the advantages of negotiated solutions to each other. Strikes and lock-outs are only a last resort.

3. Higher Wages and Reduced Working Time — The Main Goals of Strike Activity

The unions and management in West Germany are perhaps readier to fight than might generally be believed abroad. There has been a large number of disputes, but the number of workers taking part has been relatively low, owing to their regional nature. The motivation behind major strikes has not always been to do with wages, as can be seen in the following brief summary of the history of strikes and their objectives (based on material from the Bundesminister für Arbeit):

1951	Wage increases and joint management
1953–4	Wage increases
1955	5-day week
1956	5-day week and paid sick leave
1963	Wage increases
1969	Wildcat strikes for wage increases
1971	Wage increases
1974	Wage increases
1978	Protection against rationalization measures
1979	Reducing hours of work
1984	35-hour week

A reduction in hours of work has been an important issue in West German industrial disputes. In 1955–6 the struggle for the five-day week was, on the whole, successful. From the 1970s on, the length of the working week in collective agreements was around 40 hours. The number of hours actually worked has decreased steadily in line with the reduction in the working week imposed by collective agreements.

Table 8.1 describes this change. It shows that the reduction in the working week has been made possible by the growth of productivity. Productivity per man-hour has increased over the past two decades although the rate of growth has tended to decrease. Productivity growth can lead to an increase in real wages and/or a reduction in working time. Column (6) of the table shows that the increase in real wages has, on the

TABLE 8.1 *Wages and productivity in German industry (% growth), 1963–1983*

	Nominal hourly wage (1)	Cost of living (2)	Real hourly wage (3)	Hourly productivity (4)	Terms of trade (5)	Position of real wages (6)
1963	8.0	2.9	5.1	6.5	−0.2	−1.2
1964	9.4	2.5	6.9	8.5	0.1	−1.7
1965	10.5	3.2	7.3	5.2	0.0	2.1
1966	8.0	3.6	4.4	4.4	0.1	−0.1
1967	4.3	1.4	2.9	7.7	−0.1	−4.7
1968	5.7	1.3	4.4	5.9	0.3	−1.8
1969	10.2	2.1	8.1	6.7	0.4	−1.0
1970	16.9	3.2	13.7	6.6	0.1	7.0
1971	12.4	5.2	7.4	5.5	0.6	−1.3
1972	9.8	5.3	4.5	7.7	0.2	−3.4
1973	12.9	6.8	6.1	6.3	−0.3	0.2
1974	14.7	6.7	8.0	4.1	−1.8	5.7
1975	9.4	6.1	3.3	4.5	0.6	−1.8
1976	5.8	4.4	1.4	7.1	−0.5	−5.3
1977	8.6	3.5	5.1	4.3	0.0	0.8
1978	6.8	2.5	4.3	3.6	0.9	−0.2
1979	6.9	3.9	3.0	5.2	−1.0	−1.2
1980	8.4	5.3	3.1	1.5	−1.5	3.1
1981	6.4	5.9	0.5	3.6	−1.2	−1.9
1982	4.2	5.2	−1.0	2.9	0.5	−4.4
1983	2.7	2.9	−0.2	3.2	0.6	−2.8

Source: Bundesminister fuer Arbeit, Sachverstaendigenrat, 1984.

whole (with the notable exceptions of 1970 and 1974), been less than the rate of productivity growth.

In the long run, therefore, the performance of the German economy has to a certain extent allowed a reduction in working time, and collective agreements have had the effect of broadly indexing wages to the growth of productivity.

On the whole, the system of wage/labour relations has represented a good framework, and has thereby to some extent been responsible for relatively stable growth of productivity and real wages. Conflicts over the distribution of productivity growth were controlled with relative ease by the institutional framework prevailing in the 1960s and 1970s.

Those responsible for determining wages have necessarily concentrated on short-term objectives, that is, nominal wages. Forecasts of the rate of inflation have played a dominant role in negotiations between the two sides of industry. Since 1975, unemployment has also had an influence on wages, although the tightness of the labour market as expressed by the percentage of job vacancies has always played a short-term role in wage determination (see Gerstenberger, 1984, especially p. 266).

Wages, therefore, vary in line with macroeconomic variables such as the rate of productivity growth and the rate of inflation. The result is that wage differentials between sectors of trades remain very stable, even rigid. This phenomenon has been subject to criticism in that it does not take account of the need for structural change in the West German economy, especially as regards the introduction of new technology and the adaptation of training to such technology. On the other hand, the level of wages does differ between sectors according to the level of productivity. Thus, someone employed in oil-refining is about 30 per cent better off than someone working in the textile industry.

Collective agreements are concerned almost exclusively with the labour market. Most importantly, they stipulate nominal wages and, to a lesser extent, hours of work. To a certain extent, they control the laws on dismissal. In a more general respect, they set down the legal conditions for contracts of employment. To a lesser extent, they include clauses on working conditions. German unions have yet to make any significant or definitive breakthrough as far as the management of production is concerned. There are two other institutions that could potentially influence this: works councils, elected by the workers, and joint management bodies. However, so far, the role of these institutions has been largely confined to helping convince workers that identification of their interests with those of management, even if only partially, is the best means of guaranteeing increases in real wages.

4. A Constant Rate of Female Participation and the Use of Foreign Workers as a Means of Adapting to Economic Fluctuations

Against this background, it is of some interest to review changes in the working population. From the 1960s onwards this showed little change, and only at the end of the 1970s was a slight increase in its growth evident. This had an effect on activity rates, which fell between the 1960s and late 1970s and then showed a slight increase. Female activity rates, that is the proportion of women belonging to the labour force, changed in a similar way but not to the same extent. The long-term stability of female activity rates, at around 30 per cent, is a characteristic peculiar to West Germany.

In this context, it is interesting to examine employment changes by sector over the past two decades. The fall in employment in agriculture is not surprising. On the other hand, the proportion employed in industry, in the broad sense of the word, has remained relatively stable, at a far higher level than in other industrialized countries. The stability of manufacturing is even more evident. The proportion of the working population employed in this sector has remained at about 35 per cent throughout the past two decades. West Germany can be considered an over-industrialized country in which de-industrialization must eventually occur, but this is difficult to carry out in a period of stagnation. As in all other industrialized countries, the proportion of the working population employed in services is increasing, but it exceeded 50 per cent only at the start of the 1980s. From then onwards, relative de-industrialization (defined as a decrease in the numbers employed in industry and a growth of the numbers employed in services) has accelerated. The restructuring of the West German economy could add to the numbers of unemployed since it is increasingly difficult for labour to transfer from industry to services.

In West Germany the relationship between employment and economic activity is different for Germans than for so-called 'guest workers'. Employment fluctuates much less for German workers than for foreign workers. Between 1974 and 1975 the number of the latter employed in industry fell by over 20 per cent, whereas the number of German workers fell by only a few per cent (DIW, 1983, p. 25). However, the recovery of 1977–80 had much less effect than the recessions of 1974–6 and 1981–3. There is now a tendency towards growth without job creation. The dependence of foreign workers' jobs on the state of the economy also indicates the insecurity of their contractual position, whose increasing flexibility is judged desirable by employers' organizations.

The increase in wages slowed down during the 1970s and 1980s. At the start of the 1970s there was a veritable explosion of gross nominal wages, which led to a growth of net wages. In the 1980s, however, the growth of gross and net wages has been low, and in real terms, after inflation, net wages have fallen. The growth in transfers has been similar and could not, therefore, prevent the fall in growth rates or indeed the reduction in net real disposable income, which has been associated with a fall in the savings ratio.

5. The Growth of Social Spending in the Crisis

Financing the growth in the social wage has put a heavy burden on the gross wages resulting from collective agreements. Between 1960 and 1982 the ratio of income tax to gross pay increased by a factor of approximately three. The ratio of national insurance payments and employers' contributions increased considerably over the same period. As a result, there was growing hostility on the part of employers towards the 'welfare state', echoed by certain types of workers on relatively high incomes.

Changes in the social wage are linked to changes in gross nominal wages. Any increase in gross nominal wages is followed by an increase in taxes levied on wages and an increase in the social wage. This link can, to a certain extent, reduce the effectiveness of demand management policies, since to increase net wages requires — allowing for savings — a considerable increase in gross wages and leads to an increase in the social wage, which has a perverse effect on the structure of expenditure.

It seems that the fall in growth, or stagflation, means that a new method of managing the social wage is required. The lack of any relationship between the growth of the social wage and other economic variables needs to be corrected, but no solution is yet in sight. After the experience of the Nazi years, employers' organizations and unions have always been jealous of their autonomy in making collective agreements. The state has virtually no legal basis for intervening in collective bargaining, apart from a few general conditions concerning the length of the working day and week, child and female labour, night work, working on Sundays, etc. The 'industrial surveillance offices' monitor conditions at work quite effectively. From the 1960s up to the present, short-term contracts have never had a well defined legal basis.

West Germany has no legal minimum wage fixed by the state. The minimum wage is an indirect result of collective agreements. The state has no direct control over dismissals, and the opportunity for works councils' to intervene is also very limited.

The social wage in West Germany is based on institutions set up by Bismarck and is composed of old age, sickness, unemployment, and accident benefits. The development of these forms of benefit will be only briefly outlined here. The number of people paying contributions and receiving benefit increased toward the end of the 1970s. Between 1969 and 1978, the number of people covered increased from 70 to 84 per cent for old age pensions, from 63 to 79 per cent for sickness benefit, and from 60 to 80 per cent for unemployment benefit. This trend has placed an increasingly heavy burden on wages and on employers' contributions. Improvements in the system mean that an increasing proportion of the population of working age is entitled to benefits. The fact that the vast majority of the West German population is more or less protected in this way is undeniable progress. Moreover, the rate and duration of benefit have been progressively increased and its administration has improved considerably, while state participation has not risen significantly.

Old age, sickness, and unemployment benefits have developed their own momentum, partly independent of economic circumstances, although, because of the slow-down and the stagnation of economic growth, benefits were reduced in the mid-1970s.

6. Significant Changes since 1975

It is not possible here to give an exhaustive account of West German economic policy. The 1960s were a period of subtle Keynesianism, which found its apotheosis in the 'Stability Law', which outlined the objectives of economic policy and described the instruments to be used in great detail. Administrative procedures were established. Local, regional, and national administrations worked out plans, calculating internal rates of return to put into action in the event of another recession. A new classification of the budget and particularly of expenditure was introduced in order to facilitate an anti-cyclical policy.

The Stability Law was an attempt to counter what had happened in the past, but economic trends started to change, and the law became impractical and was virtually forgotten.

6.1. From the 'Stability Law' to a pragmatic conservative policy

Fluctuations in the world economy led to the abandonment of fixed exchange rates in 1973, encouraging the introduction of a subtle monetary policy in West Germany which was practical and much less dogmatic than in either Britain or the United States. A relatively modest supply-side policy gained ground, but demand management policies were still practised through investment plans. While the two oil crises posed problems and revealed weaknesses in the German economy, they were overcome (the second with more difficulty than the first, however).

From 1975 onwards, unemployment became endemic in West Germany. It was to remain the most serious economic and social problem for some years, gradually having the most important influence on economic and social change. In the long term, it weakened the unions' and workers' bargaining power, and perhaps later on it will be seen to have undermined the operation of the system of wage/labour relations and the social gains made in the past.

The advent of the centre–right government in 1982 did not bring about the promised change, with one exception: the policy of budgetary restraint was intensified. The start of the crisis in 1975 brought growth in spending to a halt, although the relative importance of the main spending blocks was not affected. To see the changes, we must look within these blocks. In the 1960s priority was given to infrastructure. During the 1970s, social spending on education and training became more important, and spending cuts have affected mainly these areas. This restrictive policy had already been started under Chancellor Schmidt. The conservative elements of the policy were strengthened, in the sense that income was redistributed from the bottom to the top, but there was not the radical change that occurred in Britain or the United States.

Dogmatic ideological monetarism has never been seriously envisaged in West Germany, but through budgetary restriction, the centre–right government did reduce the proportion of family income dependent on transfer payments. During a serious recession, a policy of trying to balance the budget is pro-cyclical, which tends to worsen the recession. This policy inevitably contributed to weakening household demand and thereby increased unemployment. On the other hand, avoiding a substantial increase in budget deficits may have spared West Germany from an even greater increase in imports, as was the case in the United States and other countries in a similar position.

By way of conclusion, it can be stated that the new government put up only a feeble resistance to the crisis in the world economy and that it is practising a form of *laissez-faire* that is hardly new or well defined. The acceptance of massive and relatively rapidly increasing unemployment, especially among the young and immigrants, is certainly the most doubtful aspect of this policy. Indeed, adult unemployment increased from 2.6 per cent in 1979 to 7.2 per cent in 1985, and youth unemployment from 3.7 to 9.7 per cent, partly owing to demographic factors. For the same reasons, other European countries have even higher rates of youth unemployment.

6.2.   Increasing re-segmentation and demands for a 35-hour week

Faced with this situation, the unions pursued their traditional policy with the help of collective agreements. Between 1975 and 1983 they were able considerably to improve the economic and social position of those in work.

Under these conditions, one question needs to be asked: does not a union policy of this kind lead to social segregation? The unionized sector of the German economy is becoming a sort of closed shop, from which young people looking for their first job — indeed, all the unemployed — are almost barred from entering. The introduction of early retirement will affect only a tiny proportion of the work-force and will have no real effect on the situation.

The unions, however, feel the threat of massive unemployment and have responded by demanding a 35-hour week. Econometric models confirmed that this would be an appropriate means of reducing unemployment, provided it were fully implemented at one fell swoop and without wage reductions. Unemployment cannot be fully eradicated by a measure like this. The printers' and metal-workers' unions led this move, but they were not strong enough to force the introduction of a 35-hour week with such radical conditions. The government took the side of the employers, which was tantamount to a straightforward rejection of the moderate policy of reducing the working week to less than 40 hours. It is unusual for the government to take sides like this in an industrial dispute in West Germany.

The gradual introduction of the 35-hour week will have only a limited effect on reducing unemployment. Management will be able to make up for the reduction in hours worked with increased productivity. The metal-workers' union indicated at an early stage that such a compromise was possible. But this tactical change implied a strategic change in negotiations. Originally, the main objective had been the creation of new jobs; the goal is now productivity agreements linked to reducing the working week and increasing wages. Indeed, recent statistics show that productivity growth began to increase because of the slight economic upturn, and that the increase in real wages was below the increase in productivity. This gap might widen — underlining the weak bargaining position of unions. The unions are thus in the process of limiting the benefits of a reduction in the working week to their members. The problems of unemployment have become an artificial argument in the negotiations, and therefore an ideological trapping.

Employers' associations adopted a very entrenched position in the negotiations, flatly refusing any reduction in the working week. An increase in productivity linked to an increase in real wages, however, provided an opportunity for compromise. The employers' and even the government's ulterior motive seems to have been to inflict defeat on the unions so as to reduce their influence and remove some of the rigidness of wage/labour relations, thereby introducing more flexibility. The employers' counter-proposals were aimed at reducing the number of years worked through early retirement. This was to be accompanied by various compensatory measures: when production capacity had been fully utilized the number of hours worked would be increased, and in times of slack the number would be reduced.

After some of the longest and hardest strikes ever in the print and metal industries, the agreements reached introduced an element of flexibility into collective agreements. The length of the working week was fixed at between 38½ and 40 hours and is variable, at least for certain categories of worker. The actual application of the agreement is to be decided by individual companies, and is partly the responsibility of the works councils.

It is, therefore, possible to speak of a form of decentralization from regional level to company level. A new mix of centralization and decentralization has been simultaneously introduced. However, there is still the danger that the application of the agreement will vary greatly from company to company and that the position of workers vis-à-vis employers will be weakened, since the latter's power has been increased as a result of current unemployment levels. The agreement also makes provision for a modest increase of 3 per cent in nominal wages, which would keep real wages unchanged. It will act as a model for other sectors and other regions.

Companies have a tendency to practise a sort of labour market segmentation. They create gangs of 'flexible' workers, preferably young and non-unionized, who have a variable working week, depending on the level of output which in turn depends on the level of domestic and external demand. These workers are in some cases complemented by workers with an inferior status, such as part-timers or workers on short-term contracts. The labour market is thus being fragmented with workers of very different status competing for the same jobs. In the long run, this competition could undermine the gains that workers have struggled to achieve and which are embodied in collective agreements.

6.3. *Various attempts at increasing flexibility*

The Ministry of Employment has passed a law under the pretext of 'creating jobs', aimed at extending legal working hours, Sunday working, night work for women, apprenticeships, and fixed-term contracts, with the purpose of injecting more flexibility into the system in the unlikely hope of creating new jobs.

Increased flexibility tends to create, on the one hand, stable employment and, on the other, insecure jobs, the increased insecurity of female employment being a good example. Female unemployment has traditionally been higher than for other sectors of the population. The increased number of part-time jobs that materialized between 1973 and 1981 were almost all filled by women, a trend that is likely to continue particularly in service industries but also in other sectors.

In this way, more organizational forms of wage/labour relations are emerging and the status of workers is being weakened. Existing institutions may eventually become nothing more than impressive façades with nothing behind them. The new insecure flexible jobs demand new forms of industrial action. One of the major issues today is the fight for 'sovereignty over the use of time', that is, the right to participate in decisions regarding working hours and free time.

As regards the process of increasing flexibility, what happens in practice has already gone beyond existing legislation and declarations of intent. A minority group in the government 'council of wise men' has underlined the fact that every year in West Germany, 5–6 million new contracts of employment (about a quarter of the total outstanding) are registered and almost as many are terminated. Around 60 per cent of these new contracts are still of no fixed length, 16 per cent are for more than three months, and 22 per cent are for periods of less than three years. So far as women with no professional training are concerned, less than 50 per cent of them obtain contracts of no fixed length (*SVR*, 1984/5, p. 190). Where will this process of increasing flexibility end? Is it necessary to have fewer fixed-term contracts? The result will be more people taken on during upswings but more losing their jobs during recessions. However, in the long run increased flexibility will probably mean increased unemployment.

6.4. *Restraint on social spending*

The social wage has been seriously affected by restrictive budgetary measures, involving the four main types of state benefit. About 250 laws or decrees have been passed since 1982; taken as a whole, they have had a considerable effect on households that rely on transfers for a large part of their income. Family budgets have fallen by 15 per cent. The government has cut unemployment benefit, allowances for handicapped people, student grants and bursaries to school pupils, allowances to large families, maternity grants, etc. Many families have been brought close to poverty because of these budgetary cuts.

The first effects of these restrictive measures were striking. In 1983 transfers declined, despite the large increase in needs, because of the crisis. Measures to restrain social security spending were relatively effective that year. The fall in receipts can be considered quite normal in a period of increasing unemployment.

The government's intentions as regards social spending are very interesting for several reasons. First, there was a provisional budget which speaks volumes about the government's intentions. Between 1977 and 1983, the different forms of social spending remained remarkably stable in relation to GDP, the exception being unemployment benefits, which grew as the number of unemployed increased. The forecast for public spending on the unemployed for the period up to 1987 was worrying, since a fall was projected, even though unemployment was expected at best to remain stable, since growth of GDP would also be limited. The government was, therefore, seriously considering a further cut in unemployment benefit. Social spending, and its main components, should fall. Budgetary restraint would continue, and state intervention in the economy would diminish. The slogan 'less state' is obviously taken seriously by the government. Nevertheless, the examples of the United States and the United Kingdom show that the long-term maintenance of such policies is very difficult.

The centre–right government has now well defined theories underlying its economic policy. It makes do with vague slogans based on neoclassical theory — less state, more market; more responsibility to individuals and families; break down rigidities, increase flexibility, and praise the value of work. Behind this smoke-screen of conservative slogans is a policy of balancing the budget which could be pursued for some considerable period of time. Introduced little by little, there is a strong chance that it will have the long-term effect of making large sections of the German population poor.

Moreover, judgements made by industrial tribunals seem to have become more restrictive and to have gone against the interests of workers and unions. One judgement considerably reduced the participation of workers councils in decisions concerning the introduction of new technology. Another judgement banned compensation for workers made unemployed indirectly as a result of lock-outs by firms supplying their company, which is contrary to past practice.

Over the past few years, the ideological climate in West Germany has been changing. There has been growing indifference to the ideas and organizations of the left. Surveys have shown that the collective consciousness of the workers in Germany has been affected by this (Zoll, 1984). Their commitment to unions seems to have declined considerably over recent years.

7. Conclusion: Flexibility by the Back Door or Enshrined in Collective Agreements?

The social features of the system of wage/labour relations in Germany (collective agreements in particular) have become increasingly synonomous with obstacles to further growth. The concept of flexibility is linked to neo-classical ideas of the Invisible Hand of unfettered market forces. Flexibility is required by the international market, which is very fluid and difficult to analyse or predict. In addition, too much rigidity prevents the introduction of new technology.

Lost market share should be regained through new high-tech products, but in this respect the German economy is not outstanding. Recent surveys have shown that Germany is having problems coping with competition from the United States and Japan on new products, while it is also under severe pressure from imports of older products from newly industrialized countries.

German technology is lagging behind in both microelectronics and biotechnology, which are considered to be the basis for future products. In the 1960s and 1970s West Germany concentrated its research expenditure on nuclear power. It has become increasingly obvious that this was a mistake, which has adversely affected the other areas. A certain degree of flexibility is also becoming evident in investment. Leasing of plant and machinery is growing rapidly, which is clearly a means of increasing flexibility. Indeed, the leasing of equipment, which represented 11 per cent of all industrial spending in 1972, touched 22 per cent in 1980.

In 1985–6, West Germany experienced a weak, but real, upturn. But the recession that preceded these years was not utilized to improve international competitiveness. Thus, the country fell further behind in the drive towards national and international restructuring.

The general increase in flexibility of the German economy could help industrial restructuring, the introduction of new technology, and the country's position in world markets. Increased flexibility of wage/labour relations, achieved by segmenting the labour market through such means as differential contracts of employment (collective agreements on one side and part-time work on the other), could also rekindle industrial disputes, even in times of massive unemployment. There seem to be many possible forms of flexibility within the framework of the collective agreements that have still not been tested or explored. The destruction of the existing system of wage/labour relations and its replacement with a system where individualized work contracts held sway would require long and arduous industrial disputes. These would hardly be conducive to essential restructuring: in fact, they would put it off even longer.

The battle for the 35-hour week shows the dangers in this area. Without negotiating seriously, the two sides became entrenched, with management having the ulterior motive of inflicting a defeat on the unions but without being able to change the system of wage/labour relations once and for all. In the long term, reductions in annual hours worked (see Fig. 8.1) and a fall in effective hours worked per week are inevitable. However, there are many possible solutions that would not necessarily destroy or discredit existing institutions. The long strikes in the printing and metal industries in 1984 showed that the transformation of wage/labour relations is taking place within, or rather bypassing, existing institutions, the total destruction of which seems unlikely. Moreover, the changes are in the direction of increased flexibility.

Because of its extension into German society, and its importance, the policy of increasing flexibility deserves careful consideration. Does it not entail a strengthening of the economic and social power of business, both within business and in society as a whole? Does not such a policy lead to a new distribution of opportunity, to the detriment of social groups that bear the brunt of increasingly insecure jobs?

Part II

Which Model Should Europe Follow?

Introduction

The chapters of Part I bring to light a central theme: the fact that since the mid-1960s changes in the system of wage/labour relations, the economic crisis, and the conduct of economic policy have been closely interrelated. On the one hand, whether because of internal factors or because of imbalances caused by the world-wide crisis, the slow-down of growth destabilized industrial relations and at times made the central principles of the Fordist system of wage/labour relations seem like rigid dogmas. Procedures for indexing wages on the basis of past inflation, the principle of sharing out productivity gains, the guarantees associated with contracts of employment, and the hierarchy of qualifications and employment rigidities have thus become the focus of debate.

On the other hand, these varied and complex changes in the system of wage/labour relations have also had an effect on the determinants of economic activity. A marked slowing-down in the growth of real wages reduces the growth of domestic demand, which is more or less completely compensated by a growth in exports. But, while a strategy of trying to increase competitiveness by this means might make sense from the point of view of each nation considered individually, it has obvious limitations when applied generally. Thus, at one stage removed, this intensification of international competition has repercussions on each country's economic policy, enforcing more restrictive fiscal and monetary policies, encouraging companies and government to look for ways of bypassing existing legislation, and stimulating a search for other more flexible ways of organizing labour, wages, and employment.

We do not claim that this description is exhaustive or that the conclusions drawn are definitive. In the first place, the structural changes currently taking place are difficult to understand, and, quite apart from changes in labour law and government legislation, we still know relatively little about how firms are managed and how they act, despite the countless monographs that have been published and the case studies that have been carried out. It is the interaction of these two factors that will either bring about a change in the Fordist system of wage/labour relations or lead to the emergence of something quite different (perhaps a two-tiered work-force or flexible specialization?). It is therefore difficult to be sure whether or not the postwar behavioural regularities in respect of the speed of adjustment of employment, the process of productivity growth, the formation of wages, and even the determinants of welfare transfers have broken down. Because of the relatively recent nature of institutional changes, the inevitable time taken to obtain statistical series, and the slow rate at which the system of regulation changes, the usual econometric methods do not show that any significant breakdown has occurred.

More research is needed. In the meantime, this part of the book will be confined to putting forward a few hypotheses and testing their relevance in the light of national studies. There are two especially important themes.

- How uniform are the changes in the system of wage/labour relations in the different countries? What effect do the particular socioeconomic history and environment of a country have on the way it reacts to the different 'shock-waves' caused by the world market?

- Although the pursuit of flexibility may be a general phenomenon, how far does the form that it takes vary according to the structure of production, the past pattern of labour relations, and the policy line adopted by companies and governments? If present trends continue, what are the foreseeable consequences of the different types of flexibility? How can present changes be reconciled with the need for a minimum degree of macroeconomic stability and social unity?

The various developments can be grouped together under the above two themes. Chapter 9 is concerned with the problem of convergence and specific national characteristics. It shows first that there is a remarkable similarity in the major institutional developments that have taken place since 1973 in the seven countries examined. Are these changes the result of economic policies lurching towards conservatism, an upheaval in the international system, and/or the limits of Fordism being reached and the type of growth that helped to propel it coming to an end? These questions are examined in Section 2 of Chapter 9. Given the scale of the changes that are occurring, it raises the question as to whether the need for flexibility is so widespread that it will determine the shape of the post-Fordist era. A comparison of the seven European countries, however, suggests a more subtle interpretation, in that the same term is being used to describe relatively different national developments and strategies — much more different, indeed, than the national variants of Fordism used to be (Chapter 9, Section 3).

Against this background, Chapters 10–12 set out some thoughts on the growing, infinitely variable, question of whether flexibility points the way to overcoming the crisis and curing the 'European disease' through a restoration of the dynamic of employment creation. It is essential to review the different meanings given to the term 'flexibility', which are so numerous that it is hardly surprising that its social and economic implications are themselves potentially very different and often poorly grasped. Second, we need to consider the apparent paradox that trade unions and workers who, in the 1960s and 1970s, challenged Fordist logic now often defend it against employers' proposals for more flexible methods of working. I intend to show that, as opposed to purely defensive strategies, there are much more progressive approaches, so that the clash between the old and the new is not necessarily the same as was depicted and popularized in France, for example, at the beginning of 1985. Since things are not economically or technologically predetermined in any rigid way, therefore, various developments and strategies for the recomposition of the system of wage/labour relations are possible — provided that the history and political compromises reached in each country allow it (Chapter 11).

It is possible, in conclusion, to draw up a balance sheet of Europe's strengths and weaknesses in search of an original model (of offensive flexibility or a post-Fordist system of wage/labour relations) that would stimulate economic recovery, create jobs, and, above all, preserve the principles of solidarity that are a part of this continent's history.

194-221

W. EUROPE
8250
8240
8300 0
2260
9243

9

Division or Unity?
Decline or Recovery?

Robert Boyer

1. The Similarity of Institutional Changes in the Different European Countries

In most countries, the last few years have been marked by significant changes in government policies and by experimentation with often conflicting economic and social strategies. One of the first things to emerge from the international comparison is that there are more similarities than the specific development of each country, considered in isolation, would lead us to think. The similarities relate to the general timing, direction, and nature of the misgivings about the Fordist system of wage/labour relations. But there are also similarities between the various factors underlying the changes that have occurred (Section 2 below).

1.1 The similarity in overall trends: consolidation followed by doubt

With only a few exceptions, economic policy can be divided into three successive phases, so that by the end of the period the way the crisis is presented and the system of wage/labour relations perceived has radically changed.

1. From the beginning of the 1970s onwards, governments at first regarded the increase in imbalances, and then the first oil crisis, as being localized and transitory disruptions (problems relating to raw materials, energy, interest rates, etc.) which would automatically disappear as time passed, with the help perhaps of the usual stabilization policies. So they sustained employment through subsidies and extended benefits to people made redundant, which meant that, for the first time since the war, the scale of such benefits became significant. The Keynesian-inspired reflation of 1975–6, moreover, made it easier to consolidate these employment guarantees in accordance with the logic inherent in the Fordist system of wage/

labour relations. Thus, in France workers dismissed as a result of the economic situation had a recognized right to an allowance equivalent to 90 per cent of their wages, and employment subsidies expanded greatly. Similarly, in Italy during the same period, the law provided a guaranteed income to employees affected by industrial restructuring, while full indexation replaced the previous system of proportional adjustment. In Belgium too, a social agreement conforming to the old way of thinking was signed in 1975, even though the recession was beginning to change the balance of power between employers and trade unions.

2. Between 1977 and the beginning of the 1980s, most of these trends began to be reversed, although the precise timing varied between countries. The European economies did not recover their previous rates of growth, as high inflation and the difficulty of regaining external balance greatly reduced the possibility of expansion, whether unilateral or co-ordinated, as in 1978. It was in this period that the idea emerged that wages were above all a *cost* detrimental to competitiveness and company profits. As the disequilibrium theory would have it, unemployment is essentially *classical* (i.e. related to real wages exceeding productivity) and no longer only Keynesian (caused by insufficient effective demand in relation to production at full-employment levels) (see Bénassy, 1984). As a result, governments tried to moderate wage demands so as to reduce inflation while reviving investment by shifting income in favour of companies. There were the first attempts to revise indexation clauses. For example, it was suggested that prices of value added instead of consumption should be used as a reference in order to neutralize the effects of changes in terms of trade. More significantly still, the government aim seemed to be to maintain the purchasing power of wages as far as possible, abandoning the old principle of sharing out productivity gains. Initially, however, this stabilization of real wages was presented as something that was to last only one or two years and not as a new and lasting rule governing the formation of incomes. At the same time, employment policy was based not so much on job creation (if only because the number of jobs in industry plummeted and the growth of the tertiary sector slowed down greatly) as on broadly based programmes aimed at reducing labour market supply (early retirement schemes, attempts to influence the pattern of female work, raising the school-leaving age, etc.) or on improving the adaptation of skills to new jobs (youth training schemes, retraining, etc.).

3. At the beginning of the 1980s, the failure of these policies to improve the situation rapidly led to a revision of the diagnosis of the crisis

and of ways of overcoming it. The emergence of this third phase can be explained largely by pressure from an unfavourable economic situation. Two examples of this can be given. First, in the United Kingdom, the last Labour government was forced to reverse its policy completely and advocate wage restraint — even before its defeat by the Conservatives, who had an explicit electoral policy of reducing the power of the trade unions in Britain. But at the beginning of the 1970s the Labour Party also had looked to the reform of labour relations as a solution to slow productivity growth. France provides a second, equally striking, example. After May 1981, the coming to power of a left-wing government led to (moderate) recovery and a desire to extend social benefits, a strategy aimed at re-establishing more sustained growth and, therefore, reducing unemployment. This attempt to bring the crisis to an end in a single country ran up against adverse developments in the world economy and internal constraints associated with continuing inflation, lost competitiveness, and, more generally, the end of the postwar phase of economic growth (see Chapter 1 above). Thus, the government was forced gradually to revise its analysis and strategy, first in June 1982 and then in March 1983 — much later, that is, than the other European countries.

In this respect, the crisis now appears to be a lasting, structural one, calling for major changes in the productive system, state management, monetary creation, and, of course, the system of wage/labour relations itself. Combating inflation has been given priority, while increased unemployment is reducing the bargaining power of trade unions. Most of the restrictive measures introduced in the second phase have thus been reinforced and extended so much that a new orthodoxy has emerged in the mid-1980s: namely, that the labour relations inherited from the past form one of the main obstacles to overcoming the crisis.

1.2. The rejection of almost all the elements in the system of wage/labour relations

The studies of the different countries agree in diagnosing four major changes.

1. The Taylorian and Fordist concepts of labour organization seem increasingly rigid, given the variability in the level and composition of demand. In fact, the pursuit of economies of scale by incorporating specialized equipment in the productive process has obvious limit-ations, either because markets become saturated or because it is difficult to manage the labour force in large production units. Thus, generally in Europe, small plants have grown in importance,

especially in Italy, where job losses in large industrial plants have gone hand in hand with the decentralization of production. The pursuit of flexibility is also important in Germany. It seems that no European country has escaped this change in what was one of the central features of postwar growth.

2. At the same time, the former hierarchy of skills and employment guarantees is being affected by the technical changes taking place and the highly changeable economic situation. Thus, the various employment developments (crisis in the primary products industry, the tendency towards stagnation of the traditional durable goods market, the growth of employment in a small number of new industries, etc.) are calling into question the structure of skills and pattern of wages. It is a change of some importance: whereas in the 1960s wage increases spread from 'locomotive' sectors throughout most of the system, nowadays relative wages are tending to become once again one of the means of micro- and macroeconomic adjustment. At the same time, the old employment guarantees are now seen by companies as hindering their adaptation to a somewhat unpredictable economic situation. Here again, Italy provides a good example of a complete reversal if we consider the position of workers in 1970 and the subsequent upsurge of small- and medium-sized enterprises not subject to this system of guarantees.

3. Converging developments have also had a significant effect on the formation of wages. First of all, most governments are trying to break the price–wage spiral by abandoning indexation, whether *de facto* or *de jure*. Either they order a reduction in the indexation coefficient (as in Italy in 1983 and in 1985), or they reject past inflation as the criterion of readjustment and replace it with an estimated inflation rate (as in France, Spain, etc.). In so far as this change occurs in a period of deflation, real wages go down in the transitional period. And a new wage formation principle comes in on top of the partial removal of indexation: in the medium term, governments are supposed to maintain overall purchasing power as far as possible. This then means abandoning the principle of sharing out productivity gains: in this new situation they are helping to rebuild company margins, although it is not clear if this means a change, in the medium term, in the rule that income gains are shared out. None the less, as the Italian case suggests, it would seem that we are moving towards a reversal of relations between wages and other forms of income. After 1973, wage formation based on the 'inflation-plus-productivity' formula brought about an increase in the proportion of income going to labour, but, because of

increased social security contributions and taxes, the balance tipped against profits. Since 1983, it has tilted the other way in favour of profits, allegedly necessary for the recovery of investment, so that wages now seem to have come down. This no doubt explains why the former clauses relating to the formation of wages have been downgraded or even completely rescinded. This has become a general phenomenon in Europe. The whole problem is knowing whether or not this change will last, something to which I shall return later.

4. Finally, the turnaround in ideas on social security is also remarkable. On average, European countries have more developed social security schemes than the United States or Japan, not to mention newly industrialized countries. In an era where international competition has revived, this has inevitably been cited as a hindrance to competitiveness. As a result, since the beginning of the 1980s, governments have tried to check the growth of welfare transfers, not so much by reducing average benefit rates as by rationalizing the different components of the system.

This is particularly so in the case of unemployment benefits, which were increased after 1973 but have been held down more recently, a development that can be seen in both the United Kingdom and France, where the principles and procedures for obtaining benefits were revised in 1984 and again in 1985. None the less, it is as well not to be too alarmist, since the welfare state that developed in the postwar years is being not so much dismantled as modified. Indeed, social benefits as a proportion of the GDP and household incomes are still growing, if not as rapidly as in the past. West Germany is a case in point; there, the relative stabilization of welfare benefits at the end of the period was associated with a continuing increase in the number of beneficiaries and a lowering of certain taxes, as was shown by G. Leithäuser in Chapter 8 above. This emphasizes the complexity of the changes affecting the Fordist system of wage/labour relations.

European countries, therefore, show a number of similar institutional changes as regards labour law and the formation of wages, collective bargaining, the organization of work and employment, and, finally, social security. We need to examine the determinants of this general trend and the precise forms it has taken in each national economy.

2. Factors Governing Changes in the Postwar System of Wage/Labour Relations

It is logical to think first of changes in the political arena, since overall economic strategy and labour legislation are *a priori* the result of the choices and preferences of the coalition in power. The fact that social democratic and conservative governments (or their equivalent) have tended to alternate might be thought to be the primary explanation for such changes. However, the different national experiences, which were the focus of Part I of this book, provide a much more subtle answer. On the one hand, it is true that doctrinal preferences play an obvious role in the management of the system of wage/labour relations and, more generally, of the economy. But on the other hand, the prevailing regulation, combined with the imbalances and constraints imposed by the international economy, exercises some control over the policy conducted and the reforms undertaken.

If we look at Britain, Italy, and France, it would seem that, over the medium term, economic factors are more important than political ones. In all three countries, both the continuation and the development of the Fordist system of wage/labour relations ran up against constraints in the form of a balance of payments deficit (United Kingdom), reductions in the efficiency of large enterprises (Italy), or continuing inflation and reductions in competitiveness in an unfavourable international climate (France). With or without political change, governments are being forced to reverse their initial policies. This does not mean, however, that any structural-type reform is bound to fail: industrialized countries have a history of institutional change playing a decisive role over the long term, provided it stimulates a move towards a broadly coherent system of regulation.

However, economic policy can no longer be based on the former kind of regulation, and this explains the difficulties encountered by almost all European governments in trying to counteract the unfavourable developments of the past decade. In their own way, the national studies confirm the above hypothesis that we are caught up in a structural crisis, and that these changes in economic behaviour are the reason why the system of wage/labour relations has been called into question (see Aglietta, 1976; Boyer and Mistral, 1978).

2.1. The limits to Fordism: the inherent consequences of its reaching maturity

The central thesis set out here is that a breakdown of such magnitude cannot simply be accidental, but is the result of the way things developed under Fordism. It is therefore convenient to start from the virtuous circle described in Chapter 1 (Fig. 1.1) and incorporate destabilizing factors into it (see Fig. 9.1). There are four tendencies, of varying importance, that threaten the further growth of Fordism.

1. *Increased organization of work is becoming counter-productive.* The multiplication and re-compartmentalization of jobs, as well as the recourse to highly specialized machinery, are making it more and more difficult to organize assembly lines. Thus, actual productivity tends now to be well below potential — all the more so because worker action can succeed in bringing whole plants to a halt. This is the other side of the Fordist coin. Problems with productivity growth threaten the very basis of the virtuous circle, the more so because workers' demands (even in relation to the organization of work) tend to end with increases in wages. Tensions over income distribution, inflationary pressures, and declining competitiveness join forces to throw the circular process of production–income– demand out of kilter. This is when a vicious circle may begin, with a slow-down of investment depressing productivity growth even further. Circuit no. I in Fig. 9.1 illustrates these crisis mechanisms schematically.

These seem to have been operating in the United States since the mid-1960s (Aglietta, 1976), with problems relating to the organization of work remaining at the heart of the US 'productivity puzzle' (Weisskopf *et al.*, 1983). The United Kingdom, in turn, has similar problems, albeit for considerably different reasons (Chapter 3). In addition, Italy is a particularly striking example of a country that has gone from an 'economic miracle' to an equally sensational standstill, largely related to Fordist labour demands, at least in the large industrial enterprises. This first crisis must be in conjunction with a second, no less fundamental, one which relates to the economic principles of Fordism.

2. *Mass production requires world markets.* The continued pursuit of economies of scale in the production sector leads logically to national markets being regarded as too small. At first, the growth of exports seems to be good for internal development, with mass consumption remaining the driving force. But at a second stage, once it becomes a general tendency, the very principle of national boundaries is threatened, since output and consumption tend to adjust to international levels. Hence it intensifies competition between countries, which also increases the penetration of the domestic market in the case of both durables and industrial goods. This is where a second destabilizing factor comes in: a national recovery (through wages or public expenditure) may be obstructed if national conditions of production do not conform with international

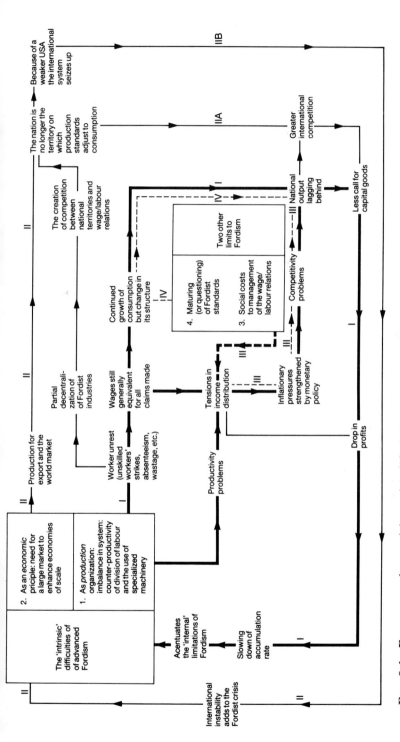

FIG. 9.1. From growth to crisis: a simplified view.

standards. Circuit II in Fig. 9.1 illustrates this second vicious circle (IIA), which may be reinforced when extended to the case of a dominant economy (IIB). The fact that Europe and Japan are catching up with US production standards helps to weaken US hegemony, and therefore to compromise the complementary nature of the growth of the different countries. This affects the international order (commercial, monetary, and financial) and makes it more difficult for second-rank countries to maintain growth.

Chapters 2–8 above confirm that the need to ensure external competitiveness made it difficult to maintain the growth enjoyed in the 1960s. Some authors see the international crisis as the main (even the sole) reason why labour relations, national Keynesian policies, and the welfare state were called into question. Indeed, previous studies of regulation encourage us to regard these two sources of crisis as part of the same process, rather than as being in conflict with one another. Two other features of Fordism also need to be taken into account in this regard.

3. *Fordism leads to growing social expenditure.* Its end purpose is none other than to incorporate wage-earners permanently not only as producers, but also as consumers, by enlarging the market. But new forms have to be found for undertaking the collective expenditure that results (e.g. education, health, pensions, urban infrastructure, housing), since the traditional means are no longer adequate. The problem is that these needs cannot usually be met by mass production, so that their relative cost tends to go up causing the proportion of public expenditure in overall consumption to increase. This becomes a problem only when the slow-down in the growth of productivity and output leads to a conflict between direct income and the social wage, private and public consumption. Hence a third crisis (circuit III of Fig. 9.1.) begins, superimposed on the others: inflationary pressures, slower growth of cash flow in companies, and so on. The studies of the seven European countries confirm that there is such a spiral, although it varies greatly, depending on how advanced the social security system is and how the growth rate has declined. In most cases this process seems to accompany the crisis rather than being its cause.

4. *Innovations in consumption diverge from standardized methods of production.* Oligopolistic competition has been associated with Fordism, based, as it is, on product differentiation, chiefly through advertising. In a second phase, consumers have been led to prefer a greater variety of use values rather than just symbolic differences. But traditional industrial processes have not found it easy to respond to this new demand, which is at odds with standardization, the basis of economies of scale, the importance of which has been indicated

above. At the same time, the postwar pattern of consumption seems to be reaching exhaustion, even if certain social groups have not yet benefited completely from it, and may still give rise to a new wave of expansion (e.g. agricultural workers, immigrants, senior citizens). The most rapidly growing items of consumption therefore no longer necessarily correspond to the old postwar 'locomotive' industries: medium- or high-technology products (videos and new electronic goods) or, on the other hand, traditional sectors which Taylorism has not succeeded in revolutionizing (e.g. medicine, education, the building industry). This is when a fourth destabilizing factor may come in: incomes distributed according to the logic of Fordism do not necessarily lead back to an increased demand for national production (circuit IV in Fig. 9.1). This divorce between production and consumption can accentuate external imbalance and make it difficult to attain previous rates of growth.

Against this background, it is possible to give a more precise explanation of three of the factors that have undermined the system of wage/labour relations.

2.2. The deterioration in the bargaining power of wage-earners

Depending on the country, this occurred either at the end of the 1970s or at the beginning of the 1980s. But, in spite of appearances, this shift in the balance of power in favour of companies is part of a number of medium- to long-term tendencies (Table 9.1).

1. *De-industrialization is affecting the strongholds of Fordism.* The new collective agreements and advances in social law started off in the motor vehicle, mechanical engineering, and basic industries. In so far as the crisis is centred on these sectors, institutional changes have affected them most of all. There can be little doubt about the reversal of trends that has occurred: since 1973 industrial investment has contracted rather than grown, and employment has fallen almost continuously for more than a decade instead of increasing slightly, as in the past (Table 9.1). Thus, slowly and gradually, one of the traditional bases of trade unionism is being eroded. What is more, the difficulties experienced by industrial enterprises often prevent them from becoming the spearhead of new wage demands.

2. *Forms of employment characteristic of the tertiary sector are gaining ground.* In one sense, the rise of services is proof of the success of Taylorist methods in industry: marketing, finance, insurance, and engineering are developing in order to keep up with mass production. However, when it comes to the system of wage/labour relations, the growth of service sector employment outside industry is not without influence.

TABLE 9.1 *Factors calling into question the wage/labour relation: deterioration in the employee situation*

	France	UK	Ireland	Belgium	Spain	Italy	West Germany
De-industrialization (average rate per annum)							
Employment							
1960–73	0.9	−0.6	2.1	0.1	n.d.	0.8	0.1
1973–81	−1.4	−2.9	2.0	−3.0	n.d.	0.0	−1.4
Creation of fixed capital							
1960–73	7.1	1.8	n.d.	4.5	n.d.	4.2	2.8
1973–81	−0.6	−2.5	n.d.	−1.9	n.d.	−2.0	0.7
Growth of the tertiary sector (% of working population)							
1973	48.9	54.6	44.2	54.7	39.0	42.5	45.2
1979	54.7	58.6	48.1	61.3	44.2	47.4	49.9
1983	58.0	63.7	51.6*	64.7*	48.4	51.6	52.4
Unemployment (%)							
1973	1.8	2.4	5.6	2.8	2.5	4.9	1.0
1979	6.0	4.9	7.4	8.4	8.5	7.5	3.3
1985	12.4	11.7	16.5	14.8	21.5	12.9	8.5
Repercussions of industrial action (no. of strikes days per 1000 employees)							
1973–79	440	501	776	238	490	1490	44
1980–82	106	313	532	69	n.d.	1095	3

* 1982

Sources: De-industrialization: Todd (1984, pp. 13–15); tertiary sector: OCDE, (1984, p. 44); unemployment: OSCE statistics in *Economie européenne*, Nov. 1984, p. 218; industrial action: ILO *Labour Statistics Handbook*, 1978–83, and *ibid. Europe sociale*, May 1984, p. 122, for the employee section.

On the one hand, the organization of work and collective bargaining are different, with subcontracting, temporary work, and part-time employment offering real competition to the Fordist type of contract. On the other hand, trade unions are encountering considerable organizational problems, because of the dispersion and the smallness of companies as much as the values that white-collar workers traditionally hold dear.

Hence the pursuit of employment growth in services far from compensates for the effect of job losses in industry, first because initiative and bargaining power lie more in the hands of management, and second because, since the beginning of the 1980s, the failure to achieve economic recovery has greatly reduced the growth of service industries. Yet the structure of employment is still undergoing a particularly rapid change: in ten years, the number of workers in the tertiary sector has gone up by between 7 and 10 percentage points, and they now account for between half (Italy) and almost two-thirds (Belgium and United Kingdom) of the working population.

3. *Unemployment has reached levels unprecedented since the interwar years.* In 1973 unemployment rates were generally less than 3 per cent in Europe, and only Italy and Ireland had levels permanently higher than this. In 1985, after a period in which countries developed rather differently, these rates were between 8.5 per cent (West Germany) and 21.5 per cent (Spain) — higher than in the United States and Japan. It is likely, therefore, that the threat of unemployment affects workers' behaviour far more than in the past: there is a clear realization that unemployment is likely to last for a long time and to be in no way comparable with anything seen in the 1960s. From a more qualitative angle, the balance between jobs and wages is becoming more and more of a consideration for companies as for governments. One of the most notable features of the Fordist virtuous circle therefore breaks down: wage increases seem to work no longer in favour of employment but against it. This is why there is a significant change in the number of industrial disputes and in the forms that they take.

4. *Fewer industrial disputes represent proof of this changed order.* At first, the crisis seems to help trade union membership, which is seen as a good way of protecting jobs and the standard of living. But, subsequently, it would seem that the influence of trade unions declines somewhat, with membership going down and their effectiveness shrinking. Even if there is no spectacular drop in membership, the failure of traditional bargaining and the difficulty in finding new aims and means of action become clear, so much so that many a specialist has described it as a crisis of trade unionism. Trade unions were necessary mediators in the old order of things, and the history of industrial action is clear proof of this. After 1978–9, the number of days lost through strikes fell considerably in almost all European countries, at least up until 1982–3 (Table 9.1). The industrial disputes in West Germany in 1984 and in the United Kingdom in 1984 and 1985 are two exceptions to this, although they

do not necessarily mark a lasting change, since they do not seem to have been resolved by a union revival!

At the same time, employers have greatly modified their management practices, as is described briefly below.

2.3. The pressure from firms to restore their financial position

The central role played in the runup to the current crisis by the growing difficulties of earning an adequate return on investment capital has already been emphasized (Fig. 9.1). In fact, these problems emerged at the end of the 1960s most clearly in West Germany and the United Kingdom, to a lesser extent in Italy, and not at all in Belgium or France, where the rate of gross profits was much higher in 1973 than in 1960 (Table 9.2). This difficulty in maintaining a high rate of investment (Table 9.1) was reinforced by the first oil crisis and became a problem in almost all European countries. Over the period 1960–82, profits tended to decline everywhere, except in Italy. Three of the characteristic features of Fordism together provide an explanation for this development.

1. *Real wages tend to grow at a faster rate than productivity.* Underlying the standard wage agreement is the notion that the standard of living can be guaranteed by explicit indexation, on the basis of an *expectation* that productivity will grow in the future. Thus, in 1974–5, and to lesser degree in 1979, the distribution of value added changed in favour of wage-earners: on the one hand, the deterioration in the terms of trade was matched by a compensatory increase in the consumer price index, and on the other hand, wages remained unaffected by lower productivity growth. As a result, the share of wages in value added rose appreciably (Table 9.2), the only exceptions being West Germany and Spain. The condition that the distribution of value added should remain broadly constant was therefore breached.

2. *Welfare transfers become a burden on the distribution of income.* At the same time, the strict application of social legislation leads to increases in social transfers to households, a significant part of which is financed directly or indirectly by businesses (Table 9.2). Thus, in the 1970s, employers' contributions as a proportion of the GDP went up by between 2 per cent (West Germany) and 5 per cent (UK). Although these contributions help, of course, to sustain final consumption and contain industrial unrest, they also have an adverse effect on rates of return, and therefore on the decision to invest. As a result, calls are made for smaller contributions and for tax relief, evidence of a fresh antagonism between self-financing and social security.

3. *As Fordism progresses, it leads to an increase in capital intensity followed by a*

TABLE 9.2   *Elements in the challenge to the Fordist wage/labour relation: company pressures and internationalization*

	France	UK	Ireland	Belgium	Spain	Italy	West Germany
Developments undermining income distribution							
Progress of real wages (ave. annual rates)							
1960–73	0.1	0.4	1.1	0.8	1.0	0.9	1.1
1973–79	1.1	0.2	0.6	1.6	−1.3	0.8	−0.3
Social transfer element: employer contributions/ GDP (%)							
1970	11.8	6.4	2.5	9.3	n.d.	13.0	10.7
1981	15.3	10.5	5.8	12.9	n.d.	14.2	12.8
Net profit rates in the mfg. industries (%)							
1960	15.6	16.4	n.d.	17.1	n.d.	17.7	26.2
1973	18.2	9.5	n.d.	17.2	n.d.	16.9	16.5
1982	13.8	5.5	n.d.	10.7	n.d.	19.2	11.7
Trend (% per annum)	−2.7	−5.3	n.d.	−4.7	n.d.	0.1	−3.0
Reinforced by the internationalization of trade							
Import penetration (%)							
Ave. 1962–72	14.2	21.7	n.d.	47.8	13.8	16.4	17.4
1973–78	20.4	29.2	51.3	54.6	16.1	24.5	21.2
1979–84	24.0	29.4	64.7	69.4	18.9	28.2	26.0
Relative competitivity index							
1960	116.0	109.5	81.7	89.8	n.d.	82.3	74.1
1973	96.8	91.2	99.8	98.3	n.d.	95.2	110.8
1979	98.3	109.2	96.5	94.0	n.d.	88.0	112.1
1984	89.1	120.3	89.1	72.2	n.d.	92.3	98.2

Definitions and sources: 'Progress of real wages' = gap between real wages and productivity, *no* account being taken of variations in the terms of trade. 'Profit rates' = gross surplus in running costs expressed as % of gross capital. Taken from Chan-Lee and Sutch (1985, p. 24). 'Import penetration' = ratio of imports to GDP *en valeur* as an average for the periods considered. Figures based on Ralle (1984). 'Relative competitivity index' = relative wage costs for industry expressed in one currency, reference year 1975. *Economie européenne*, Mar. 1984, pp. 199–31.

slow-down in labour productivity growth. Immediately after the war, new production methods were doubly important, both because they were relatively capital-saving and because they allowed major productivity gains to be made. But once the essential part of this change has been carried out, it becomes more and more expensive to maintain previous trends *within the Fordist scheme of things*, and no longer possible at all by changing from Taylorian to Fordist methods. Profit rates suffer as a result of this lower output/capital ratio, a change that accompanies and reinforces a reduction in the share of profits in value added. This fall is further aggravated when the slower rate of growth brings about a decline in capacity utilization.

Under the pressure of these three factors, company rates of return fall significantly, and the effect of this is to reverse investment trends and worsen company finances, especially in the case of manufacturing industry. Subject to the need to remain financially solvent (made more difficult by the post-1981 increase in interest rates), management is forced to reconsider how to organize staff in a way that will restore profitability as well as ensure a speedy adjustment to an uncertain economic environment. We have seen that, under these circumstances, indexation clauses are the first to be affected. As to the need to quickly adjust employment (which has been declining for the first time), all sorts of efforts are being made in the search for flexibility and I shall come back to these later (Section 3). A third structural change reinforces the need for these policies.

2.4. *From a predominantly national market to international competition*

The tendency for the European economies to become more integrated, partly as a result of the advance of Fordism, became much stronger in the 1960s. A much greater proportion of goods produced went into exports, especially of capital goods and durable consumer goods. In qualitative terms, a high degree of specialization develops within industries (e.g. in the motor vehicle industry in Europe) and this reduces the extent to which the productive system and the standard of living develop in parallel. Consequently, a strategy of increasing exports is accompanied by increased penetration of the domestic market, which is the counter-part of the specialization policy. Thus, the multiplier effects of a Keynesian policy are reduced in scale, first because surges in imports reduce the extent to which domestic production is stimulated, and second because foreign manufacturers exert pressure on domestic price formation.

The extent of these changes is shown by three kinds of indicator.

1. *The degree of internationalization* continued to increase between 1962 and 1984 in all European countries (Table 9.2). This applies both to countries with medium-size home markets and to those whose mode

of growth is governed by what happens internationally (Ireland and Belgium). In addition, contrary to what had been observed in the interwar years, the worsening crisis (at least up until now) has not interrupted this trend: even after 1979, penetration of internal markets has continued to increase.

2. As a result, *controlling production costs* has become one of the central objectives of companies and governments. The key indicator is becoming the index of relative competitiveness, which expresses in a common monetary unit cost prices in industry (Table 9.2). As we have seen, the priority accorded this criterion is not without consequence for the process of wage formation. Belgium offers a prime example of this change in the Fordist logic, since in recent years the price index of foreign competitors has tended to take the place of consumer prices in wage bargaining.

3. Once *flexible exchange rates* become generalized, the former wage formation procedures may reduce the potential of a change in parity to restore equilibrium. A fall in the value of a national currency may make non-substitutable imports more expensive, accelerate inflation, generalize unfavourable expectations about the future exchange rate, and increase the burden of foreign debt — without, however, stimulating real growth very much. The pressures exerted by the international monetary system then make it difficult to maintain the old established, nationally based system of wage determination.

In short, in the 1980s the need to adjust to competitive forces has become the governing philosophy (circuits IIA and B in Fig. 9.1) as opposed to the nationally based Fordist process of development (Fig. 1.1). Final evidence of this can be found in the breakdown of the economic regularities established in the 1960s.

2.5. *The end of growth*

All the indicators combine to emphasize the scale of the changes that have occurred. This can be clearly seen if we compare the periods 1973–9 and 1979–85 (Table 9.3) with the period 1960–73 (Table 1.2).

Growth, productivity, and real wages have all been affected, and these have had repercussions on employment. With the exception of Ireland, rates of growth were halved between 1973 and 1979, with an equivalent reduction also occurring after 1979. Thus, at the end of this period, the medium-term growth rate was no more than 1–2 per cent a year for output as well as real wages, far removed from 5–7 per cent of previous years. In so far as productivity growth has fallen less than demand, total employment (and not just in industry) has declined continuously since

TABLE 9.3. *After 1979: breakdown of growth processes: annual average rates, (a) 1937–1979; (b) 1979–1985* (%)

		France	UK	Ireland	Belgium	Spain	Italy	West Germany
Growth of GDP	(a)	3.1	1.4	4.1	2.4	2.5	2.6	2.4
	(b)	1.1	1.0	2.1	1.0	1.5	1.3	1.1
Per capita productivity	(a)	2.9	1.1	2.7	2.3	4.2	1.6	2.9
	(b)	1.6	1.8	2.3	1.8	3.3	0.9	1.6
Real wages	(a)	4.0	1.3	3.3	3.9	2.9	2.4	2.6
	(b)	1.5	1.8	−0.1	0.2	1.2	1.2	0.2
Employment	(a)	0.2	0.3	1.4	0.1	−1.7	0.8	−0.5
	(b)	−0.5	−0.8	−0.2	−0.8	−1.8	0.4	−0.5
Balance of payment on current account/GDP	(a)	−0.6	−1.3	−5.5	0.2	−1.6	−0.2	1.0
	(b)	−1.5	1.3	−7.5	−0.8	−1.2	−1.1	0.03
Government financing capacity/GDP	(a)	−0.9	−4.0	−9.7	−5.2		−9.1	−3.0
	(b)	−2.4	−3.0	−12.6	−11.2	−4.7	−11.8	−2.6
Rate of inflation	(a)	10.4	15.6	14.9	7.8	18.3	17.1	4.6
	(b)	9.9	8.6	13.5	7.0	12.5	14.7	3.9

Sources: Economie européenne, Nov. 1984, pp. 225–7, Jul. 1984, Table 2, p. 11; for Spain, Toharia (1984). 'Changes in the wage/labour relationship in Europe, 1973–1984', FERE report, Vol. 1, pp. 81–124, Sept. 1984.

the beginning of the 1980s. In contrast to the postwar period of growth, productivity has thus worked *against* employment.[1] Three kinds of constraint have emerged which might explain this change.

1. *Maintaining external balance seems to be more and more difficult.* Whereas in the 1960s there were surpluses on the current balance, persistent deficits now mean that austerity measures have to be taken to limit the growth of demand on the home market, and interest rates have to be raised to attract foreign investment. Only West Germany and the United Kingdom have managed to achieve surpluses, but by different means (oil exports in one case, competitive advantage in the other). Whereas in the 1960s the openness of the economy had a broadly neutral effect on growth and employment, in the 1980s it seemed to have a negative effect (see Boyer and Ralle, 1986a, 1986b).

2. *The end of growth jeopardizes the operation of automatic fiscal stabilizers.* The budget tends, in fact, to be in deficit throughout the economic cycle, since periods of (only moderate) growth cannot make good the finances run down during recession. Consequently, in spite of efforts to limit public spending, the public deficit varied on average between 2.5 and over 12 per cent of GDP in the period 1979–85, according to country. In so far as welfare transfers are the main source of increased government spending, governments and administrators have reacted, as noted above, by trying to revise and 'rationalize' systems of social security (see André and Delorme, 1984; BIT, 1983, OCDE, 1985).

3. *Combating inflation takes precedence over the reduction of unemployment.* One of the features of the monopolistic system of regulation was that an increase in inflation served as a means of restoring full employment (see Aglietta, 1976; Boyer and Mistral, 1978; and most *régulation* studies). But at the end of the 1960s this process came up against two constraints. First of all, the position of the dollar as the international currency was called into question (the withdrawal of convertibility having been declared in 1971). Second, the widening divergences between national rates of inflation led to a system of floating exchange rates, more or less controlled by the central banks. Creditors thus returned in force to change the direction of monetary policy (see Aglietta and Orléan, 1982); the interest rate explosion that began after 1981 in the United States spread, via the international monetary system, to almost every other country. After inflation accelerated in the mid-1970s, therefore, there was a very

---

[1] This is confirmed by detailed studies (e.g. Boyer and Petit, 1980, 1981b). This does not mean that productivity should be slowed down in the pursuit of full employment (see Ch. 10).

marked decline at the beginning of the 1980s, although the average figures for 1979–85 do not show this very clearly (Table 9.3). The change in monetary policy accompanied and then reinforced the end of postwar growth.

In accordance with good Keynesian logic, attempts at monetary and budgetary controls and the adjustment of the balance of trade have led to a fall in real demand and hence to increased unemployment — contrary to the neo-classical view of things, which saw these measures as a necessary and sufficient condition for a return to full employment. Thus, since 1979, unemployment has gone up rapidly to reach levels not seen in Europe since the 1930s.

How have the different European economies reacted? What social groups have suffered most from underemployment? What significance should be accorded to the much-vaunted concept of flexibility?

3. The Race for Flexibility, but the Re-emergence of Specific National Factors

One of the main lessons to be learnt from this international comparison is that each country has its own way of adapting to a lower, less stable, rate of growth. If we were to believe the statements made by employers' organizations and trade unions as well as by governments, there would be little doubt about the universal nature of the search for greater flexibility. However, if we look in detail at institutional and economic developments, the changes that have taken place in the system of wage/labour relations are by no means totally identical. In fact, the historical development of each country and the specific nature of its economic and social framework, as well as its particular international position, determine how it responds to the crisis. Forgotten or obsolete forms of wage/labour relations may be revived, stimulated by the constraints to which companies have been subject for a decade. Confirmation of this hypothesis can be found in both quantitative and qualitative studies.

3.1. Mechanisms of employment adjustment that vary from country to country

The word 'flexibility' is, in fact, too often used without being precisely defined; effecting a more rapid adjustment of employment, adapting hours of work to the economic situation, varying activity rates to labour market prospects, and increasing part-time work, fixed-term contracts, and temporary jobs are some ways of adjusting activity to developments in production. But it is also possible to cite the variability of flows into and out of employment, adjustments in training and retraining schemes, or the way wages react to the financial position of firms and the general economic situation.

From a strictly quantitative point of view, we have to break down the possibilities of adapting the system of wage/labour relations into different components. The results of recent studies emphasize the diversity of forms taken by the pursuit of flexibility in each country (Table 9.4).

Thus, in Italy the high elasticity of the length of the working week to the level of activity seems to be the favoured form of adaptation, while (no doubt because of labour legislation) the labour force seems particularly inflexible and the concept of part-time working little developed, at least in large companies and the sector covered by legislation. At the opposite end of the scale, West Germany seems to use many means of adjustment, from the speed of adaptation of employment and a high degree of sensitivity in the activity rate (a 1 per cent fall in growth reduces the activity rate by 0.4 per cent) to the increase in part-time employment which, at the end of the period in question, accounted for over 12 per cent of total employment (Table 9.5). It is not surprising, therefore, that long-term unemployment is so low in West Germany — not much different, for example, from the level in the United States.

France (as is often the case) occupies an intermediate position, since an average speed of adjustment of employment and elasticity accompany a female activity rate that varies counter-cyclically and a moderate increase in part-time working that accounts for only half the jobs created between 1973 and 1981. Finally, the British position is somewhat paradoxical, given the fact that many analysts regard its system of wage/ labour relations as extremely inflexible. However, the adaptability of working hours seems to make up for the relative immobility of the labour force, while male and female activity rates and the significant increase in part-time working (17.9 per cent of employment in 1981) makes it much easier to adapt to depressed, unstable economic conditions.

It would seem, therefore, that the crisis is bringing to light the specific characteristics of each country's system of wage/labour relations which the regularity and strength of growth in the 1960s concealed. Each of the preceding chapters has analysed the effects of these difficulties on the growth of employment, productivity, and wages. Another indicator is presented here to support this thesis: over and above a general increase in unemployment, there are different social groups bearing the associated costs.

3.2. *Specific types of inequality in the crisis*

A first approach is to compare the reasons why people become unemployed in the different European countries (Gambier and Szpiro,

TABLE 9.4 *An evaluation of the different components of employment adjustments*

	Employment mobility between firms[a]		Employment adjustment rate after 1 yr[b]	Cyclical elasticity of working wk[c]		Cyclical sensitivity of activity rates[d]			Elasticity of unemployment rate/GDP[e]	Long-term unemployment (% of total unempl.)[f]
	% of work-force employed for less than 2 yrs	Ave. no of yrs. in job		Mfrs	Overall	Men	Women	Total		
Belgium	24.8	8.0	0.46		0.537				−0.29	59.5
Italy	20.0	7.1	0.12	**0.610**	0.310	0.1	0.1	0.1		
France	17.8	8.8	0.43	0.363	0.342	0.1	−0.4	−0.1		39.8
W. Germany	25.0	8.5	**0.56**	0.538	0.545	0.4	0.2	**0.4**	**−0.46**	**8.5**
UK	24.4	8.6	0.32	**1.055**		0.01	0.5	0.2	−0.66	33.3
Japan	21.2	11.7	0.27	0.390	0.280	0.04	0.5	0.2	−0.09	
Canada	33.1	7.5	0.44	0.079	0.047	0.3	0.6	**0.4**	0.40	5.3
USA	38.5	7.2	0.38	0.384	0.203	0.2	0.3	0.2	−0.46	7.7

Sources:

[a] OCDE, *Perspectives économiques*, Sept. 1984, p. 119.
[b] ATLAS Model, Statistics & Financial Studies, no. 62 (1984), p. 36.
[c] OCDE, *Perspectives économiques*, Sept. 1983, p. 105.
[d] OCDE (1983), p. 98.
[e] OCDE (1984), p. 119.
[f] OCDE (1983), p. 46.

1982). There is a clear contrast between Italy, where more than 70 per cent of the unemployed are young people looking for their first jobs, and Belgium, where increased redundancies, i.e. job losses, account for 90 per cent of the growth of unemployment. Ireland, France, the Netherlands, the United Kingdom, and West Germany present a different picture in which the four types of unemployment (first employment, redundancies, resignations, and voluntary unemployment) combine in varying proportions, with West Germany, without doubt, constituting the most balanced example.

In social terms, these differences are not without effect on the different ways in which employees collectively protect their interests (more easily achieved in cases of collective redundancies than in cases where young people are unable to join the work-force) and, therefore, on their bargaining power *vis-à-vis* the state or on the different forms of compensation given (often more generous when there are collective redundancies for economic reasons, as was the case for a long time in France and Italy, for example).

A second approach makes it possible to pinpoint the mechanisms of discrimination by showing who the unemployed are and who the holders of atypical types of employment are, i.e. those without unlimited-term and full-time employment contracts (Table 9.5). If some types of inequality are general (the young), others are much more specific (part-time, immigrant labour).

- The seven European countries have one thing in common: by and large, the *young* are twice as likely to be unemployed as the rest of the population. However, discrimination is greatest in Italy and least marked in West Germany, with Belgium, the United Kingdom, and France coming in between. Among the young, women are even more disadvantaged, except in West Germany and the United Kingdom.

- However, contrary to common belief, *women* in general are not as badly off as the young. Of course, unemployment levels among them are higher than for men, but the discrimination coefficient remains low, except in Italy, and there is some tendency for activity rates to change in their favour. Female activity rates rose by between 5 and 3 percentage points from 1973 to 1982 (though by less in West Germany), whereas, because they tended to join the labour market later and leave it earlier, the rate among men declined over the same period.

- *Part-time working* has developed quite rapidly since 1973, especially in the service sector, where a new pattern of work seems to have emerged, in many respects the exact contrary of that observed in manufacturing. Thus, while part-time working has declined in importance in industry, it has become more widespread in services (CEPII, 1984a; Boyer and Ralle 1986b). And women are more likely than men to have part-time jobs (Table 9.5). Even if this does not represent a shift towards a more precarious form of

TABLE 9.5 *Some indicators of inequalities in employment and unemployment*[a]

	France	UK	Ireland	Belgium	Spain	Italy	West Germany
Young people							
Unemployment rates							
(1) among young people	21.7	25.9	n.d.	30.0	38.9	35.7	13.3
(2) average	9.0	13.3	n.d.	16.2	17.9	11.0	7.5
Discrimination coefficient ((1)/(2))	2.4	2.0	n.d.	1.9	2.2	**3.2**	1.8
Young women							
(3) Unemployment rates	27.1	23.9	n.d.	34.7	n.d.	43.2	12.2
Discrimination coefficient ((3)/(2))	3.0	1.8	n.d.	2.1	n.d.	**3.9**	1.6
Women							
(4) Unemployment rates	12.6	13.0	n.d.	23.2	n.d.	19.8	8.2
Discrimination coefficient ((4)/(2))	1.4	1.0	n.d.	1.4	n.d.	**1.8**	1.1
Unequal developments in activity rates, 1973–82							
(5) Men	−1.8	−1.0	−1.7	−1.1	n.d.	0.5	−0.3
(6) Women	3.8	3.3	2.7	5.3	n.d.	5.0	1.7
'Positive discrimination' in favour of women ((6)−(5))	5.6	4.3	4.4	6.4	n.d.	5.5	2.0

Part-time							
Proportion of total employment in 1981 (%)							
Total	8.3	17.9	n.d.	6.4	n.d.	5.1	12.0
Men	2.3	3.1	n.d.	1.3	n.d.	2.9	1.6
Women	17.4.	**40.0**	n.d.	16.3	n.d.	10.1	28.9
Foreigners							
Proportion of total employment (%)							
in 1974	10.8[b]	3.4[b]	1.7[c]	6.4	n.d.	0.07	10.3
in 1981	7.1[d]	3.5	2.2[d]	6.2	n.d.	0.06	8.6
Employment development differential: foreigners/total (average annual rate) (%)	**−10.2**	0.5	7.6	−0.3	n.d.	−0.6	**−3.0**

[a] April 1983 (unless otherwise indicated).
[b] 1975.
[c] 1976.
[d] 1979.

Sources: Unemployment rates: EUROSTAT (1984), Employment and Unemployment, p. 176. Activity rates: EUROSTAT (1984), Employment and Unemployment. Part-time: EUROSTAT (1984), Employment and Unemployment. Foreign labour: EUROSTAT (1983), Survey of the Workforces, p. 4. Foreign labour: EUROSTAT (1984), Employment and Unemployment, pp. 168, 169.

employment, the increased employment of women, the spread of service-type jobs, and the move away from formal contracts of employment seem to be associated with a new kind of segmentation.

- *The unequal treatment of foreign workers and nationals* represents another kind of disparity. The countries in which the proportion of immigrants was the highest before the crisis (France and West Germany) have made greatest use of this to reduce total employment. On the other hand, there is not the same discrimination in Italy and Belgium and still less in the United Kingdom and Ireland.

- Accordingly, each country, depending on its historical development, is following quite distinct ways of increasing flexibility: similar opportunities for employment for men and women, provided that women accept part-time work (United Kingdom); less underemployment among young people, where an immigrant work-force enables rapid adjustment of employment to occur (West Germany and, to a lesser degree, France); pronounced discrimination against the young and women (Italy).

If the process of wage formation is taken into account, this conclusion is reinforced: from a strictly theoretical viewpoint, the cyclical variability of wages represents, in some cases, an alternative to variations in employment. But the experience of different European countries varies tremendously (see Chapter 10 below). Moreover, the position of different categories of wage-earners is far from being identical, but varies according to whether they work in large modern companies with a certain degree of monopoly power or in small firms more affected by cyclical variations in activity. Even social security (for which relative uniformity remains the goal in Europe) has not provided equal protection to the different categories of beneficiary. Depending on the exact form of legislation and the bargaining position of employees, unemployment benefits vary greatly according to whether they go to those made redundant in the Fordist sector, those in politically sensitive areas hit by recession, those rejected by small firms, or women and young people entering the labour market.

There is a surprising twofold paradox in all this:

1. At a time when segmentation theories are losing ground, European societies (but also the United States) are exploring *new forms of differentiating wage/labour relations*.

2. While *statements of intent* and declared policies indicate a general rush for flexibility, the actual forms of flexibility differ greatly from country to country, from sector to sector, and from one kind of worker to another.

3.3. The need for flexibility: from broad compatability to open conflict with the Fordist system of wage/labour relations

A comparison of the national studies reveals that countries have responded in diverse ways to the same series of international and internal upheavals. Without exaggeration, what has been witnessed at one extreme is the incorporation of margins of flexibility into the postwar system of wage/labour relations; while at the other extreme, what has been seen is a 'frontal assault' on its most rigid manifestations. In between these two extremes, there has been a virtual continuum of strategies towards increasing flexibility.

- West Germany provides a good example[2] of the possibilities open to a system where the legal guarantees accorded to wage-earners are compatible *a priori* with the need for technical and economic change. Thus, wages remain sensitive to disequilibrium in the labour market, making adjustments possible within the Fordist scheme of things. Similarly, individual wages are not tied to a rigid and immutable definition of a skill or job, so that worker mobility is compatible with maintaining the level of wages. In this way, in West Germany the largely decentralized nature of bargaining, the traditionally strong and unified trade union movement, and the internationally integrated nature of its industry all combine to explain how the country coped much better with the first oil crisis than other countries, with the earlier reversal of economic policy also playing an important part. The second oil crisis and the rising dollar, however, were dealt with less successfully, if only because the German economy came up against a shift in trends of international trade. Having greater flexibility than foreign competitors does not, therefore (except in the case of Japan), seem to be a sufficient condition for a return to full employment. It is perhaps the trade union movement's awareness of this that led to their call for a huge and rapid reduction in working time. In fact, the industrial dispute of spring 1984 seems to have been ended, at least for the time being, by a reaffirmation of the need for competitiveness and flexibility.
- Next, Spain and France provide an example of the state trying to go along with the company line and to incorporate a minimum degree of flexibility in legislation. Since the 1970s, French governments have tried to organize labour mobility by laying down rules for those moving from unemployment to vocational training and for new entrants moving into permanent employment for the first time (see Rose, 1984). Early retirement, various kinds of so-called solidarity contracts, and youth training schemes are all aimed at restoring the qualitative and quantitative balance of labour supply and demand. Contrary, therefore, to the current feeling that flexibility and market forces go together on the one hand, and rigidity and government intervention on the other, employment policy might also be one of the means of adjustment. In some cases, this socialization of mobility could even be one of the conditions for economic efficiency and reduction in inequality. Spain is a good example of this: in less than ten years, the labour market has moved from a corporatist system to one encouraging a certain amount of

---

[2] Japan would provide another. It is not considered here because it was not included in the comparative research.

flexibility, without the Fordist model having ever been stabilized as in other European countries.

- Italy, on the other hand, seems to have had a legislative system with complete and binding rules enforcing an 'ultra-Fordist' system of wage/labour relations at least for the largest enterprises, and at the same time to have been particularly innovative in specializing in a flexible way (see Piore and Sabel, 1984). There is, therefore, an increasingly clear departure from the rules that in 1970 were aimed at establishing a statute for workers. The particularly wide-ranging guarantees given to the employees of large undertakings seem to be hampering the process of accumulation and adaptation to a changing international environment. Consequently, employment in small- and medium-sized enterprises (not subject to this legislation), and the growth of family work in the black or grey economy, are just so many ways of undermining the victories won by worker struggles in the past. Thus, after ten years a legislative system aimed at standardizing jobs has had the opposite effect: it helps to create or revive a dual labour market and, therefore, to segment the industrial work-force. Chapter 7, furthermore, shows the apparently beneficial effects of the 'Cassa Integrazione Guadagni' on the modernization and restructuring of companies most affected by the crisis, and the guarantee of income by the state seems to be one of the conditions for reducing manpower surpluses created by modernization in circumstances where there is a high degree of conflict. State-paid unemployment benefits therefore may be helpful, rather than harmful, as those neo-classical economists who emphasize the negative effects of a minimum wage and unemployment benefits consider. The complexity of the Italian system serves to remind us of how fallacious can be the simple idea that the state and markets, welfare transfers and competition are in conflict with each other.

- Finally, the United Kingdom[3] provides an example where the scale of structural problems and the persistence of the recession have encouraged a radical reassessment of the compromise between employers and trade unions. Chapter 3 shows that the reform of industrial relations has been the order of the day since the beginning of the 1970s, but neither the Conservative nor the Labour Party has been able to demolish the hard-won trade union and social guarantees achieved after more than a century of worker struggle. It would seem, however, that the extent of de-industrialization and the vigorous efforts in this direction since the Conservatives returned to power have finally had their effects on the system of wage/labour relations. In Britain, important aspects of the compromise that used to prevail are at odds with each other, even if the TUC still maintains its power (albeit defensively), and we are, therefore, a long way from a return to a mythical state of pure and perfect competition in the labour market.

This same kind of change seems to be emerging in the United States, with, however, important differences. In the first place, it is employers, rather than the federal government, who are taking the lead in rejecting the

---

[3] And also, up to a point, the United States, not studied here (but see Boyer, 1985a).

compromise between wages and productivity. Second, bargaining there is much more decentralized and trade unions have less to do with the way economic policy is conducted. Because of this, in 1982–3 collective wage agreements were suspended and new negotiations were begun following procedures that break away completely from the former standard type of contract as used in the automobile industry (see Piore and Sabel, 1984; Coriat, 1985; Lacombe and Conley, 1985). Trade unions are being forced to accept significant wage cuts in the hope of achieving fewer job losses and the financial recovery of industries in crisis. If these trends were to continue (although it is too soon to say whether they will), they would mean the gradual decline of the postwar accord between capital and labour and the beginning of a period of experimentation with new forms of wage/labour relations (see Chapter 11 below, Sections 3 and 4).

Two major conclusions can be drawn from this brief overview.

1. First, re-segmentation of the labour market is the order of the day in almost every country where the Fordist system of wage/labour relations inherited from the 1960s did not permit adaptation to the new conditions of international competition and the instability of macroeconomic developments.

2. Second, and above all, strategies to increase flexibility vary from one country to another and follow different paths, depending on the history of industrial relations, industrial specialization, and the country's position in world markets. Beyond the universal 'pursuit of rigidity', there are particular components (wages, working time, or levels of employment) and particular groups (the young, foreign workers, women) that have borne the burden of the adjustment implied by the crisis.

At this stage of the analysis, it is time to discuss in greater detail the foreseeable effects of the changes that are taking place. For certain people, flexibility tends to be synonymous with a way out of the crisis and therefore has decidedly favourable connotations. Does not the notion of 'rigidity' denote old habits and backward-looking attitudes? Others, by contrast, see the various pressures imposing flexibility by force, rather than by choice, as an explanation of the worsening crisis and of the plunge into the vicious circle of stagnation. The following two chapters examine these issues.

10

Defensive or Offensive Flexibility?

Robert Boyer

The use of the term 'flexibility' has become so common that it cannot simply be dismissed as something not worth attention. Furthermore, both the concept and the strategies that it encompasses deserve more than to be routinely trotted out as a panacea for all the ills affecting firms. Is it a clearly defined idea, or an amalgam of different aspects of change in the system of wage/labour relations? Can the effects of different strategies to increase flexibility (of wages, employment, contracts of work, etc.) be foreseen with sufficient certainty? Can we be sure that enhanced flexibility at the microeconomic level is a solution that is valid at the macroeconomic level, both in economic and in social terms? In particular, are the gains from flexibility unevenly distributed, offering more to the best-placed firms, sectors, or countries, or are they more general in their impact and thus capable of reducing international disequilibrium? What lessons can be drawn from economic history?

These are very large questions, and the answers to them are well beyond the scope of this chapter. Furthermore, the literature on the subject has been growing steadily since the early 1980s. This chapter will therefore confine itself to an introduction to the subject and a suggestion of themes for more extensive research.

1. A Generic Term, of Particular Ambiguity because of its Mutability

The comparision of the experience of the different European countries has already demonstrated the vast range of methods used to adjust the amount and distribution of work to falling growth rates. It showed that the search for flexibility took very different forms. This conclusion is in no way accidental: if we look at the issue in terms of the systems of wage/labour relations, there is a temptation to identify as many types of flexibility as there are elements of the systems.

1.1. Five main definitions

The wealth of literature on the subject suggests that 'flexibility' can be defined with reference to so many objectives that *a priori* appear to be unrelated, that the only common denominator is the term itself (see Table 10.1).

1. *The degree of adaptability of productive organizations* constitutes one definition. This depends largely on the decisions made about technology and organizational methods when the production unit was set up, which in turn were determined by the size and stability of the market. The principle Fordist industries were based on the expectation of rapidly expanding markets, justifying extreme specialization of plant, the preferred method of achieving large returns to scale. It is hardly surprising, therefore, that the greatest problems of adaptation are experienced in steel, heavy chemicals, and the automobile industry, while the less Fordist industries are managing to adapt without a significant fall in productivity growth. At the same time, new adaptable machinery, designed to cope with uncertain demand fluctuating in volume and in nature, is being introduced and becoming more widespread. It should be noted that such flexibility can be introduced without having to modify many of the characteristics of the former system of wage/labour relations. At the risk of over simplification, the key word of this form of industrial organization would be 'plant flexibility', with a high level of automation, and incorporating in the very principle of its organiz-ation more or less total adaptability as regards the volume and variety of products demanded by the market.

2. The second possibility concerns *the ability of the workers to move from one job to another* within a given overall production process, or eventually within a process that can switch rapidly between products (which ties in with the first definition). This kind of flexibility requires skill and competence from the work-force, and specifically requires an ability to master different aspects of the same production process. It has already been emphasized that these qualities are the exact opposite of those demanded first by Taylorism, then by Fordism. Thus, the 'unemployability' of some skilled workers in more variable jobs in certain cases is due strictly to management persisting in a policy of no training. In contrast, the key word here is 'work-force versatility': this entails the ability of employees to work at different jobs, having had a sufficiently broad general and technical training; financial incentives to involve workers in the quality aspects of their jobs; and the absence of insuperable divisions between supervisors and technicians. The

TABLE 10.1 *Flexibility: five basic principles*

	Organization of production	Range of labour specialization	Work-force mobility	Wage formation	Social cover
Definitions	Ability to adjust plant to variable demand in volume and products	Adaptability of workers to various tasks, whether complex or not	Possibility of varying jobs and working time according to the local or world economic situation	Sensitivity of wages to the company's position and the labour market	Elimination of conditions unfavourable to employment in the fields of taxation and social transfers
Components	• Plant with multiple applications • Subservience to the production line and optimum management of flux • Adaptation of the product to the needs of the consumer and to instant demand	• Extent of general and technical training • Job rotation within a company • Relatively close links between production and quality control • No management/work-force barriers	• No major constraints to the right to work • Ease of interregional migration (housing) • No rights specific to one company (social benefits, pensions) • Link between jobs and wage differences	• At macroeconomic level: — ave. wage in terms of productivity, unemployment, and exchange terms — no enforced min. wage • at microeconomic level: — continuous revision with changes in local economic situations — less respect for the parity argument	• Absence of contributions that make labour more expensive in relation to capital • No social security and tax thresholds • Reduction of contributions paid by employers • Greater choice between private insurance and nat. schemes
Key symbol	Flexible plant[a]	The proudhonist worker[b]	The temporary work-force[c]	Links between wages & productivity[d]	The two-tier work-force[e]

[a] See Besson (1983); Coriat (1985); Kundig (1984).
[b] See Archier and Serieyx (1984); Piore and Sabel (1984); Schumacher (1976).
[c] See Gattaz (1984); Gilder (1985).
[d] See Weitzman (1985).
[e] See Harris and Seldon (1979).

symbol of this new approach to industrustrial work would simply be a modern version of Proudhon's 'ideal worker' (*l'ouvrier proudhonien*).

3. According to a third definition, greater flexibility depends on the *laxity of legal constraints governing the contract of employment*, and in particular dismissal. In contrast to the above definitions, this focuses on the institutional aspects pertaining to employment law and the details of collective agreements. Many observers are eager to spotlight this as the key to regaining flexibility. This ability to vary the volume of employment can also be achieved by being able freely to vary the length of the working week and the annual distribution of hours worked during the year according to the volume of orders. By extension, this third model could include all the factors that contribute to workers' mobility between companies, jobs, or regions. All those measures that reduce workers' ties with a particular establishment or company are steps towards this kind of flexibility. If the contract of employment binds the worker to a large conglomerate company, this mobility can be achieved by *internal* transfer from one production line to another. But usually the debate focuses on *external* flexibility: in this case the ideal type seems to be a contract of employment with conditions that can be amended from one day to the next. This form of flexibility ideally would be achieved through the extension of *temporary employment* to society as a whole.

However, this type of flexibility does not fit in with the two preceding types: it could even be in conflict with them. The possibility of rapidly adjusting the work-force is likely to inhibit research into flexible mechanization, while rotating workers too rapidly is in itself detrimental to their adaptability and, in general, to their commitment to the firm's goals and therefore (most probably) to its performance.

4. Flexibility can however assume a fourth meaning: it can relate to the *adaptability of wages* (nominal and/or real) to the economic situation facing each company or the labour market as a whole. On the argument put forward above as an interpretation of the 1930s, it was resistance to wage reductions that explained the scale of (primarily classical) unemployment observed at the time. Unemployment could therefore be reduced by removing the restrictions that prevented wages from falling to their 'natural' level. Following another line of argument, the fact that wages do not adapt to deteriorating terms of trade, slowing productivity growth or rising unemployment, favours a belated and inflationary adjustment, which in turn necessitates austerity measures. And to back this up, those countries with the greatest wage flexibility are also those with

the smallest growth in unemployment from 1973 to 1983 (the United States and Japan, as opposed to most European countries). This notion of flexibility therefore advocates increased *competition* in the job market, wage differentiation according to either the firm's financial position and the productivity of individuals, or the abolition or relaxation of legislation on minimum wages (the introduction of a considerably lower minimum wage for young people than for adults, for example).

This flexibility is essentially a variation on the theme of the *incentive wage*, which can, moreover, assume a variety of forms: a return to the old methods of linking pay to individual effort, the reintroduction of competition, or even, last but not least, some kind of *participation*, whereby employees are involved in profit-sharing schemes. Beyond the obvious institutional and socio-political differences, there is one common theme: to call into question those agreements that prevent wages from being a function of *ex post* productivity.

In a sense, this fourth variant is a substitute for the third: if the employees are prepared to work for lower pay, it is then less, or even not at all, necessary to dismiss them. At the risk of being somewhat simplistic, two different models could be put forward. One would give virtually guaranteed employment, but would require acceptance of variations in wages including reductions (the Japanese ideal of 'employment for life'). The other, with wages fixed at a higher level, would entail laying off workers for a short, or sometimes long, term of unemployment (the American model of the 1960s?). Once again, it can be seen how widely concepts of flexibility differ.

5. According to the fifth and final definition, flexibility is seen as *the possibility for companies to relieve themselves of some of their social and fiscal payments* and, more generally, of legislation that limits freedom of management. In this case, the aim is to reduce the difference between the worker's take-home pay and the total wage cost to the company; this differential was introduced after the Second World War, and has increased particularly since 1973. In more general terms, the fiscal system and legislation often emerge from an accumulation of 'institutionalized compromises', culminating in a particularly complicated system, which is difficult for the economic agents to master and which can, moreover, sometimes end up being counterproductive, even frustrating the intended aims of the legislators. Flexibility is therefore synonymous with reforming and rationalizing state intervention for the sake of greater efficiency, particularly in the area of job creation. This category could include the abolition of social contributions that penalize labour and favour

capital-intensive industries, the legalization of outlawed working practices when it is in the interest of the companies and employees concerned, etc.

The symbol of this kind of flexibility could be either the *black economy* on the Italian model, or a return to *minimum state intervention* dear to the disciples of liberalism, or — which is the most likely possibility — a *two-tier work-force*, divided on the criteria of social security and employment rights.

1.2. A plethora of partial indicators

It is unusual for the debate to be conducted in such general terms, concerned as it is with much more specific aspects of flexibility. In this respect, there is a fairly impressive range of measures that are difficult to relate to each other. The most important of these are summarized in Table 10.2, which, however, is by no means exhaustive. Leaving readers to work through the definitions of these indicators one by one, I shall confine myself to a few observations relevant to the subsequent analysis of the effects of flexibility.

- Paradoxically, *the aim of flexibility is to maintain the stability of certain aspects of economic life*. Thus, the aim of plant flexibility and worker versatility or mobility is to control capitalized labour productivity — and therefore financial performance. It is appropriate at this point to emphasize that other forms of flexibility (in the financial system, in the organization of firms, etc.) can also be envisaged whose aim might be, for example, to stabilize employment.

- *The number, and therefore relativity, of indicators is evident*: in so far as flexibility is defined very broadly as the ability of a system or sub-system to respond to a variety of disturbances, as many kinds of flexibility can be identified as there are variables and external shocks. The same applies to the deterioration of wages: the degree of indexation in relation to prices, the degree of dependence on unemployment or productivity, and the scale of sectoral differences are all possible indicators. Alternatively, one common characteristic of wage rigidity is that real wages often increase more rapidly than productivity, corrected for the terms of trade. But from a strictly theoretical point of view these measures are not comparable, and this poses considerable problems, for example in describing the relative situation in the United States, Japan, and Europe.

- *It is important to distinguish between the consequences of flexibility and the means of achieving it*. A second feature of wage rigidity is that the degree of rigidity can be related to the degree of protection against being employed, the scale and predictability of economic cycles, whether or not collective bargaining is centralized, etc. However, it must then be shown how these factors do, *or do not*, influence wage flexibility. By the same token, it is not enough simply to point to a few pieces of social and fiscal legislation: it is also necessary to

TABLE 10.2 *On the variety of indicators delimiting flexibility at work*

	Organization of production	Range of labour specialization	Mobility of work-force	Wage formation	Social security
Indicators	R1 Stability of plant productivity gains when faced with changes in product and procedure R2 Upturn of the curve showing productivity, in relation to Fordist methods	R3 Stability of work-force productivity gains in relation to changes in product and processes R4 Upturn of the training/Fordist curves	R5 Variability of labour and working hours in response to changes in demand and profitability	R6 Variability of average wage according to the economic situation R7 Absence of a gap between productivity and terms of trade R8 Elasticity of the wage structure	R9 System of compulsory deductions neutral as regards employment R10 Small gap between take-home pay and total cost of labour
Indicators of methods	M1 Proportion of production carried out by adaptable plant M2 Degree of variation admitted by the production processes as regards: (a) volume of production of a given model (b) changes of specifications for a given range (c) change of the range itself (d) restructuring of plant and machinery	M3 Weakness in the rate of permanent employment M4 Rate of mobility — workers, supervisors, technicians M5 Low wage differential within the firm M6 Proportion of workers with technical/general training M7 Scale of internal training programme	M8 Rapidity of adjustment of labour M9 Elasticity of length of working hours M10 Rate of rotation of work-force M11 Elasticity of activity rate M12 Regional and sectoral mobility M13 Counter-cyclical variation of labour supply and demand M14 Low rate of long-term unemployment M15 Existence of large wage differentials between firms and branches	M17 Low level and time lag of price M18 Dependence of wage on unemployment M19 Dependence of wage on productivity M20 .Dependence of wage on profitability M21 Minimum of relatively unrestrictive wage M22 Redundancy payments as a small proportion of industrial revenue M23 Large differentials in wage trends	M24 Gap between compulsory deductions from wages and other sources of income M25 Level of subsidies for employment or exemption M26 Absence of fiscal, social, and legal regulations M27 Size of underground economy; level of illegal and semi-legal work M28 Proportion of voluntary insurance cover in total social security

explain how they influence decisions about employment and investments. It is equally striking how many indicators of employee mobility there are. The estimates made for the European countries show the range of possible permutations (Table 9.4 above).

- *Certain contradictions can be perceived between the micro-and macroeconomic level, and internal and external flexibility.* To give an example, large sectoral and regional disparities are not necessarily evidence that average wages respond to certain macroeconomic fluctuations. Thus, considerable microeconomic flexibility can go hand in hand with notable macroeconomic rigidity (the United Kingdom?). On the other hand, the stabilization of labour relations through contractual agreements can be the path to a broad range of adaptability (Japan?).[1] Equally, the external mobility of workers can be in conflict with the conditions for internal flexibility, which entails investment in training specific to the company. Yet again, we see how misleading it is to lump all these factors together under the same heading.

- Finally, against the background of crisis, schemes for *introducing flexibility have sometimes become a euphemism for downgrading most of the rights of wage-earners.* This ignores the fact that the same principle of competition that requires a reduction during a slump implies an increase during a boom, perhaps greater than would result from the implementation of a wage agreement smoothing changes over the full cycle. It has long been recognized that wages in the secondary sector show more extreme variations — both upward and downward — than wages in the primary sector, so that, over the long term, their relative position changes only slowly. In other words, the stabilizing effects of wage agreements cannot be assessed over a short period of time.

From this example it will be appreciated that maximum flexibility is not always the optimum. It is this central idea that the following three sections aim to substantiate.

2. Strategies for Increasing Flexibility: Dimly Perceived, Uncertain, and Controversial Effects

Beyond this classification, what are the consequences of these different types of flexibility and the ways of achieving them? Rather than summarize the wealth of recent research on this subject, an almost Promethean task, I shall concentrate on three aspects that clarify the options open to the countries of Europe.

2.1. *Flexibility and productivity: from conflict to complementarity?*

From the very definition of plant and work-place flexibility, it is clear that

[1] Weisskopf (1985) demonstrates, in this connection, that the security enjoyed by employees in this country is favourable to the dynamics of productivity, contrary to the tendency observed in the United States and other OECD countries generally.

the aim is precisely to stimulate overall productivity. Therefore, in principle, flexibility and productivity go hand in hand and have a stabilizing effect, since, to a large extent, the present crisis stems from the fact that the Fordist methods of attaining these productivity gains have been exhausted. Furthermore, the development of electronic capital equipment should increase the coefficient of plant utilization, thereby reducing the coefficient of capital, the growth of which has in the past aggravated problems of profitability (cf. Chapter 9, Section 2.3). By the same token, even a moderate restoration of the position of labour should reduce the imbalances inherent in the rigidity of Fordist production lines. It would therefore be tempting to view flexibility of production as a means of surpassing mass production on Taylorian lines, as do Piore and Sabel (1984).

Closer examination, however, challenges this view.

- In theory, the factors governing productivity growth in the short term are different from those determining its rate of development in the medium/long term. Certainly, the level of utilization of productive capacity is the primary factor explaining the 'productivity cycle'.[2] However, in the medium term it is the rate of investment, the growth of the market, and the skill of the work-force that condition the rate at which technical change is incorporated into the economic system. In the long term, it is only the emergence of a coherent technological system that will enable cumulative growth of productivity to be achieved (Freeman, 1983; Perez, 1983).

  From the available material (Coriat, 1984, for example), it can be seen that factory robotics are certainly a factor in increasing short-term productivity growth, but there is nothing to show that they form a principle of organization as powerful as Fordism. Indeed, it is difficult to predict how widespread such new kinds of flexible automation will become. So it is not absolutely certain that this is a new principle of obtaining increasing returns to scale. Admittedly, widespread computerization in the tertiary sector brings significant potential increases in productivity. But we could equally reach an impasse in which the short-term reduction in the costs of production becomes an obstacle to changes in socio-productive organization, which offers the best chance of a cumulative fall in relative prices. In a nutshell, the introduction of flexibility could be a defensive measure aiming to cope with the unpredictability of the crisis, but not necessarily to overcome the crisis itself.

- The possible contradiction between flexibility in production and economic

[2] The US recovery at the end of 1982 again gives a striking example. The fact that productivity gains were initially so large has less to do with the entry of the United States into a new age of technology and the final restoration of work discipline, than with the unprecedented growth of the GNP. In fact, if industrial performance is taken over a full cycle, it is lower than the average for other postwar cycles. The problem of productivity remains unresolved.

performance is borne out by the *history* of industrial systems. Broadly speaking, two courses of development can be identified (see Boyer and Petit, 1981b).

The first would seek to achieve the *greatest increasing returns to scale* through specialization of plant, integration of production processes, and a pronounced division of labour. Fordism in the process industries falls into this category: in periods of rapid growth, productivity gains were particularly large. However, the other side of the coin is the difficulty of reacting to a drastic and unexpected contraction in the market. It is inherent in the very nature of production processes that only a very small percentage of the work-force can be shed and that is difficult to switch machinery to other kinds of production. Consequently, any recession means a collapse, or at least a notable decline, in productivity. When viewed from this angle, what was yesterday the very keystone of modernity and technical progress within the existing organizational structure now appears to represent a damaging rigidity.

In contrast to this, the other course is based on a low degree of mechanization, little exploitation of returns to scale, and small-scale enterprise. This *divisibility* has the advantage of allowing rapid and total adaptation to the economic situation: the work-force is composed primarily of direct labour, and it is relatively easy to make plant idle. It also exhibits remarkably stable productivity growth, more or less the same in periods of expansion as in periods of recession. During the oil crises and the monetary disturbances that have recurred since 1973, this particular advantage has helped to rehabilitate flexible production processes. However, the other side of the coin in these sectors is that long-term productivity growth is lower, and economic performance more generally is significantly worse than in the Fordist industries.

So this would imply that there is a *compromise between flexibility and long-term trends in productivity*. There are two further points in favour of this argument. First, the history of technical change suggests that certain restrictions limiting an extensive use of labour (legislation on the reduction of the working week/year, minimum wages, etc.) have promoted industrial modernization by favouring capital-intensive methods (see CEPREMAP-CORDES, 1977). Second, a comparison of the development of industries in the United States and Europe since the end of the 1960s would seem to indicate the existence of *two models*: one relying on flexibility (of employment and wages), but at the expense of productivity (the United States), the other continuing to increase productivity rapidly to meet the problems posed by lower real wages elsewhere (Europe) — even though there have been some reductions since 1980 in European countries.

Against this backdrop, it is easier to appreciate why *people are going for flexible automation*: for the first time in almost a century of industrial history, it could combine productivity and flexibility, which in the past have tended to be contradictory terms. The effects of easing legal constraints need to be put into perspective in a similar way.

2.2. Abolition of barriers to dismissal and of statutory controls: miracle cure or illusion?

The first of these strategies for flexibility is seductively paradoxical: the reason why companies (particularly in Europe) are not taking on more workers is that they can no longer lay them off. Restore this freedom to hire and fire, and jobs will mushroom! Usually neoclassically inspired macroeconomics abhors such sophistry. The dramatic entry of this argument into current debate is to be welcomed — as the equivalent of the savings paradox dear to the Keynes of *The General Theory*: in order to increase production and employment, the propensity to save has to be reduced in order to increase savings.

The fact that under Fordism employment had tended to become almost a *fixed factor* has already been emphasized repeatedly. This development, a distinct change in comparison with the nineteenth century, is far from being absolute since mass redundancy schemes are still numerous. Redundancy has been effected largely by companies in sectors worst hit by the crisis. Accepting this form of mobility does cause a contraction of employment in these sectors, but it also enables workers to move to new jobs that are more in line with demand and therefore probably are more secure. But there is still the question of determining whether the long-term *advantages* for employment derived from lifting restrictions imposed by legislation and agreements are greater than the short-term *disadvantages*. Four sets of reasons indicate that the beneficial effects are not as great as anticipated by the advocates of this kind of liberalization.[3]

1. Given this mobility , it would be logical for workers to move from *low-* to *higher-productivity* sectors. But if, as a first approximation, it is assumed that this shift of the work-force does not affect effective demand, determined for example by the external constraint, the net effect on employment appears to be *negative*. Even supposing significant elasticity of demand in relation to relative prices, there is no guarantee that increases in competitiveness will be adequate to offset the initial job losses. This would seem to be the case on the whole for European countries (Boyer and Petit, 1981a).

[3] This refers specifically to the French employers' proposal (known in France by the acronym ENCA), a scheme that is supposed to create over 400 000 jobs. There has been heavy criticism of the opinion poll on which this estimate is based, so it seems at the very least to be somewhat optimistic.

2. It must however be asked whether this freedom to fire encourages employment in those sectors that resort to redundancy (or whether it at least limits the reduction). In fact, it would seem that fluctuations in employment are simply magnified, without, at first sight, having any effect on medium-term trends. Indeed, reducing the costs of taking on and laying off employees leads firms to react more hastily to variations in demand, thus weakening the traditional productivity cycle and lessening the consequences of an error in forecasting (Nickell, 1979). In the same way, variations in working hours would be reduced, with periods of unemployment becoming more frequent but shorter. In so far as productivity trends are determined primarily by investment and the speed of integration of technical innovations, medium-term employment is not affected, since demand is determined by disposable income and relative prices, which are unchanged by assumption.[4]

3. The following two hypotheses can be put forward. On the one hand, a more rapid response to economic conditions may make it possible to satisfy demand at a lower cost, thus 'capturing' it from competitors. On the other hand, abolition of redundancy payments would reduce the overall cost of using labour and should lead to a substitution of labour for capital, thereby favouring employment. From the available research, it would seem that these effects are particularly difficult to quantify and are small in relation to present unemployment rates.

It is, for example, significant that econometric studies of the United Kingdom (conducted by the same investigator) gave quite different results depending on the method used. In 1979 Nickell came to the conclusion that British legislation might have been responsible for a 20 per cent rise in unemployment between 1970 and 1976. In 1982, using a different statistical formulation, he concluded the opposite: that the *same* legislation had *positive* effects, with the reduction in the rate of new entry on to the unemployment register outweighing the reduction in the rate of new job creation.

Even on the most favourable combination of assumptions, the stimulus to employment associated with the reduced cost of labour attributable to the abolition of redundancy payments is not on the same scale as the rise in unemployment figures registered since 1973. The effect would be between *0.1 and 1 per cent of total employment*

---

[4] This is illustrated by such sectors as the construction industry. For a long time, the work-force and working hours have varied according to the requirements of the season and the economic situation. Nevertheless, in this sector, which is now suffering a major crisis in most European countries, employment is still not exempt from macroeconomic determinants. A high degree of work-force flexibility does not therefore prevent cyclical job losses (Boyer, 1985b).

and would be once and for all, which means it would have little impact on medium-term tendencies.[5] It would be as well, then, to revise downwards substantially the estimates referred to in the Introduction.

4. Finally, it is important to remember that, in most European countries, the clauses covering redundancy payments come from agreements between unions and management. They are therefore independent of state intervention. Admittedly, in France plans for laying off workers are subject to the approval of the Inspection du Travail (a government labour agency). At the most, this can delay dismissal for two to three months but cannot prevent it altogether. It is, however, true that paying the extra wages due can aggravate the losses already incurred by the company, thereby necessitating *more* redundancies. On the other hand, the companies can take this delay into account when planning. Furthermore, let us not forget that since 1980 redundancies have run into six figures in Europe.

That being the case, in what way could unemployment be significantly affected? Since the abolition of legislation is being interpreted as the dawn of a new era, eminently beneficial to firms, could it increase confidence in the future, and therefore bring investment and lead to sizeable job creation? But this would come rather from political action than for any economic reason. The same conclusion seems to follow if we examine two other aspects of legislation.

1. It is supposed that the *abolition of statutory and welfare obligations* would enable small businesses which have proved their dynamism over the past decade, to take on more labour. A preliminary statistical analysis of the distribution of firms (Lang and Thelot, 1985) suggests that only between 15 000 and 50 000 extra jobs would be created, i.e. less than 0.25 per cent of the total work-force. The effects are therefore minimal in relation to expectations.[6] Moreover, it entails a *downgrading of social rights* — a movement that

[5] Taking the case of Britain, where legislation is judged to be restrictive, the research of S. Nickell (1979) allows the following, very approximate, calculation to be made. Since redundancy payments in the mid-1970s were equivalent to a month's wages (i.e. 8.3 per cent of the annual cost of a worker), since total redundancies per year numbered 300 000 out of a working population of 23 million (i.e. a probability of dismissal of 0.013), and since the long-term elasticity of unemployment in respect of the real cost of wages is at best -0.7, a total abolition of redundancy payments would enable fully rationalized businesses to increase their work-forces by $0.7 \times 0.013 \times 8.3\% = 0.7\%$. Even supposing that redundancy amounted to two months' wages and that the probability of dismissal was estimated by the firms to be 0.1 (a quite remarkable figure!), the increase in employment would hardly rise above 1 per cent.

[6] It will be remembered that the draft agreement between the CNPF (the French management federation) and the unions (which was ultimately rejected by the rank and file) included clauses that provided for the abolition of regulations concerning representative bodies and union rights.

tends to be viewed as inevitable because of the deepening crisis. The reverse could equally be argued: that this disruption of social legislation should be met by an adjustment in the opposite direction, i.e. extending the general obligations of employers (regarding training, for example) to small and medium businesses, as advocated by the Centre des Jeunes Dirigeants (1985). The difference between *defensive* and *offensive* strategies of flexibility, a dichotomy that will be developed further below (Chapter 11, Section 3), can be seen. The initial negative effects on unemployment in small businesses could be offset only by more rapid modernization.

2. Similar caution is called for so far as the *reduction of the legal working week* is concerned, although this issue is even more complex. In France, at least before 1981, the 40-hour barrier was seen as an obstacle to the redistribution of employment through a large reduction in working time. Theoretical simulations using macro-economic models implied that it would have significant effects on employment (of the order of hundreds of thousands). The implementation of a 39-hour working week in 1982, however, has led *ex post* to much lower estimates (around 10 000–40 000) (Colin *et al.*, 1984; *Travail et emploi*, 1984). Undoubtedly other schemes, better managed, could create significantly larger numbers of jobs. This experience does not mean that other analyses, far more thorough than those based on a purely arithmetic calculation of employment/working/income, should not be undertaken.

In these three areas of employment legislation — redundancy payments, abolition of statutory and welfare obligations, and reduction in the working week — the gap between forecasts and the actual job creation attainable from amending legislation can be measured; and relaxing legislation is not enough to affect unfavourable macroeconomic trends automatically and miraculously reverse them.

2.3. Wage 'rigidities' as the cause of unemployment

In analysing the roots of the crisis, the disruption caused by the opposing trends in productivity and real wages has been very much emphasized. Proposals for increased wage flexibility are therefore, quite logically, the focal point of the debate today. Since the beginning of the 1980s, a threefold characterization has tended to emerge.

1. Over the long term, wages have become less and less sensitive to changes in economic conditions.

2. The prime difference between Europe on the one hand and the United States and Japan on the other is the fact that the labour market in Europe is less flexible.

3. Government intervention must therefore be focused on making wage determination more competitive again.

Thus, in the mid-1980s a *new orthodoxy* seems to be asserting itself: it is the inertia of labour markets that is seen to account for the fact that Europe benefited so little from the US recovery in 1983–4. An impressive array of statistics would appear to bear this out.

- Because of the *slowness of real-wage adjustment*, income distribution has been detrimental to profits, a phenomenon described by the term 'anticipatory wage gap'. Various OECD reports (e.g. December 1982) and academic research (Branson and Rotemberg, 1980; Sachs, 1983) come to the conclusion that the development is particularly disadvantageous for European countries

- In line with the general hypothesis of *classical unemployment*, the excess of wages over productivity seems to be one of the factors accounting for the growth of unemployment rates in France, West Germany, the United Kingdom and to a lesser degree the United States (Sachs, 1983, p. 264). In Sachs's view, this gap can be made good by demand reflation so long as productivity responds more quickly than wages. For the majority of neo-classically inspired economists, however, it is real wages that have to be reduced.

- There is a dual factor behind European rigidity. First, wages are much better indexed in relation to prices than in the United States, where, owing to multi-year contracts, there is significant nominal intertia, even though this corresponds to high flexibility in real terms. Second, in Europe unemployment and market flucutations play a lesser role in wage determination. Combining these two characteristics, it has become accepted practice to construct indicators of wage rigidity. They measure the increase in unemployment that would theoretically be necessary to stabilize nominal wage increases in the face of an external shock to consumer prices. This is one of the central arguments of the June 1985 OECD report, and of many similar works (Coe and Gagliardi, 1985; Grubb *et al.*, 1983).

- At the same time, Europe is said to be suffering from *smaller sectoral and regional wage differences*, evidence of greater restriction on the working of market forces, and therefore on the possibility of adapting to a new distribution of jobs, industries, and locations (Blanchard *et al.*, 1985).

The consensus of opinion on this diagnosis is impressive. In 1984 and 1985, just about all the international organizations (OECD, EEC, IMF, Bank for International Settlements, etc.) as well as the 1985 *Economic Report of the President* (US Government, 1985), devoted significant study to this difference between US flexibility and European rigidities in the functioning of the labour market. And yet this received wisdom, culminating in the idea of 'Eurosclerosis', seems to be based on shaky grounds even if we accept that there are quite distinct systems of wage/labour relations in the three OECD zones.

2.4. A new orthodoxy on the agenda

These claims must be dealt with one by one.

1. *The notion of an anticipatory wage gap lacks a firm theoretical basis.* It is difficult to establish in theory what distribution of income should serve as the point of reference. Besides, variations can be caused by many factors other than changes in wages: the growth of productivity, changes in the terms of trade and in relative prices between industry and the economy as a whole, the rate of investment, etc. (Blanchard *et al.*, 1985). Even a freeze on reductions in employment can cause a variation (Krugman, 1982). Consequently, it comes as no surprise that the categorization of the different countries is turned upside down when a different base year is chosen — which is necessarily an arbitrary choice, since there is no golden rule as regards income distribution — or when industry rather than the economy as a whole is examined. This is how Gordon (1984) is able to demonstrate, on the contrary, that the anticipatory wage gap is large in the United States and Japan, and moderate in Europe! So far as Le Dem and Pisani-Ferry (1984) are concerned, this indicator is so variable that it has little significance. Moreover, it would seem that the differences between Europe and the United States begin to dwindle at the beginning of the 1980s (McCallum 1984).

2. *The link with employment and unemployment turns out to be equally tenuous.* Sachs (1983) himself acknowledges that the United States is a striking exception to the theory that it is classical unemployment that is predominant, while Le Cacheux and Szpiro (1984) detect a significant relationship of the expected sign for France, West Germany, and the United Kingdom; on the other hand, in the United States and Japan the wage bill and employment vary together! The work of Le Dem and Pisani-Ferry bears out the absence of any general rule, since all possible permutations can occur. Japan created jobs despite a record distortion of the distribution between wage and profits, while a stable distribution led to job losses in West Germany — but to massive job creation in the United States. Gordon (1984) also concludes that there was no standard international relationship between 1972 and 1979. In short, the temptation to contrast United States and Japan with Europe, or Keynesian unemployment with classical unemployment, does not seem to stand up to closer scrutiny.

3. Similarly, *there are serious reservations about the concept and extent of 'wage rigidity'.* First, the theoretical basis of the measures proposed, which hinge on the concept of the natural rate of unemployment, known to be a tenuous concept, can be disrupted, as is shown by Thirlwall

(1983). Second, the relative importance to be accorded to nominal and real-wage rigidity is arbitrary. These two indicators refer in fact to different theoretical concepts: Walrasian equilibrium with expectations in the case of the first, and classical disequilibrium as regards the second. The labels of 'flexibility' and 'rigidity' can be applied alternately to Europe or the United States, depending on the criteria. Indeed, the econometric estimation of wage equations is one of the most erratic areas of applied macroeconomics, which means that minor changes in specification can sometimes alter completely the rank order of the different countries. Thus, McCallum (1984) finds that there is little difference between countries in the 1980s. Equally, the OECD report (OCDE, *Perspectives économiques*, 1985) and Grubb *et al.* (1983) both agree on the two extremes of flexibility and rigidity (Japan and the United Kingdom, respectively). But most of the other classifications are quite different: France is deemed to be relatively rigid according to the OECD, but flexible according to Grubb *et al.*; in one case the United States is considered almost as flexible as Japan, and in the other as rigid as Italy. Thus, Europe seems to be neither homogeneous[7] nor significantly more rigid than the other countries, and the very concept of rigidity becomes uncertain.

4. Lastly, *greater regional differences in wage rises are not necessarily indicative of a greater possibility of regulating rates of unemployment through adjusting the structure of wages.* Thus, a systematic comparision of US and British regions (NIER, 1984) certainly reveals larger differences in the United States. However, the variation in rates of unemployment is even greater than in wages, and there is no evidence of the expected correlation between wages and unemployment. In short, the United States is no more successful than the United Kingdom in eliminating regional imbalances in the labour market. This shows that a large degree of decentralization does not automatically create a competitive market, and that today's unemployment is not merely frictional,[8] even on the other side of the Atlantic.

In conclusion, two far more general criticisms can be levelled at those characterizations that depict Europe as the breeding ground of classical unemployment.

1. Implicitly or explicitly, they tend to see the determination of wages as being primarily responsible for a possible anticipatory wage gap — without taking into account the multitude of mechanisms and

---

[7] This backs up the conclusions of Chapter 9, Section 3.

[8] It is enough to note that the ratio of job seekers to available jobs in the 1980s is on a totally different scale to the figures recorded in the 1960s.

trends that could also be responsible: a sharp fall in productivity or deterioration in the terms of trade, the consequences of under-investment and the impact of the choice of technology, the importance of elasticities of substitution and contraction of demand, etc. Yet in terms of economic policy, these differences can lead to *confcting strategies*.

2. The series of effects that tend to *stabilize* the wage share over the medium term are further underestimated: price increases, so far as they are allowed by international competition (mechanisms that, as we know, tend to eliminate classical unemployment); the influence of the distribution of income on investment, productivity, and therefore employment; shifts in international specialization and changes in structures of production; etc.

   Furthermore, the most recent econometric research, which formalizes certain dynamic models of this kind for France (Lambert *et al.*, 1984, and Artus *et al.*, 1985, are among the most recent), draws the conclusion that there is a recurring cycle of inflation, Keynesian unemployment, and classical unemployment. Thus, underemployment, which had been predominantly Keynesian from 1963 to 1968, became primarily classical from 1968 to 1973, reverted to being Keynesian from 1974 to 1975, before once again becoming classical in 1976 and 1979. From the beginning of the 1980s, however, Keynesian underemployment is said to have become predominant again. In so far as these results appear to be fairly reliable, the difficulties encountered by the hypothesis that classical unemployment has pertained over the whole period from 1968 can be appreciated.

In conclusion, it is not at all certain that the European countries are in a worse situation simply on account of the way in which their labour markets are organized. Given that, what kind of strategy should they adopt?

3. The Pursuit of Flexibility: A Moderate rather than Maximum Effort

In setting out these results, it is intended to demonstrate that the conventional view, which has gradually gained currency during the first half of the 1980s, is highly debatable. Basically, it sees the crisis as a significant and protracted deviation from the outcome to which the socio-political processes are leading, which would require an equilibrium of pure and perfect competition. Consequently, it would seem that the most fast-acting and far-reaching adjustment would be the best treatment. To be more specific, the recommendations of economic policy hinge on three proposals:

1. *to reduce wages* until an adequate distribution of income is restored;
2. *to restrict budgetary and monetary policy*, to complement this new lowered wage;
3. *to promote, over the medium to long term, labour relations* favouring restoration of a competitive labour market.

In fact, these notions are very largely discredited by macroeconometric studies and other more theoretical analyses.

3.1. The effects of wage restraint in Europe: uncertain and contradictory

What would happen if every country in Europe independently reduced wages by 5 per cent in relation to their trend growth? This question can be answered thanks to work done recently by the European Community (*Economie éuropéenne*, 1984d) and by Wharton Econometrics (1985). Since the formation of these models is as much (if not more) a reflection of the authors' views as of the structural features of the economies studied, the contradictory nature of the effects of wage reductions will be emphasized, as some mechanisms work to stimulate employment while others aggravate it.

- According to a *classically inspired argument based on competition*, such a reduction would trigger disinflation, which boosts national growth by improving competitiveness. This trend may facilitate a fall in interest rates and a growth of real balances, thereby having a beneficial effect on consumption and investment. Beyond these short-term effects, the change in the distribution of income favours profits, which are a positive factor in stimulating capital formation and therefore productivity growth. At the same time, in so far as the elasticity of substitution of labour for capital is significant, the reduction in real wages increases employment as it favours labour-intensive methods of production. The interaction of these mechanisms sets up a 'virtuous circle' whereby an improvement in the external position leads to a revival of growth in internal demand.

- Following the *logic of the Keynesian circular process of income–demand–production determination*, the short-term effects are usually negative: wage restraint depresses consumption, all the more so when allowance is made for the lower propensity to consume out of non-wage income. To the extent that investment decisions are largely based on expected demand, investment is also depressed, even though there may be an upturn in profits. The decline in internal demand may therefore outweigh the improvement in the balance of trade, which, in addition, moderates productivity growth because of the underutilization of productive capacity. It is therefore possible that these Keynesian effects will inhibit the effects of an increase in competitiveness and profits, with the result that the *ex post* level of employment remains

permanently lower than the initial level. This very Fordist chain of logic
therefore leads to an unfavourable outcome.

It is significant that some of the national models used emphasize
classical effects more, while others stress the Keynesian mechanisms. The
Sysifo model in West Germany and the *Oxford* model in the United
Kingdom fall into the first category. In the first year the negative effects
on consumption predominate, but thereafter a 'virtuous circle' is
generated, which is quite dynamic in West Germany but fairly weak in
the United Kingdom. On the other hand, the *Metric* model depicts a fall
in employment in France up until the second year, and when the upturn
finally does occur it is so gradual that by the end of the fourth year
employment is still lower than it would have been with no wage restraint.
Lastly, in Italy the short-term Keynesian effects are overridden by the
effects on competitiveness, apparently because of the high level of non-
wage income.

To some extent, these contrasting results are due to the different
national *economic structures* (composition of disposable income, relative
international position, price-fixing mechanisms, etc.). However, another
prime reason for these discrepancies is the use of opposing theoretical
models. To take the case of France, the *DMS* model, defining the
determinants of production and employment differently and ascribing
importance to the role of profits in the investment decision, paints a
somewhat different picture from the *Metric* model. Similarly, in the *Oxford*
model, the introduction of an elasticity of -0.5 of employment with
respect to real wages is enough to raise the number of jobs created
significantly. Third, if the EEC results are compared with the estimates
made by Wharton Econometrics, although the average effects on growth
for the EEC as a whole are similarly negative during the first year,
afterwards they become positive in one case, while remaining negative in
the other.

What better way of illustrating the uncertainties hanging over such a
crucial issue, even despite the vast quantities of research undertaken by
economists? Bearing this in mind, is it wise to recommend substantial
wage reductions as the answer to the unemployment problem in Europe?
Moreover, the long-term elasticity of employment with respect to initial
wage reductions is at best around 0.5.[9] Furthermore, effects on the
balance of trade are minimal because of the influence of re-equilibrating
mechanisms which preclude the possibility of basing lasting growth on a
cumulative surplus in foreign trade.[10]

---

[9] According to the *Sysifo* model, because of disinflation, the fall in real wages is less than the
initial nominal reduction of 5%. Consequently, overall wage restraint of 1.9% *ex post* would
facilitate the creation of 2.7% extra jobs, which is a substitution rate of 1.4%. The results are far
lower in the other countries.

[10] According to the *Sysifo* model, there would even be a deterioration of trade in West

3.2. Benefits of a co-ordinated accompanying policy

These rather disappointing results lead on to the investigation of other elements of the fight against unemployment. In view of the fact that wage restraint improves public finances, it is possible to envisage a *policy of support* through public spending or fiscal measures. This is the gist of the second alternative.

- If it is assumed that nominal capital GDP is thus kept constant (by means of growth in public investment in proportion to the gains from disinflation), production picks up very significantly, exerting a locomotive effect on employment, which is then maintained at a higher level than would have been achieved with a continuation of previous trends. This Keynesian recovery therefore has a *multiplier effect* on the gains obtained through wage restraint. Admittedly, there are two pre-conditions for this policy: first that governments accept a deterioration of the public sector accounts, and second that countries can finance an increased external deficit. So it comes as no surprise that two of the obstacles to expansion of demand crop up again, even in a context of disinflation and wage restraint. The interdependence between the management of wages and financial and monetary aspects of general economic policy can once more be seen.

  Contrary to the belief spread mainly by conservative ideology,[11] wage austerity *should not* be accompanied by restrictive budgetary measures, because this could cause a cumulative contraction in demand, to the extent that the beneficial effects of improved competitiveness are more or less wiped out. In line with the theory advanced by Malinvaud (1982), in the current situation, restoring an equilibrium in the distribution of income favourable to profits should be supported by an active demand policy. In short, *incomes policy and management of demand should be conducted in opposite directions*.

- But what would happen if all countries in Europe were to adopt the same policy of wage restraint, *at the same time*, without supporting global demand? Quite logically, they would lose any competitive advantage over their European partners, with the result that part of the gains in foreign trade would be wiped out. However, the effects of disinflation would spread via internal trade within the Community, improving real wages, which then would fuel extra consumption. In the short term, the negative effects seem to be predominant; after three or four years, the effects seem to have more or less balanced out or ended up marginally positive.

These results, in so far as they are borne out by other multinational

Germany after four years. It would seem that the dynamics of demand, fuelled by disinflation, pulls up imports, which grow more than foreign competitivity.

[11] Indeed, the recovery in the United States in 1983–4 owes a great deal to this principle: wage restraint combined with increased growth in public expenditure and a large budgetary deficit, resulting from changes in collective bargaining and the beneficial effects of the strong dollar on disinflation.

simulations,[12] dissipate possible concern at the prospect of a policy of wage reduction leading to the export of unemployment. This is always assuming that a downward spiral, with each country attempting to gain a differential advantage through a fresh round of wage reductions, would not be triggered — an issue that I shall have occasion to take up again in Section 4 below.

- The advantages of *co-ordinating support policies* to back up wage restraint can now be emphasized. Concurrent expansion enables employment to be maintained, while limiting the deterioration in the external and public sector accounts. It can also mitigate the effects of competitive rivalry in the reduction of wage costs. This is preferable to all three preceding alternatives on many counts. Moreover, it embodies a belief close to the heart of any Keynesian economist: international co-operation pays dividends,[13] especially where economic recovery is concerned.

Three conclusions may be drawn from this exercise. First, the effects of wage restraint are ambiguous and ambivalent, since the mechanisms of the 'Fordist cycle' combine with competitive forces in varying proportions according to the country and the period. The greatest of caution should therefore be observed as regards proposals to slash wages: they rest on particularly shaky methodological and empirical foundations. Second, budgetary policy should be inversely, rather than directly, linked to wage policy, so as to avoid any cumulative spiral which would depress internal demand without any guaranteed export-led growth. Lastly, paradoxically, the flexibility of wages in an upward direction would limit the positive effects of recovery, whereas an incomes policy that succeeded in preventing a wage and price explosion as expansion took place would, on the contrary, make it more effective.[14] Thus, stabilization of the distribution of income is more favourable to employment than greater flexibility.

This distribution could of course register the effects of structural change and certain developments at the international level. But, contrary to one common belief, *maximum* wage flexibility is not necessarily the *optimum* as far as employment is concerned. The same conclusion can be reached from a more theoretical model.

---

[12] The CEPII's *Sachem-Ouest* model, or the Department of Economic Forecasting's *Atlas* model, tend to corroborate this.

[13] This is in fact the title of a study by the European Trade Union Confederation (Confédération Européenne des Syndicats, 1984), which does not, however, touch on the issue of wage restraint.

[14] Without any such policy, the increase of inflationary pressures in fact reduces the results of recovery by over half (1.6% for GDP against 3.5% with a policy of wage restraint).

*3.3. Microeconomic flexibility and overall employment: no general,
uniform relationship*

Very broadly, the arguments for flexibility have one major flaw: the
assumption that, since flexibility is beneficial at *the individual company level*,
it is automatically beneficial at the national level also. There is little
doubt that a company records better results if it is more competitive and
flexible than its competitors. However, the answer is by no means as
clear-cut once these attributes are generalized and have repercussions on
the level of economic activity. For those who believe in a perfect self-
regulating market, these effects cannot fail to be favourable, since they
consider the overall economy to be only an extension of the representative
firm and employee. This view had already been put forward between the
wars by Professor Pigou, who believed that a downward adjustment of
the nominal wage was a sufficient condition for a return to full
employment. On the other hand J. M. Keynes and his successors held
that there are certain situations where the spontaneous actions of the
economic agents cannot absorb unemployment, and may even aggravate
it. Indeed, when the level of effective demand determines employment, a
reduction in wages (the perennial problem with flexibility!) either has no
effect or is detrimental (see Keynes, 1936, ch. 19).

This reference to the controversies stirred up by the Depression in the
1930s is of more than just anecdotal interest. In the 1980s a belief that is
not so very different from that maintained by Professor Pigou has gained
general acceptance: that any kind of flexibility at the microeconomic level
cannot fail to benefit overall employment. But most of the Keynesian
arguments still hold good. These will now be put into the present context,
by turning from the issue of reducing nominal wages to the issue of
linking them more closely to changes in economic conditions.

Suppose that firms face a situation where effective demand is declining
— possibly because of a fall in expected profitability — which leads to a
reduction in employment. There may also be a deterioration in their
competitiveness, since it is assumed that it is an open economy. Because
of these factors, certain firms will press for re-negotiation (or imposition)
of wage agreements, laying down new, more competitive, mechanisms.
Because of the forces of competition, the other companies in the same
sector will be encouraged, or compelled, to follow suit. All things being
equal, improved control of prices will at first facilitate the acquisition of
market shares, particularly abroad. But once agreements have become
the norm and are reflected in average wages, wage income will be
depressed, with consequent effects on consumption and investment.
What will be the net effect on employment once this process has worked
through, i.e. once there is an increase in the elasticity of nominal wages

with respect to employment, the variable used here to measure the degree of competition? A simple macroeconomic model, constructed on these hypotheses, gives conflicting results (Table 10.3).

TABLE 10.3 *Effects of greater responsiveness of wages to the economic situation: the lessons of a theoretical model*

Structural Characteristics	Initial conditions: autonomous demand and productivity such that:	
	Employment decreases	Employment increases
Fordist logic dominant	I Increased fall in employment; flexibility has a destabilizing effect and does not favour employment	II The growth of employment increases: flexibility has a destabilizing effect but favours employment
Competitivity logic dominant	III Checked decrease in employment but limited value at best zero for the rate of variation; flexibility has a stabilizing effect and favours employment	IV Decreased growth in employment, limited value of zero for rate of variation; flexibility has a stabilizing effect but does not favour employment

Note: For an illustration of the corresponding model see CEPREMAP (1985).

- The *same* increase in wage flexibility does not always produce the same results, irrespective of time and place. It all depends on the relative strength of Keynesian effects (wage income–consumption–investment), on what happens to external competitiveness (production costs–exports and imports–production–income), and on the economic situation at the outset (employment growing or declining). Whether greater competitiveness is beneficial to *overall* employment or not can be determined by the structural parameters of the economy under consideration.[15] This puts into perspective the claims of neoclassical theories to demonstrate that wage flexibility is the optimal solution. The results are a repetition of those produced from econometric simulation of European models.

- If at the outset the components of autonomous demand and productivity are such that employment is falling, and if the Fordist effects are also greater than the effects on competitiveness, a policy of increasing flexibility

[15] Some of the most important of these limitations are the elasticity of the volume and value of foreign trade, the propensity to consume, the coefficient of acceleration of investment, the margin, and the proportion of the various elements of demand in total production.

aggravates job losses and tends to destablize the economic system (quartile I in Table 10.3). In this case, flexibility, which, *ex ante*, promises to be beneficial *at the microeconomic level*, actually turns out to have the opposite effect *ex post at the macroeconomic level*. This is ominous, since the interests of firms lead to the deflationary factors being accentuated, in a cumulative way. The end result therefore is equivalent to that elaborated by Keynes regarding nominal wage reductions, although the mechanisms differ significantly. So it will benefit employment if the employees reject these new mechanisms, or if the state blocks this deflationary spiral by imposing minimum wage norms (New Deal policy?).

- If, on the other hand, the impact on foreign trade proves greater than the impact on wage income, flexibility improves the level of production, thereby *slowing down job losses* and stabilizing the economy (quartile III in Table 10.3). In this second case, the microeconomic interests of the firms coincide with improvements in overall employment. The structural changes in wage agreements effected by the firms are therefore in line with restoring equilibrium.

- Even in this case, firms do not succeed in reversing previous tendencies and creating jobs. Total flexibility (i.e. wages tending towards zero as soon as employment contracts — a highly unrealistic hypothesis) would, at best, stabilize employment. In fact, a return to employment growth would require action on the components of autonomous demand (trends in world trade, public spending, credit, etc.) and on technical change (trends in productivity), all factors that companies cannot influence individually. In these conditions, flexibility *cannot* challenge the constraints imposed at the level of the economic system as a whole: at most, it allows adaptation while limiting the unfavourable consequences. *In theory*, therefore, there is a clear division of responsibility between businesses and economic policy. *In practice*, there is a possible illusion at the firm level: as the introduction of flexibility initially slows down the contraction of employment, there is a great temptation to reinforce it as it comes up against the *barrier of effective demand*.

This brings us a long way from the original argument. On the one hand, under conditions of Fordist growth, flexibility tends to be unfavourable, since it exaggerates the rise as well as the fall in employment and can exacerbate economic fluctuations. On the other hand, when growth is based essentially on foreign trade, flexibility cushions the negative effects on employment of the constraints on the level of effective demand. But it is then a *defensive adjustment*, a 'shoulder to the wheel' policy, whereby wage-earners have to bear the brunt of costs incurred elsewhere (because of disturbances in the international system, say, or the thrust of budgetary policy). This is unfortunate in both economic and social terms, and moreover does not seem to provide an answer to the problem of mass unemployment.

Such a conclusion is sufficiently important to merit a discussion of its premises. First, it is not just a reformulation of the Keynesian argument quoted earlier. It differs on two counts: on the one hand because it is the principle of wage determination rather than nominal wages that is at stake, and on the other hand because, given an open economy, the inadequacy of effective demand and of competitiveness combine to explain unemployment, so the results are not purely tautological. Second, the model could be extended and refined by, for example, introducing an economic policy that is either pro- or anti-cyclical. Moreover, it is highly probable that expectations will reinforce the trends previously described, once a deflationary spiral has been initiated.

It may therefore be that the arguments in favour of a 'moderate flexibility' transcend the framework of the model on which these analyses have been based.

4. The Lessons of History: Not to be Forgotten

A survey of growth in the capitalist economies over the long term does indeed produce some confirmation.

4.1. Wage rigidities and rising growth rates: the postwar period

Certain econometric studies have effectively demonstrated that the labour market was more flexible during the nineteenth century or the interwar years. Thus, both France and the United States have experienced increased rigidities, although in my view that gives a dubious, not to say erroneous, description of the Fordist system of wage/ labour relations. After the Second World War, wages became less sensitive to variations in employment (see Boyer, 1979b and Basle *et al.*, 1982, for France; Sachs, 1980, for US), the speed of adjustment in which declined considerably at the same time, especially in the countries of Europe (see Boyer and Mistral, 1978b). Was this period adversely affected by the institutionalization of the management of employment and the determination of wages? On the contrary, it would seem that these developments were largely beneficial.

Particularly in Europe, *growth became so much more sustained and regular* that it guaranteed virtual full employment up to the mid-1960s. This was no chance occurrence, as is shown in the introductory chapter to this volume. Basically, the growth of wage income was planned *ex ante* to correspond with the growth of productivity capacity and, thereby, stimulated it further.

Adjustment of overall supply and demand no longer entails massive falls in production and employment. Consequently, it operates through simply causing recession, during which the stability of wages and the

traditional productivity cycle stabilize the economy. Thus the potential
for large productivity gains, inherent in Fordism, can be realized. To take
this argument to its logical conclusion, reduced 'flexibility' in the labour
market proves beneficial both to employment and to economic growth, in
contrast to current conventional wisdom.

But it could be objected that flexibility assumes new relevance when
sustained growth gives way to a period of structural crisis.

4.2. *Flexibility — and yet no end to the crisis: the interwar years*

The experience of the 1930s, however, *refutes* the notion that all that is
required to preclude all risk of persistent stagnation, and to find a
spontaneous way out of the crisis, is for the economies to be flexible. For a
start, the crash of 1929 occurred at a time when labour markets were still
remarkably competitive, with the possible exception of the United
Kingdom. Given that the productivity growth associated with Taylorism
is such that employment growth is quite small and therefore holds down
wage income, inadequate wage growth could even be viewed as one of the
causes of the crisis in 1929 both in the United States and in France.
Thereafter, once the crisis had set in, massive job contraction and the
collapse of nominal wages proved incapable of pushing up profits or
investment: a vicious circle was initiated, in which unfavourable
expectations and the collapse and subsequent stagnation of demand fed
on each other. As prices fell more than wages, real wages grew from 1929
to 1932,[16] and at the time gave the impression of real-wage rigidity, the
source of unemployment. The order of events and of cause and effect was
in fact the other way round: it was the *crisis* that caused the shift in the
distribution of income. Besides, this shift served instead to *correct* the
excessive level of profits in relation to effective demand (Boyer, 1979a),
even though it was insufficient to initiate an endogenous recovery
in activity.

Lastly, the flexibility of employment — specifically, the absence of
legal restrictions on dismissals — is far from being a necessary or
sufficient condition for the recovery of job creation: a far greater speed of
adjustment than we have today (quartile II of Table 10.3) did not
prevent the persistence of unprecedented rates of unemployment. This is
hardly surprising, since, at least in the first instance, employment
depends on the interaction of changes in effective demand — or profitable
supply — with productivity trends. And flexibility can have conflicting
effects on these three variables: positive or negative on demand
depending on circumstances (cf. previous model), always positive on

---

[16] See S. Bonell, quoted in Sachs (1983, p. 272). The USA is the only exception.

profitable supply, and an ambiguous effect on productivity (generally favourable in the short term, but uncertain in the medium term as it all depends on the type of flexibility — whether it involves plant and machinery, work-force versatility, or wage reduction).

Faced with the uniformity of these conclusions, readers may be forgiven for believing that one crucial issue has been omitted: does international competition not demand the introduction of flexibility, as an element of competitiveness in largely open economies?

4.3. Wage restraint: the equivalent of competitive devaluation in the past?

The close correlation between the breakdown of the old system of wage/labour relations and the burgeoning of the international crisis was repeatedly emphasized in Chapter 9 (Sections 1 and 2.4). In view of the ever increasing unpredictability of changes in demand, exchange rates, and interest rates, flexibility of production and adaptability of the work-force appear to be vital, and largely distinguish one national system of production from another.

Flexibility of working time, job mobility, and the sectoral shift of labour from sectors in decline to those in ascendance allow rapid response to changes in the volume and distribution of world demand. This is one way to gain a larger market share in circumstances where the end of the period of rapid growth of international trade in industrial goods no longer makes it possible for the various economies to grow simultaneously.

Control of labour costs — through a boost to productivity or a reduction in real or nominal wages — is a second way of increasing exports, or reducing penetration of the domestic market, and therefore of generating a balance of trade surplus, beneficial to growth and (under certain conditions) employment.

There is little doubt, therefore, that flexibility is advantageous for *any given country*. But this does not necessarily hold true when the strategy is adopted by *all countries together*, just as its spread from a few high-performance firms to the national economy may result in a contraction of employment and/or a destabilization of the economy (quartiles I and IV of Table 10.3). It is possible, in effect, to use the results above, substituting nation-states for firms and the international system for the national economy. In this case, if external transactions are invalidated, we are left with the Keynesian system. It is clear from this that increased flexibility always has destabilizing effects (quartiles I and II of Table 10.3). If at the outset effective demand is such that world-wide employment is contracting, this is reinforced by the restoration of a more competitive system of wage determination. This spiral may be further aggravated if all governments decide to cut budgetary expenditure and to adopt a restrictive monetary policy.[17] Although theoretical and relatively extreme, this process is potentially disturbing, since it reproduces the worst interactions of the 1930s. Even though numerous Fordist safety nets still exist, in the past decade certain tendencies have emerged which, if they continue, can only lead to increased international instability.

For the European countries, *extending competition to the most basic products*, the markets for which are naturally determined by price and production cost, is perhaps a questionable way of safeguarding jobs, because it entails using unfair advantages against economies where the standard of living, the level of wages, and social legislation are very different. On the contrary, in the long term everything seems to indicate that competitiveness is based on the ability constantly to renew the advantages associated with quality, new products, mastery of the means of production, etc. So price competition is no longer the essential thing, and the mainspring of commercial warfare has less to do with lowering relative wages than with improving the skill and competence of the work-force, and with innovation in the methods of production and organization. Resort to the easiest forms of flexibility could therefore mean a retrograde step as regards the international division of labour — and, correspondingly, *growing difficulties in maintaining the old system of wage/labour relations.*

Even in this case, it is *impossible*, by virtue of the basic accounting principle that one country's exports must correspond to another country's imports, for all national economies to enjoy *greater relative competitiveness* and therefore also to enjoy growth through exports and foreign trade surplus. That is stating the obvious, no doubt; but it seems to have been forgotten by the advocates of flexibility in all possible areas and by those who see the import and world-wide diffusion of the 'Japanese model' (or American model!) as *the* answer to present difficulties. In this regard, it is striking to note that, from the end of the 1970s, just about all European countries seemed to be vying with each other to control labour costs (Table 9.2 above). There is no doubt that this tactic has curbed inflation significantly. Nevertheless, no virtuous circle of export-led growth has been initiated, if only because the measures taken regarding wages and employment have *also* affected the growth of consumption and of the European market, and because economic policies have been more restrictive than expansionary.

As a third line of argument, it is in fact conceivable that flexibility is more than just a means of competing for a share in existing international markets, and that potentially, because of its global implications, it contributes to a *contraction of world demand*. It is possible to think of it, in

---

[17] This result does not contradict the simulations for wage restraint in Europe, quoted earlier (Section 3 above). Economic policy had either remained unchanged, or had shifted to expansionary measures gradually as disinflation took effect.

effect, as a mechanism similar to competitive devaluation — or protectionism. In the initial phase, those countries that are more competitive because of their flexibility exploit the markets of their weaker competitors. Faced with the consequent foreign trade deficit, the latter are then compelled to adopt stabilization polices: wage restraint and the search for variability then take effect on their growth rates. Since the initiating and dominant countries continue to strive for increased competitiveness, the position of each country relative to all others and market shares settle back more or less to their initial position — but at a generally lower level of growth and employment.[18] Things are made worse if governments also introduce wage controls and austerity measures, because in so doing they contribute to a reduction of world demand, thus making the net effect *negative* rather than simply *neutral*. Hence there may be a rise in unemployment which makes it possible for further efforts to be made to increase flexibility. Particularly unfavourable expectations can prolong this process, bringing about a vicious circle which is the equivalent, at the international level, of the process that explains the resistance of Keynesian-type recession in a national economy.

The dangers may, however, be even greater, because it is still in the interests of each country to pursue its drive for competitiveness[19] — at the risk of aggravating the overall situation — when there is no supranational body (the counterpart of the nation state) generally empowered to impose or introduce adequate agreements or rules of fair play. In a nutshell, the pursuit of flexibility, a rational response to the crisis, may actually exacerbate it, by undermining international trade. There is, of course, no need to be excessively alarmist. Other mechanisms can help to reverse these unfavourable tendencies, for example maintaining public demand in each country at a sufficient level, granting loans to debtor countries for modernization purposes, etc.

Protectionism and competitive devaluation are subject to almost unanimous disapproval, while flexibility has, for several years, been presented in a distinctly favourable light. But what if certain types of flexibility were as pernicious as these other two strategies that are so widely denounced?

---

[18] Cf. Table 9.2 above. Given co-ordinated wage policies, employment is up by only 0.2% over its base level, while it rose by 0.6% with independent measures. As far as the balance of trade is concerned, there is no change, which exemplifies the futility of policies aiming to export unemployment, both as regards employment and external equilibrium.

[19] One example of the Prisoners' Dilemma (see Chapter 11, Section 1).

11

The Search for New Wage/Labour Relations: Complex and Contradictory, but Crucial

Robert Boyer

In the light of the above discussion about methods of flexibility in theory and in practice, it can be seen that the challenge for the 1980s is not just a simple adjustment in the economy, but very probably a total redefinition of wage/labour relations, and of other forms of organization as a whole, in order to work out an alternative method of development. But this interpretation immediately runs up against an *apparent paradox*: have not the industrial disputes of the past decade been typified, on the contrary, by increased union determination to defend the old Fordist compromise in its entirety? After all, does not managerial success as regards flexibility point up strongly the difficulty of unions in drawing up alternative proposals appropriate to the 1980s, which are not the same as the 1960s?

It is important to clarify some of the reasons for this paradox, and then to describe the development of industrial relations, emphasizing the new course that they have taken since the beginning of the 1980s. This then makes it possible to chart some of the changes in wage/labour relations, which may augur a general reform.

1. The Trade Union Defence of the Fordist Compromise: Not so Irrational — But Difficult to Maintain in the Long Term

In so far as a structural crisis is marked by the demise of the old and the difficulty of the new becoming established and defining a coherent system, a common, and understandable, response to this situation is to extol the virtues of the past, perceived as the 'Golden Age' or the 'good old days'. Although it means glossing over some of the imbalances or even the contradictions inherent in the old system of regulation, the behavioural features of the period of expansion are seen to promise a revival of growth on bases tried and tested over a long period of time. This accounts for the return to the gold standard after the First World War, and also for fears of a new period of stagnation, once most of the post-Second World War reconstruction had been completed! Indeed, it was difficult for people at the time to conceive of a banking system based on credit — or the possibility of a high and sustained growth rate from the transition to mass production and consumption.

Mutatis mutandis, the controversy surrounding the present upheaval in wage/labour relations is not free from such nostalgia. As already seen most governments react like this in the first years of a crisis. Up until very recently, the strategy of the trade unions was to defend the old compromise in its entirety, and in addition to fight for jobs. Why give up achievements for which workers had been struggling since the advent of industrial capitalism — achievements, moreover, that in the 1960s were compatible with a rapid rise in not only the standard of living but also profits and investment? It is not hard to appreciate why unions have energetically defended the postwar consensus, the basis of their strategy, their internal organization, and their credibility in the eyes of workers and wage-earners.

But reference to the past does not by itself explain what is sometimes described with a derogatory nuance as the 'defence of acquired interests'. The overall interests of unions and employers' organizations may quite rationally imply the maintenance of old demands and practices, at least so long as the crisis does not radically destabilize economic regularities. To clarify this, it is useful to look briefly over the history of industrial relations from the beginning of the 1960s. *Four major phases* can be identified.

The first phase coincides with the period of the 'glorious three decades' (1945–75). Throughout this period, industrial labour disputes did occur, but they were tightly channelled within the Fordist compromise. Virtually all demands (including those concerned with jobs or production lines) culminated in wage rises. Faced with these rises, businesses reacted by stepping up productivity growth or, failing that, by putting up prices. To the extent that wage growth spread through the whole economy and competition was oligopolistic, demand did not suffer any unfavourable repercussions because of this inflationary spiral. Labour disputes were thus based on an agreed division of roles: the unions took the initiative on wage issues, while businesses were free to raise prices. Unemployment was very low and, in general, employment was growing, so these issues hardly ever surfaced in industrial disputes, unless there were sectoral or regional problems.

The second stage went unnoticed by all sides at the start, since it began with the progressive destabilization of the monopolistic system of regulation (see Chapters 1 and 9 above). On the one hand, reorganization of work no longer necessarily brought productivity gains on a par with the nominal wage increases. Consequently, only an increase in inflation, made possible by an accommodating monetary policy, could temporarily maintain profitability. On the other hand, the internationalization of trade and production had reached the stage where national companies were no longer in sole control of fixing their own prices. From then on companies suffered a drop in profitability and a loss of markets, and in certain cases they had to resort to shedding jobs. Calls for an incomes policy, based on reciprocal moderation of wage and price rises, date from this period. The decline in inflation was to stimulate national competitiveness and to promote growth and employment.

These invocations of the virtues of moderation, however, generally got caught up in the cross-fire between employers and unions. In effect, it is in the clear interest of both sides to continue with their existing strategies. To simplify matters, let us suppose that unions have the choice between two options, a high or a low wage claim, and that companies have an analagous choice, of a moderate or a large price increase.[1] What happens if both sides of industry *lack confidence in each other*, and fear that the other party will fail to implement a possible compromise? It would then be in the interests of the unions to put in a high claim. If the firms do, in fact, curb their prices, employees will gain an increase in real wages; if, on the other hand, they increase them markedly, the workers will be protected from a fall in their standard of living. *Mutatis mutandis*, it is the same for companies: they pre-empt the consequences of the union strategy by choosing the option of high price rises. The end result is a high level of inflation, with adverse effects on the external balance and therefore on growth, including the growth of real wages. The result is less beneficial, both to employees and to the companies, than that which would have been produced by moderation of nominal income. And yet neither the employers nor the employees have an interest in revising their strategy. Informed readers will doubtless have recognized the equivalent of the 'Prisoners' Dilemma':[2] the pursuit of individual self-interest leads to the worse results for both.

This is one explanation of the continued defence of the Fordist

---

[1] Assume also a single union strategy (or a single union), and a single company policy, so that the wages and prices they agree correspond to the mean value for the whole economy.

[2] Game theory, and its application to economics, often uses this example. Two suspects are being separately interrogated about a crime they jointly committed. They know that if they both stay silent they will receive a light prison sentence. If one stays silent while the other confesses, the first will receive a long prison sentence while the other will go free. If both confess they will both receive a medium prison sentence. Each person can choose only once — which means that, if one chooses to stay silent while the second confesses, the first cannot then confess upon learning of his sentence. This is what creates the dilemma. Their joint interest is for both not to confess, but the outcome is that both do confess. From the point of view of either one of them, staying silent while the other confesses would give the worse outcome, and confessing at least ensures that this outcome is avoided, while it also allows the possibility that the confessor will go free if the other stays silent.

compromise (particularly as regards wage elements). It does not just come down to inertia and habit in the union strategy. It is also the *best strategy* in a social context which precludes open and natural co-operation between employers and unions. The economist cannot afford, any more than the politician, to remain impassive when faced with such a situation, which is frustrating, to say the least. The history of labour relations since the war suggests three ways of overcoming this dilemma.

1. First, the recurrence of this paradoxical situation may convince both sides of the benefit of *co-operation and a kind of consensus*. In this case, the main aim is to create mutual trust, which would prevent a relapse into a purely individual strategy to minimize the losses incurred. It would seem that this is what has happened in Austria, Japan, Norway, Sweden, etc. — those societies that vacillate between corporatism and social democracy. Comparative studies demonstrate that these countries, where disputes are least frequent, have the best macroeconomic performance in terms of unemployment and inflation (Cameron, 1982; McCallum, 1983). Such a consensus, however, is forged through a long historical process, not itself free from upheaval: it is clearly less feasible for the traditionally less co-operative societies to import this model when the crisis promotes confrontation and is far from nuturing the necessary climate of confidence. Hence the recourse to two other solutions, which are somewhat imperfect and costly.

2. The state may resort to a *prescriptive or authoritarian incomes policy*. Thus there are many instances in the United States, as well as in the United Kingdom and France, of wage and price norms, often imposed in conjunction with plans for economic stabilization. With very few exceptions, however, the measure cannot be pursued for very long, and flounders under the renewed convergence of business and union interest in free wage negotiations. In addition, this approach often alternates with a third, quite different, strategy.

3. Firms under financial pressure may go on the offensive with a *change in the rules of the game* imposed by pressure, threat, or persuasion. It is indeed conceivable that redundancies could be the management response to union wage claims considered to be excessive. This new development, after a period of virtually guaranteed employment, cannot but alter the nature of the strategies followed previously. In so far as there are massive job losses — particularly affecting hard-core union members — wage restraint *can* become the best way of defending wage income, thereby changing union behaviour. The early 1980s provide many examples of this third strategy.

2. Labour Relations: From the Iron Fist to More or Less Forced Co-operation?

This marks the beginning of a *third phase*, characterized by an abrupt reversal of initiative and relative strength. The further the crisis has progressed beyond alternating periods of recovery and recession, the more rapid has been the upheaval in industrial relations. Indeed, there has been an accumulation at the macroeconomic level of all those conditions that make it impossible for firms to continue their previous policy on employment. Increased penetration of the domestic market, difficulties in exporting, shifts in the location of manufacturing industries, an upsurge in real rates of interest, the onset of decline in the traditional Fordist sectors — all combine to disrupt standard practices in industrial relations. The reversal of company policy is often accompanied or precipitated by a change in the government or its policy. For example, in the United States, the 'monetarist shock' in Reagan's first term of office played a part in undermining many features of US postwar collective bargaining. The businesses hardest hit are the first to negotiate wage concessions, often on a substantial scale, in exchange for fewer job losses (see Lacombe and Conley, 1985). Other businesses then follow their lead, citing the concessions already obtained. Thus movement is in a downwards rather than an upwards direction.

All things considered, the United Kingdom provides an analogous example. The shift in favour of firms is spectacular, less as a result of negotiated settlements beneficial to companies than because of the virtually unilateral imposition of new conditions (the miners' strike of 1984–5). Even where circumstances are less inflammatory, industrial relations tend to grind to a halt, since it is no longer a question of bartering concessions for advantages, but rather of minimizing the loss of existing rights, while satisfying economic criteria determined completely outside the framework of consultation, and of getting the workers to accept it. The failure of negotiations on flexibility in France (February 1985) is an example of the middle way between defending the Fordist logic and drawing up new agreements that are favourable to employment. It is this that is the priority in what appears to be a *fourth phase* in industrial relations.

In the long term, it is not necessarily in the interests of firms to make terms of employment and pay dependent on short-term economic conditions and to accentuate factors making for instability in the management of their labour force. The loyalty and commitment of workers to the company, and therefore to productivity and economic performance, may well be damaged by this shortening of future employment prospects. Furthermore, maintenance of skill levels in any company requires a minimum degree of stability for a large part of the work-force. In addition, the fourth phase sees the beginning of negotiation of a *new set of rules of the game*. There is then a real trade-off of advantages against concessions: reduction in working time against freedom to distribute working hours over the year, internal worker mobility against participation in and/or control over the introduction of new technology (e.g. West Germany), virtual job security for a small number of workers in exchange for improvements in productivity and quality, suppression of outdated jobs against large-scale internal training schemes (e.g. 1984 agreements in the US car industry).

So the diagnosis would be that we are now entering a new phase of labour relations. In comparison with what went before, this is now based on at least three conditions:

1. a new agreement on the objective of increasing productive efficiency through co-operation between workers and management;

2. the negotiation of reciprocal concessions (jobs, training, working hours, wages, etc.) in exchange for these undertakings;

3. recognition that there is a range of forms of organization and methods of management that can be used to achieve the same objective of competitiveness. Information can be made available about the alternatives, and the choice made after consultation and negotiation with the employees.[3]

There is no doubt that it was the absence of these three aspects that led to the failure in France of the first talks on flexibility, whereas some — admittedly, very local — progress was made in the United States. In short, today's national economies have entered an era of intense experimentation, of trial and error in pursuit of the possible outline of a new system of wage/labour relations.

3. The 1980s: Innovation, Regeneration, or the New Combined with the Old?

These developments emphasize that Fordism may not after all be the high point in the history of labour relations. Certainly, Fordism has today come under fire largely because of the pressure of financial and economic difficulties, rather than because of the express wishes of workers, although they do play a part in shaping the various elements of the system of wage/labour relations. Indeed, the crisis brings out its

---

[3] The break with Taylor's 'one best way' is thus, in theory, obvious.

limitations and encourages a host of experiments seeking an alternative. The crisis is not, therefore, wholly *negative* just because it is *destructive* of the old order. It can also be *positive*, by being the catalyst for the *reconstruction of 'the wage-earning society'*, which ultimately transcends some of the conflicts and contradictions that have been stumbling blocks to growth since the Second World War.

Indeed, the forces at work are particularly complex because there is no guarantee that the succession of 'models' (US, Japanese, etc.) put forward by the experts, or the host of 'breakthroughs' on the part of management, will all produce viable options or paths for the future. Most of the 'miracle cures' are, in fact, proved wanting by changes in economic circumstances that are common during crises. Second, the overall socio-political and economic coherence of these schemes has yet to be tested. Lastly, even supposing that these models were fully integrated and could be exported (which is doubtful), how can we make the transition from the Fordist system to this other model without total chaos?[4] The aim of this chapter is far less ambitious: to outline some of the innovations and resurrected methods that have marked the system of wage/labour relations over the past decade (Table 11.1).

3.1. The organization of labour: revolution, revision or regression?

The new principles of *flexible automation*, which have already been discussed, are compatible with change. By making small-scale production competitive and improving the profitability of multi-purpose plant and machinery, they *theoretically* embody one of the potential methods of industrial production in the future. The extension of these methods could open up a whole new chapter of history, as illustrated by the title of the work by Piore and Sabel (1984). But computerization can also perpetuate some of the old tendencies of the scientific organization of labour. In the past, this has happened in processing industries. In the future, large sections of tertiary labour may be subject to a form of rationalization, which has so far been delayed because of a lack of social and technical means of controlling workers.

To go from one end of the scale — radical innovation — to the other — resurrection of regressive methods — we find Taylorian and Fordist methods being exported to newly industrialized countries. This involves transferring forms of organization rendered inappropriate in the developed countries, by the general level of training and awareness of young people, to geographical areas that are more amenable to them (Rubino, 1983).

---

[4] See Boyer (1986) and Boyer (1984a). As regards the divergences between theoreticians and practising managers in their quest for new principles of firms' organization, see the ironic retrospective 'Business Fads' (*Business Week*, 20 January 1986).

TABLE 11.1 *The transformations of the wage/labour relation*

	Organization of production	Hierarchy of qualifications	Work contract	Wage formation	Social protection
Innovation	• Work-shop flexibility • Robotics • Computerization of tertiary work	• Self-employed groups • Quality circles	• Job security against concessions on productivity and variability of the work-force • Transfer of labour from one firm to another • Job-sharing	• Wage funds • Profit-sharing within the company • Collective agreements sharing effective productivity gains (rather than anticipated gains)	• Health Maintenance Organizations: an alternative way of satisfying collective needs • New means of intervention (incorporation of young people in to the work-force)
Blend of the old and the new	• Electronification of mass production • Scientific organization of work in the tertiary sector • Export of Fordist production lines to other countries	• Redefinition of jobs and re-evaluation of middle management • Emphasis on general and in-house training • Promotion of a distinction between conception work and execution work	• Firms' responsibility as regards retraining • Part-time work • Two alternative contracts: (1) virtually guaranteed work, against wage concessions (2) fixed-term contracts, but with higher pay • Subcontracting, temporary work	• Trinomial wage: minimum legal wage, performance of firms, individual merit • Wages no longer linked to consumer price, but to competitors' prices	• Financial contributions to social security to be rationalized and made more widely applicable • Extension of cover to larger sectors of the population and, in some cases, increase of lump-sum payments • Subsidies for creating and/or preserving jobs
Resurgence	• Relative boom of medium- and small-scale enterprises • Traditional cottage industries	• Tapping relatively unskilled labour for certain stages of production	• Fixed-term contracts • Illegal and semi-legal work • Easing of the legal or structural limitations on redundancies	• De-indexation • Differential wages (at a lower rate) for newcomers • General (and sometimes substantial) drop in wages under threat of total closure and relocation • Changes in legislation on the minimum wage (for young people, etc.)	• Exemption from welfare liabilities • Cuts in certain benefits • Move towards a dual system: basic security provided by the state, supplemented by more comprehensive private cover • No provision for illegal or semi-legal work

But even within old industrial countries, the crisis enables methods of work from the distant past to be revived and put into practice. To take just one example, home working has re-emerged, not only in traditional areas (the clothing trade) but also in modernized, or even truly modern, areas (e.g. 'cottage electronics'). Nor does this take into account the large numbers of traditional tertiary jobs that are organized on relatively primitive lines. Nevertheless, it would seem, in terms of employment, that the 'regressive' methods are at least as important as those methods associated with the most technologically advanced sectors.

3.2. Qualifications: more training versus the attraction of unskilled labour

Today the whole structure of wages is subject to the repercussions of these many diverse innovations. On the one hand, there is the opportunity to mitigate some of the worst features of Fordism: less need for a hierarchy exercising authoritarian control, the possibility of doing away with tedious, dangerous, or purely repetitive jobs, opportunities of raising qualifications through general and adequate technical training. This opens up new dimensions in job negotiation: the redefinition of recognized qualifications, ways of progressing up the salary scale, work regulations corresponding to these new social and technological circumstances. This would also cover the self-employed (somewhat neglected these days). Furthermore, it is conceivable that the position of middle management, etc., could be called into question.

But on the other hand, not all companies or sectors are in a position to adopt this strategy: falling back on cheap, unskilled labour is a great temptation — and a very real danger, particularly as minimum wage levels are lowered or eliminated. Persistent reliance on immigrant labour in Europe and the influx of a new generation of immigrants into the United States demonstrate the dimensions of this phenomenon. Equally, it is not certain that computerization will undermine the historical division between manual labour and intellectual work. If some repetitive tasks can be abolished and others made potentially more varied and interesting, the rationalization and Taylorization of intellectual work itself may also occur. To summarize, the present changes seem to be relatively open-ended: they are so diverse and contradictory that they cannot be rigidly determined solely by what is technologically possible.

3.3. The work contract: some steps forwards, as well as backwards

The course of the first half of the 1980s paints a rather bleak picture: the proliferation of insecure jobs, the reduction or total evasion of legal safeguards, the proliferation of exceptions to full-time and long-term

employment, the black economy, the growth of jobs not covered by legislation, etc. Conservative doctrine tends to portray these developments as
beneficial — and inevitable — which lends credence to the idea of wage
reductions pure and simple as a general prescription. This impression is
further reinforced by the problems encountered by social democratic
governments in their attempts to extend the rights of wage-earners.

This does not, however, take into account those innovations and
original ideas that have been shown to be particularly relevant by the
crisis. Is it not significant that in 1985 there is talk of granting a degree of
job security in exchange for increased adaptability and productivity of
the work-force in large enterprises? By the same token, transfers of work
from one group to another undoubtedly herald greater consideration of
social issues in employment decisions. Furthermore, are those government
policies that in Europe enable workers in declining industries to be
retrained not an anticipation of an extension of the monopolistic system
of regulation?

As stated above, the new and the old can blend together. This also
applies to the new twin-option work contracts, the first option giving job
security (unless economic results are catastrophic) against wage concessions (previous wage levels can be. re-established only through above-
average productivity) and the second having fixed-term contracts, but
higher wages.[5] But once again, there are no preordained (in this case
economic) criteria to determine *a priori* which group of workers would
come under which of these two contracts.[6]

3.4. Wages: a move towards complex hybrid systems?

One of the most inventive schemes in this field is the establishment of
wage funds, which have been hotly debated in Sweden. In one sense, it
provides a way of extending the time scale that unions take into account,
a way of dealing with the constraints associated with modernization and
more generally with economic efficiency. With this institutional method
of proceeding, employees can be assured that savings from wage restraint
are in fact channelled into launching new investment projects. At the
same time, from a strictly macroeconomic viewpoint, the extension of

[5] Proposed 1985 contract for the US car industry. It should be stressed that this would
preclude any union representation, the workers' claims and grievances all being expressed
within the enterprise itself (see Blandin, 1985).

[6] Thus, within certain firms, the second type of contract (or 'wage concession') is restricted to
new employees. In this case segmentation would differentiate between experienced steady
workers and young workers with access only to temporary or low-paid employment. In the
preceding model, this division would be a function of life-style preferences (and of greater or
lesser risk aversion, as the neo-classical theorists would put it), without discrimination with
respect to age. One can imagine other possible divisions between wage earners: stable domestic
workers *v.* unstable immigrant worker, etc.

such a system ensures that a temporary lull in consumption does not lead to a contraction of investment (a traditional accelerator effect) or the spread of adverse expectations as regards plans for the future, developments that usually result in recession and persistent underemployment.[7] In theory, therefore, wage funds could be a possible updated version of an incomes policy, superceding those authoritarian, centralized, state-controlled incomes policies that, as has been emphasized, have met with little success.

There are, however, other less innovatary variations, which combine old Taylorian forms of the *effective* incentive wage, with some Fordist safeguards (wages rising in part with the cost of living). In this respect, proposed binomial or trinomial wage schemes (a third element being determined by company results) are gaining ground. Lastly, at another extreme, the resurgence of a variety of schemes based on competitiveness must be emphasized: plans for lower wages for young people, attempts to get wage-earners to agree to concessions even during recovery (United States in 1984 and 1985), pressure on those not covered by employment legislation, relocation to low-wage areas, exclusion of any general agreement on indexation, etc. This list gives an idea of the range of formulae potentially available and therefore of the economic and social dynamics that can be envisaged: wages, a component of demand as well as one of the costs of production, are at the heart of the process of finding ways out of the crisis.

3.5. Social security: if crisis were the mother of invention!

The difficulty in balancing the social security budget in a period of sluggish growth and soaring unemployment at first resulted in the raising of compulsory deductions and attempts to 'rationalize' the range of benefits. But these measures have repercussions on the level of activity: an increase in employees' and household contributions depresses disposable income and therefore consumption; higher taxation of companies reduces their financial reserves, and therefore their incentive to invest and, in certain cases, to expand employment when social contributions are based largely on the number of employees. Thus, the global crisis and the financial problems of the welfare state reinforce each other, to the point where the division between those who believe that over-generous social security is to blame and those who believe the opposite (that extension of the system as it stands should be enough to pull us through the crisis) becomes irrelevant.

In fact, it seems that it is the integration of social security with the

---

[7] This process is at the heart of Keynes's analysis in his *General Theory* (Keynes, 1936).

economic system as a whole — i.e. its structure and funding — that is the root of the problem, and not simply its day-to-day administration. As a result, attention in all countries is now turning to the respective advantages of nationwide private insurance schemes and collective and contractually based social security. In those countries with centralized state systems, there is no shortage of people attempting to find alternatives — based on local support networks, for instance, or the privatization of some of the risks. Conversely, the crisis highlights the limitations of a decentralized system administered by individual companies[8] and calls for a return to a far wider safety net. Furthermore, it may be that intermediate systems (a Health Maintenance Organization, the establishment of a general budget for hospitals, etc.) could internalize some of the externalities associated with the provision of community services (such as health care), while maintaining the incentive of competition.

At another extreme, proposals to make a sharp division between state welfare backed by public funds and private insurance lead towards a multi-tier social security system, which would tend to accentuate inequalities in direct income. Would the outcome be an updated and integrated system, or inefficient and fragmented social security? Herein lies one of the great questions of this decade: what is the *desirable* way forward for social security, given that, because of the non-recovery of growth, it is *impossible* to continue administering a system on the margin, when that system was set up in the 1930s and 1940s and is designed for a completely different mode of development? This is a very general question, which applies to wage/labour relations in their entirety.

4. From Defensive Flexibility to the Active Pursuit of New Principles

It would be futile to try to define the many variations as there are permutations of the five elements examined above. In fact, the available options hinge basically on two major questions:

- What is the crisis? Nothing more than a *delayed reaction to change*, or an extended phase of *structural transformation*?

- Is greater flexibility merely a means of adjusting *downwards*, or does it offer a *positive principle of economic and social organization*?

---

[8] Thus, there were social policies among firms after the Second World War which sought to retain their work-force by offering housing, company training schemes, pension schemes, etc. These advantages are inherently incapable of transfer to another firm, which causes problems when a region or an entire industry is hit by crisis (e.g. the steel industry in the East and North of France).

From this, four possible strategies emerge, depending on whether defensive or offensive methods of flexibility are implemented, and on whether the crisis is considered to be transitional or structural (Table 11.2).

TABLE 11.2   *The price of flexibility: differing interpretations*

Phenomenon considered to be:	Strategy employed	
	Defensive flexibility	Offensive flexibility
Transitional	I Policy aimed at absorbing previous imbalances (particularly in wages) is sole pre-condition required for a return to previous levels of national and international growth	II Means of improving the international ranking of the country and revival of growth, within the framework of a system that continues to be cohesive and dynamic
Structural	III In theory, when taken to extreme, flexibility = return to actual or idealized mechanisms of competition (drawn from the 19th century and from Walras, respectively): in practice, further wage segmentation	IV The issue at stake here is no less than the attempt at establishing a new wage/labour relation, which is: ● Proudhonist? ● neo-Fordist?

1. In one argument (quartile I in the table), the crisis is caused by the failure to adapt rapidly enough, particularly in the area of wages, to a series of 'shocks', the effects of which have not yet been absorbed by the economic system; the potential for growth remains unaffected. There is a great temptation here to hold that a *defensive form of flexibility* is all that is needed to bring about recovery. The theoretical justification for this is that unemployment is predominantly classical. As already seen, this interpretation is generally applied to Europe, with the many limitations that have been emphasized (cf. Chapter 10, Section 3).

2. Still supposing the crisis to be transitional, there is a second strategy which relies on the modernization of production, training, etc., as an alternative way of improving the country's position *vis-à-vis* other nations. It differs from the previous strategy in that there is no necessary recourse to wage reductions, or restrictions on workers'

rights; instead, it brings into play the potential for offensive flexibility offered by the new methods of organization and production. Japan would be the classic example of this strategy. This is based on the implied assumption that the international order is not in crisis and that this strategy could therefore be applied generally. The flaw in this second argument is that it does not acknowledge that the current state of international relations hardly constitutes a system and therefore can no longer transmit the potential for growth from the most dynamic to other economies. Besides, it is an elementary truth that it is impossible for every country to enjoy technological supremacy and the best demand opportunities.

3. If, however, it is held that the crisis affects virtually all postwar structures and forms of organization, defensive flexibility assumes a wholly different significance. In this case it entails an *attempt to restore competitive forces*, idealized by the theory of market self-regulation. Flexibility would then be synonymous with a plea for competition, and more generally for liberalism as the only feasible form of organization. The intention is to dismantle most of the Keynesian forms of state intervention in economic activity, in line with the wishes voiced so often since the 1970s by Professor F. Hayek. In practice, turning the myth into reality would undoubtedly entail further segmentation of labour markets and a division of the work-force by a plethora of different regulations.

4. But there is a fourth course (quartile IV in Table 11.2): confronted by a crisis in the mode of development, only a general transformation of all forms of organization — and not just of wage/labour relations! — is capable of promoting a return to growth and hence a reduction of the present mass unemployment. This differs from the preceding option in that it assumes that developments in social and economic structures are *largely irreversible*, which precludes a return to nineteenth-century capitalism, first because it is necessary to deal with the new contradiction between fully developed norms of production and consumption, which did not exist before, and second because the competitive system of regulation in the nineteenth century was not in fact as efficient as is now thought, entailing as it did alternating phase of expansion and depression, which were often brutal and pronounced, a low rate of growth over the long term, economic instability acting as a brake on potentially beneficial technical change, etc.

In brief, although the crisis popularizes the idea of the inexorable march of technology and economics, it could be concluded that the situation is not so cut and dried, is *relatively open*, and is determined by the structural and historical traits of each country on the one hand, and by the decisions made as regards overall strategy on the other. How far does this apply to the European economies and the Community as a whole?

5. Adaptability and Acceptance of Change as a Result of the Stabilization of New Agreements

It is clear that there are certain dangers in equating the introduction of flexibility and a return to competition in the labour market. Admittedly, in the crisis sharper competition is an incentive to innovation in businesses and can demonstrate the inadequacy of the rules previously governing wage/labour relations. This development, which is one of destruction (when activities rendered obsolete by the crisis go bankrupt or are abandoned), evasion (when companies are not constrained by legislation, or when the black or grey economies flourish), or amendment (when collective agreements are suspended and/or revised, or when employees accept, *de facto* or *de jure*, certain kinds of mobility and restructuring), can give the impression of the absolute predominance of market forces over economic, social, and legal structures, which, *by their very nature*, *lag behind* the transformations that are taking place. In varying degrees, this is the liberal analysis — and also the neo-Schumpeterian view.

Pushed to the extreme, this view can lead to an exaggeration of the self-regulatory capacity of competition, favouring a relatively passive approach in economic policy: if state interference with market forces is kept to a minimum, entrepreneurial initiative will soon lay the foundations for renewed growth. As regards wage/labour relations, it would be as well to remember the arguments in favour of a more measured approach, whereby agreements within the private sector and state intervention, the market, and regulations work together to establish a viable form of wage/labour relations. In particular, it could be that in present-day societies the much sought after mobility requires new types of collective organization as much as a restoration of market forces.

For their part, the 1930s are a reminder that, when the growth of production is impeded by structural factors at the *macroeconomic level*, there is no point in expecting to find a solution in rapid and flexible *adjustment at the microeconomic level*. On the contrary, New Deal type developments, which were ultimately to culminate in the Fordist system of wage/labour relations — a strengthening of the legal position of trade unions, the creation of a minimum wage, planned growth of purchasing power, etc. — came about *in reaction to spontaneous market adjustments*. It is on the basis of such institutionalization that competition could recover its effectiveness and be compatible with a return to full employment.

Basically, the crisis of 1929 highlighted the shortcomings of the forces of competition in a situation where a largely *indivisable* system of production and investment was emerging. All the evidence indicates that the subsequent development of wage/labour relations has further reinforced *these factors of indivisibility*: convergence between norms of production and consumption, concentration of capital equipment necessary for the growth of private consumption, close links between direct and indirect wages, a blurring of the division between company and state management, etc. Here again, it could be that market forces alone are incapable of reconciling the contradictory factors that govern the development of wage/labour relations. To limit the argument to the issue of flexibility, there is no guarantee that the combined effects of private initiatives in this area, all of which are 'well reasoned', will not finally lead to an impasse, i.e. to a destabilization of the economy and more generally of the social system itself. The nature of wage/labour relations is of such significance for the overall system of regulation that it concerns the community as a whole just as much as the firms and workers directly affected. Moreover, state intervention, perhaps limited but directed at dealing with market failings, seems to be more vital than ever.

The final point, which has been emphasized repeatedly, is that those forms of flexibility that are *most effective in the long term* do not necessarily correspond with those that are in line with the somewhat shortsighted logic of the adjustments wrought by market forces. Redundancies and wage reductions are more of an admission of defeat, an ignominious method of adaptation, than a triumphant march out of the crisis: when new technology can open possibilities of satisfying previously unexpressed demands, and promote productivity growth, how can sustained reliance on such types of flexibility be justified? In contrast to this, other forms of adjustment, which probably offer better prospects — and are more acceptable socially — could be developed by pursuing a method of working and a process of production that implemented flexible specialization, by aiming to increase training and skill of the work-force to make for greater versatility, by re-orienting state intervention, and through labour legislation. Surely the effectiveness of mobility and retraining schemes is all the greater since they are based on negotiated and informed, and therefore voluntary, acceptance of the changes precipitated by the crisis? For their part, collective agreements incorporate these issues more and more frequently, alongside pay, qualifications, and union rights.

At the same time, the increasing number of government schemes aiming to facilitate industrial change (training, employment of young people, early retirement, etc.) testifies to the importance of *collective forms of managing flexibility* today.

I shall now attempt to draw out some ideas for the future from this analysis, and to indicate a few questions concerning Europe.

6. Possible Developments in Wage/Labour Relations: Five Scenarios

The international comparisons undertaken produce rather a surprising conclusion: although wage/labour relations are subject to the same kinds of pressure in each country, the *particular features* of the historical development of each nation, and the decisions made regarding political and social issues, come very much into play when seeking ways out of the crisis. This suggests that, beyond acute financial constraints and apparent economic determinism, the present decade is much more *open* than is often believed.

It is not, in fact, a matter of re-establishing 'proper management' of the labour market, based mainly on greater flexibility of wage/labour relations and decreased state intervention. It is a matter of seeking and *creating* a system of wage/labour relations that could fit in with trends in the international division of labour and encourage the emergence of a new mode of development. This is undoubtedly the way in which the problems of Europe should now be approached: does the crisis lead to a degree of uniformity, or, on the contrary, to a divergence of wage/labour relations in each country?

But first, a word of caution. My intention is not to describe the most likely courses of development or to set current changes in a supposedly definitive analytical framework. My more modest objective is to draw some conclusions of relevance for the future from the above results. My aim, therefore, is to test the coherence and relevance of the arguments applied, rather than to make any predictions. The analysis will focus on five scenarios which are meant largely as representative and involve differing degrees of probability.

6.1. Scenario A: A world-wide Keynesian system ensures a revival of growth so that only marginal changes in Fordist wage/labour relations are required

This first scenario rests on the premise that the breakdown in stable international relations is the root cause of the collapse of the postwar compromise. Co-ordination of the economic policies pursued by different countries would allow a return to full employment, without any significant institutional changes. The mode of development would remain essentially Fordist, although the motive force would come from new products and technologies.

Taking into account the close interrelationship between wage/labour relations and the mode of development, this scenario seeks to adjust the dynamics of the economy in such a way as to consolidate Fordism. It may be, however, that relations between nation-states and conflicts of interest at the international level make it impossible for this to be achieved.

In addition, certain Keynesian economists suggest a variant, whereby a form of protectionism is intended to create the conditions for national growth that is, if possible, independent of the current state of international relations (Scenario A'). The declared or implied intention of this protectionism is often the maintenance of the kind of labour relations and competition that were prevalent in the 1960s.

There is no doubt that this scenario has obvious attractions, particularly for those sectors worst hit by the crisis. But the whole problem is to create the conditions required to bring it about, for they will not occur spontaneously in present circumstances. Besides, is it possible simply to resurrect the kind of development that occurred after 1945? These are doubts voiced by the proponents of a very different strategy.

6.2. Scenario Z: Restoration of the market, deregulation, and disengagement of the state as the basis for a new system of labour relations

The hypothesis is that the market is the only effective tried and tested means of co-ordinating individual decisions. By their nature, legal agreements and state intervention lag behind industrial innovation. This is particularly true for most employment legislation (union rights, minimum wage, social security, etc.). The simple answer is therefore to prune these institutional measures thoroughly, so that the unfettered adjustment of employment, wages, and working time and conditions will produce new jobs, a rise in the standard of living, and a return to full employment.

This scenario could be described as one of *competitive flexibility*, since it rests specifically on greater competition in the labour market. It therefore assumes that pure market economies are essentially stable and self-regulatory, which provokes historical as well as theoretical objections from contemporary neo-Keynesians: what accounts for mass unemployment during previous major crises when flexibility reigned virtually supreme, or at least was not restricted by 'union power' and regulations?

An alternative Scenario Z' can also be envisaged, which in contrast to Z would involve a *relative* rather than an *absolute* shift to market forces: it would temporarily introduce *more* competition into wage/labour relations, although without seeking to restore a mythical (and probably unattainable) perfectly competitive labour market.

These two scenarios Z and Z' differ from A and A' in that they concentrate all the changes made in response to uncertain economic developments and wide fluctuations in activity on wage/labour relations. Their gamble is that adapting to the instability engendered by the crisis through flexibility will in fact stabilize the economy and boost growth. This paradoxical approach is undoubtedly open to dispute — which is why the US recovery at the end of 1982, which seems to have derived more from Keynesian mechanisms and the price of the dollar on world markets than from changes in labour relations, excited so much interest.

Between these two extremes, there is a whole range of possibilities, which depend on the nature of *simultaneous* changes in wage/labour relations and in the overall system of regulation. It is of interest to examine another scenario where flexibility assumes a completely different aspect.

6.3. Scenario R: Flexible specialization — the start of a change in technological direction, in wage/labour relations, and in the mode of development

This encompasses all the implications of the hypothesis that Fordism, as the dominant method of organizing production, is facing a crisis of a *structural* nature. Confronted by the counter-productive effects of compartmentalizing work and conceiving of plant and machinery in terms of the mass production of the past, there is an incentive for firms to undertake a thorough revision of their choice of technology and organization. 'Rigidity' has less to do with the restrictive nature of past collective agreements — if only because they can be re-negotiated — or with state legislation — which can be beneficial if it stabilizes competition and forces firms to seek 'progressive' solutions, in order to maintain most of the social advantages — than with the inappropriate design of machinery and failure to tap the skills and know-how of workers. Thus, as *flexibile machinery and attempts at achieving versatility become more widespread*, and as workers are given more responsibility, *a system of wage/labour relations totally divorced from Fordism* could take root, which could be described as a *Proudhonist* alternative. The model would then be one of groups of generally skilled employees operating machinery that is capable of reacting without delay or excessive costs to changes in the nature of products and the volume of demand.

Although this alternative is based primarily on flexibility of employment or wages or a reduction of social security, these could be necessary but *temporary* steps on the way to a far-reaching change in the way firms are managed and, still more, in the direction of technological change. Here, the main point of reference could be the Italian brand of 'decentralization of production', although it could also be the type of management employed by large Japanese companies. The difference between these two models could, moreover, distinguish two variants of the same scenario: R, in which large-scale units of production would decline to be replaced by a whole host of small and medium-scale businesses (the so-called 'Proudhonist' scenario), and R', in which flexible specialization and workers' mobility would operate within large companies, possibly being supplemented by a network of modern and efficient subcontractors (a Japanese scenario?).

There is no doubt that this type of change would run into many problems. Is it plausible that the trends that have operated since the Industrial Revolution could be reversed? Does it not imply a complete shift in the balance of power and in social and economic structures? Is it conceivable that all the indivisibilities that characterize contemporary society could thus be reduced — the persistence of mass production in basic industries, and the need for a large-scale infrastructure in transport, energy, housing, and social facilities? What role would the unions play in this kind of scenario, and would it not risk provoking resistance from organized labour? Is it certain that this *internal* change in company management would be enough to counteract the macroeconomic causes of instability? In particular, what should be the direction of economic policy — Keynesian or minimalist? Are there not very many different ways of applying this type of flexible specialization, all depending on the socio-political context (ranging from self-management through an updated brand of social democracy, all the way to pure hard-line liberalism)?

The very novelty of this type of scenario prompts the exploration of two further kinds of development in which the old and the new are combined to shape a new system of wage/labour relations that is somewhere between the previous two types.

6.4. Scenario L: Re-segmentation of labour markets: towards a multi-tier system of wage/labour relations?

This starts from the contention that, in the past, the transition to Fordism was compatible with the persistence of different forms of wage/labour relations in the sectors that were not at the centre of the new mode of development. In a similar sense, the competitive nature of wage determination and the flexibility of employment were the necessary complement to institutionalizing labour relations in large firms (sub-contracting, temporary labour, etc.) or the consequence of the particular features of the organization of production and the variability of demand (e.g. construction and public works). This is the reality that theories of segmentation and dualism of the labour market set out to analyse.

Faced with the transformations necessitated by the crisis, with increasing economic instability and growing uncertainty, firms would react by limiting the hiring of workers (covered by the system of wage/ labour relations in force) to the most vital and permanent jobs, and would fill other vacancies with workers under a host of different terms and conditions of employment. Part-time work, fixed-term contracts and jobs deemed 'insecure' in general have already been on the increase for a decade, as we have seen. The comparison of the studies of the different countries suggests, moreover, that this shift is all the more significant because the safeguards granted under Fordist wage/labour relations are absolute and put a stranglehold on most elements of mobility (for example, compare Italy and West Germany). Furthermore, in the case of redundancy and retraining for other jobs, workers from the 'hard-core' of industry have greater bargaining power, which enables them to negotiate a better deal than those made redundant from smaller companies, not to mention young people looking for their first job. In short, in this scenario economic trends and the power relations would tend to lead to a two-, or rather a multi-tier work-force, and thus towards a system of wage/labour relations characterized by a plethora of different regulations. The models outlined in the preceding scenarios would simply be components in the kaleidoscope that labour relations would then become: marginal adjustment of Fordism where it remains irreplaceable, a Proudhonist system in certain new sectors (or old sectors that have been renovated by new technology), and competitive mechanisms wherever variability of employment and wages is the most obvious way of managing work.

However, this scenario itself has two extreme variants. In the first case (Scenario L), this 'patchwork' of wage/labour relations could succeed in containing unemployment, or even in re-stimulating growth, thereby moderating the latent social tensions inevitably created in such a scenario in the European countries. In the other scenario, L', this fragmentation is associated with a gradual slide into stagnation and social *anomie*; it is therefore fertile ground for potential conflicts. The turning taken will be decided by a subtle blend of employment policy and general economic policy and the greater or lesser benefits of each country's area of specialization. These risks could lead different countries to explore another way, which avoids divisions in the labour market and widening inequalities while counteracting tendencies towards stagnation.

6.5. Scenario N: Incorporation of flexibility into the organization of production, with negotiation over the forms that it takes, and maintenance of the old system of wage determination

In some ways, this scenario combines *certain* features of Scenario R to enable *some* of the objectives of Scenario L to be achieved (but by different means) so as to prevent segmentation, which is a distinct possibility if the trends of the last decade continue. It presupposes that the groups concerned attach highest priority to the avoidance of increased inequality and social marginalization, and that workers accept changes in the method of production — in the skills and tools used — in exchange for having some say in the technological and organizational transformations that are taking place. The means to this end could be negotiation between management and unions on the forms of *offensive flexibility* (training of workers and acquisition of new skills, more rapid introduction of new adaptable machinery, etc.), with the intention of being better equipped in the future to avoid the more unfortunate forms of defensive flexibility that have been experienced (e.g. loss of legal safeguards in the contract of employment, drastic wage cuts, savage job losses). Further-more, this option is based on the assumption that the embryonic system of wage/labour relations incorporates solidarity with the jobless, so that at the macroeconomic level they can once again bring about a virtuous circle, whereby modernization boosts employment and vice versa (for example through some kind of scheme for the reduction of working hours, in so far as this is consistent with creating more jobs). Under these conditions, an agreement could be sought, through negotiation, concerted action, and state intervention, on the principle of sharing productivity gains, which would be the counterpart of the agreement on which the success of Fordism was founded. Equally, the principle of extensive social security could be reaffirmed and made possible by a progressive recovery of growth and a detailed review of its organization, if this proves inadequate given the requirements of the period or the objectives pursued.

This transformation of wage/labour relations is not enough by itself, however, to guarantee a return to growth. General economic policy must also ensure the co-ordination between plans for modernization and restructuring on the one hand, and management of overall demand on the other, as well as a minimum level of co-operation to establish a new set of rules at the international level so that foreign trade once again acts as a stimulant and not as a factor spreading and deepening the crisis.

In summary, this scenario is by no means easy to achieve, and it therefore remains highly improbable today, although the germ of some of the required ingredients can be found in various European countries (e.g. consultation on the introduction of new technology, projects for reconversion, and emphasis on training).

12

Europe at the Crossroads

Robert Boyer

It is time to draw a few conclusions and indicate possible developments concerning European institutions and policies that would permit the emergence of a specifically European, post-Fordist, system of wage/labour relations. If the chances of success were proportionate to the magnitude of the challenge, Europe's position would be enviable. If, on the other hand, one had to predict the future of Europe over the long term as a continuation of the years 1979–85, there would be some cause for concern. At the same time, one of the few possible solutions seems to lie in appealing to the achievements of Europe and its traditions of unity to turn the obstacles facing it into levers for economic recovery. The following brief sketches will revolve around these three ideas.

1. Three Unprecedented Challenges

The time has long since passed when admiring US researchers came to study the European 'miracle': exceptional rates of growth and low levels of unemployment, rapid industrial modernization and changes in life-style, and progress towards European unity. In the mid-1980s the situation is precisely the opposite. Businessmen, politicians, and economists are rushing to the United States in order to glean understanding and, above all, 'recipes' that will enable them to copy the 'American way out of the crisis'. In fact, Europe today is confronted with imbalances that have intensified for more than a decade and are on a different scale from those observed in the 1960s.

1.1. *The spread of mass unemployment and accompanying social inequalities since 1973*

The upsurge in unemployment was contained until 1979, but it increased thereafter and in 1985 was more than 10 per cent of the active population (Table 12.1). This is in significant contrast to the much more moderate growth in underemployment in the United States and Japan. It is a

TABLE 12.1   *Unemployment, 1960–1985 (% of labour force)*

	EEC	USA	Japan
1960	2.5	5.5	1.7
1973	2.5	4.9	1.3
1979	5.5	5.8	2.1
1985	10.2	7.2	2.5

Sources: Economie éuropéenne, November 1984, p. 218; OCDE, December 1985, p. 30.

disturbing phenomenon that the European countries are no longer creating jobs although the active population is continuing to grow. Virtually all five- to ten-year projections suggest that, without a reversal of economic policy and major structural changes, Europe will be the only region in which unemployment will continue to increase right into the 1990s.

In the absence of job creation, the big question concerns the accessibility and distribution of employment. Consequently, a relatively new phenomenon has appeared which is now of quite significant proportions: labour market segmentation going beyond the old division between nationals and immigrant workers. The young seem to have been the very first victims of this rationing process. At the same time, the increasing number of women in employment and the tertiarization of jobs are changing wage/labour relations, which have hitherto been essentially industrial and male-oriented.

Will European societies, traditionally committed to unity, be able to tolerate for long this *re-emergence of inequality* and the spread of poverty? This is the *first challenge* facing Europe.

1.2. The difficulty of industrial regeneration and the threat to the international position of Europe

These problems are proportionate to the importance of old industries in Europe and to the difficulties of modernizing Fordist sectors such as the motor industry. Hence, national industrial policies are often 'hobbled' by the servicing of substantial deficits and have access to few resources to assist those sectors seen as the industries of the future. This process is evident from the dramatic fall in high-technology exports, particularly since 1979 (Table 12.2). In these circumstances, the EEC is encouraged to go for the competitiveness associated with low production costs of traditional goods or medium-technology products, areas in which competition is governed essentially by price. In this respect, the

Robert Boyer

TABLE 12.2   *How does Europe stand in comparison with its competitors?*

	EEC		USA		Japan
Share of world production[a]					
1960	26.4		25.6		4.4
1973	25.3		21.8		5.7
1979	24.1		20.6		5.7
1985	22.1		20.0		8.2
Technological position High technology (HT) in the world HT market[b]					
1973	10.2		7.8		7.4
1979	9.2		7.0		9.2
1984	6.3		4.6		13.0
Balance of trade in high and medium technology goods/GNP[c]					
1973	1.5		0.7		3.4
1979	2.1		0.8		6.9
1983	1.1		−1.1		10.1
Competitiveness in terms of costs[d] Industry					
1960	80.3		172.1		76.4
1973	98.0		111.4		100.4
1979	105.6		95.4		97.0
1984	87.2		130.3		90.3
Scale of recovery[e] Growth of GNP: cycle started in:					
1970	5.4		8.7		
		(0.62)		(1.0)	
1975	6.8		8.0		
		(0.85)		(1.0	
1980	1.7		3.9		
		(0.43)		(1.0)	
1982	2.3		11.0		
		(0.20)		(1.0)	
(elasticity, Europe/USA, in brackets)					

Notes to TABLE 12.2

Definitions and sources:

[a] In volume, purchasing power parity exchange rates. CEPII–CHELEM in CGP (1985), May, p. 11.
[b] CGP (1985) p. 14.
[c] OCDE, *Perspectives économiques*, no. 37, p. 25.
[d] Wage costs in a common unit compared with the weighted average of competitors. Index of 100 in 1975. *Economie éuropéenne*, Mar. 1984, pp. 130–1, 119.
[e] Growth of real GNP. OCDE, *Perspectives économiques*, Dec. 1984, p. 16.

improvement of its competitive position since 1979 is quite evident — even if it is essentially dependent upon the overvaluation of the dollar (Table 12.2).

However, these efforts have not managed to arrest Europe's decline in terms of world production, a decline that is gathering momentum as compared with 1970–3 (Table 12.2). The contrast with Japan, which seems to be the winner on all counts, is striking: remarkable breakthroughs in the field of high technology (nearly doubling that country's market share in ten years), lower average production costs than competitors, a rise in the share of world production by an amount more or less equivalent to the losses recorded by the United States. It should be emphasized in passing that the US position is not as brilliant as one might have imagined: losing momentum in the production of high-technology goods, the country is suffering from high costs. In spite of the strength of the recovery at the end of 1982, it is managing to do little more than stabilize its share of world production.

Can the European countries accept such a relegation in the international division of labour and join battle with low-cost countries? Is Europe missing the opportunity of playing its part in the new and changing system of technology? The *second challenge* facing Europe, therefore, is that of modernizing successfully at a time of recession and not as a consequence of the devastation of a world war.

1.3. Policies of 'self-interest' and the threat to European society

If, in previous chapters, much has been made of the common characteristics of countries, the emphasis now must be on the elements that are different and can lead to competitive struggles within Europe itself. It has been shown that each country has developed *quite specific institutions* for introducing and nurturing its own version of Fordist wage/labour relations. Now, quite logically, these peculiarities are reappearing and are most significant in times of recession: a breakdown in the conditions for 'consensus' growth makes national differences a key factor in competitiveness and in gaining market shares, whence the common path to flexibility, which spreads from the best-placed countries to the others by the polarizing action of external deficits and surpluses. Thus, the temptation to adopt a policy of self-interest is strong, and bears not upon protectionism (excluded by the rules of the Treaty of Rome), nor upon the practice of competitive devaluation (which membership of the European Monetary System makes difficult), but upon making wage/labour relations more flexible. Moreover, the strength of extra-European competition further reinforces this tendency which is quite logical even though it may work to destabilize Europe.

One might gain the impression that in these circumstances each one of the countries is constrained — or tempted — to explore a different policy: Scenario A[1] for France after May 1981, then, after an attempt at A′, swinging between Scenarios L and N; Scenario Z for the United Kingdom, which, in a sense, anticipates Reaganism; Scenario R for Italy — at least in the eyes of foreign observers, who have made themselves the apostles of flexible specialization. For its part, West Germany seems to be best placed for exploring Scenario N, without ruling out a strategy of re-segmentation (Scenario L). Belgium appears to be exploring a similar strategy. As for Spain, now admitted into the Community, particularly rapid changes are in progress, with the country endeavouring to combine Scenario Z in the short term with elements of a Scenario N-type policy.

In short, it may be that the actual strategies are appreciably more heterogeneous than the declarations of intent and common references to the imperative for flexibility and competitiveness would indicate. Henceforth Europe will be facing a *third challenge*: to prevent the crisis from leading to a *divergence of interests and policy* between member-states, thus precipitating the collapse of Community institutions.

2. From Euro-pessimism to Euro-realism

Faced with the magnitude of these problems, business circles and international organizations have hastened to describe Europe as a drowning continent, a new Atlantis. The numerous causes of sclerosis include rigidity of the labour markets, outdated trade unions, and the absence of entrepreneurial drive.

Is Europe the 'sick man' of the world economy, a new victim of the 'English disease'? In fact, it is usual, especially during crises as deep as the one we are experiencing, for views of the future to swing from visions of darkest depression to those of uncontrollable optimism. Without denying the gravity of the situation, it is important to strike a balance

---

[1] See Chapter 11, Section 6, for details of these scenarios.

between the undoubted weaknesses, and also the strengths, of the Old Continent.

2.1. *Europe: cornered between the Green Giant and the Samurai?*

Since 1979, the three major OECD blocs have developed in contrasting ways, which for Europe mark a break with the past. The pattern of its economic growth does not resemble that of either the United States or Japan (Table 12.3).

- It is striking that since 1967 the *US economy* has been in a phase of *predominantly expansionary* growth, with medium-term stabilization of the per capita GNP, semi-stagnation of real wages, but sustained growth of employment. In spite of the often triumphant declarations, the years 1979–85 conform, for the moment, to past trends. We know that jobs have chiefly been created in the service industries, and have often involved part-time work. Furthermore, the trend growth of productivity has not been recovered since 1982, despite the exceptional strength of the recovery.

- *Japan* is a long way from being a simple variant of the 'American model'. Indeed, it seems to be the only major country (with certain newly industrializing countries (NICs) of South-east Asia, such as Korea) still benefiting from the virtuous circle of productivity–competitiveness–employment–real wages. Contrary to the situation in the United States, job creation is achieved not at the expense of productivity, but, on the contrary, because of productivity. At the same time, wages continue to grow, adjusting when necessary to the changes of the international economy — in 1979–80, for example. As for the growth rate, although much lower than that of the 1960s, it is still greater than that of the other two blocs.

- *Europe's problem* seems to be not to have explored either of these two models, and to be the loser on both accounts. Productivity growth is much more sustained than in the United States, but it does not ensure sufficient competitiveness to enable industrial employment to grow. The growth in services is not sufficient to compensate for de-industrialization, so that productivity growth in the context of the current system of regulation seems to militate against employment. The growth rate has continued to decline, first in 1973–9, and then from the beginning of the 1980s, scarcely reaching 1 per cent per annum. In short, Fordist growth has come to an end without a replacement being discovered. There is no doubt that this best characterizes the situation. Here, then, is good reason for expressing pessimism about Europe's future.

However, this assessment requires qualification in the light of other considerations.

2.2. *The mote and the beam: the need to recognize the limitations of the US and Japanese models*

It seems that Europeans are allowing themselves to be convinced of their

TABLE 12.3 *Europe, the United States, and Japan: three contrasting models (% per annum)*

	EEC				USA				Japan			
	GDP (q)	Productivity (μ)	Real wages (s/p)	Employment (N)	q	μ	s/p	N	q	μ	s/p	N
1979	3.5	2.5	1.9	1.0	2.3	−1.0	−0.5	3.3	5.1	3.7	2.4	1.3
1980	1.1	0.7	1.4	0.4	−0.2	−0.5	−0.5	0.3	4.9	3.8	−0.4	1.0
1981	−0.3	1.1	0.9	−1.4	3.0	2.1	0.6	0.9	4.0	3.2	1.9	0.8
1982	0.5	1.6	0.5	−1.1	−2.4	−0.6	2.0	−1.8	3.2	2.2	1.6	1.0
1983	0.9	1.6	1.3	−0.7	3.8	3.1	2.2	0.7	3.0	1.3	5.9	1.7
1984	2.2	2.2	0.9	0.0	6.0	2.0	1.4	3.9	4.7	3.7	2.4	1.0
1985	2.3	2.2	1.0	0.0	2.5	0.6	1.3	1.9	3.7	2.5	2.1	1.2

The problem: despite wage restraint, reduction of growth and increased unemployment

Irregular, predominantly *expansionary* growth, stable employment

The last virtuous circle, sustained and simultaneous growth in productivity, employment, and real wages

Source: *Economie éuropéenne*, November 1984, annex of statistics.

probable decline even to the extent of no longer perceiving either the fragility of the US recovery (a recovery which does not necessarily mean that structural problems have been left behind) or the contradictions that permeate this 'model'.

• To begin with, it may be that the structural position of the *United States* is much more fragile than it seems. In the first place, is it so wonderful for the country that was in the vanguard of Fordism to record, over a period of 20 years, a weakening of productive potential? What should we think of recovery occurring principally through stagnation of post-tax real wages? On the basis solely of these indicators, the conclusion would have to be that the United States is returning to a mode of development like that of the nineteenth century. Certainly, the IMF continues to revolve around the dollar, which because of this benefits from substantial asymmetrical effects. Thus, the rise of the dollar that occurred between 1979 and 1984 played a major disinflationary role, permitting a rise in real wages independently of a relatively mediocre productivity performance.

On the other hand, this prolonged overvaluation has destroyed whole sections of US industry, so that the recovery at the end of 1982 was undermined by a rocketing of imports at a rate hitherto unknown. This, it seems, is one of the reasons for the recovery running out of steam at the beginning of 1985. Now, in spite of brilliant performances and its dominance in areas of advanced technological research, the United States is recording a continuing deterioration in the mass *production* of these kinds of product (cf. Table 12.2). The difference is, therefore, significant in relation to Japan, which is a past master at producing and marketing new products. If the two chosen indicators are to be trusted, Europe is in the better position in 1983, even if the long-term tendencies (1963–83) are less favourable.

Comparisons of the United States and Europe bring to mind a sort of schizophrenia rather in the vein of the old definition of the optimist and the pessimist. It would seem that many observers deplore the fact that the European bottle is half empty, while noisily celebrating the success of having a bottle that is half full.

Certainly *Japan*, the super-star, has many more trumps to play. In 25 years it has almost doubled its share of world production; in 10 years the contribution of its trade surplus in high- and medium-technology products to GNP has trebled; it has remarkable control over its costs of production; and its international trade performance has been outstanding. Its only weakness is its dependence upon the opening up of frontiers to its goods and capital, and, therefore, its vulnerability to the risk of a protectionist reaction, which would spread first from the United States and from there to Europe. Furthermore, Japan's stature in the world economy is not such that it can organize and stabilize it for its own benefit, the role traditionally ascribed to a hegemonic power.

However, that is a 'rich man's disease', for the moment hypothetical, and of a different order to the attacks of quite genuine industrial weakness in *Europe*. This situation is all the more worrying, since the hypothesis of excessive real wages is becoming less and less plausible; since 1981, real wages have grown less quickly than productivity. In the same way, thanks to the undervaluation of European currencies, Europe enjoyed quite a significant cost advantage in 1984. If unemployment had been simply of the classical kind, it ought to have benefited a great deal more than it did from the US recovery. In short, unemployment in Europe would seem more Keynesian (linked to insufficient effective demand) than Marxist (due to prolonged inadequacy of investment), with its structural aspect (the result of incompatibility between technical change and the system of economic regulation) remaining open. The problem, therefore, is not to be found where the reports of the OECD, the IMF, and the BRI in 1984 and 1985 located it.

Europe's situation, therefore, is serious but perhaps not hopeless.

2.3. *Exploiting Europe's advantages — without ignoring its weaknesses*

It would be opportune for the EEC to explore a strategy of offensive adaptation to the socio-technical systems currently emerging, with the dual aim of maintaining its international position and forging a model to replace Fordism. In this search, Europe is not as badly placed as one might have thought (Table 12.4).

- First, since the end of the 1970s, the major European countries, with the exception of the United Kingdom, have caught up with and then overtaken US *productivity levels*. Contrary to what a simple 'catching-up' hypothesis would imply, it is now countries other than the United States that seem to be exploring the most efficient new methods of production. Second, even if the value of the dollar returned to a more sustainable long-term level, the countries of Europe would still possess a certain competitive edge (Table 12.2). In addition, expenditure on research and development has been increased since 1979, even if its contribution to GNP continues to be less than in Japan and the United States. So long as the corresponding technological gambles bear fruit, Europe can anticipate certain competitive advantages in the area of high technology.

  Finally, the flexibility and the reorganization of work that have enabled the United States to increase employment by millions[2] have been much vaunted. On purely quantitative indicators, it would seem that the European countries have fared just as well in redistributing jobs and working time. One of the major differences — apart from the downward adjustments of wages — may be the amount of extra freedom that stewardship of the international reserve funds opens up. A comparison of recoveries in France in 1981 and in the United States in 1983–4 is enlightening in this respect: rapid reversal of policy in one case, continuation in the other, despite an external disequilibrium that, in relative terms, was every bit as considerable.

[2] However, in the USA opinion is divided about the extent of the adaptation allowed by collective agreements. For a refutation of European views on the USA, see Piore (1985).

TABLE 12.4   *Some factors favouring an offensive strategy vis-à-vis the wage/labour relation*

	France	UK	Italy	West Germany	USA	Japan
1. Level of industrial productivity[a] (at 1975 exchange rates)						
1973	88.8	47.9	80.3	91.9	100	55.7
1979	109.7	48.1	89.3	109.6	100	74.8
1982	113.6	50.2	94.5	110.1	100	85.9
2. Growth of industrial productivity[b] (working hours, mean annual rate)						
1960–73	6.7	4.4	6.9	5.7	3.0	10.7
1973–82	4.5	1.8	3.7	3.6	1.7	7.2
3. Market share for high-technology products[c] (%)						
1972	11.0	14.0	n.d.	26.0	32.0	13.0
1983	8.0	10.0	n.d.	17.0	37.0	25.0
4. R & D expenditure[d] (% of GNP)						
1973	1.75	2.15	0.85	2.10	2.45	1.95
1979	1.80	2.25	0.85	2.40	2.30	2.10
1983	2.15	2.40*	1.10*	2.55	2.75	2.50
5. Company development[e] (%)						
Rate of creation	1.9	n.d.	n.d.	3.4	3.7	4.0
Rate of failure	1.2	n.d.	n.d.	1.2	3.6	3.6
6. Human potential[f] Scientists and engineers in industry (%)	6.8	10.5	4.0	9.0	23.0	14.0
7. Balance of work/ employment time[g] Share of working time in total decrease in hours worked in industry, 1973–82	0.47	0.15	0.38	0.36	0.44	0.32

* 1982.

Sources:
[a] Bureau of Labor Statistics and OCDE; from Chan-Lee and Sutch (1985, p. 62).
[b] Alvarez and Cooper (1984).
[c] Bundesbank, in *US News and World Report*, 27 May 1985.
[d] OECD, in *The Economist*, 16 March 1985
[e] Ergas, OECD, in *The Economist*, 24 November 1984, p. 103.
[f] OECD, in *The Economist*, 24 November, 1984, p. 19.
[g] Statistics calculated from EUROSTAT (1984, pp. 247, 99).

- And yet, the weaknesses in industrial organization and specialization are obvious (Table 12.4). In *all* the major European countries, the market share in high-technology exports has been reduced over the course of the last decade, in a relatively modest way in France and the United Kingdom and very significantly in West Germany. Even if the indicators remain tenuous, it would seem that the choices that operated in the 1960s and 1970s have been less fruitful than elsewhere. This poor performance is itself consistent with the weakness of the links between scientific research and industrial activity: it is not so much the total number of research workers as that of those working for and in industry that is the problem (cf. the indicator in Table 12.4). By adopting a Schumpeterian viewpoint on the process of recovery, it can be seen that one of Europe's handicaps is the low rate of new business creation. However, if business failures are taken into account, the balance relative to the United States or Japan is not so unequal. It would seem that in these countries competition between businesses is as destructive as it is creative. Europe is further restricted in its options by two other structural weaknesses.

    Since the Second World War, Europe has occupied *a middle position in the international division of labour*: the trade balance of industrial products, in surplus in relation to the Third World and the other less advanced economies, has been in deficit *vis-à-vis* Japan and the United States. This corresponds to the specialization of an intermediate country, which enjoys a technological advantage only over countries less advantaged than itself. There is a great danger that Europe may thus be squeezed between, on the one hand, the strategy of the NICs for industrial advancement and the debt problems of the developing countries, and, on the other hand, the extraordinary technological thrust of Japan and the financial power of the United States. Any delay in an offensive redeployment will entail, in time, the need to lower the production costs of basic goods in direct competition with countries where Fordist wage/labour relations are at best embryonic. After losing the first battle to stay in the leading group, Europe would be caught in a woefully defensive struggle, with scant promise of economic or social advance. Imagine if free trade zones were to be introduced in Europe, to compete with those in South-east Asia!

- Finally, and this is not a minor point, the *monetary dependence* of Europe on the United States introduces an additional weakness. In the first place, this is because monetary policy is largely conditioned by the decisions of the Federal Reserve Board, thus depriving the Old Continent of the financial intermediation that would allow it to pursue its own policies outside the international monetary maelstrom. A joint programme for European recovery runs the serious risk of running up against financial constraints, since the European Currency Unit (ECU) is not the dollar, and the City is not Wall Street! Indeed, one can imagine the effect that a sudden and uncontrolled fall of the dollar would produce, entailing, as it would, a pronounced recession in the United States. Europe has benefited very little — less than ever (Table 12.2) — from economic developments in the United

States, highly favourable as they were from 1982 to 1984 (strong demand and the weak competitiveness of US industry). What would happen if there were a significant policy reversal, if European governments decided to adjust their budgets to boost employment?

In short, weaknesses — and strengths — are not always where we are wont to see them. But what can be done?

3. The Art of Judo: Transforming Obstacles into Levers for European Reconstruction

The fortunes and misfortunes of Europe have been studied so much over the last decade that one hesitates to return to the subject. Nevertheless, in the light of this study of wage/labour relations, four propositions can be put forward for discussion.

3.1. Promoting European social unity — or, failing that, a code of conduct on defensive flexibility

The tradition of European workers' movements, the state of social legislation, trade union conflicts, and the orientation of economic policies have prevented harsh downward adjustments in employment and wages. Inasmuch as the distribution of incomes in 1985 has returned to a pattern compatible with a restoration of incentives to invest, it would be useful to lay down a few *basic principles* as to the desirable criteria for determining wages.

- In the first place, smoothing the changes that occur is not necessarily the worst of methods, as long as, within the space of two or three years, an adjustment of incomes to economic changes is guaranteed. However, should salaries be adjusted to the economic circumstances and to productivity, or should, on the contrary, *firm rules* be laid down first for determining wages in such a way as to favour productivity and/or to stabilize the economic situation? In the first category are two- or three-part formulae in which wages are settled on the basis of a social minimum, company results, and individual merit. They bring up to date and extend a long tradition in the systems of payment (piece-rates, Taylorian formulae, etc.) and economic theory: wages should be established on the basis or marginal or, failing that, average productivity. However, most significantly, certain managers and theorists have proposed the opposite: that *high wages would contribute to a rise in productivity*. A greater interest of workers in their work, loyalty to the company, incentives to improve working methods, and pressure to find new technologies and markets would all justify high wages and qualifications. This is one way of expressing the significance of the central difference in the present study between *defensive flexibility* and *offensive policies for refashioning wage/labour relations*.

- It may be, therefore, that the particular features of Europe represent a trump card in terms of the exploration of the second alternative. Moreover, paradoxically, certain US experts emphasize how much the flexibility of wages in the United States compromises the research into, and the implementation of, more efficient techniques. It must be emphasized, however, that, unless care is taken, such a policy can also lead to *segmentation in the labour market*, since only the most productive workers see themselves rewarded with high wages, the remainder continuing to do less productive and poorly paid jobs. Loss of a sense of solidarity among wage-earners is therefore the Achilles heel of this scenario. Only efforts pursued with perseverance, imagination and pragmatism will ensure the avoidance of this danger, which is particularly significant in the long term.

- If this programme seems too ambitious, it is worth noting that the countries of the European Community are already working towards a 'Gentleman's Agreement' on the *renunciation of options for a purely defensive kind of flexibility*. It would be a matter of avoiding — except in unforeseen circumstances — recourse to the customary expedient of lowering nominal wages, destroying the right to work, or, again, cutting essential social services. And yet, even this quite minimal solution would pose problems. In order for the EEC to be competitive *vis-à-vis* other countries, is not this downwards revision in employment necessary, and will it not, eventually, be beneficial? What if the blocking of industrial modernization prevents wage rises? After all, the competition that the European countries engage in between themselves can be beneficial: would not the EEC re-emerge from this rivalry in a better position?

In short, the very idea, and still more the actual success, of European social unity presupposes a reconstruction of *regional growth* to create an *industrial and technological Europe* — indeed, a true *common economic policy*. Three other propositions follow from this.

3.2. *Making regional and national differences the source of new complementarities*

It would seem that, until the mid-1960s, the progress of European integration had rested upon the exploitation of complementarities between the national economies. Conversely, the increasing internationaliz-ation and openness observed ever since has caused a shift towards greater competition: the structure of production is tending to become increasingly similar, and the products produced in each country more interchange-able. In these circumstances, any European policy dealing with wage/labour relations must avoid falling from the frying pan into the fire.

- On the one hand, the wish for a thoroughgoing harmonization of labour legislation, apparently desirable for reasons of social equity and equality in competitive conditions, could have the opposite effects to those envisaged. Indeed, the most dynamic economic zones would be favoured, since they could adapt without too much difficulty to a system close to that already in operation. On the other hand, the backward zones and areas of depressed employment would be greatly penalized, at the very least in the short/medium term, since their industrial structures would be still less competitive because of more advanced social legislation and increased labour costs. To picture this, one has only to imagine the consequences of an alignment of wages between southern Italy and the Ruhr!

- On the other hand, the acceptance of a growing disparity in wage/labour relations between countries would have the consequences already stressed. First, it would aggravate the competitive struggles within Europe. Examples of this are to be found in the competitive bidding and counter-bidding indulged in by the various regions with a view to attracting foreign investors and the jobs they bring. Today, competition is related to the size of subsidies and allowances, but in the future it could also concern the right to work and social cover itself. The relocation of US businesses from the *snow belt* to the *sun belt* (and into states where labour legislation is more recent) provides an example worth pondering. The accentuation of inequalities in standards of living within as well as between European countries would not fail to have social and political consequences. Moreover, it is not certain that transfers of public funds to depressed zones — assuming that the transfers were acceptable to the rich regions — could compensate for a decline in key areas of their industry.

In consequence, a European policy would have to negotiate between these two hazards and to combine both diversification and harmonization. The necessity for this equilibrium becomes apparent when one reflects upon the problem of the new sectors of high technology. Nowadays, each region and each town is trying to attract industries in the fields of information technology, robotics, and microelectronics, in the hope of becoming a centre of high qualifications. But not everybody can be dominant in the industries of the future, in which, moreover, the potential for creating jobs is relatively weak. Therefore the ideal solution would be, in time, to make the old disparities and those created by the present crisis open out into new complementarities on a European scale.

3.3. *Offensive reconstruction of industry and new specialization*

In fact, in the long term, a high standard of living and social protection can be assured only by efficient structures of production and the capacity to resist renewed international competition. It must be recalled that, historically, the social democratic model, in both its Scandinavian and its Austrian form, rests precisely upon this twin feature. However, the whole problem is that of easing the move from Fordism to a new socio-technological system of which the outline as yet remains fluid. In terms of European policy, this would lead to three propositions.

1. Given the inertia of institutionalized compromises, *the allocation of*

funds from the Community budget is directed chiefly towards the support of agriculture and the primary sectors corresponding to what were the first Community institutions. It is much more difficult to favour new industries, as innovators have not, as a rule, the same power as the long-established pressure groups. And yet, the future demands a substantial, if not massive, redeployment in favour of these industries. After much trial and error, it would seem that the Europeans are now conscious of this necessity, as witnessed for example by the ESPRIT and EUREKA programmes, among others.

2. In order to be achieved, this transformation requires substantial funds to be devoted to *training and retraining the work-force*. The present study has shown repeatedly that the forces of competition (making surplus workers unemployed and leaving them to find alternative jobs) are particularly inefficient, short-sighted, and harmful in social terms. On the other hand, planned or mixed economies can assure this job transition at a lower cost. In this regard, the various countries in Europe are rich in institutions that can make this *offensive flexibility* possible.

3. The fundamental problem, therefore, is to combine support and extension of the social elements necessary to wage/labour relations with the stimulation of industrial modernization. International comparisons suggest that success requires a *subtle balance between co-operation and competition*. Thus, the Japanese method of organization combining government, major companies, and subcontractors alternates phases of co-operation when major projects are chosen and conceived with phases of competition for the mass production of new products. Similarly, the Italian decentralization of production provides another example of co-operative interaction between the spirit of enterprise, local co-operative networks, and public organization of commercial provision and social security.

At the level of the European Community, this analysis raises two questions. On the one hand, how can we avoid competition between the various national industries undermining the development of production on a European scale, for example by seeking special links with Japanese or US capital to the detriment of joint European ventures? The question is not only hypothetical, bearing in mind the low level of intra-European direct investment as opposed to the growth of collaborative ventures with countries outside the EEC. On the other hand, once certain European joint ventures have been launched, how can sufficient stimulus be achieved from competition to ensure that the resulting production proves competitive relative to that of other regions?

3.4. The need to define new common economic policies

Changes in wage/labour relations are narrowly conditioned by the general policy pursued by member-states and the Community. The present study has emphasized many times that the questioning of wage/labour relations was something fundamental and provided the chance to go beyond Fordism. However, it is neither an adequate nor an acceptable means of compensating for the prejudicial effects of ill-considered and defective budgetary and monetary policies. If we imagine, for example, the outbreak of a financial crisis bringing a fall in the dollar, recession in the United States, and contraction of the world market, it would be a bad strategy to 'pay' in terms of living standards and social security for a collapse that is in fact the result of international financial disorder. In the event, the lessons of the New Deal and of the emergence of Scandinavian social democracy are still valid. On a more positive note, three lessons emerge from the numerous studies made by European economists.

1. First, *budgetary policy must not be restrictive when a policy of wage austerity is pursued*. On the contrary, if moderation of nominal wage growth is combined with compensatory action on public expenditure in order to maintain an acceptable level of activity, the beneficial effects on employment are multiplied. However, the temptation for governments, especially conservative ones, is precisely the opposite. Care must be taken not to create circumstances which, in the event of the dismantling of most of the safety nets created under Fordism, could lead to a vicious circle as it did in the 1930s.

2. *It pays to follow concerted policies at a European level.* On the one hand, this provides a policy of exporting unemployment being followed by countries perpetually trying to achieve a competitive advantage by reducing wages, taxation, social contributions, or any other element of the costs of production. On the other hand, it brings the benefit of additional multiplier effects and helps in managing the external constraint in order to proceed in every country to a joint policy of expansion (public expenditure) and restraint (nominal incomes).

3. Finally, *any additional degree of monetary or financial autonomy is a trump card* in the search for an offensive transformation of structures of production and industrial relations. Thus, stabilization of the exchange rate between the ECU and the dollar, and a freeing of certain interest rates from the international market, could only favour the transition towards a new system of wage/labour relations. From a general point of view, it could be that the discovery of new methods of monetary management, together with that of a successor to Fordism, constitute two of the main challenges of the present decade.

4. Fledgling Institutions: A Concept for the Future

On the time scale of history, most Community institutions are in the bloom of youth — and yet, some of them are already almost in their death throes (the Common Agricultural Policy?). The present economic situation in Europe is, to say the least, paradoxical. On the one hand, the realization is dawning that major forces of regulation no longer operate on a national scale: the concept of Europe as a major regional zone and as a pole for the reorganization of the international system appears intellectually seductive. However, on the other hand, any attempt at putting it into practice runs up against a host of obstacles that, alas, are not only contingent: the defence of political autonomy and national characteristics, the temptation to form more fruitful alliances outside Europe, opposing and conflicting views about what ought to be the objectives and institutions for a new phase of European integration.

Given the difficulties encountered by unification of the market for agricultural and industrial products, it is easy to imagine those that would arise on the path towards European social and industrial unity. All the more so now that the '30 glorious years' have passed and the dividends of growth no longer permit easy payment of the costs of reciprocal concessions. On the contrary, *new compromises must precede the economic revival*. Each person may interpret this process, which is more contradictory than ever, quite differently according to his or her own preferences and beliefs. Pessimists will stress that greater European unity is virtually unattainable and will expand the list of examples of European failures. Optimists, for their part, will tend to set much store by the few innovations that have succeeded and the plans for the future that have been recently launched.

In any event, the years to come will probably be overshadowed by two major questions.

1. Will the countries of Europe manage to come up with an original form of wage/labour relations, as much an alternative to the solutions tried in the United States as to the Japanese model? Or, failing this, will they be able to modify and develop these examples in order to take account of the traditions of the Old Continent and the value attached to consensus?

2. In the race between the repercussions of the international crisis — which doubtless still holds plenty of surprises — and the establishment of new Community institutions, will the innovations that allow a more conscious political control prevail over the primitive and somewhat anarchic system of regulation?

The future is open — but in terms of the time scale, it is already late.

BIBLIOGRAPHY

NB. Bibliographical references are to 'OECD' (i.e. the abbreviation for the English-language Organization of Economic Co-operation and Development), except where page numbers cited in the text refer to the French-language publications of the Organization, which take a different pagination: in that case, the French-language abbreviation 'OCDE' is used instead.

Adler, P., and Bowers, N. (1984), 'On Productivity, Work Intensity, and Supervision'. OECD, July. Mimeo.

Agglietta, M. (1976), *Régulation et crise du capitalisme*, Calmann-Lévy, Paris.

—— (1980), 'Crise et transformations sociales', *Histoire*, 6.

—— (1986), 'Etats-Unis: persévérence dans l'être ou renouveau de la croissance', in R. Boyer (ed.), *Capitalismes fin de siècle*, PUF, Paris.

—— and Brender, A. (1984), *Les Métamorphoses de la société salarial*, Calmann-Lévy, Paris.

—— and Orléan, A. (1982), *La Violence de la monnaie*, PUF, Paris.

Alvarez, D., and Cooper, D. (1984), 'Productivity Trends in Manufactory at Home and Abroad', *Monthly Labor Review*, 107.

André, C. (1984), 'Les Evolutions spécifiques des diverses composantes du salaire indirect à travers la crise', *Critiques de l'économie politique*, no. 26–7.

—— and Delorme, R. (1984), 'Les Evolutions des déficits des finances publiques et sociales: comparison internationale et interprétation', Convention d'Etudes Commissariat Général du Plan-CEPREMAP 54–83, December. Mimeo.

Andreani, E., Crosnier, M. A., Okba, M., and Poret, P. (1984), 'La Protection sociale dans les pays développés: l'essor du dernier quart de siècle. Tensions et incertitudes', *Cahiers de l'IRES* 2: 'La Protection sociale dans le monde'.

Archier, G. and Serieyx, H. (1984), *L'Enterprise du trosième type*, Seuil, Paris.

Artus, P. (1983), 'Formation des prix et des salaires dans cinq grands pays industriels', *Annales de L'INSEE*, 49.

—— (1984), 'Contrats de travail et degré d'indexation des salaires aux prix'. Workshop on Price Dynamics and Economic Policy, Château de la Muette, Paris, 6–7 September, OECD. Mimeo.

——, Laroque, G., and Avouyi-Dovi, S. (1985), 'Estimation d'une maquette macro-économique trimestrielle avec rationnements quantitatifs', *Annales de L'INSEE*, 57.

Bachet, D., Guglielmo, R., Garnier, J. P., and Lautier, F. (1984), 'Démocratie industrielle et compétitivité de l'entreprise', CESTA, May. Mimeo.

Bacon, P., Durkan, J., and O'Leary, J. (1982), *The Irish Economy: Policy and Performance, 1972–1981*, Economic and Social Research Institute, Dublin.

Bacon, R., and Eltis, W. (1976), *Britain's Economic Problem: Too Few Producers*, Macmillan, London.

Baglioni, G. (1982), in G. P. Cella and T. Treu, *Relazioni industriali: manuale perl'analisi dell'esperienza italiana*, Il Mulino, Bologna.

Banco de España (1984), *Informe Anual 1983*, Apéndice estadístico, Banco de España, Madrid.

Barou, Y., and Rigaudiat, J. (1983), *Les 35 heures et l'emploi*, La Documentation Française, Paris.

Basle, M., Mazier, J., and Vidal, J. F. (1980), 'Formation des salaires, reproduction des revenus et accumulation en longue période', *Économie appliquée*, 2.

—— (1982), 'Emploi, revenu salarial, prix et profit', *Économie et prévision*, 54.

—— (1984), *Quand les crises durent . . .* , Economica, Paris.

Begg, I., and Rhodes, J. (1982), 'Will British Industry Recover?' *Cambridge Economic Policy Review*, 8, no. 1.

Belleville, J. (1985), *L'Avenir a changé*, Syros, Paris.

Bénassy, J. P. (1984), *Macro-économie et théorie du déséquilibre*, Dunod, Paris.

——, Boyer, R., and Gelpi, R. M. (1979), 'Régulation des économies capitalistes et inflation', *Revue économique*, 30.

Berger, S. (1980), *Organizing Interests in Western Europe*, Cambridge University Press.

Berthelot, Y., Fouet, M., and Pisani-Ferry, J. (1985), Report of the Working Group, 'Configurations prospective de l'économie mondiale', Commission Prospective des Échanges Internationaux, Commissariat Général du Plan, May. Mimeo.

Bertrand, H., (1978), 'Une nouvelle approche de la croissance française de l'après-guerre: l'analyse en sections productives', *Statistiques et études financières*, Orange Series, 35.

—— (1981), 'Les deux crises des années trente et des années soixante-dix', *Revue economique*, 32.

—— (1983), Accumulation, régulation, crise: un modèle sectionnel théorique et appliqué, *Revue economique*, 34 (2).

Besson, P. (1983), 'L'Atelier de demain'. *Perspectives de l'automatisation flexible*, Presses Universitaires de Lyon, Lyon.

Beveridge, W. H. (1944), *Full Employment in a Free Society: A Report*, Allen & Unwin, London.

BIT (Bureau International du Travail) (1978–83), *Annuaire de statistiques de main-d'oeuvre*, ILO, Geneva.

—— (1983), *Sécurité sociale: quelle méthode de financement? Une analyse internationale*, ILO, Geneva.

—— (1984), *Le Travail dans le monde*, ILO, Geneva.

Blanchard, O. *et al.* (1985), *Employment and Growth in Europe: A Two-handed Approach*, Centre for European Policy Studies Papers, no. 21.

Blandin, C. (1985), 'Les Concessions des syndicats américains de l'automobile: Démissionaires ou modernes?' *Le Monde*, 13 July.

Boyer, R. (1978), 'Les Salaires en longue période', *Économie et statistique*, no. 103. Published in abridged form as 'Wage Formation in Historical Perspective: the French Experience', *Cambridge Journal of Economics*, 3 (2).

—— (1979a), 'Determinantes et évolution probable de la productivité et de l'emploi: un essai de synthèse de travaux récents', CEPREMAP no. 7922, September. Mimeo.

—— (1979b), 'La Crise actuelle: une mise en perspective historique', *Critiques de l'économie politique*, no. 7/8, May.

—— (1980), 'Rapport salarial et analyses en terme de régulation: une mise en rapport avec les théories de la segmentation du marché du travail', *Économie appliquée*, 33.

—— (1981), 'Les Transformations du rapport salarial dans la crise: une interprétation de ses aspects sociaux et économiques', *Critiques de l'économie politique*, 15/16.

—— (1982), 'Stratégie syndicale, rapport salarial et accumulation: de mai 1968 à juin 1982', CEPREMAP Note no. 8222, published in M. Kesselman (ed.), (see Boyer, 1984b).

—— (1984a), 'L'Introduction du taylorisme en France, à la lumière de recherches récentes: quels apports et quels enseignements pour le temps présent?', in de Montmollin and Pastre (1984).

—— (1984b), 'Rapport salarial, accumulation et crise: 1968–1982', in M. Kesselman (ed.), *Le Mouvement ouvrier français*, Editions Ouvrières, Paris; published in English as 'Wage Labor, Capital Accumulation, and the Crisis, 1968–1982', *Tocqueville Review*, 5.

—— (1985a), 'Les Nouvelles Formes du rapport salarial dans la crise: une bibliographie comparative et internationale', CEPREMAP, July, Mimeo.

—— (1985b), 'Productivité et emploi dans le BTP: à propos de quelques recherches récentes', in *Le Travail en chantiers. Plan construction*, La Documentation Française, Paris.

—— (ed.) (1986), *Capitalismes fin de siècle*, PUF, Paris.

—— and Mistral, J. (1978), *Accumulation, Inflation, Crises* (1983 edn), PUF, Paris.

—— and Mistral, J. (1983a), *La Crise actuelle: d'une analyse historique à une vue prospective*, PUF, Paris.

—— and Mistral, J. (1983b), 'Politiques économiques et sortie de crise: du carré infernal à un nouveau New Deal', *Futuribles*, 70.

—— and Petit, P. (1980), 'Emploi et productivité dans la CEE', *Économie et statistique*, 121.

—— and Petit, P. (1981a), 'Le Progrès technique dans la crise: ses déterminants, son impact sur l'emploi', CEPREMAP, July. Mimeo.

—— and Petit, P. (1981b), 'Progrès technique, croissance et emploi: un modèle d'inspiration kaldorienne pour six industries européennes', *Revue économique*, 32 (6).

—— and Ralle, P. (1986a), 'Croissances nationales et contrainte extérieure, avant et après 1973, *Cahiers de L'ISMEA, Économie et Sociétés*, séries P29, no. 1.

—— and Ralle, P. (1986b), 'L'insertion internationale conditionne-t-elle les formes nationales d'emploi? Convergences ou différenciations des pays européens', *Cahiers de L'ISMEA, Économie et Sociétés*, séries P29, no. 1.

Branson, W. H., and Rotemberg, J. J. (1980), 'International Adjustment with Wage Rigidity', *European Economic Review*, 13 (3).

Brepoels, J. (1981), *Wat zoudt gij zonder 't werkvolk zijn* (2 vols,), Fritak, Louvain.

Bullock, Lord (1977), *Report of the Committee of Inquiry on Industrial Democracy*, HMSO, London.

Bureau du Plan (1984), 'La Flexibilité du marché du travail', Bureau du Plan, Brussels, May. Mimeo.

Business Week (1984), 'Boosting Shop-floor Productivity by Breaking All the Rules', 26 November.

—— (1986), 'Business Fads', 20 January.

Cambridge Economic Policy Group (1980), 'Urban and Regional Policy', *Cambridge Economic Policy Review*, 6 (2).

Cameron, D. R. ([1982), 'Social Democracy, Corporatism, and Labor Quiescence: the Representation of Economic Interest in Advanced Capitalist Society', Stanford University, October. Mimeo.

Cassiers, I. (1986), 'Croissance, crise et régulation en économie ouverte. La Belgique entre les deux guerres', Ph.D. thesis, Université Catholique de Louvain.

Cellier, F. (1981), 'Les Transformations sociales du système économique capitaliste', *Économie appliquée*, 34.

——, Le Berrer, R., and Misqueu, D. (1984), 'Le Modèle multinational *Atlas*, 1ʳᵉ. partie: Les modèles par pays', *Économie et prévision*, 62.

Centre des Jeunes Dirigeants (1985), 'Catalogue des rigidités: actuers du changement', summarized in *Les Échos*, 5 May.

CEPII (1983), 'Dualité change et contraintes extérieures dans cinq économies dominantes: le projet *Sachem-Ouest*', *Economie prospective internationale*, no. 13–14.

—— (1984a), *Économie mondiale: la montée des tensions*, Report of CEPII, Economica, Paris.

—— (1984b), *Économie mondiale, 1980–1990: la fracture?* Report of CEPII, Economica, Paris.

CEPREMAP (1985), 'Flexibilités des marchés du travail et/ou recherche d'un nouveau rapport salarial', Working Paper no. 8522, September. Mimeo.

CEPREMAP-CORDES (1977), 'Approches de l'inflation: l'example français', vol. III, CEPREMAP. Mimeo.

CERC (Centre d'Etude des Revenus et des Coûts) (1982), *Rapport Annuel*, La Documentation Français, Paris.

CFDT (1985), 'Colloque sur la flexibilité', *CFDT Aujord'hui*, 1985.

CGP (Commissariat Général du Plan) (1985), *Configurations prospectives de l'économie mondiale*, CGP, Paris.

Chan-Lee, J. H., and Sutch, H. (1985), 'Profits et taux de rendement dans les pays membres de l'OCDE', Working Paper, May. Mimeo.

Chavance, B. (1984), 'Les Formes actuelles de crise dans les économies de type soviétique', *Critiques de l'économie politique*, 26–7.

Coe, D., and Gagliardi, F. (1985), 'Détermination des salaires nominaux dans dix économies de l'OCDE', OECD Working Paper no. 19, June. Mimeo.

Colin, J. F., Elbaum, M., and Fonteneau, A. (1984), 'Chômage et politique de l'emploi 1981–1983', *Observations et diagnostics économiques*, no. 7.

Colpaert, T. (1984), 'Flexibilteit en deregulering', ABVV Working Paper, October. Mimeo.

Commission of the European Communities (1983), 'Amélioration de la flexibilité du marché', Direction Générale des Affaires Économiques et Financières no. II/411/83-F, 25 November. Mimeo.

—— (1984), 'L'Amélioration de la flexibilité des marchés du travail', Comité de Politique Économique, July. Mimeo.

Confédération Européenne des Syndicats (1984), *Conference sur l'emploi. L'alternative syndicale: un emploi pour tous*, Strasbourg, 5–6 April, CES, Brussels.

Confindustria (various years), 'Economic Situation Report'.

Conniffe, D., and Kennedy, K. A. (1984), *Employment and Unemployment Policy for Ireland*, Economic and Social Research Institute, Dublin.

Conseil Économique et Social (1983), 'Le travail clandestin', official publication, La Documentation Française, Paris.

—— (1984), 'Productivité, croissance, emploi', *Journal officiel*, Reports and Suggestions to the Economic and Social Council, 16.

Coriat, B. (1979), *L'Atelier et le chronomètre*, C. Bourgois, Paris.

—— (1982), 'Relations industrielles, rapport salarial et régulation', *Consommation*, 3.

—— (1984), 'Crise et électronisation de la production: robotisation d'atelier et modèle fordien d'accumulation du capital', *Critiques de l'économie politique*, 26–7.

—— (1985), 'L'Emploi dans les stratégies d'automatisation: le modèle automobile américain', report, January. Mimeo.

Coulaures, J., and Fremeaux, P. (1985), 'Modernité ou rentabilité?' *Alternatives économiques*, 26.

Coutts, K., Tarling, R., and Wilkinson, F. (1976), 'Wage Bargaining and the Inflation Process', *Cambridge Economic Policy Review*, 2.

CRISP (1983), 'Les Relations collectives du travail en Belgique', *Dossiers CRISP*, no. 18.

—— (1984), 'La Sécurité sociale: genèse, mutations, reformes', *Dossiers CRISP*, no. 20.

Crouch, C. (1979), *The Politics of Industrial Relations*, Fontana, Glasgow.

Daems, H. (ed.) (1981), *De Belgische industrie: Ein Profielbeeld*, De Nederlandse Boekhandel, Anvers.

Daneo, C. (1975), *La Politica Economica della Riconstruzione 1945–49*, Einaudi, Milan.

Davies, R. J. (1983), 'The Comparative Political Economy of Wage Determination: A Quantitative Analysis for "The Group of Ten"', Association Internationale de Relations Professionnelles, Sixth World Congress, 28–31 March 1983. Mimeo.

Dayon, A. F., Galibert, A., and Mazier, J. (1981) 'Les Ajustements internes et externes des économies européennes face à la crise: une étude sectorielle (1970–1979)', vols. I and II, GRESP, December, Convention d'Étude no. 20–80 avec le Commissariat Général du Plan, Rennes I. Mimeo.

De Bernis (Destanne), G. (1983), 'Théorie de la régulation et historique des crises', in GRREC, *Crise et régulation*, PUG, Grenoble.

Delattre, M., and Eymard-Duvernay, F. (1984), 'Le Progrès des PME dans la crise: signe d'un relâchement du tissu industriel', *Critiques de l'économie politique*, 26–7.

Delorme, R., and André, C. (1983), *L'État et l'économie*, Seuil, Paris.

Delors, J. (1984), '1984, l'année zéro des politiques d'individualisation des salaires', *Intersocial*, 98.

Department of Employment (1979–83), *Gazette*, London.

De Swert, G. (1983), 'Van overleg naar onderleg', *De Nieuwe Maand*, 6.

De Vroey, M. (1984), 'A Regulation Approach Interpretation of the Contemporary Crisis, *Capital and Class*, 23.

DIW (Deutsches Institut für Wirschaftsforschung) (1983), *Erhönter Handlungs bedarf im Strukturwandel*, Duncker & Humblodt, Berlin.

Donovan, Lord (1968), *Royal Commission on Trade Unions and Employers' Associations*, HMSO, London.

Dosi, G. (1984), *Technological Change and Industrial Transformation*, Macmillan, Hong Kong.

Drache, D. (1984), 'The Formation and Fragmentation of the Canadian Working Class 1820–1920', *Studies in Political Economy: A Socialist Review*, 15, Autumn.

EEC (various years), *National Accounts*, 1964–1981, and *Income Statistics of Community Countries*, 1965–1982, Brussels.

Économie européenne (various years), *Economie européenne*, Commission of the European Communities, Brussels.

Économie politique (1985), 'Les Gâchis de la flexibilité du travail', June.

The Economist (1984a), 'Europe's Technology Gap', November.

—— (1984b), 'Real Wages in the Real World', December.

—— (1985a), 'Into Intrapreneurial Britain: Twenty-five Suggestions', 16 February.

—— (1985b), 'Welfare State: Trouble in Store', 9 March.

Elliot, J. (1978), *Conflict or Cooperation? The Growth of Industrial Democracy*, Kogan Page, London.

Emons, V. (1968), *L'Interessement des travailleurs belges à la productivitè*, Institute technique des salaires, Paris.

EUROSTAT (1983), *Enquête par sondage sur les forces de travail*, Commission of the European Communities, Brussels.

—— (1984), *Emploi et chômage*, Commission of the European Communities, Brussels.

Eyraud F., and Tchobanian, R. (1984), 'Tendances et evolution des relations professionnelles en France: la tentation de l'enterprise', LEST, Document 34/3. Mimeo.

Foa, V. (1983), *La Cultura della CGIL*, Einaudi, Turin.

Frank, D., and Kergoat, J. J. (1983), 'Une politique active en matière d'emploi et de lutte contre le chômage a marqué 1982', *Bulletin mensuel des statistiques du travail*, supplement no. 104.

Frank, R. H. (1984), 'Are Workers Paid Their Marginal Products?' *American Economic Review*, 74.

Freeman, C. (ed.) (1983), *Long Waves in the World Economy*, Butterworth, London.

Freyssinet, J. (1981) 'Nouvelles tendances dans les politiques des entreprises en matière de gestion du personnel', Comité de la main d'oeuvre, May. Mimeo.

Galibert, A., Delage, B., and Mazier, J. (1983), *Analyse des restructurations industrielles dans les économies dominantes (1973–1974)*, Rapport convention d'études no. 3–83, Commissariat Général du Plan-Centre de Recherche en Économie Industrielle, Université Paris-Nord, September.

Gambier, D., and Szpiro, D. (1982), 'Une analyse comparative des structures du chômage en Europe', *Observations et diagnostics économiques*, 2.

Gaspard, M., and Frank., D. (1981), 'Les Effets des pactes nationaux pour l'emploi sur l'évolution du chômage', *Économie et prévision*, 47.

Gaspard, M., Loos, J., and Welcomme, D. (1985a), 'Aménagement et réduction du temps de travail dans les enterprises: au service de l'emploi et de l'efficacité économique, *Travail et emploi*, 23.

—— (1985b), 'Onze pays industrialisés et dix ans d'expériences: le "partage du travail" en question', *Travail et emploi*, 23.

Gattaz, Y. (1984, 1985), 'Les ENCA', *Intersocial*, 109, 110, 113.

Gemeentekrediet en NM KN (1981), *De industrie in België: twee eeuwen ontwikkeling 1780–1980*, Snoeck-Ducaju, Ghent.

Georcakopoulou, V. N. (1984), 'Crise, économie parallèle, formes atypiques de production et d'emploi: le cas de l'Italie', preliminary report, SET-Paris-I, December. Mimeo.

Germe, J. F., and Michon, F. (1979), *Stratégies des entreprises et formes particulières d'emploi* (2 vols.), SET, Université Paris I.

Gerstenberger, W. (1984), *Struckturwandel unter Verschlechterten Ranmenbedingungen Ifo*, Institut für Wirtschaftsforschung, Duncker and Humblodt, Berlin.

Gilder, G. (1985), 'The Real Economy', *Impact*, 2.

Ginsbourger, F. (1985), 'L'Émergence d'une division séquentielle du travail. Louage de main-d'oeuvre et sous-traitance', Ph.D. thesis, Paris VIII.

Gordon, R. J. (1984), 'Wage–Price Dynamics and the Natural Rate of Unemployment in Eight Large Industrial Nations', Workshop on Price Dynamics and Economic Policy, Château de la Muette, Paris, 6–7 September, OECD. Mimeo.

Gorz, A. (1984), 'Emploi et revenu: un divorce nécessaire?' *Alternatives économiques*, 23.

Grando, J. M., Margirier, G., and Ruffieux, B. (1980), 'Rapport salarial et competitivité des économies nationales; analyse des économies britannique, italienne et ouest-allemande depuis 1950', part i, doctoral thesis, Université des Sciences Sociales, Grenoble II.

Graziani, A. (1979), *L'Italia dal '45 ad oggi*, Il Mulino, Bologna.

Groux, G., and Levy, C. (1985), 'Mobilisation collective et productivité économique: les cas des "cercles de qualité" dans la sidérurgie', *Revue française de sociologie*, 26.

Grubb, D., Jackman, R., and Layard, R. (1983), 'Wage Rigidity and Unemployment in OECD Countries', *European Economic Review*, 21.

Guinchard, P. (1984), 'Productivité et compétitivité comparées des grands pays industriels', *Économie et statistique*, January.

Gutierrez Garza, E. M. (1983), 'L'Accumulation du capital et le mouvement ouvrier au Mexique: 1950–1960', doctoral thesis, Université Paris VIII.

Hansard (1983), *Parliamentary Debates*, 23 November, HMSO, London.

Harris, R., and Seldon, A. (1979), *Over-ruled on Welfare*, Hobbart Paperback no. 13, Institute of Economic Affairs, London.

Hausmann, R. (1981), 'State Landed Property, Oil Rent and Accumulation in

Venezuela: an Analysis in Terms of Social Relations', doctoral thesis, Cornell University.

Henry, B., and Ormerod, P. (1978), 'Incomes Policy and Wage Inflation: Empirical Evidence for the UK, 1961–1977', *National Institute Economic Review*, 85.

Henry, B., Sawyer, M., and Smith, P. (1976), 'Models of Inflation: the UK', *National Institute Economic Review*, 77.

Hickman, B. G., and Klein, L. B. (1984), 'Wage–Price Behaviour in the National Models of Project Link', *American Economic Review*, 74.

HM Treasury (1976), *Public Expenditure in 1978–1980*, Cmnd. 6393, HMSO, London.

—— (1979), *The Government's Expenditure Plans, 1980–81*, Cmnd 6393, HMSO, London.

—— (1983a), 'Income Distribution: Effects of Budgets', in *Report from Treasury and Civil Service Committee, Session 1982–1983*, HMSO, London.

—— (1983b), *The 1983 Budget*, HMSO, London.

Hollard, M., Refeldt, U., Ruffieux, B., and Servais, O. (1984), *Emploi et informatisation: éléments pour une réflexion methodologique à partir des études quantitatives sur les effets des technologies de l'information sur l'emploi*, Report to the Director-General of Employment, Social Affairs and Education of the Commission of the European Communities, contract 830183, Université des Sciences Sociales de Grenoble, IREP-D, July.

Huyse, L., and Berting, J. (eds.) (1983), *Ais in een Spiegel? Een Sociologische Kaart van Belgie en Nederland*, Kritak, Louvain.

ILO (various years), *Labour Statistics Handbook*, ILO, Geneva.

INE (various years), *Encuesta de Población Activa*, INE, Madrid.

—— (various years), *Contabilidad Nacional de España*, INE, Madrid.

INSEE (Institut National de la Statistique et des Études Economiques) (various dates), *Données sociales*, La Documentation Française, Paris.

Institut Syndical Européen (1981, 1983), *Négociations collectives en Europe occidental 1979–80 et 1982. Perspectives pour 1981 et 1983*, rd. Günter Köpke, ISE, Brussels.

—— (1985), *Flexibilités et emplois: mythes et réalités*, Report, ISE, Brussels.

Intersocial (1983), 'J. Borel: temps partiel et polyvalence "tirés" par la modernisation', no. 94.

—— (1984a), La Tribune, 'Faut-il lier l'amélioration des conditions de travail à l'amélioration de la qualité des produits et de la productivité du travail', no. 98.

—— (1984b), La Tribune, 'Faut-il placer au centre des négociations salariales la productivité dans l'enterprise, comme le suggère J. Méraud', no. 105.

—— (1984c), 'Les flexibilités chez Gitane, IBM et Proscop', no. 104.

—— (1984d), '1984 l'année zéro des politiques d'individualisation des salaries', no. 98.

—— (1985a), 'La crise du syndicalisme a-t-elle dépassé son point de non-retour? Va-t-on vers de nouvelles règles du jeu dans l'entreprise', no. 109.

—— (1985b), 'L'échec des négociations sur "la flexibilité" a-t-il notamment pour cause la crise que traverse le syndicalisme?', no. 110.

Jobert, A. (1974), 'Vers un nouveau style de relations professionelles?' *Droit social*, 9/10.

Joyce, L., and McCashin, A. (1981), *Poverty and Social Policy*, Institute of Public Administration, Dublin.

Kahn, G. A. (1984), 'International Differences in Wage Behaviour: Real, Nominal, or Exaggerated?' *American Economic Review*, 74.

Kato, T. (1984), 'Work Sharing, Layoffs, and Intra-firm Labour Transfers', Discussion Paper no. 656, Queen's University, Canada.

Kennedy, F. (1975), *Public Social Expenditure in Ireland*, Economic and Social Research Institute, Dublin.

Kergoat, J. (1985), 'Les Distortions de la "flexibilité", *Le Monde*, 16 July.

Keynes, J. M. (1936), *The General Theory of Employment, Interest, and Money*, Macmillan, London.

Kilpatrick, A., and Lawson, T. (1980), 'On the Nature of Industrial Decline in the UK', *Cambridge Journal of Economics*, 4 (1).

Klodt, H. (1984), *Produktivitatschwäche in der deutschen wirtschaft*, Kieler studie 186, Mohr, Tübingen.

Krugman, P. (1982), 'The Real Wage Gap and Employment', *Annales de L'INSEE*, 47–8.

Kundig, B. (1984), 'Du taylorisme classique à la "flexibilisation" du système productif: l'impact macro-économique des différents types d'organisation du travail', *Critiques de l'éconmie politique*, 26–7.

Lacombe, J. J. II, and Conley, J. R. (1985), 'Major Agreements in 1984 Provide Record Low Wage Increases', *Monthly Labor Review*, 108.

Lambert, J. P., Lubrano, M., and Sneessens, H. R. (1984), 'Emploi et chômage en France de 1955 à 1982: un modèle macro-économique annuel avec rationnement', *Annales de l'INSEE*, 55/6.

Lang, G., and Thelot, C. (1985), 'Taille des établissements et effets de seuil', *Économie et statisque*, 173.

Lawson, T. (1982), 'On the Stability of the Inter-industry Structure of Earnings in the UK, 1954–1978', *Cambridge Journal of Economics*, 6 (3).

Layard, R., and Nickell, S. (1985), 'The Causes of British Employment', *National Institute Economic Review*, 43.

Leborgne, D. (1982), '1930–1980: 50 ans de croissance extensive en URSS', *Critiques de l'économie politique*, 19.

Le Cacheux, J., and Szpiro, D. (1984), 'Part salariale et emploi, *Observations et diagnostics économiques*, 8, July.

Le Dem, J., and Pisani-Ferry, J. (1984), 'Crise et politiques économiques dans les grandes économies industrielles: permanences et changements', *Critiques de l'économie politique*, 26–7.

Lemennicier, B., and Levy-Garboua, L. (1984), 'Dépenses publiques et politiques sociales efficientes', CREDOC no. 4912, November. Mimeo.

Lemoine, M. (1985), 'Les Illusions de la flexibilité', *Le Monde diplomatique*, March.

Leroy, R. (1983), *Un scénario égalitaire: la distribution des revenus en perspective*, Ciaco, Louvain-la-Neuve.

Letourneau, J. (1984), 'Accumulation, régulation et sécurité du revenu au

Québéc au début des années soixante', Ph.D. thesis, Université de Laval (Canada).

Levi, M. (1984), 'Les Politiques d'emploi de la gauche, bilan et enseignements de trois années d'experiences', *Critiques de l'économie politique*, 28, September.

Levy, M. L. (1985), 'Rapport salarial et transition démographique', INED, Paris. Mimeo.

Linhart, D. (1985), 'Flexibilité: syndicats en porte-à-faux', *Politique aujourd'hui*, 8.

—— and Linhart, R. (1985), 'La Participation des travailleurs: une cote difficile à tailler', *Le Monde diplomatique*, July.

Lipietz, A. (1978), *Crise et inflation, pourquoi?*, Maspero, Paris.

—— (1983), L'Enrol inflationniste, La Découverte/Maspero, Paris.

—— (1986), 'Réflexion autour d'une fable', CEPREMAP no. 8530. Mimeo.

Lorenzi, J. H., Pastre, O., and Toledano, J. (1980), *La Crise du XXe. siècle*, Economica, Paris.

McCallum, J. (1983), 'Inflation and Social Consensus in the Seventies', *Economic Journal*, 93.

—— (1984), *Unemployment in OECD Countries: Tests of Alternative Explanations*, University of Quebec, Montreal.

Malinvaud, E. (1982), *Emploi et chômage*, Presses de la Fondation Nationale des Sciences Politiques, Paris.

Margirier, G. (1983), 'La Crise en Italie: un cas exemplaire', IREPD, no. 83/10, Université Grenoble II.

—— (1984), 'Quelques aspects des transformations récentes du rapport salarial', *Critiques de l'économie politique*, 26–7.

—— (1985), 'Crise et nouvelle organization du travail', *Travail et emploi*, 1985, no. 1.

Maurice, M., Cellier, F., and Silvestre J. J. (1982), *La Politique d'éducation et d'organisation en France et en Allemange*, PUF, Paris.

Metcalf, D. (1984), 'On the Measurement of Employment and Unemployment', *National Institute Economic Review*, 42.

Michon, F. (1982), 'Partage du travail et flexibilité: analyse des conditions technologiques, économiques et sociales d'une politique de partage du travail', Séminaire d'économie du travail, Paris I-Tolbiac. Mimeo.

Midler, C. (1984), 'Les Concepts au concret: réflexions sur les liens entre systèmes techniques et systèmes de gestion dans l'industrie automobile', Communication à la Table Ronde CNRS-INSEE: 'Les utils de gestion du travail', October. Mimeo.

Mistral, J. (1982), 'La diffusion internationale iñegale de l'accumulation intensive et ses crises', in H. Bourguinat (ed.), *Économie et finance internationales*, Economica, Paris.

de Montmollin, M., and Pastre, O. (eds.) (1984), *Le Taylorisme*, La Decouverte, Paris.

Morville, P. (1985), *Les Nouvelles Politiques sociales du patronat 'Repères'*, La Découverte, Paris.

Naisbitt, J. (1984), *Megatrends: Ten New Directions Transforming our Lives*, Futura, Macdonald, London.

National Bank of Belgium (1980–1), 'Het veries aan levenskracht van de

Belgische economie in het voorbije decennium', *Tijdschrift van de Nationale Bank van België*, Brussels.

National Planning Board (1984), *Proposals for Plan 1984–1987*, The Stationery Office, Dublin.

Nickell, S. (1979), 'Unemployment and the Structure of Labor Costs', in K. Brunner and A. Meltzer (eds.), *Policies for Employment, Prices, and Exchange Rates*, North-Holland, Amsterdam.

—— (1982), 'The Determinants of Equilibrium Unemployment in Britain', *Economic Journal*, 92.

NIESR (National Institute of Economic and Social Research) (1984), 'The Economic Situation: Some Aspects of Labour Markets in Britain and the United States', *National Institute Economic Review*, 42.

O'Brien, J. F. (1981), *A Study of National Wage Agreements in Ireland*, Economic and Social Research Institute, Dublin.

OCDE (various years), *Perspectives économiques*, no. 37.

—— (1982), *Le Défi du chômage*, Report of Ministers of Labour, OCDE, Paris.

—— (1983), *Les Mises à pied et le travail à temps réduit: dans quelques pays de l'OCDE* (by B. Grais), OECD, Paris.

—— (1983–5), *Perspectives de l'emploi*, OECD, Paris.

—— (1984, 1985), *Perspectives de l'OCDE*, OECD, Paris.

—— (1985), *Les Dépenses sociales, 1960–1990*, OECD, Paris.

Odhner, C. E. (1984), 'Flexibility: Origins and Significance', paper prepared for the Trade Union Advisory Council of the OECD. Mimeo.

Ominami, C. (1980), 'Croissance et stagnation au Chili: éléments pour l'étude de la régulation dans économie sous-développée', Ph.D. thesis, Université Paris X-Nanterre.

—— (1986), *Le Tiers monde dans la crise: essai sur la transformation récente des rapports Nord-Sud*, La Découverte, Paris.

Panitch, N. (1980), 'Recent Theorisation on Corporatism: Reflexion on a Growth Industry', *British Journal of Sociology*, 31.

Pépin, M., and Tonneau, B. (1982), 'Réglementation sociale et vie des entreprises: mise en oeuvre des ordonnances de janvier 1982 sur les 39 heures et la 5e. semaine de congés', *Économie et prévision*, no. 59.

Perez, C. (1983), 'Structural Change and Assimilation of New Technologies in the Economic and Social Systems', *Futures*, 15.

Petit, P. (1984), 'Progrès technique, croissance et tertiarisation', note presented at the CNRS-PIRTEM seminar, 'Productivité et mesure de la productivité dans les activités de services', 27 September. Mimeo.

—— (1986), *Slow Growth and the Service Economy*, Frances Pinter, London.

—— and Tahar, G. (1984), 'L'automatisation du travail industriel: une mise en questions de ses relations à l'emploi', Convention ADI 83/500, CEPREMAP (Paris)-CEJEE (Toulouse), September. Mimeo.

Pigou, A. C. (1978), *Employment and Equilibrium: A Theoretical Discussion* (2nd edn), Augustus M. Kelley, Fairfield, Conn.

Piore, M. J. (1982), 'Convergence dans les systèmes nationaux des relations professionnelles', *Consommation*, 3.

—— (1985), 'The U.S. Can Be Inflexible Too', *Financial Times*, 8 May.

—— and Sabel, C. F. (1981), 'Italian Small Business Development, Lessons for US Industrial Policy', MIT Discussion Paper no. 288.

—— (1984), *The Second Industrial Divide: Possibilities of Prosperity*, Basic Books, New York.

Plettinckx, F. (1984), 'Het effect van de matigingswetten op de evolutie van de lonen', *Oriëntatie*, 3.

Polekar, 1981a), 'De zekere weg naar de jaren 50', *De Nieuwe Maand*, 10.

—— (1981b), 'Loonmatiging: om wat te doen?' *De Nieuwe Maand*, 1.

—— (ed.) (1985), *Het Laboratorium van de crisis*, Kritak, Louvain.

Prais, S. J., and Wagner, K. (1985), 'Schooling Standards in England and Germany: Some Summary Comparisons Bearing on Economic Performance', *National Institute Economic Review*, 43.

Quinn Mills, D. (1984), *The New Competitors*, John Wiley, Chichester.

Ralle, P. (1984), 'Performances économiques, structures de l'emploi et degré d'ouverture: une étude comparative de pays européens', memoir ENSAE CEPREMAP, November. Mimeo.

Reviglio, F. (1975), 'La Congiuntura più longa', *Materiali per una Analisi della Politica Economica Italiana 1972–74*, Il Mulino, Bologna.

Reynaud, J. D. (1978), *Sur la négociation collective en France, les syndicats, les patrons, l'État*, Éditions Ouvrières, Paris.

Romani, C. (1983), 'La Productivité comme déformation structurelle: les industries françaises et allemandes dans la crise', Ph.D. thesis, Université d'Aix-Marseille-II.

Rose, J. (1984), *En quête d'emploi: la transition professionnelle*, Economica, Paris.

Rubery, J., Wilkinson, F., and Tarling, R. (1984), 'Flexibility in the Use of Labour and Fixed Wage-costs', University of Cambridge. Mimeo.

Rubino, A. (1983), 'Generation Change: A Study on the Structure of the Labour Force', Ph.D. thesis, European University Institute, Florence.

Sabel, C. F. (1983), 'From Austro-Keynesianism to Flexible Specialization: the Political Preconditions of Industrial Redeployment in an Astemainschaft', paper delivered to the Oesterreichische National-bank, Vienna, 20 May.

Sachs, J. (1980), 'The Changing Cyclical Behaviour of Wages and Prices', *American Economic Review*, 70.

—— (1983), 'Real Wages and Unemployment in the OECD Countries', *Brookings Paper on Economic Activity*, no. 1.

Salette, G. (1968), *La Flexibilité de l'économie*, Éditions Cujas, Paris.

Salvati, M. (1975), *Il sistema economico italiano: Analisi di una crisi*, Il Mulino, Bologna.

—— (1978), *Alle origini dell'inflazione italiana*, Il Mulino, Bologna.

Schmidt, K. D. *et al.* (1984), *Im Anpassungsprozess zurückgeworfen*, Institut für weltwirtschaft, Keiler studie 185, Mohr, Tübingen.

Schmitter, P. C. (1974), 'Still the Century of Corporatism?' *Review of Politics*, 36.

Schor, J. B. (1985), 'Changes in the Cyclical Pattern of Real Wages: Evidence from Nine Countries, 1955–1980', *Economic Journal*, 95.

Schultz, C. L. (1984), 'Cross-country and Cross-temporal Differences in Inflation Responsiveness', Brookings Institution, Washington, DC.

Schumacher, E. F. (1976), *Small is Beautiful*, Blond and Briggs, London.

Serroyen, C. (1985), 'De versukkeling van het sociaal overleg', *De Gids op Maatschappelijk Gebied*, 3.

Slomp, H., and Van Mierlo, T. (1984), *Arbeidsver houdingen in Belgie* (2 vols.), Aula Pocket Spectrum, Utrecht.

Socialist Economists (1983), *Jobs and Wages: The True Story of Competitiveness*, Socialist Economists, Dublin.

Soria, V. (1985), 'Reproduction, Crisis and Regulation in the New Spain 1571–1720', Second report of work in progress, CEPREMAP, February. Mimeo.

Stankiewicz, F. (1984), *Économie du chômage et de l'emploi*, Cujas, Paris.

Strassman, P. A. (1985), *Information Payoff: the Transformation of Work in the Electronic Age*, Free Press, New York.

Sudreau Report (1975), *Le rapport Sudreau*, La Documentation Française, Paris.

SVR *Sachverständigenrat zur Begutachtung der Gesamwirtschaftlichen Entwicklung, Jahresgutachten, versch, jahrgange* (various years), Verlag Heger, Bonn.

Tarling, R., and Wilkinson, F. (1977), 'The Social Contract', *Cambridge Journal of Economics*, 1 (4).

—— (1982), 'Changes in the Inter-industry Structure of Earnings in the Post-war Period', *Cambridge Journal of Economics*, 6 (3).

Thirlwall, A. P. (1983), 'What Are the Estimates of the Natural Rate of Unemployment Measuring?' *Oxford Bulletin of Economics and Statistics*, 45.

Todd, D. (1984), 'Un point de vue sur les performances de production industrielle dans la Communauté', *Économie européenne*, 20.

Toharia, L. (1984), 'Les Transformations du rapport salarial en Espagne 1979–1983', in 'Les Transformations du rapport salarial en Europe, 1973–1984', FERE report, Vol. I. Mimeo.

Trades Union Congress (1983), *The Battle for Jobs: TUC Economic Review*, TUC, London.

Travail et emploi (1984), 'La réduction du temps de travail', 19.

US Government (1985), *Economic Report of the President*, US Government Printing Office, Washington, DC.

US News and World Report (1985), 'Europe: A Most Disquieting Technological Delay', 27 May.

Vandenbroucke, F. (1981), *Van crisis tot crisis: Een Socialistisch alternatief*, Kritak, Louvain.

Veltkamp, G. M. J. (ed.) (1978), *Inleiding tot de sociale zekerheid en de toepassing ervan in Nederland en Belgie*, vol. I, Kluwer, Deventer.

Verdier, F. (1984), 'Droit et changement social: du droit du travail à un droit de l'emploi?' Commisariat Général du Plan, Seminar on the Social Conditions for Technical Change. Mimeo.

Vilrockx, J., and Hancké, B. (1985), 'Crisisgedrag in cijfers. Verhoudingen werkgever-werknemer sinds 1973', *De Nieuwe Maand*, 2.

Weisskopf, T. E. (1985), 'Worker Security and Capitalist Prosperity: an International Comparative Analysis', University of Michigan. Mimeo.

——, Bowles, S., and Gordon, D. M. (1983), 'Hearts and Minds: A Social Model of US Productivity Growth', in *Brookings Papers on Economic Activity*, no. 2.

Weitzman, M. L. (1984), *The Share Economy*, Harvard University Press, Cambridge, Mass.

—— (1985), 'The Simple Macroeconomics of Profit Sharing', *American Economic Review*, 75.

Wharton Econometrics (1985), 'Could Europe Grow Faster?' *The Economist*, 11 May.

White, M. (1982), 'Shorter Hours Through National Agreements', *Department of Employment Research Paper*, no. 35.

Zarifian, P. H. (1983), *Le Redéploiement industriel*, Le Sycomore, Paris.

Zoll, R. (1984), *Die Arbeitslosen, die könnt ichs alle erschiessen*, Bund verlag, Cologne.

Zylberberg, A. (1981), 'Flexibilité incertaine et théorie de la demande de travail', *Annales de l'INSEE*, 42.

INDEX